Key Stage 3

Classbook

Science

for September 2000

First published 1998
Second edition 2000

Reprinted 1998 (three times)

Letts Educational
9–15 Aldine Street
London W12 8AW
Tel 020 8740 2266
Fax 020 8740 2280

Design and page layout: Ken Vail Graphic Design

Illustrations: Graeme Morris (Ken Vail Graphic Design)

Colour reproduction by PDQ Repro, Bungay, Suffolk

Picture research by Brooks Krikler Research

British Library Cataloguing-in-Publication Data

A CIP record for this book is available from the British Library

ISBN 1 84085 418 9

Printed and Bound in Spain

Letts Educational Limited, a division of Granada Learning Limited.
Part of the Granada Media Group.

Acknowledgements

The authors and publishers are grateful to the following for permission to reproduce photographs:

Courtesy of the Trustees of the British Museum: 49.2; BUPA: 107.3; Caterpillar: 82.1; Bruce Coleman Collection: 2.3b; 32.1; 32.2; 33.1; 33.2; 38.2; 39.3; 46.1; 95.4; 110.3; James Davis Travel: 80.4; 85.1; 107.1; Eye Ubiquitous: 5.2; 26.4a,c,d; 33.3; 70.1; 80.1; 88.5; 98.4; 100.1; 107.5; 108.1; 112.1; Ford Ka: 114.2a; Robert Harding Picture Library: 14.4; 27.1; Holt Studios: 28.3; Hulton Getty: 29.3; Jo Kemp: 97.1; Magnum: 12.3; 36.2; NASA: 83.4; 84.1; 87.3; Richard Noble: 77.1; Oxford Scientific Films: 16.1; 96.5; Pictor International: 51.1; 53.2; 92.1; 111.1; Planet Earth: 35.3; 37.2; 57.3; 61.3; Rex Features: 64.1; Science Photo Library: 1.1a; 2.3a; 8.2; 9.1; 10.3; 11.3; 13.2; 17.1; 18.2; 20.1; 20.2; 25.3; 45.1; 46.3; 60.1; 66.1; 67.1; 67.5; 72.1; 76.2; 83.1; 85.4; 86.2; 87.2; 88.3; 89.4; 94.3; 96.1; 99.1; 99.2; 106.1; Solution Pictures: 108.2; 109.4; Spectrum Colour Library: 1.1c; 5.1; 26.2; 26.4b; 29.4; 38.1; 47.2; 48.3; 56.1; 57.1; 69.2; 75.2; 100.3; 104.1; 109.3; Frank Spooner Pictures: 1.1b; 15.1; 15.3; 19.2; 19.3; 28.1; 29.1; 39.1a; 44.1; 51.3; 52.3; 65.1; 66.3; 72.2; 74.1; 79.3; 81.1; 90.2; 95.1; 101.1; 112.5; 113.1; Still Pictures: 49.1; 58.3; 61.2; 75.3; 113.2b; Tony Stone/Getty Images: 54.1; 92.2; 93.1; Superstock: 88.1; Trip Photo Library: 12.1; 19.1; 39.1b; 50.1; 59.1; 62.2; 65.3; 68.1; 71.2; 73.1; 76.1; 87.1; 91.5; 102.2; John Walmsley: 42.1; Williams Renault 80.4b.

Contents

Materials and their properties 82

Physical processes 162

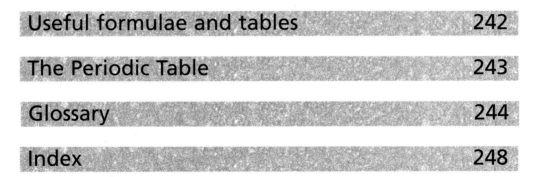

Introduction

This Letts Science Classbook has been written to help you to learn and understand the science you need during your Key Stage 3 studies. It covers all of the content of the National Curriculum in one volume and it is designed to help you prepare for the tests at the end of Key Stage 3.

The book is split into three main parts:

1. Life processes and living things
2. Materials and their properties
3. Physical processes

Each of these parts has an introduction that explains the science you will be covering. At the end of each part is a summary. This covers the ideas and topics that you should have become aware of as you worked through that part.

The three main parts of the book are themselves split into sections. Each section contains a series of two-page topics called units. The book contains 114 units, each containing the important ideas that you will need to know. The units begin with a list of topics that you will study in the unit. The information that follows is written clearly so that you can read through the unit yourself. There are also many diagrams and photographs for you to examine. These are as important as the writing, so study them carefully. Each unit contains some questions that are intended to encourage you to stop reading for a while and to think about the science you are learning. There is also a review activity at the end of each unit. This has been written to help you to develop some of the ideas further, as well as to revise the ideas you have just studied. Try them – they should be enjoyable as well as helping you to learn.

It is very important that you realise that the book builds on work you did at Key Stage 2 and the units should help to refresh your memory of this. The units should also be valuable preparation for your studies at Key Stage 4. In this sense, this part of your science education is a very important bridge between earlier study and your GCSE course.

We hope that you find this book interesting to read and full of useful information. Remember to think carefully about each of the units. As well as helping you to be successful in tests and examinations we hope that you will enjoy the challenge and fascination of science and grow to appreciate how important science is in understanding the world around you.

Life processes and living things

This part of the book is written to help you understand life processes and living things. The ideas should build on those you have already studied, but much of the work will be new to you. There are five main sections.

Life processes and cell activity

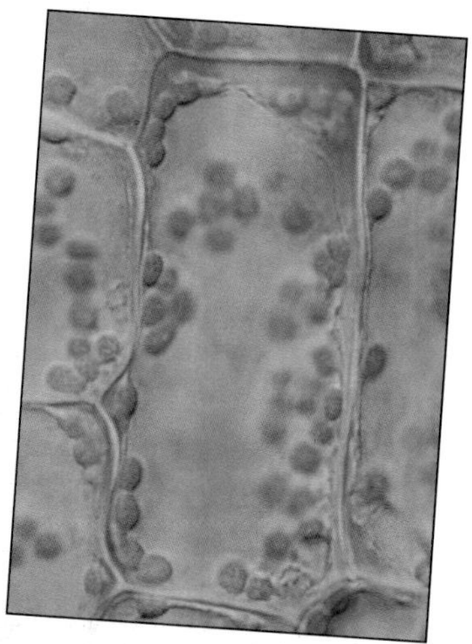

In this section you will study the life processes of plants and animals. You will also find examples of different plant and animal cells. Two units explain how animal and plant cells can become specialised to carry out specific jobs. You will learn about the structure of a single cell and how its different parts work. The differences between animal and plant cells are explained, and the roles played by a plant's chloroplasts and cell wall. This section also shows how cells come together to form tissues, and how tissues are arranged into organs and organ systems.

Humans as organisms

This section is about your own body and life. You will learn why you need a healthy diet and the main components of a healthy diet for people in different situations. You will then discover what happens to food after it is eaten, how it is digested and used by your body. Next, you will learn about blood and the circulatory system. There are units that explain how food and oxygen are transported around the body, and how waste materials are taken away from cells. Breathing comes next. In these units you will learn why we breathe and how, as well as why we should take care of our lungs. You will then learn about the way bones and muscles enable us to move. The next four units describe human development and reproduction. The section ends with a discussion of how our bodies fight disease and how we can stay healthy.

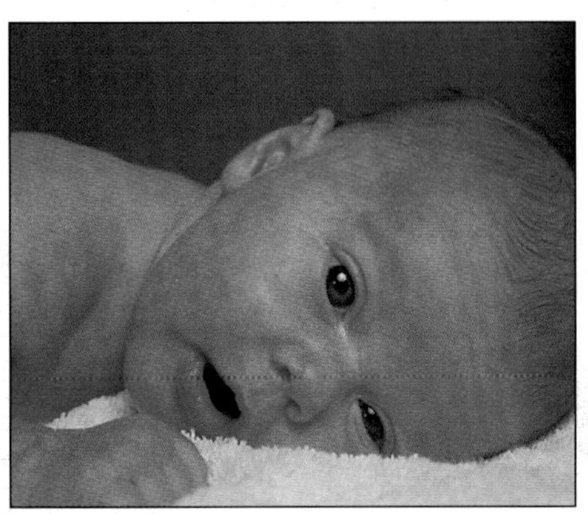

Green plants as organisms

This third section begins by examining how plants make food with the aid of sunlight. You will learn in more detail why chlorophyll is essential and how leaves are constructed to help the process. You will see how leaves absorb some of the light from the Sun and use it as energy. It may be useful to dip into the section on light and colour in the third main part of the book at this point. After learning about leaves you will look at roots in detail and discover how their structure helps them to collect nutrients from the soil. Finally, you will find out how plants reproduce and how this process depends on the assistance of wind and insects.

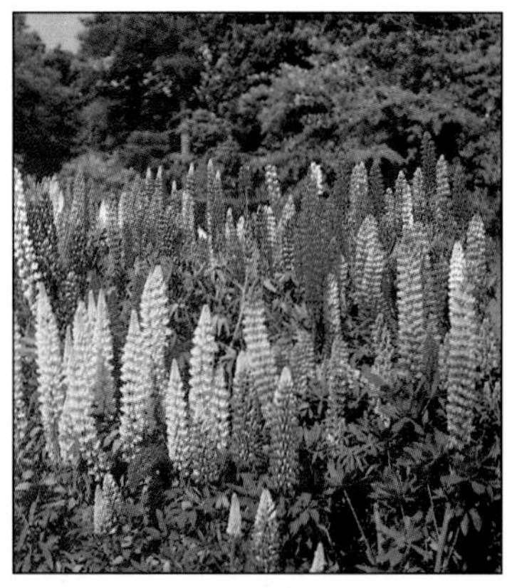

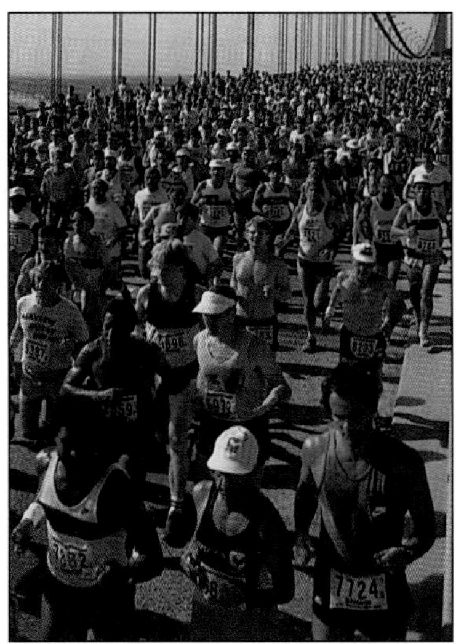

Variation, classification and inheritance

Section four begins by discussing the general differences between individual living things. You will learn the meaning of the word 'species' and how variations arise between and among species. This is followed by an explanation of the way characteristics are inherited and how this knowledge can assist us in producing better food crops. Finally, you will learn how scientists classify plants and animals, and how you can identify living things for yourself by using keys.

Living things in their environment

In this final section you will learn what a habitat is. You will also discover how and why different habitats support different plants and animals. This is followed by a unit exploring how animals and plants adapt to daily and seasonal changes. Relationships between different species are explored in detail. Two units explain the meaning and importance of food chains, food webs and pyramids of numbers. The way energy travels along a food chain and the way toxic materials can follow the same route are also explained. The section ends with a review of populations and competition between species. This includes predator and prey relationships and the reasons why some species are better adapted to survive hardship than others.

1 How living things are organised

In this section of the book you will learn the following things:

- **the characteristics or functions of living things;**
- **that some organisms are made up of only one cell;**
- **that most animals and plants contain many cells working together;**
- **what the words tissue, organ and organ system mean.**

The processes of life

It is easy to decide whether most objects are living or not. A brick is obviously not living and has never been alive. A dog running around is obviously alive. But what about a leaf that has fallen from a tree? To answer a question like this we need to think about what all living things must do to be alive.

All living things must carry out seven processes to stay alive.

1 All living things obtain energy from their food by a process called **respiration**.
2 All living things obtain food by a process called **nutrition**.
3 All living things rid themselves of waste materials by a process called **excretion**.
4 **Growth** is another important function of living things. All living things grow.
5 All living things respond to their environment. They therefore require **sensitivity**.
6 All living things move. **Movement** is an important part of life.
7 All living things get old and die. Replacements are made by the process of **reproduction**.

▲ ***Fig 1*** *The apple trees are alive, the fir trees are dead, and the silver cup has never been alive.*

These seven functions are discussed in more detail later in the book.

Single celled organisms

The simplest living organisms have just one **cell**. An organism made of only one cell is called **unicellular** or **acellular**. A single cell has to be good at everything. It needs to be an 'all-rounder'.

A single cell cannot grow bigger than a certain size. If it becomes too big, chemicals cannot move through it quickly enough (Fig 2). Most unicellular organisms are so small that you need a microscope to see them. Amoeba is one example.

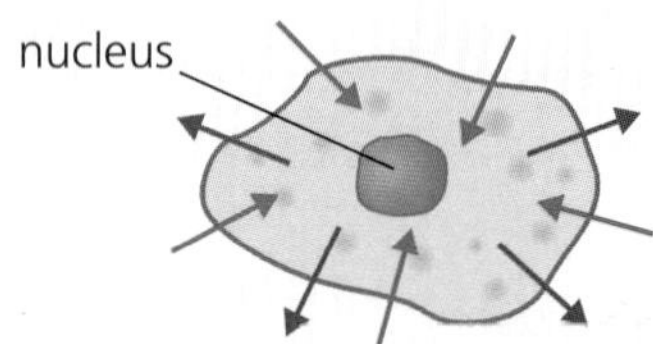

Materials can reach all parts of the cell. Waste materials can leave easily.

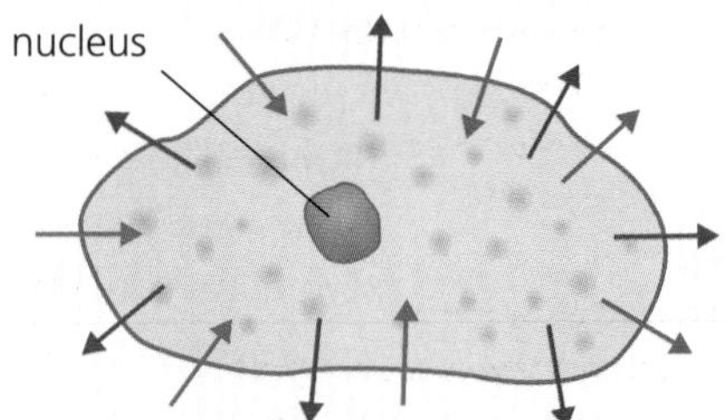

Materials have difficulty reaching all parts of the cell. Waste materials cannot leave easily.

▲ ***Fig 2***

Q1 What are the seven processes needed for living things to survive?

Q2 What prevents amoeba from growing as large as fish?

Multicellular organisms

Bigger organisms need to have more than one cell working together (Fig 3).

Plants and animals made up of more than one cell are called **multicellular**. Some of their cells can become **specialised** to do particular jobs (see Units 3 and 4). However, when an organism becomes more complicated its cells need to be carefully organised.

Cells are often grouped together. Groups of cells of the same type carrying out the same tasks are called **tissues**. Two examples are nerve and muscle.

Different tissues can work together to carry out more complicated jobs. Groups of tissues working together are called **organs**. One example is the heart, which is made up of muscle tissue, nerve tissue and connective tissue.

Groups of organs work together as **organ systems**. The heart works together with arteries, veins and capillaries to form the **circulatory system** (Unit 9). Other examples are the **reproductive system** (Unit 16) and the **digestive system** (Units 7 and 8).

▼ *Fig 3*

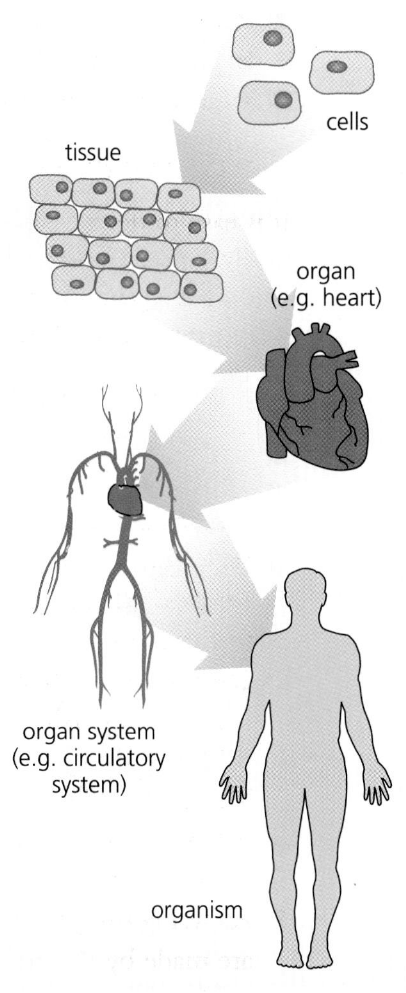

Q3 What does the term organ system mean?

Q4 List three examples of organ systems.

Key Words

acellular – made of one cell. Also unicellular

cell – the basic building block of living things

multicellular – made of more than one cell

organ – a group of tissues working together

organ system – a group of organs working together

tissue – a group of similar cells grouped together

SUMMARY

- The seven vital processes of life are respiration, nutrition, excretion, growth, movement, sensitivity and reproduction.
- Organisms made up of only one cell must carry out all the functions of life. There is a limit to how big a single cell can grow.
- Larger animals are made up of more than one cell. Their cells can be specialised to work more efficiently.
- Cells of the same type grouped together are called tissues. Groups of tissues combine to form organs. Organs can also join up into organ systems.

SUMMARY *Activity*

Study the list of the seven processes of life. For each process, try to make a list of the organs and tissues of your body that make the process possible.

2 Animal and plant cells

In this section of the book you will learn the following things:

- that animals and plants are made up of cells;
- the vital functions of the cell membrane, cytoplasm and nucleus in animal and plant cells;
- that animal and plants cells are similar but that they have some important differences.

What are cells?

Cells are the building blocks of living things, or **organisms**. They are often called the basic unit of life. Cells come in thousands of different shapes and sizes but they all have the same basic jobs to do. They must all be able to:

- obtain energy from foods;
- make new chemicals for the organism;
- control their own chemical reactions;
- reproduce to make new cells;
- keep their contents together and safe from the environment.

These special roles are carried out by different parts of the cell.

Animal cells

An animal cell is made up of **cytoplasm**, a **nucleus** and a **cell membrane**.

The cytoplasm is the liquid part of the cell. Chemicals in the cytoplasm can break down molecules to release energy. They can also join small molecules together to make larger ones. In your own body the chemicals made in the cytoplasm of your cells finish breaking down the food you eat and build the protein for your muscles.

The nucleus is the cell's control centre. It contains genetic material which allows the nucleus to control the chemical reactions taking place in the cytoplasm. The nucleus is also responsible for cell reproduction.

The cell membrane is the outer skin of the cell. This is a thin and flexible covering that keeps the cell contents together. The cell membrane also controls the movement of chemicals in and out of the cell. Some chemicals can pass through easily and others cannot. The membrane is therefore described as **selectively** or **partially permeable**.

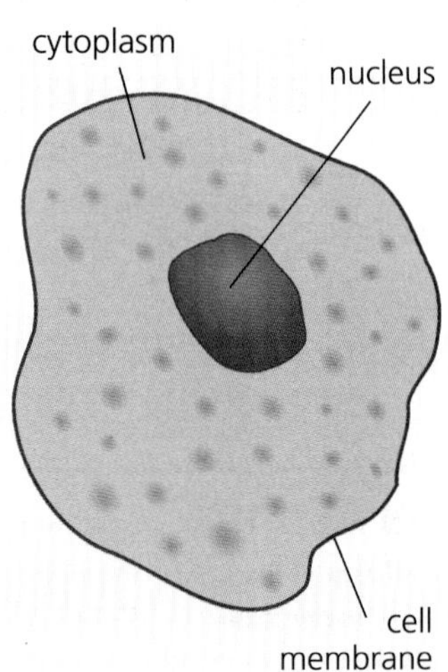

▲ ***Fig 1*** *A typical animal cell.*

Q1 What do we call the part of the cell that controls the rest of the cell?

Q2 What does selectively permeable mean?

Plant cells

Plant cells must carry out many of the same functions as animal cells so they also have cytoplasm, a nucleus and a cell membrane. Plant cells are surrounded by a thick, rigid **cell wall** made of **cellulose** and contain a space called a **vacuole** filled with watery sap. They also contain structures called **chloroplasts** filled with a green chemical called **chlorophyll**. Chlorophyll allows plant cells to use energy from sunlight to make small chemical molecules (Unit 22).

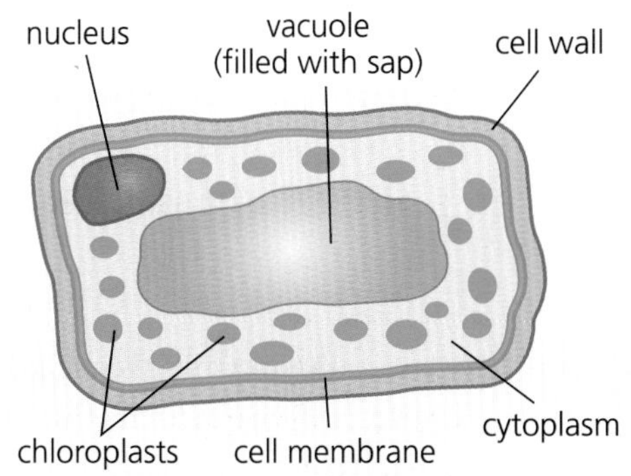

▲ ***Fig 2*** *A typical plant cell.*

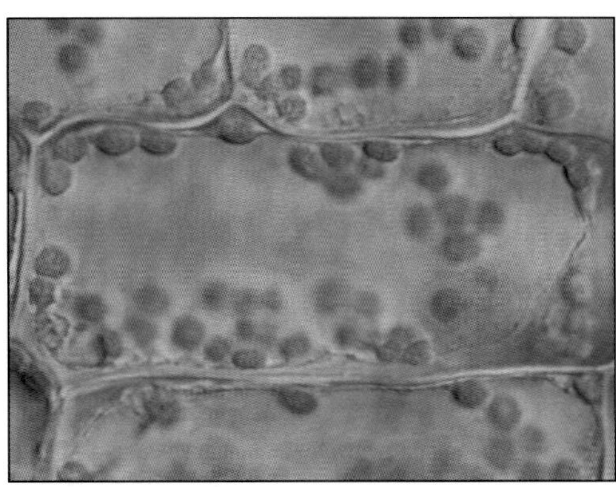

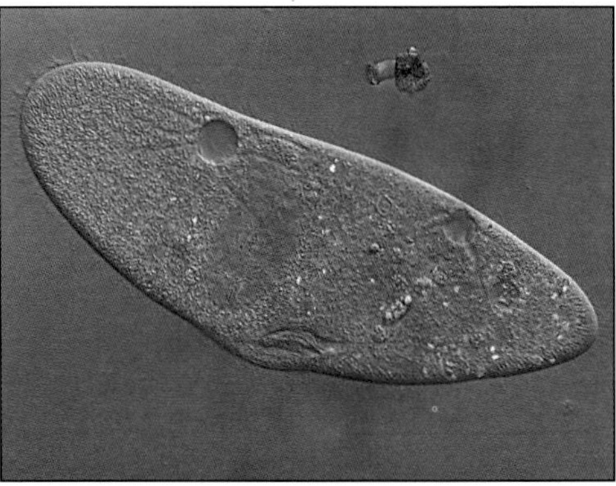

▲ ***Fig 3*** *Plant cells and an animal cell seen through the microscope.*

Q3 List some of the differences between plant and animal cells.

Q4 What is the role of the cell wall in a plant cell?

Q5 Which processes do chloroplasts play a vital part in?

Key Words

cell membrane – flexible covering of the cell
cellulose – the substance plant cell walls are made of
chlorophyll – green chemical in plant cells
chloroplast – a structure in a plant cell that contains chlorophyll
cytoplasm – the liquid part of a cell
nucleus – the control centre of the cell
selectively or **partially permeable** – allowing only some chemicals through

SUMMARY

- Organisms are made up of one or more smaller units called cells.
- Cells contain three basic parts: cytoplasm, a nucleus and a cell membrane.
- The cytoplasm contains the chemicals needed to maintain life.
- The nucleus controls the activity of the cell and is responsible for reproduction.
- The cell membrane keeps the cell contents together and controls what passes in and out of the cell.
- Plant cells also have a rigid cell wall of cellulose and chloroplasts which contain a green pigment called chlorophyll.

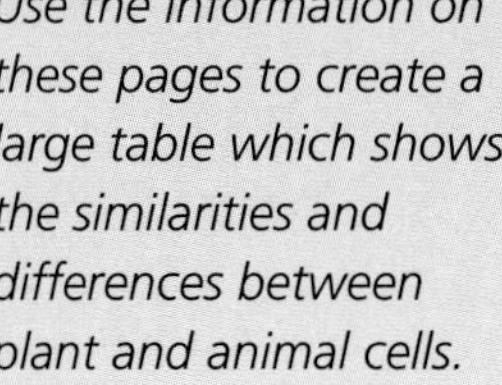

SUMMARY *Activity*

Use the information on these pages to create a large table which shows the similarities and differences between plant and animal cells.

3 Some specialised animal cells

In this section of the book you will learn the following things:

- that some animal cells are specialised to carry out special jobs;
- how some cells are adapted in this way;
- that specialisation of cells is essential for the survival of multicellular animals.

Each to its own job

Multicellular animals are made up of many cells. These cells are not all the same. Some are adapted or specialised to do special jobs within the organism. They work together like a team to share the job of living. This is called **division of labour**.

Some cells and their special jobs are shown below.

Epithelial cells

Epithelial cells cover outer surfaces such as skin and inner surfaces such as mouth and intestines. Epithelial cells need to:

- protect the organism from wear and tear and chemicals;
- allow wanted substances to pass into the organism;
- allow unwanted substances to pass out of the organism;
- guard against water loss;
- allow the organism to sense the environment.

Epithelial cells are found in places where they get worn away. They divide rapidly so that lost cells can be replaced. Many of them are flat so that they can be arranged like tiles on a roof. Some make protective oils or mucus. Some have surface hairs called **cilia** that wave backwards and forwards to move particles that could harm the organism. Dust particles in the lungs are removed in this way. These are called **ciliated epithelial cells**.

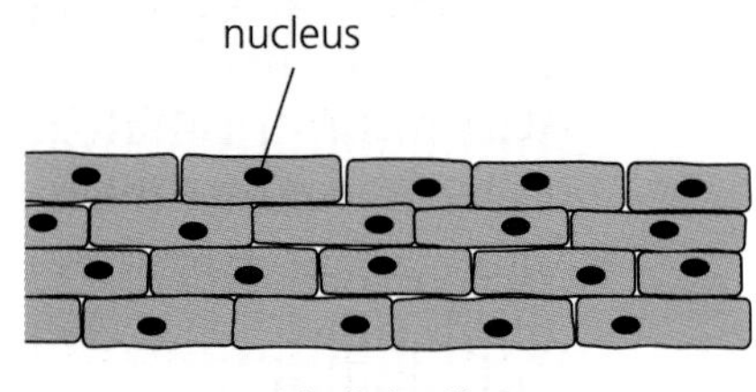

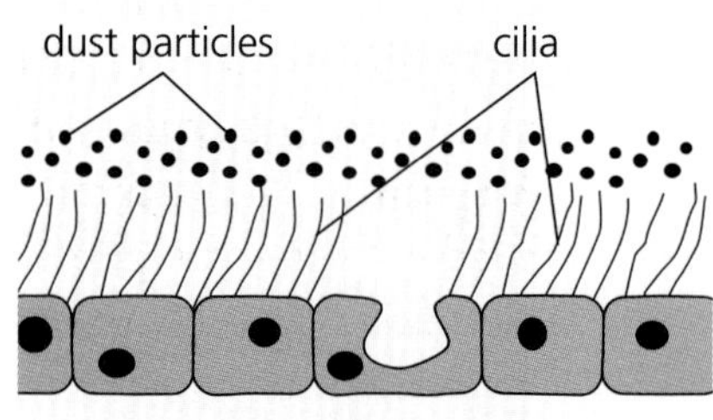

▲ ***Fig 1*** *Epithelial cells.*

Q1 How does the shape of epithelial cells help them to do their job?

Q2 What type of cell makes mucus? Where in your body do you think these cells can be found?

Cells that carry oxygen

Blood carries oxygen in specialised cells called red blood cells. The strong current of the bloodstream carries them around. Red blood cells are adapted to carry oxygen and can do little else. They have lost their nucleus, making more space

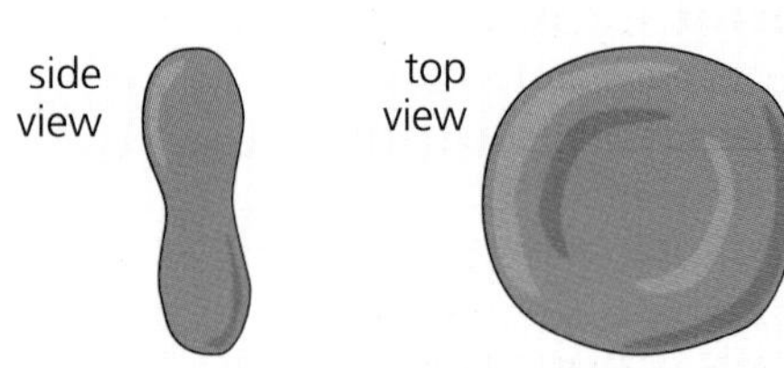

▲ ***Fig 2*** *Red blood cells (x5000) are round and flat.*

for a chemical called **haemoglobin**. They are also very flat and thin. This makes the cell surface larger. The cells can also bend and squeeze through very narrow blood vessels.

Cells specialised for reproduction

Eggs cells and sperm cells play a vital role in the reproduction of animals.

Eggs, or **ova** (singular, **ovum**), contain one half of the genetic material needed to make a new organism. They also contain a food store which makes them amongst the largest cells known.

Sperm cells contain the other half of the genetic material needed to make a new organism. Unlike ova, they do not have a large food store. A sperm cell is adapted for swimming. The head contains the genetic material and energy. The tail drives the sperm through liquid towards an ovum.

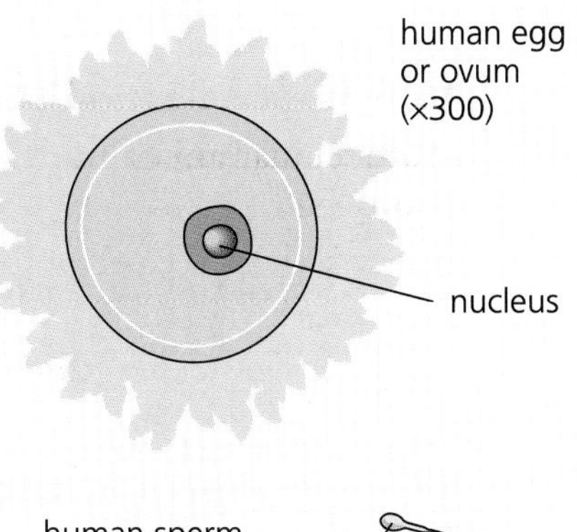

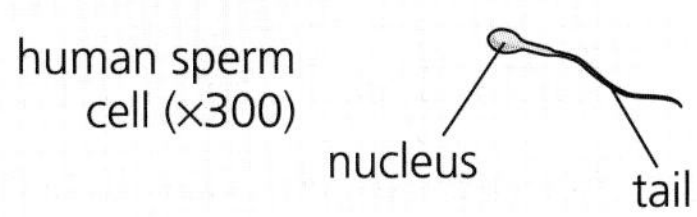

▲ ***Fig 3*** *Human ovum and sperm.*

Q3 How are red blood cells and sperm cells adapted to carry out the jobs they do?

Q4 Why does a red blood cell have no need for a tail?

Q5 What makes ova amongst the largest cells known?

Passing the message

When your hand touches something unpleasant or painful you move it away very quickly. The information about the object passes from your hand to your brain along nerves made of specialised nerve cells. The nerve message is like electricity travelling along a wire and each cell has a long thin arm very like a wire with insulating material around it.

Key Words

cilia – tiny moving hairs attached to cells
ciliated – having cilia
division of labour – sharing out the functions needed to maintain life
epithelial cells – cells lining outer and inner surfaces of the body
specialised – adapted to do a special job

SUMMARY

- The cells in multicellular organisms are specialised to share out the functions of life by division of labour.
- Epithelial cells line body surfaces and help to protect the organism.
- Some more examples of adapted and specialised cells are red blood cells, ova, sperm and nerve cells.

SUMMARY *Activity*

Describe how the cells on the surface of your skin are adapted to do their job.

4 Plant cells are specialised too

In this section of the book you will learn the following things:

- **that some plant cells have become specialised to carry out special jobs;**
- **how some cells have become specialised in this way;**
- **that specialisation of cells is essential for the survival of multicellular plants.**

Plants are not as active as animals but they must carry out all the functions of life. Plants also contain many cells that are specialised to help them do this.

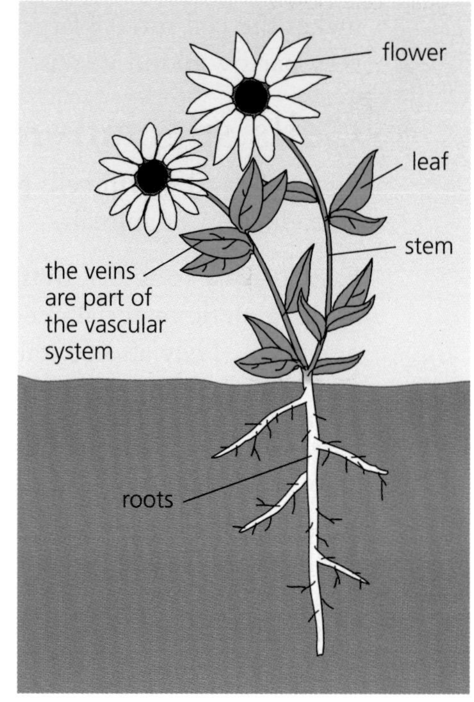

▲ ***Fig 1*** *Plants have tissues and organs specialised to do different jobs.*

Plant organisation

Plant cells are limited in size as animal cells are. A growing plant must make more cells, not bigger cells. Like animals, multicellular plants are made up of different types of cells. There is also division of labour in plants.

Cells with the same function are gathered together into tissues. Plant tissues work together in organs. The major tissues and organs of a flowering plant (Fig 1) must all work together to carry out the seven functions of life and keep the organism alive.

Plants also need to move food and water from place to place. Instead of blood and a heart, they have a system of tubes called **vascular tissue**.

Q1 Why are there organs and tissues in plants that do similar jobs to those in animals?

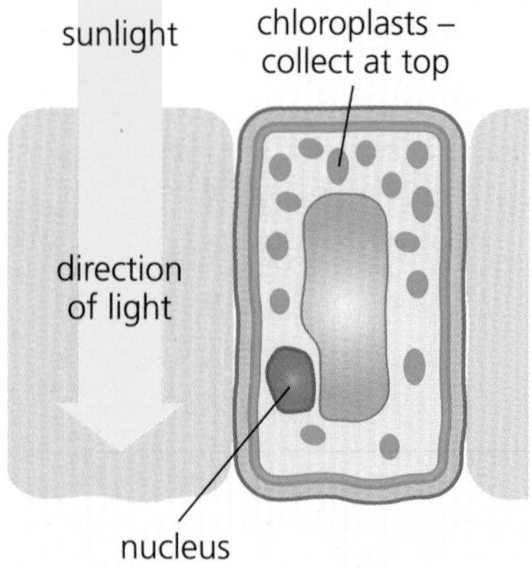

▲ ***Fig 2*** *Sunlight travels deeper into palisade cells because they are this way up.*

Cells in leaves

Plant leaves contain many cells adapted to make food. They use energy from the sun to turn water and carbon dioxide gas into sugar. This process is called photosynthesis (Unit 23).

Palisade cells are especially well designed for photosynthesis. These cells contain many chloroplasts filled with chlorophyll and form a layer just beneath the upper protective covering of the leaf. When the sun shines on the leaf the energy from the sunlight passes directly into them. They are also tall and arranged in regular rows, to help the sunlight to shine deep inside.

Q2 How are palisade cells adapted to help the plant make food?

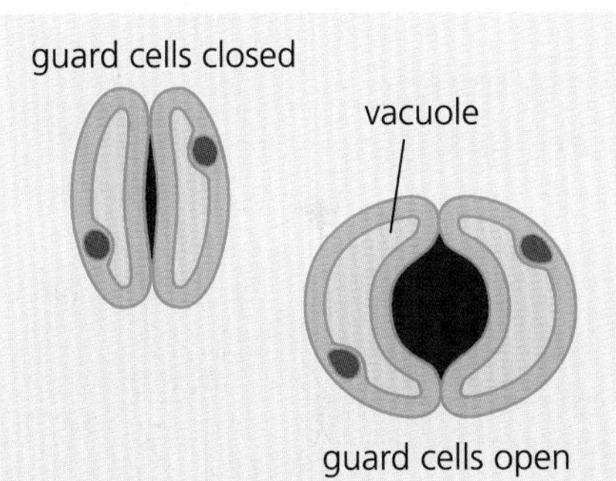

Guard cells are some other very specialised leaf cells. They control the small pores called **stomata** (Unit 22) on the underside of leaves. Full, fat guard cells open a stoma and thin, empty ones close it. In this way the guard cells control the amount of water and gases that pass in and out of the leaf.

◀ ***Fig 3*** *Hard, fat guard cells open the stoma. Soft flabby cells close it.*

Q3 How do guard cells work to open and close a stoma?

Under the soil

Some very important cells are found in plant roots (see Fig 4). Root cells do not normally contain chloroplasts for photosynthesis because they are under the soil where no sunlight can reach them. The root controls the flow of water and minerals into the plant. Near the tip, roots are covered by a protective layer of cells called **epidermal cells**. Some of them have tiny outgrowths. These cells are called **root hair cells**. Root hairs have very thin walls and make the outer surface of the root bigger, which increases the amount of water the roots can take in.

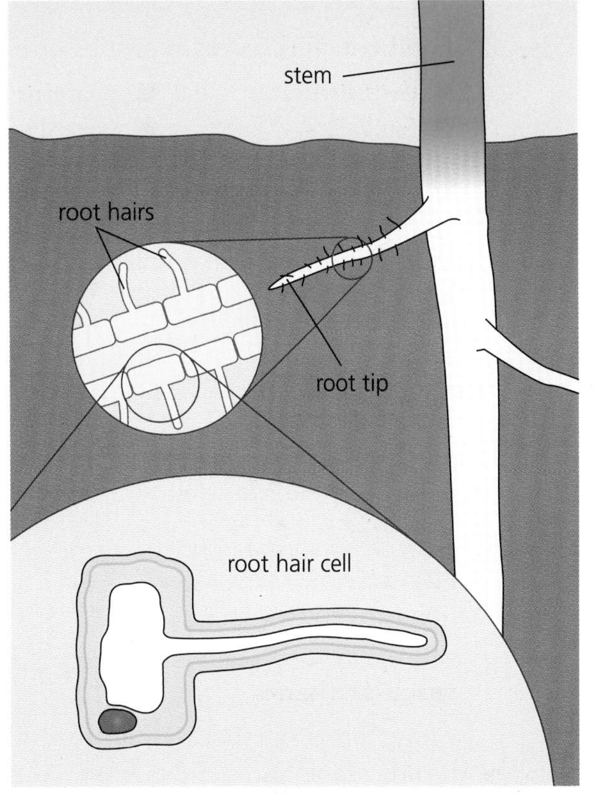

▲ ***Fig 4***

Q4 Which cells in animals do the same job as a plant's epidermal cells?

Q5 Why are root cells not green?

Key Words

epidermal cells – the outer protective cells that cover a plant
root hair cells – epidermal cells with hair-like outgrowths
stoma (plural: **stomata**) – a pore in the lower surface of a leaf
vascular tissue – the circulation system of a plant

SUMMARY

- Many plant cells are adapted to carry out special jobs.
- Cells in multicellular plants are organised into tissues and organs.
- Palisade cells in leaves are adapted for photosynthesis.
- Guard cells in leaves control the movement of water and gases.
- Root hair cells help the plant to take in water and minerals.

SUMMARY *Activity*

Look very carefully at a leaf. List the number of different cells and tissues you can see using only your eyes or a hand lens.

5 A balanced diet

In this section of the book you will learn the following things:

- **that a balanced diet contains carbohydrates, proteins, fats, minerals, vitamins, fibre and water;**
- **how your body gets these substances;**
- **why these substances are important to you.**

The food that you eat is broken down in your body to give you energy and the materials you need to grow strong and stay healthy.

What is in your food?

Food contains six main groups of essential chemicals or **nutrients**:

- carbohydrates
- fats
- proteins
- vitamins
- minerals
- water

Different foods contain different amounts of these nutrients so we need to eat a variety of foods (see Fig 1). This is called a **balanced diet**. What you need to eat will not be exactly the same as what someone else needs. You must decide what is a healthy diet for you. Knowing about the science of food will help you to make sensible choices.

Why do we need different nutrients?

Carbohydrates such as sugars and starches give your body energy (Unit 6).

Fats form a vital part of cell membranes. Fat is also stored in your body as an energy reserve. Eating too much fat can sometimes cause health problems. This is why doctors advise us to keep the total fat content of our diet low, but it would be dangerous to stop eating fats altogether. Most plant oils cause fewer health problems than fats from animal sources.

▲ *Fig 1*

Q1 Which of the foods in Fig 1 are rich in fats or oils?

Q2 Why would it be unhealthy to eat no fat or oil at all?

Proteins are used for growth and repair of body tissues. You need protein to grow, and to replace damaged cells after you stop growing. Muscles are mostly protein. Enzymes (Unit 7) are also proteins.

Foods that are rich in protein include meat, eggs, fish, cheese, wholemeal bread, lentils and beans. There are also processed protein foods, such as tofu (made from soybeans) and Quorn (made from a fungus).

Q3 Why do body builders need a lot of protein in their diet?

Vitamins and **minerals** are also essential. Vitamins help your cells to work properly. Minerals are needed to build some of the molecules in your cells. Eating a varied diet (lots of different foods) helps you to get all the vitamins and minerals you may need.

The minerals and vitamins in Table 1 are only a few of the ones essential for good health.

Q4 What might happen to a person who did not eat enough green vegetables?

▼ *Table 1*

Vitamin	deficiency problems	some sources
vitamin A	dry skin, night blindness	carrots, liver, eggs, green vegetables
vitamin C	scurvy (bleeding gums, bruising, tender skin)	citrus fruit, potatoes, tomatoes
vitamin D	rickets (soft bones)	milk, butter, cheese, sunlight on skin

Mineral	deficiency problems	some sources
calcium	weak teeth and bones	milk, cheese,green vegetables
iron	anaemia (blood deficiency)	nuts, meat, eggs
iodine	thyroid problems (cold, tired, overweight)	shellfish, green vegetables

About 70% of your body weight is **water**. Every chemical reaction in your body needs water. It is also the main part of blood. You use water to dilute poisonous waste and excrete it as urine. You lose water when you breathe and when you sweat. The water that leaves your body through excretion, sweating and breathing must be replaced. You could survive for up to a month without food, but would die in a few days without water. We get most of our water by drinking liquids and a little from our food.

▲ ***Fig 2*** *All living things need water to survive.*

Key Words

carbohydrate – a sugar or starch
protein – a body building material
mineral – an element needed to make some body chemicals
nutrient – any food substance needed by the body
vitamin – a ready-made chemical essential for health

SUMMARY

- The six main nutrients are carbohydrates, fats, proteins, vitamins, minerals and water.
- Carbohydrates and fats provide energy. Fats are also needed for cell membranes. Proteins are needed to build tissues and make enzymes.
- Small amounts of vitamins and minerals are also essential to health.
- Your body is 70% water. Water lost through excretion, sweating and breathing must be replaced.

SUMMARY *Activity*

Information about the nutritional contents of foods can be found on labels. Check the labels on 10 food substances at home and decide which ones would be good sources of protein, carbohydrate and fats. Which ones contain the most vitamins?

6 Energy for life

In this section of the book you will learn the following things:

- that cells use food to give them energy;
- that different activities and lifestyles demand different amounts of energy;
- that some important carbohydrates are not used for energy.

What do we need energy for?

All living things must have energy to survive. Approximately 70% of the energy you use every day keeps your body working. This includes your heartbeat and all the chemical reactions that take place in your cells. The remaining 30% is used for extra work and activities. So the total amount of energy used in a day depends on how active you are. It may be influenced by:

- age – growing children need more energy than older people;
- size – larger people may need more energy;
- gender – men generally need more energy than women;
- occupation – people with active jobs need more energy;
- activity – people who take part in active sports need more energy;
- motherhood – pregnant women and women who are breast feeding need more energy.

Energy is measured in **kilojoules** (**kJ**). Heat energy was once measured in **calories** (**c** or **cal**) or **Kilocalories** (**C, Cal** or **Kcal**), which you sometimes see on food labels.

Q1 Why do you think growing children use up a lot of energy?

Q2 Why do you think a pregnant woman needs a lot of energy?

Q3 What do you do each week that needs a lot of energy?

Activity	Kilojoules per day	Kilocalories per day
mountain climber	23 000	5 400
building worker	21 000	5 000
athlete	19 000	4 500
footballer	16 000	3 800
teenage boy	12 500	3 000
secretary	11 000	2 600
teenage girl	9 500	2 300

◀ ***Table 1*** *Energy needed by some different people.* *

Q4 Where would you place the following people in the table?
a) a retired man who watches television a lot.
b) a female ballet dancer.

* *The calorie has been replaced by an energy unit called the joule (J). One calorie (c) = 4.2 J. One kilocalorie (C) = 4.2 kilojoules (kJ).*

Food	Energy in 100 grams (kJ)
celery	35
sugar	1 600
lard	2 700
breakfast cereal	1 500
toast	1 000
mashed potatoes	400

◀ ***Table 2*** *Amounts of energy in some different foods.*

Q5 Which of the foods in Table 2 are:
a) rich in carbohydrates? **b)** rich in fats?

Q6 List five other foods that would contain an amount of energy similar to celery.

Q7 What is fat used for in your body?

Some very big carbohydrates called **dietary fibre** cannot easily be broken down by your body. Dietary fibre helps food to pass through your digestive system (Unit 7). Cellulose from plant cell walls is an important source of dietary fibre.

Food	fibre	starches	sugars
wholemeal bread	✔✔✔	✔✔✔	–
cereals	✔✔✔	✔✔	–
vegetables	✔✔✔	–	–
white rice	✔	✔✔✔	–
potatoes	✔	✔✔✔	–
jam	–	–	✔✔✔
grapes	✔	✔	✔✔✔
chocolate	–	–	✔✔✔
honey	–	–	✔✔✔

◀ ***Table 3*** *Carbohydrate in some different foods.*

Q8 Why does eating a chocolate bar give you energy?

Q9 Name two foods that would give you dietary fibre.

Key Words

calorie – a unit once used to measure heat energy*
dietary fibre – indigestible carbohydrates (roughage)
digestion – chemically breaking down food into smaller molecules
kilojoule – the unit for energy

SUMMARY

- All living things need energy to survive.
- The amount of energy you need depends on how old you are and how active you are.
- Different foods contain different amounts of energy. Foods rich in fats and carbohydrates contain a lot of energy.
- Some carbohydrates called dietary fibre keep us healthy but do not give us energy.
- Energy is measured in kilojoules.

SUMMARY *Activity*

Make a list of the foods you eat during a full day. Use food labels to try to work out how many kilojoules of energy the food contained.

7 Breaking down food

In this section of the book you will learn the following things:

- that food is broken down into smaller molecules by a process called digestion;
- that enzymes play an important role in the breakdown of foods;
- that foods need to be broken down because many food molecules are too big to pass into your blood;
- that digestion occurs in the digestive system.

Digestion

Nutrients are often large and complicated molecules. Before they can be used by your body they must first be broken down into smaller ones. This process is called **digestion**.

Food molecules and enzymes

A protein molecule (Fig 1) is made up of a long chain of much smaller molecules joined together. The smaller molecules are called **amino acids**. The bonds between amino acids can be broken by **enzymes**. An enzyme that breaks down a protein will have no effect on starch. Each type of enzyme only works on one type of food.

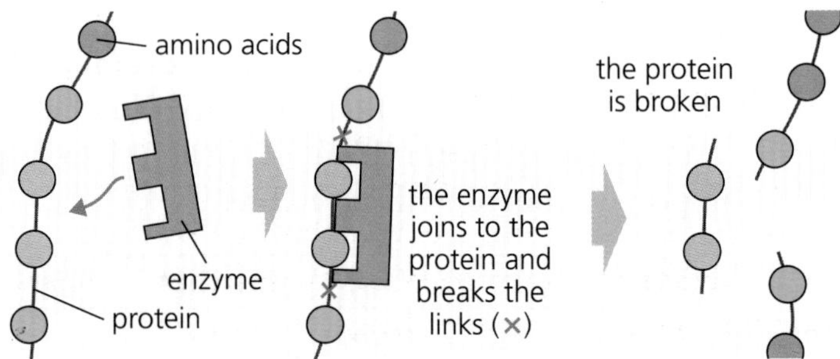

▲ ***Fig 1*** *The enzyme is breaking the protein down into amino acids. An enzyme that breaks down proteins is called a* ***protease****.*

Q1 Why does your digestive system contain many different enzymes?

Q2 What is a protease? Why do you think some washing powders contain protease?

The digestive system

The food you eat passes from your mouth to your anus through a long tube called the gut. As the food makes this journey it is broken down by two processes:

- physical action
- chemical attack

Breakdown of food begins in your mouth. Your teeth grind food up while enzymes in your saliva begin to digest it. Teeth are shaped to do different jobs. Sharp chisel shaped teeth (incisors) can bite a piece from a big chunk of food. Flat teeth (molars) can grind it up so that is easy to swallow.

Food is moved down by squeezing movements, not by gravity. Mucus made by the gut also helps the food to slide down.

In your stomach the food is churned and mixed into a paste with water, acids and enzymes.

More enzymes are added as the food moves around the first bend in your gut.

When it reaches the small intestine it is a well digested watery fluid. Here, the digested nutrients pass through the gut wall into the blood (see Units 8 and 9).

Q3 Why do humans have a set of differently shaped teeth?

Q4 What parts do the stomach and small intestine play in digestion?

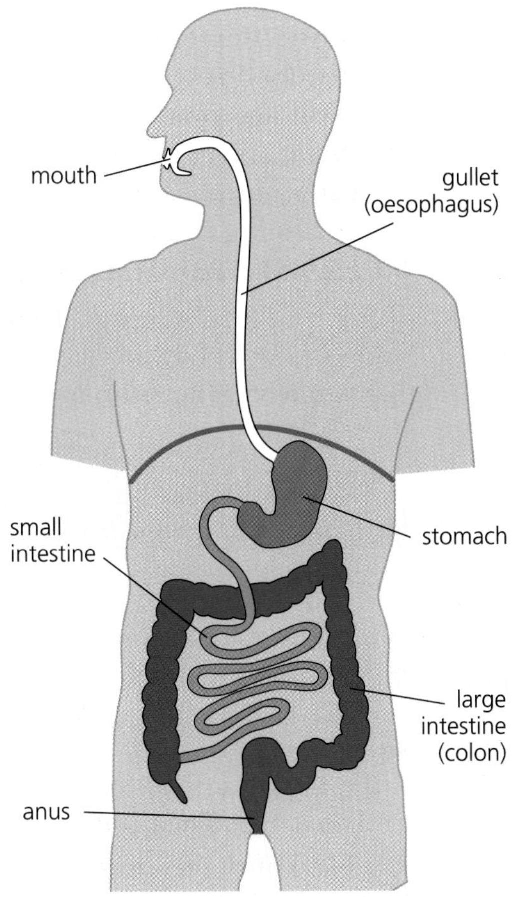

▲ ***Fig 2*** *The human digestive system.*

After the nutrients have been taken out, the gut contains waste material (e.g. fibre) and water. The **colon**'s main job is to reclaim water. Some diseases, such as cholera, force food to 'run' through your gut too quickly for the water to be recovered. One reason why cholera is a very dangerous disease is just because it makes a person's body lose water.

Finally, the nearly-solid unwanted material is **egested** from the gut through the anus. It is now called faeces. When flushed down the toilet, faeces become part of the **sewage**. Faeces can be a source of disease because they contain billions of bacteria. This is why sewage must be purified before it flows into rivers or the sea. It is also the reason why we wash our hands after using the toilet.

Q5 Why is water taken into the body in the large intestine?

Q6 Why is washing your hands after using the toilet so important?

Key Words

colon – a part of the large intestine where water is absorbed

egestion – unused food and fibre passing out of the anus

faeces – unused food and fibre that passes out the anus

sewage – waste material, including some from toilets, that must be purified before it goes into rivers and the sea

SUMMARY

- Nutrients in food must be digested before they enter the blood.
- The digestive system contains a long tube called the gut that runs from the mouth to the anus.
- Water is reclaimed in the large intestine before waste materials (faeces) pass out of the anus.
- Faeces can cause disease. Sewage must be purified and hands washed clean.

SUMMARY *Activity*

How are human teeth adapted to do their job? Look at your own teeth in a mirror.

How do you think your teeth compare with the teeth of:

a) a lion; b) a sheep?

8 How nutrients enter the blood

In this section of the book you will learn the following things:

- that food is absorbed into the blood as it passes through the small intestine;
- that the wall of the small intestine is specially adapted to help this process.

The small intestine

After your food is broken down it passes through the gut walls into your blood. The blood will take the food to all the cells of your body. The passage of vital nutrients from the gut to the blood is called **absorption**.

The small intestine is specially adapted to do this job.

- The small intestine is very long and narrow. Food can only squeeze through slowly. This gives the nutrients time to be absorbed into the blood.
- The walls of the small intestine are lined with thousands of fingers and folds which increase its surface area.

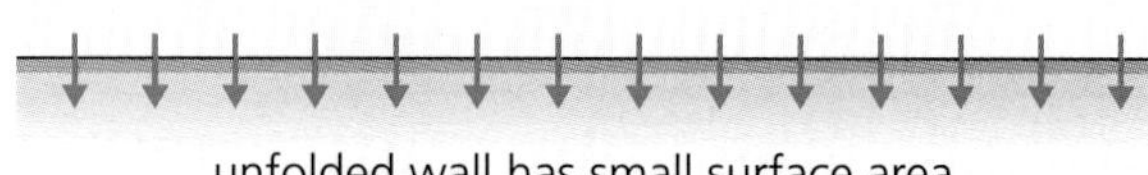

unfolded wall has small surface area

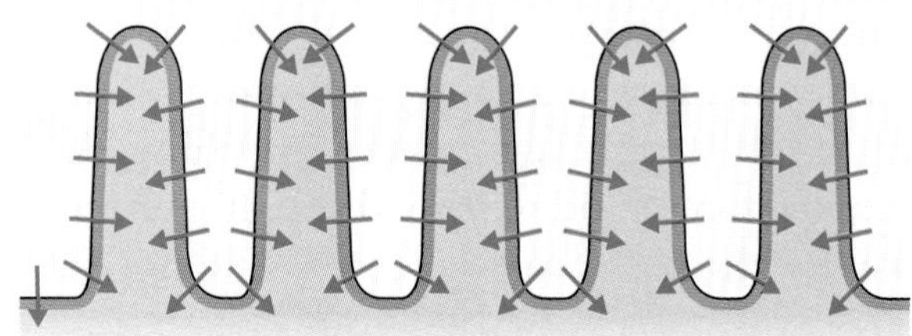

within the same distance a folded wall has a much greater surface area

▲ ***Fig 1*** *Use a piece of string to measure the surface.*

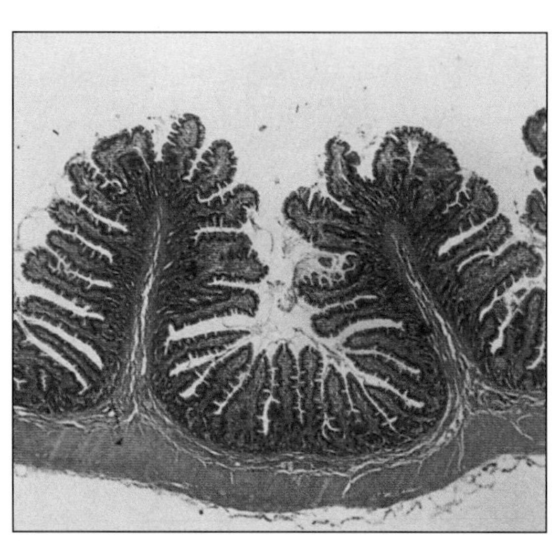

The small intestine of an adult person is between six and seven metres long. The walls are lined with finger-shaped folds called **villi**. By increasing the surface area on the inside of the small intestine, villi greatly increase the amount of food that can be absorbed as it goes along. The small intestine is very narrow so that as much food as possible is pressed against the walls. This also helps absorption.

◀ ***Fig 2*** *Villi.*

Q1 What is the word that describes food passing from the small intestine to the blood?

Q2 Why is the small intestine long and narrow?

Q3 What are villi?

The small intestine has a very good blood supply. This also helps nutrients to go into the blood. Tiny thin-walled blood vessels called **capillaries** run inside the villi.

Moving on

Blood leaves the villi of the small intestine full of simple sugars, amino acids and nutrients from broken down fats. Some of the food goes to be stored. Fat is stored under your skin and around some body organs. Some sugar is stored as glycogen in your **liver** and muscles. Fat stores help your body to survive without food for a while. Glycogen stores are a fast energy reserve for extra activity.

Most of the food is pumped around your body in your bloodstream. This is how it reaches the tips of your fingers and toes, your brain and your heart. This is also how it reaches places where fat is stored.

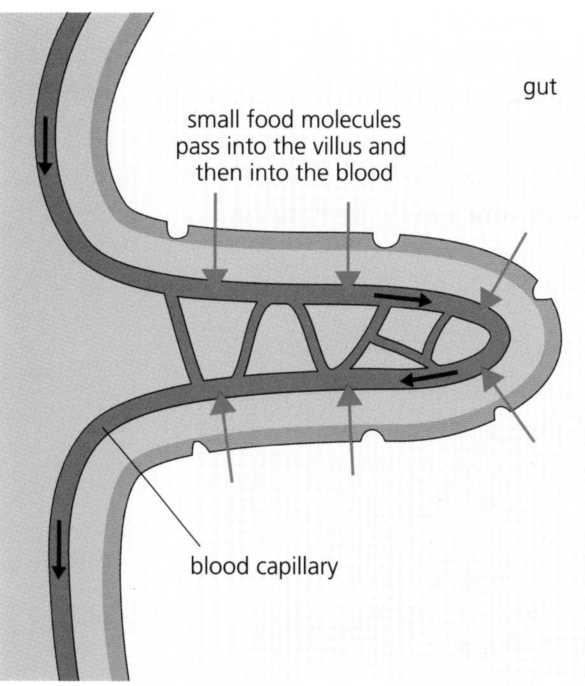

▲ ***Fig 3*** *Villus.*

Q4 Why must the small intestine have a good supply of blood?

Q5 Why does the body store some nutrients?

Key Words

absorption – the passage of nutrients from the gut to the blood
capillaries – very small blood vessels
liver – a very important organ in your body
villi – small folds in the lining of the small intestine wall

SUMMARY

- Nutrients pass from the gut to the bloodstream through the walls of the small intestine. This process is called absorption.
- The small intestine is adapted for this process in three main ways.
- Fats are stored under the skin and around some organs. Sugar is stored as glycogen in the liver and muscles.

SUMMARY *Activity*

Describe the journey taken by a single molecule of sugar between your mouth and a muscle cell in your finger.

9 The body's transport system

In this section of the book you will learn the following things:

- **that your blood carries essential gases and nutrients to all parts of your body;**
- **that your heart is a muscular pump that pumps blood around your body;**
- **the differences between arteries, veins and capillaries.**

Cells need nutrients and oxygen in order to survive and grow. They also produce waste materials that must be taken away. The circulatory system brings food and oxygen to every cell of your body and takes away waste products. It also carries other things your body needs.

What is blood?

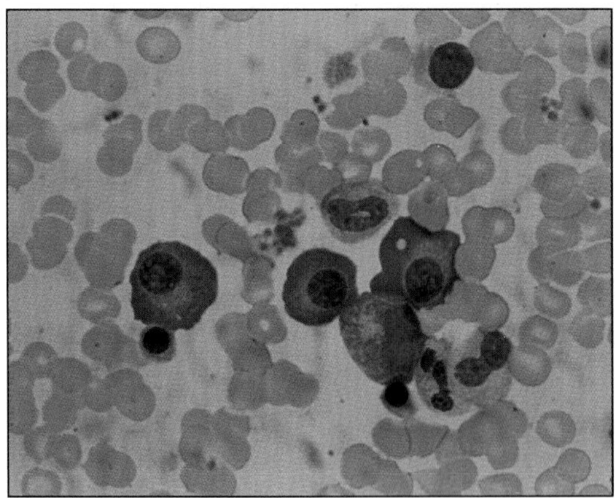

▲ *Fig 1*

Blood is made up of two main parts. A liquid called **plasma** carries dissolved gases, foods and waste materials. Plasma flows easily because it is mainly water. This enables blood to flow along the narrow tubes called capillaries.

Q1 Why do humans need a circulatory system?

Q2 Why must blood be watery?

The plasma contains **red blood cells**, **white blood cells**, and some tiny granules called **platelets**.

Red blood cells

Red blood cells are flattened and have no nucleus. They are filled with a red substance called **haemoglobin** that can catch oxygen. This is how the red blood cells carry oxygen around the body. (Also see Unit 3.)

White blood cells

White blood cells protect the body from diseases caused by bacteria that enter the blood. One type of white blood cell can wrap itself around bacteria and digest them. Another type helps your body to make defensive chemicals called **antibodies**, which protect you from future attacks from the same bacteria (Unit 20). You can see at least three different white blood cells in Fig 1.

Platelets

These tiny granules pack themselves together whenever a blood vessel is damaged. They help to seal cuts and make the blood clot into a scab. Messages from white blood cells send out the alarm which tells the platelets where to go.

Q3 What makes red blood cells red?

Pumping the blood

The heart is a pump made of powerful muscle. Each time it beats, it sends a spurt of blood around the body. You can feel this as a pulse.

Blood travels out of the heart in blood vessels called **arteries** with strong, thick, elastic walls. Arteries become narrower and narrower as they go away from the heart.

When they are so tiny that red blood cells have to fold double to get through, they are called **capillaries**. The walls of capillaries are very thin so that nutrients and oxygen from the blood can leak out into the cells around them. At the same time, waste materials pass in the opposite direction.

Blood returns to the heart in **veins**. Veins do not need thick walls because the blood in them is not being forced hard by the heart. There is even a danger that the blood could stop flowing altogether. Veins therefore have **valves** to keep the blood moving and prevent it from going backwards.

Q4 Which vessels allow materials to pass between the blood and the body cells?

Q5 List two differences between arteries and veins.

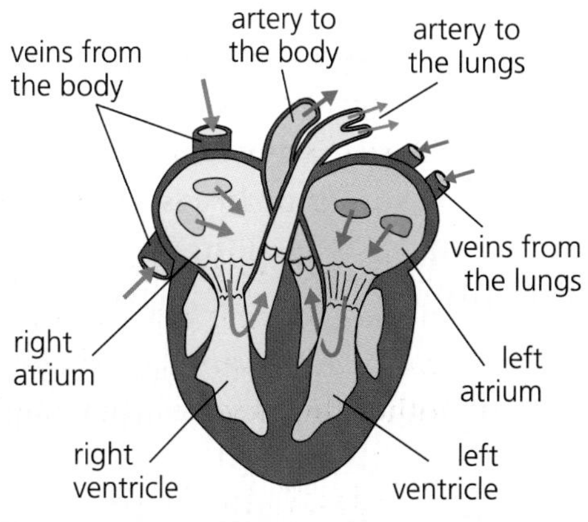

▲ ***Fig 2*** *Vertical section of the human heart.*

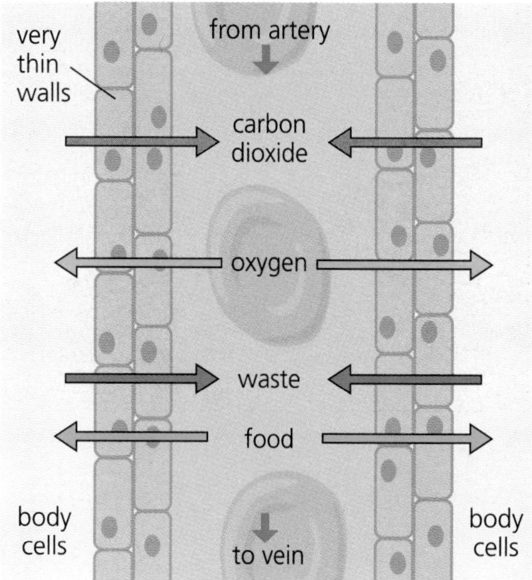

▲ ***Fig 3*** *Capillary in tissue.*

Key Words

artery – a blood vessel that carries blood from the heart

capillary – a tiny thin-walled blood vessel

haemoglobin – the red pigment inside red blood cells

plasma – the liquid part of blood

platelets – small components of blood that are essential to clotting

valve – a mechanism that allows a liquid to flow in one direction only

vein – a blood vessel that carries blood back to the heart

SUMMARY

- Blood is the body's transport system.
- Plasma carries food, gases and other soluble substances.
- Red blood cells carry oxygen. White blood cells fight disease. Platelets help blood to clot.
- The heart is a muscular pump that drives blood around the body.
- Arteries are thick-walled vessels that carry blood from the heart.
- Veins are thin-walled vessels with valves. They carry blood back to the heart.
- Thin-walled capillaries link arteries and veins.

SUMMARY *Activity*

Find out how to take your pulse. Take your pulse for one minute before exercise and for one minute after. What happens to the pulse? Why do you think this happens?

10 How we get our oxygen

In this section of the book you will learn the following things:

- that the oxygen we need to stay alive comes from the air;
- that air enters our lungs by a process called breathing;
- how our lungs are adapted to allow oxygen to pass into the blood;
- that our lungs also play an important part in removing waste gases from our body.

Your body cells need oxygen to obtain energy from sugars (Unit 6). Oxygen is transported by the blood (Unit 9). This oxygen enters the blood in your lungs.

Inhaled air	
oxygen	21%
other gases (mainly carbon dioxide)	1%
nitrogen	78%

Exhaled air	
oxygen	17%
carbon dioxide	4%
other gases	1%
nitrogen	78%

▲ ***Fig 1*** *Your body has changed the composition of the air between breathing in and breathing out.*

Taking air into the lungs is called **breathing**. Breathing in is called **inhalation**. Breathing out is called **exhalation**. Every breath you inhale contains a mixture of gases. Every breath you exhale also contains a mixture of gases but the proportions have changed.

Q1 How has the air changed between inhaling and exhaling?

How do we breathe?

Every time you inhale, the muscles between your ribs tighten. This lifts your ribs upwards and outwards. At the same time, your diaphragm tightens and moves downwards. This increases the space inside your chest, which pulls air in to fill up the extra space inside your lungs.

Every time you exhale, the muscles between your ribs relax and allow your ribcage to collapse. At the same time, your diaphragm relaxes and moves upwards. This reduces the space inside your chest and pushes air out of your lungs.

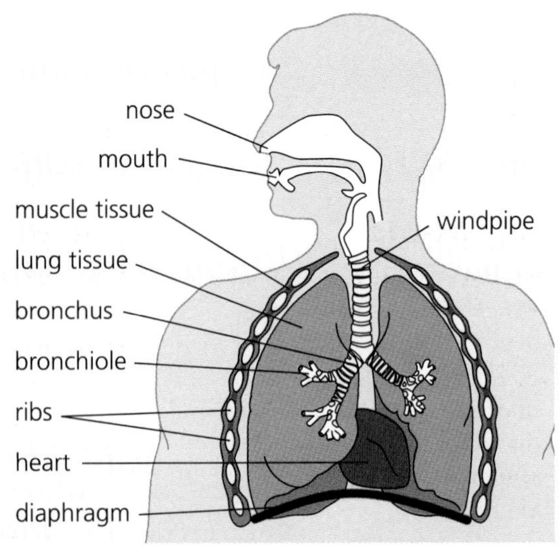

▲ ***Fig 2*** *Inside your chest.*

Q2 Why are the ribs important for breathing?

Q3 What is the job of the diaphragm?

The structure of your lungs

When you inhale, air flows from your nose or mouth into your windpipe. This divides into two smaller tubes called **bronchi**. One bronchus goes to each lung. There they divide into smaller tubes called **bronchioles**. The bronchioles carry on branching until they finally end in tiny air sacs called **alveoli**. Alveoli make the lung tissue spongy (Fig 3).

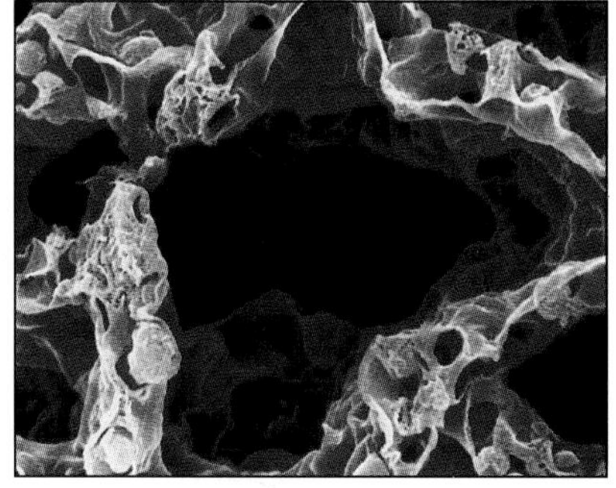

▲ *Fig 3*

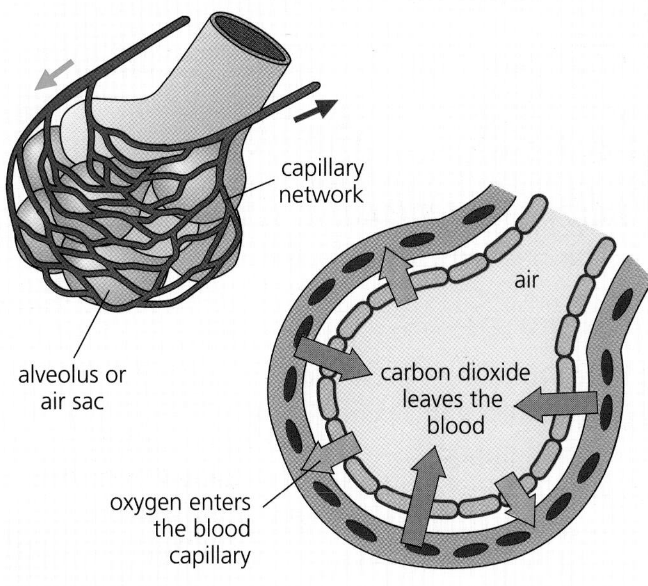

▲ *Fig 4*

The alveoli increase the surface area of the lungs many times. Each alveolus contains a net of blood capillaries (see Fig 4). The walls of the alveoli are very thin and the walls of the capillaries are very thin so it is easy for gases to pass between them. It is here that oxygen from the air enters the blood and unwanted carbon dioxide leaves the blood. This is called **gas exchange**. Oxygen in the blood is sent from the lungs to the heart and then pumped around the body. Carbon dioxide in the alveoli is exhaled.

Q4 Why must the walls of the alveoli and capillaries be thin?

Q5 Place the following list in order of size with the largest first: windpipe; alveolus; bronchiole; bronchus

Key Words

alveolus – a tiny air sac in a lung
bronchiole – a small air tube in a lung
bronchus (plural: **bronchi**) – one of two main tubes branching off the windpipe
capillary network – the tiny blood vessels surrounding an alveolus
gas exchange – the process of oxygen entering the blood and carbon dioxide leaving the blood

SUMMARY

- The oxygen we need to stay alive comes from the air.
- Breathing in is called inhalation. Breathing out is called exhalation.
- Exhaled air contains less oxygen and more carbon dioxide than inhaled air.
- Lungs are specially adapted to allow oxygen to pass into the blood.
- Alveoli are tiny sacs in the lungs where gas exchange takes place.

SUMMARY *Activity*

Count how many times you breathe every minute. This is your breathing rate. Take some gentle exercise and then count your breathing rate again. What happens? Why do you think it happens?
Repeat the activity in Unit 9 and compare the results.

11 Smoking and lung disease

In this section of the book you will learn the following things:

- **that the lining of the windpipe has special cells that help to clean the air as it enters the lungs;**
- **that tobacco smoke is a mixture of very harmful chemicals;**
- **that the chemicals in tobacco smoke can damage cells in the windpipe;**
- **that the chemicals in tobacco smoke can make gas exchange less efficient;**
- **that tobacco smoke can cause cancer.**

Lungs are where oxygen enters our blood. Without oxygen, a person dies very quickly. Anything that interferes with the way our lungs work is bad for our health. It is important to keep our lungs clean, undamaged and free from infection. Smoking causes serious damage and makes our lungs work less efficiently. Non-smokers who breathe in other people's smoke can suffer from the same health problems as smokers. This is called **passive smoking**.

The normal cleaning service

The cells lining your windpipe are adapted to remove particles from inhaled air before it reaches the bronchioles and alveoli. Some cells produce sticky mucus which traps dust and **bacteria**. Other cells have tiny hairs called **cilia** which beat in waves to push the mixture back up to your throat. If the mixture of mucus and dirt is swallowed it can be destroyed by acid in your stomach.

Q1 List two ways in which particles are prevented from entering your lungs.

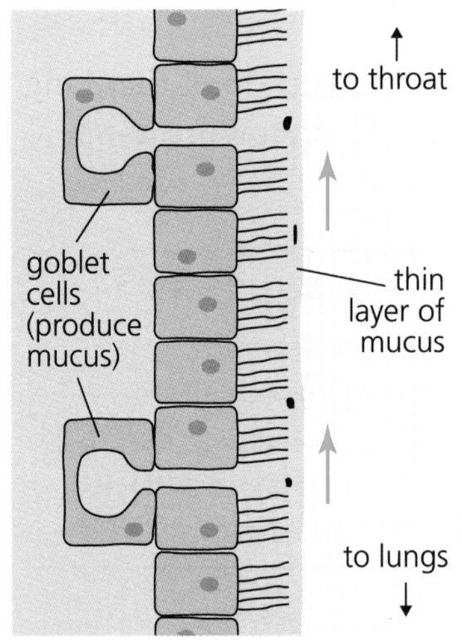

▲ ***Fig 1*** *The cilia beat to remove particles. The mucus traps particles and is then swallowed.*

Cilia and smokers

The tar in tobacco smoke damages the cilia in the windpipe so that they stop working. This means that bacteria, dirt and mucus can build up deep inside the lungs. Bacteria in your lungs can cause infections such as bronchitis. Mucus and dirt in the bronchi and bronchioles make you cough. Eventually the alveoli become blocked and damaged. This reduces the working surface of the lungs and makes it harder to breathe.

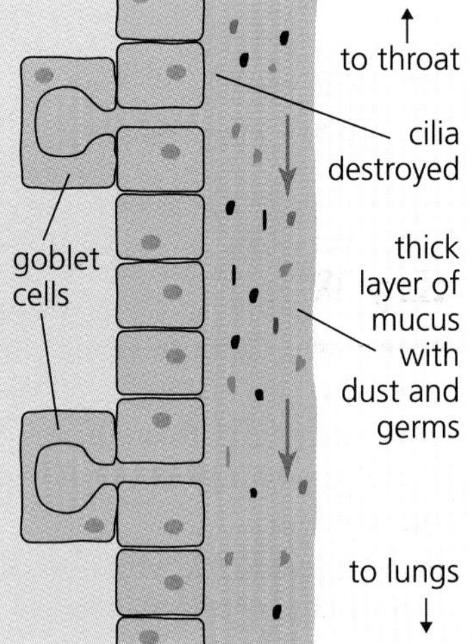

▲ ***Fig 2*** *Damaged and destroyed cilia cannot protect the lungs.*

Q2 Where do you think the disease bronchitis gets its name from?

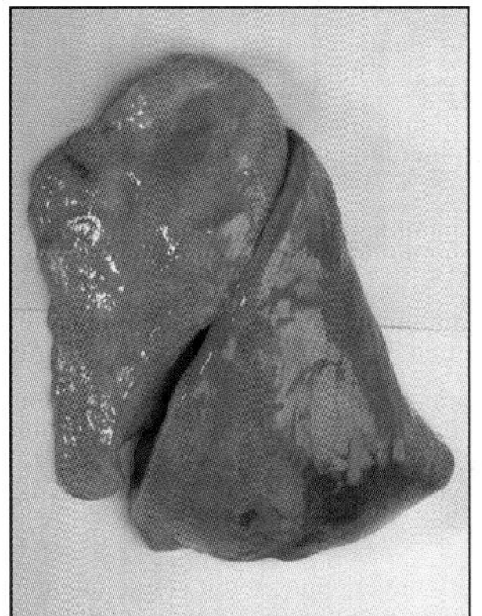
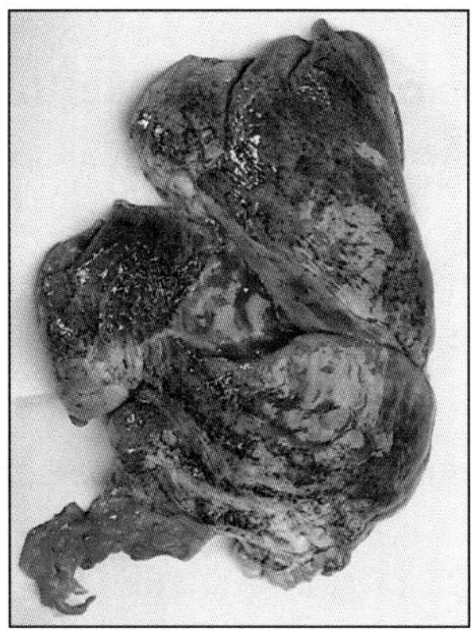

▲ *Fig 3 Which lung would you rather have inside you?*

Blocking blood cells

One of the chemicals in tobacco smoke is a gas called carbon monoxide. This gas can pass through the lungs and into the blood. Carbon monoxide links to haemoglobin, as oxygen does, but unlike oxygen it does not easily let go. Once a red blood cell is full of carbon monoxide it cannot carry oxygen. This makes the blood of smokers less efficient.

Lung cancer

Cells are always dividing to replace cells that become old and die. Sometimes this normal process can get out of control. If too many cells are made they can grow into a lump called a tumour. Tobacco smoke contains chemicals that can cause cells to divide and form tumours.

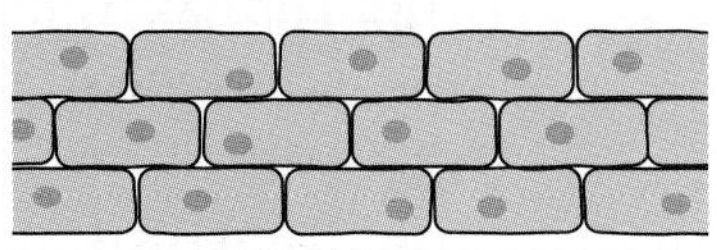
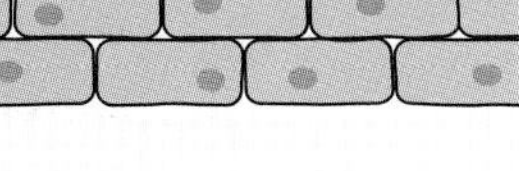

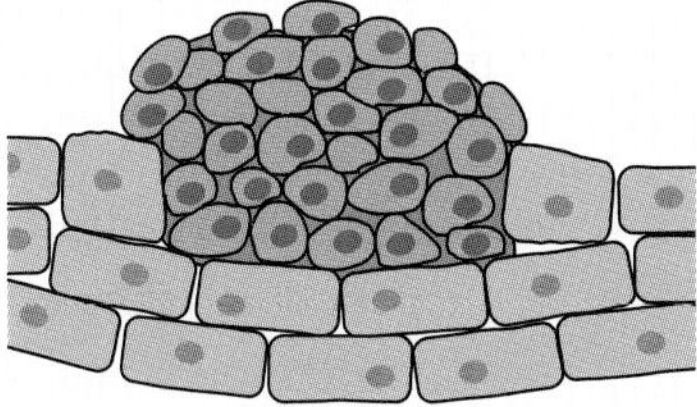

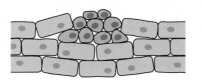

normal cells — one cell divides quickly — a tumour forms

▲ *Fig 4 Fast-growing tumour cells may spread to other parts of the body.*

Q3 How does tobacco smoke damage lungs?

Q4 Why is carbon monoxide a problem for smokers?

Q5 Why do you think that lung cancer is one of the most common types of cancer?

Key Words

bronchitis – an infection of the bronchi

cilia – tiny hairs. Cilia in the windpipe beat to remove dirt and germs

passive smoking – breathing in someone else's tobacco smoke

tar – a dark, sticky material found in tobacco smoke

tumour – a lump made by cells dividing too quickly

SUMMARY

- Tobacco smoke can damage cells that normally remove dirt and bacteria from the air we breathe.
- Carbon monoxide in tobacco smoke links with haemoglobin in red blood cells to prevent it from carrying oxygen.
- Many people think that chemicals in tobacco smoke can cause tumours.
- Non-smokers who breathe in tobacco smoke from other people can also have their health damaged.

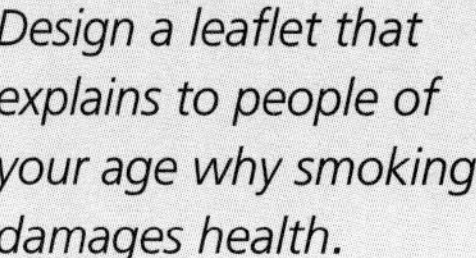

SUMMARY *Activity*

Design a leaflet that explains to people of your age why smoking damages health.

12 Getting energy from food

In this section of the book you will learn the following things:

- how oxygen is used to break down food in your cells and release energy;
- that this process is called aerobic respiration;
- that glucose is the food most commonly used in aerobic respiration;
- that glucose is broken down to carbon dioxide and water during aerobic respiration.

Energy from sugars

A glucose molecule can dissolve in blood and is small enough to pass into cells. It also releases energy very easily. If glucose catches fire, a flash of heat is released.

Cells do not burn glucose by setting fire to it but the end result is the same. Cells release energy from glucose gradually, in stages. At each stage the energy is either used to stay alive or stored to be used later. To do this the cell must:

- use enzymes to break down the glucose slowly;
- store the energy that is released in a large molecule that works a little like a battery storing electricity.

The energy storage molecule can stay in a cell until it is needed. Cells that need large amounts of energy in a hurry, e.g. muscle cells, contain many of these molecules.

▲ ***Fig 1*** *Glucose burns in air to give* ***carbon dioxide*** *and* ***water****. The energy is released in one step.*

Q1 Why must glucose be broken down carefully in your body?

Q2 Why is the energy storage molecule important?

Respiration

Glucose is broken down in stages (Fig 2). First the molecule is broken in half to make two smaller molecules. This gives out a small amount of energy. Before it can break down the glucose any further the cell must have oxygen.

▼ ***Fig 2***

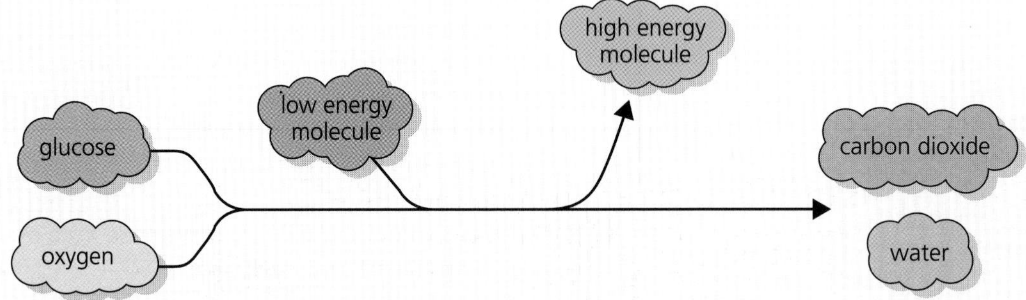

Oxygen allows the cell to break the glucose down completely. This process is called **aerobic respiration** because it uses oxygen. **Aerobics** is a form of exercise that is slow enough to allow glucose to be completely broken down by oxygen but fast enough to make your body work hard to do it.

In aerobic respiration, all the **hydrogen** from the glucose joins up with the **oxygen** to make **water**. This is already a normal part of your body. All the **carbon** joins up with **oxygen** to make **carbon dioxide**. Carbon dioxide dissolves in the blood and goes to the lungs to be breathed out. A word equation for respiration is given below.

Glucose + oxygen → carbon dioxide + water + **energy**

Q3 Why is oxygen vital for respiration?

Energy without oxygen

If you run very fast your muscles use up a lot of energy. Your blood tries to carry as much oxygen to your muscles as it can but sometimes it cannot work fast enough to keep up. When this happens, the sugar in your muscle cells cannot break down completely. The cells turn the half broken down glucose into an acid that can give you cramp.

Q4 Why do we sometimes get muscle cramps?

Q5 Why do cells have to break down glucose step by step?

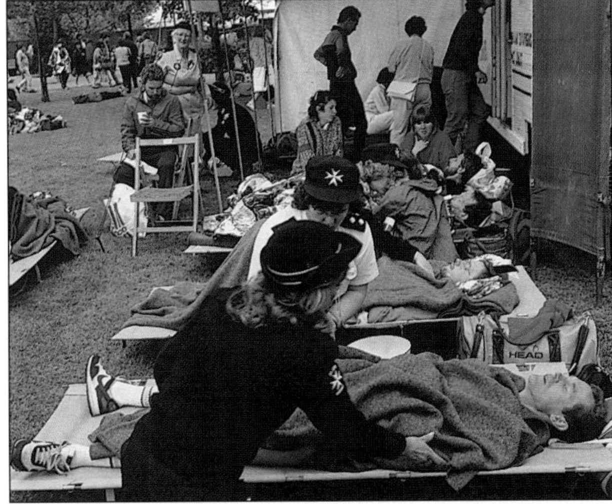

▲ ***Fig 3*** *Regular exercise helps to keep you fit, which keeps your heart and lungs working well. Exercising hard when you are unfit can cause exhaustion.*

Key Words

aerobic respiration – using oxygen to get energy from glucose

carbon dioxide – a combination of carbon and oxygen created by burning or respiration

hydrogen – a chemical element that combines with oxygen to make water

SUMMARY

- Glucose is normally broken down in your body to give carbon dioxide and water.
- The oxygen links to hydrogen from the glucose to form water. The carbon dioxide must be sent out of the cell.
- If your muscles work too hard, an acid can be made which gives you cramp.

SUMMARY *Activity*

Explain to somebody who knows nothing about science why your arms will get cramps if you hold a heavy weight for a long time.

13 Supporting your body

In this section of the book you will learn the following things:

- **that your skeleton is a frame of bones that supports and protects body organs;**
- **that joints between bones allow the skeleton to move and bend;**
- **that different parts of your skeleton have different jobs to do.**

The human skeleton contains more than 200 bones. Some parts of the skeleton protect organs. Other parts support our body and allow us to move. Bone is a mixture of soft living material and hard non-living mineral salts. This makes bone hard but prevents it from being brittle.

Q1 Why is it important to have minerals such as calcium in our diet?

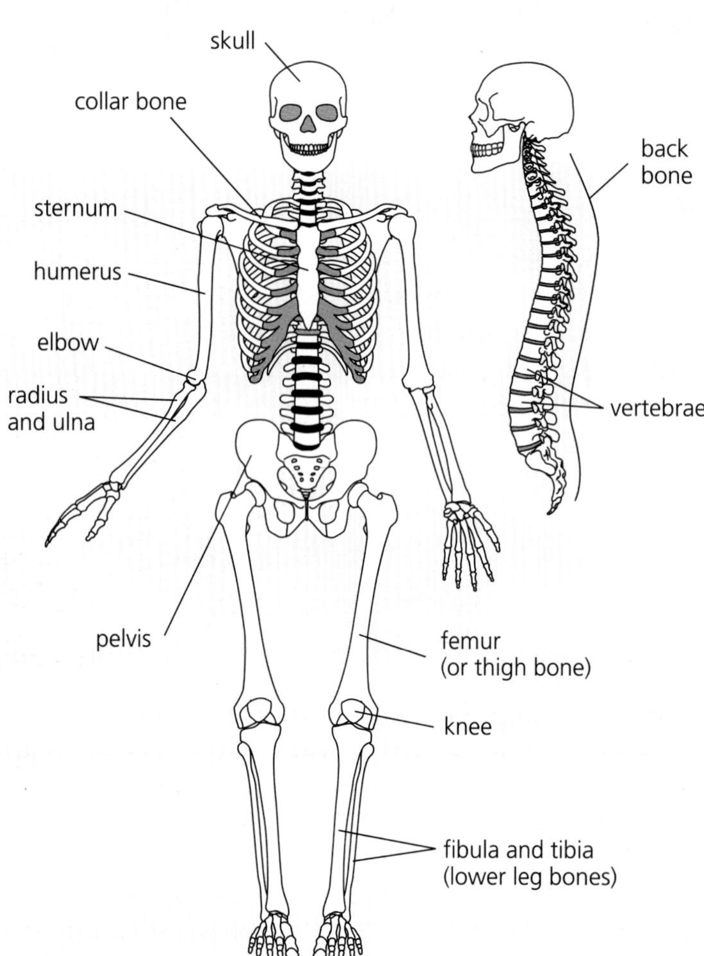

▲ ***Fig 1*** *The human skeleton.*

The skeleton

The **skull** is a rigid box made up of plates of bone firmly joined together. They work like a crash helmet to protect the brain.

The **rib cage** is a flexible case around our heart and lungs. Each rib curves round the sides of the chest from the backbone and is joined in front to a plate of bone called the **sternum**. Ribs are connected to one another by the muscles that help us to breathe.

The backbone, also called the spine or **vertebral column**, is a chain of chunky bones called **vertebrae**. It protects the spinal cord, which carries messages between your brain and body. It also supports the skull, ribs and limbs.

Arms and legs are limbs made of long bones with joints that allow them to move. They are mainly for support. Legs allow us to stand and walk. Arms allow us to move objects and take care of our body.

Q2 List three parts of the skeleton that protect vital organs.

Q3 List two parts of the skeleton that support the body.

How do joints work?

Different joints work in different ways. There are three main types of joint:

- hinge joints;
- ball and socket joints;
- gliding joints.

Hinge joints

A typical hinge joint is found in the knee. It allows the bones to move backwards and forwards like the hinge on a door. Hinge joints are not designed to move from side to side. The ends of the bones are coated with a smooth substance called **cartilage** which prevents them from grinding together. A slippery fluid inside the joint helps it to move easily.

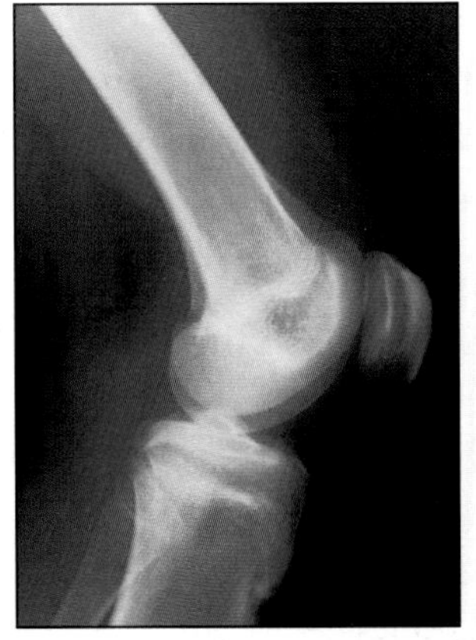

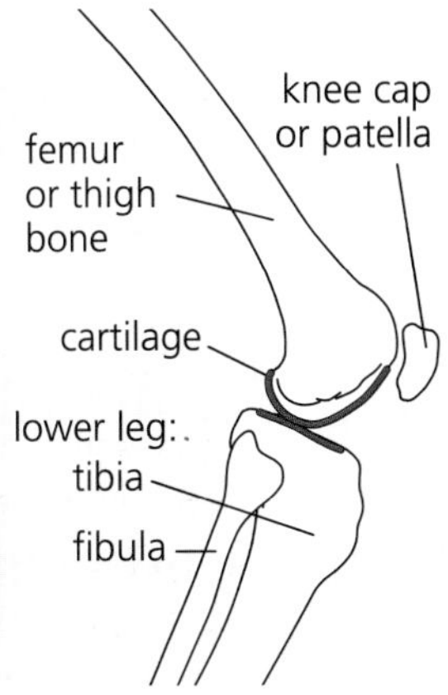

▲ ***Fig 2*** *Unless the cartilage is damaged the bones will move smoothly.*

Q4 Can you name a hinge joint, other than the knee, in your body?

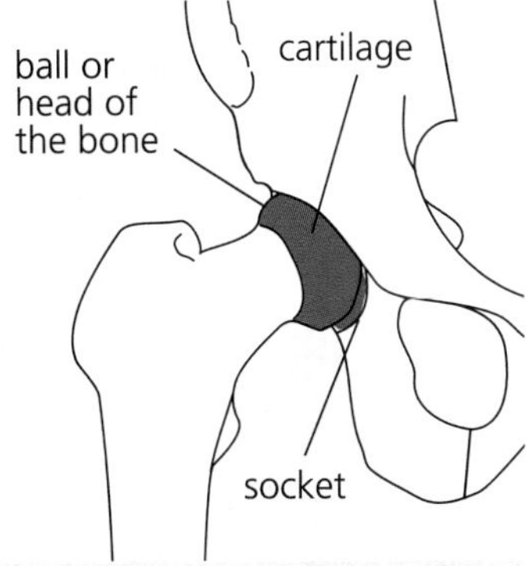

Ball and socket joint

Some parts of our body need to move more freely than a hinge would allow. For example, the shoulder can move in a full circle. The type of joint that permits a circular movement is called a ball and socket (Fig 3).

◀ ***Fig 3***

Q5 Why does damaging cartilage in a joint make it painful to move the joint?

Gliding joints

Some joints are designed to allow bones to slide a little way. The small bones inside our wrists (Fig 4) and feet are arranged this way.

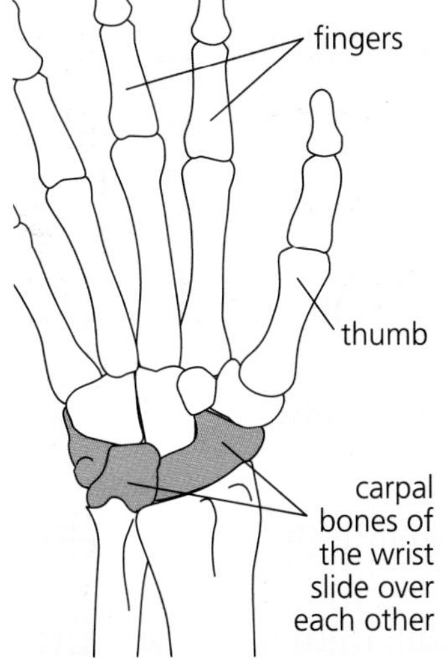

▲ ***Fig 4***

Key Words

cartilage – a strong smooth material, also called gristle
rib cage – the flexible cage protecting your heart and lungs
skull – a round bony box protecting your brain
spinal cord – the nerves that run down the backbone
sternum – a plate of bone at the front of the chest

SUMMARY

- Your skeleton contains more than 200 bones which support and protect your body.
- Bones are strong and do not bend easily.
- Bones are linked together by three different types of joints.
- Joints are protected from wear by cartilage at the ends of the bones and fluid in between.

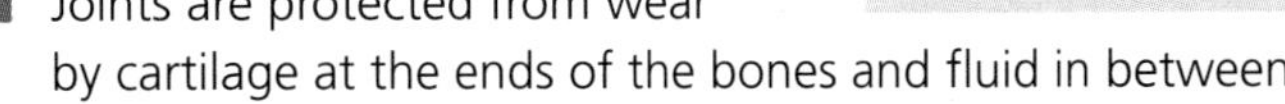

SUMMARY *Activity*

Make a table that shows which of the following contain hinge joints, gliding joints or ball and socket joints: elbow; toes; ankle; fingers; vertebrae; jaw.

14 Bones on the move

In this section of the book you will learn the following things:

- **that muscles pull on bones to make them move;**
- **that muscles often work in pairs called antagonistic muscle pairs.**

A skeleton cannot move without muscles to work the joints. Muscle is an elastic meaty tissue that makes up a large part of your body. The kind of muscle that moves joints is called skeletal muscle. Muscles work by **contraction**, getting shorter and fatter. This uses up energy.

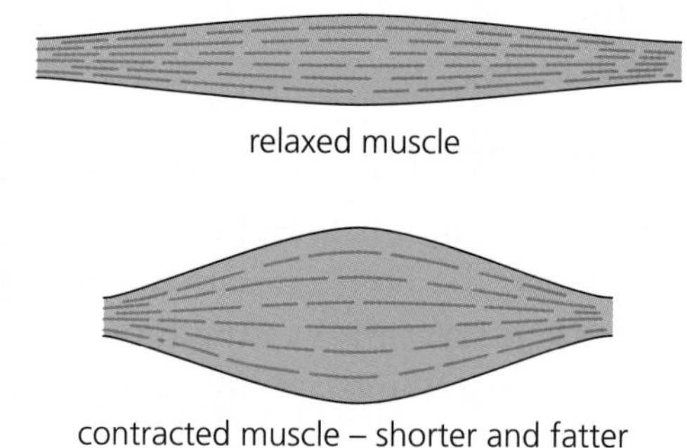

▲ ***Fig 1*** *A muscle will pull anything its tendons are attached to.*

Muscles and joints

Muscles are attached to bones by strong fibres called tendons. When a muscle contracts, its **tendons** pull on the bones and make the joint move. Muscles cannot push. They can only pull. This means that one muscle can only move a joint in one direction (Fig 2).

Q1 What is skeletal muscle?

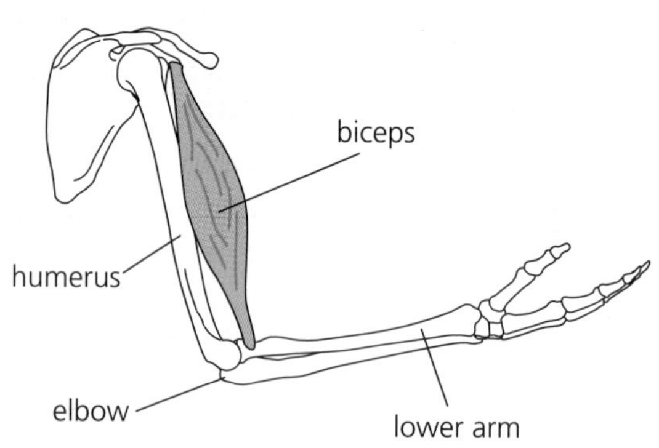

▲ ***Fig 2***

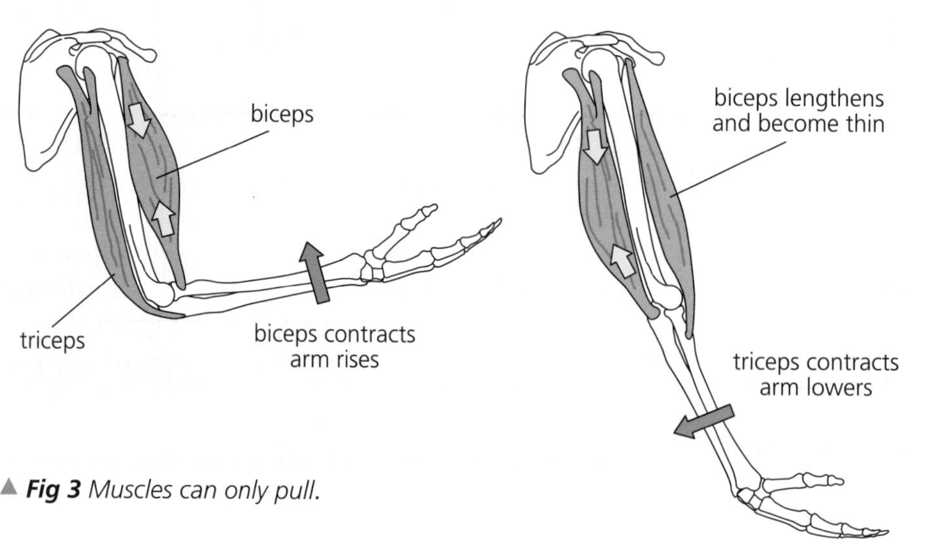

▲ ***Fig 3*** *Muscles can only pull.*

Your biceps can pull your hand towards your shoulder but it cannot push the bones apart again. Muscles on the other side of your arm, called the triceps, work the opposite way. They can pull the lower arm down but cannot push it up. Between them, the biceps and triceps can move the lower arm up and down. Muscles that work against one another like this are called **antagonistic muscle pairs** (Fig 3).

Q2 Why is it a problem that muscles pull but do not push?

Q3 Why must skeletal muscles work in pairs?

Q4 Where in your body are the biceps and triceps muscles?

▲ ***Fig 4*** *A bodybuilder learns to tense antagonistic muscle pairs at the same time to make them bulge.*

Other jobs for muscle

We can decide when we want to move a joint. Our brain sends a message along nerves to the muscle and tells it to contract. Because we volunteer to do this the muscles are called **voluntary**.

Not all the muscles in your body are used to move joints. Your diaphragm (see Unit 10) is a sheet of muscle that makes you breathe, even if you try not to. Another kind of muscle you cannot control is found in your heart. The walls of your intestines and blood vessels also contain muscles. This helps them to contract and push materials along. We do not tell these muscles to work. Our heart beats and the walls of our intestines carry on working when we are asleep. Because we do not volunteer to make these movements the muscles are called **involuntary**.

Q5 What is the difference between voluntary and involuntary muscles?

Key Words

antagonistic muscle pair – two muscles working in opposite directions
involuntary – muscle that is worked by the body automatically
tendon – a tough strand that joins a muscle to a bone
voluntary – muscle that we can move when we wish

SUMMARY

- Skeletal muscle moves the joints in your body.
- Muscles can only pull. Skeletal muscles work in pairs.
- Other muscles in our body make our heart beat and move food along our gut.
- Muscle we can control is called voluntary muscle.
- Muscle we cannot control is called involuntary muscle.

SUMMARY *Activity*

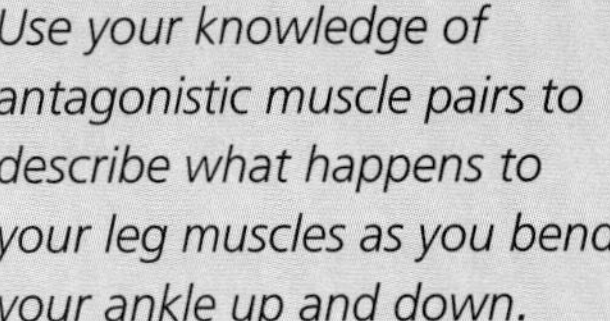

Use your knowledge of antagonistic muscle pairs to describe what happens to your leg muscles as you bend your ankle up and down.

15 Human development

In this section of the book you will learn the following things:

- **that important emotional and physical changes occur as humans change from being children to being adults;**
- **that these changes are controlled by chemicals called hormones;**
- **that the changes are part of preparing for reproduction.**

Humans reproduce by a process called **sexual reproduction**. In sexual reproduction genetic material from the male is combined with genetic material from the female. The genetic material from the male is carried in cells called sperm. The genetic material from the female is in the egg (Units 16, 17, 18, 27–29).

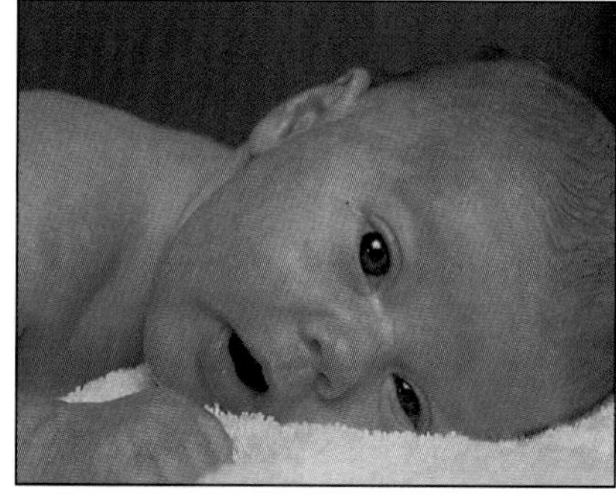

▲ ***Fig 1*** *Babies need a lot of time, care and love.*

Babies are born with sex organs already formed but they are not ready to work yet. Before sexual reproduction can take place human males must be able to produce sperm and females must be able to produce eggs. This will not happen until they are almost old enough to take on the responsibility of bringing a new life into the world.

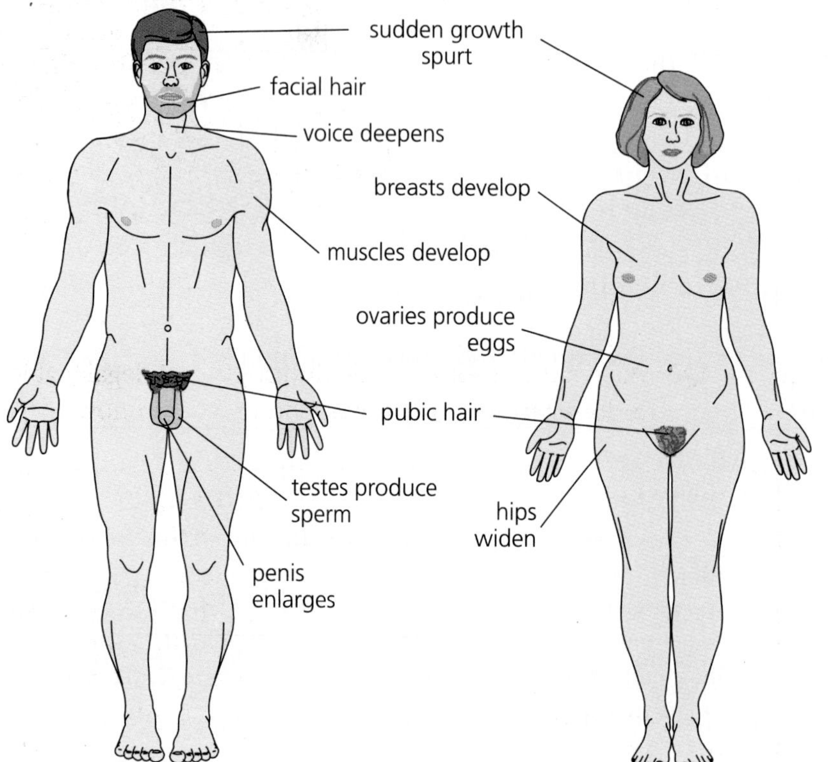

◀ ***Fig 2*** *General differences between adult man and woman. Nobody looks exactly like this.*

Puberty

The stage of life when human sex organs begin to work is called puberty. Puberty generally starts between 11 and 15 years old for a girl and between 13 and 15 years old for a boy. Everyone is different so it may occur before or after these ages. During this important stage of life many changes take place in young men and women.

Q1 What is puberty?

The changes at puberty are controlled by sex **hormones**. Hormones are chemical messengers that are produced by glands and carried in the blood. Some of the important changes are shown in Fig 2.

Q2 List the changes that occur in males during puberty.

Q3 List the changes that occur in females during puberty.

Many of the differences between males and females are called **secondary sexual characteristics**. These visible changes start to develop at the same time as the female sex organs start producing eggs and the male sex organs start producing sperm. The period of time when secondary sexual characteristics develop after puberty is known as adolescence. Adulthood is usually reached in the late teens or early twenties. Boys may continue growing up to the age of 23. Girls may continue growing up to the age of 20.

Q4 What is the difference between puberty and adolescence?

Physical changes

Both girls and boys change shape. A girl develops breasts and her body shape softens. A boy's shoulders broaden and his penis grows larger and can become erect. A boy's voice becomes deeper and facial hair starts to grow. Boys and girls grow **pubic** hair around their sex organs. At some point a girl will start to menstruate (Unit 17). Boys and girls may also suffer from spots.

▲ ***Fig 3*** *Adolescence brings more freedom, but freedom brings more responsibility.*

Emotional changes

As they grow, adolescents become more independent from their parents. They begin to think and act for themselves, become more aware of people of the opposite sex, and take on more responsibility for their actions. These changes can be exciting but they can also be confusing and difficult.

Q5 What are some of the changes that adolescents experience?

Q6 Make a list of some of the things you will legally able to do when you are 18 that you cannot do now.

Key Words

adolescence – the period of life between puberty and adulthood

puberty – the time when sex organs begin to work

secondary sexual characteristics – body changes that develop during adolescence

sex hormones – chemicals that cause the changes of puberty

SUMMARY

- Puberty is the time when sex hormones become active.
- Adolescence is the time following puberty. This is a period of much physical and emotional change.
- Secondary sexual characteristics include breasts in women, facial hair in men, and pubic hair in both.

SUMMARY *Activity*

List some reasons why you think adolescence is an exciting but a confusing time for many people?

16 The reproductive system

In this section of the book you will learn the following things:

- **the structure and function of the male reproductive organs;**
- **the structure and function of the female reproductive organs;**
- **where sperm cells are produced;**
- **how sperm cells enter the female reproductive system.**

Sex cells are also called **gametes**. Sperm cells are male gametes and eggs or ova are female gametes. Sexual reproduction occurs when a male gamete combines with a female gamete to make a new organism. The organs that produce gametes and bring them together are called the reproductive or sex organs. The sex organs make up the **reproductive system**.

▲ ***Fig 1*** *Fish sperm can swim through the water to the eggs.*

Fertilisation in water

Animals that live in water, such as fish, can shed their eggs or sperm into the water and let them mix there. Land animals cannot do this because sperm cells need to swim to an egg. Most land animals, including humans, solve this problem by arranging for the egg and sperm to meet inside the female's body, where the new organism will also grow.

The human male

The human body is too warm for sperm cells to survive. This is why the testes, where sperm are made, need to be kept outside the body in a bag of skin called the **scrotum**. The testes also make sex hormones. The penis is made of soft, spongy tissue. It is normally limp but can fill with blood and become hard and erect.

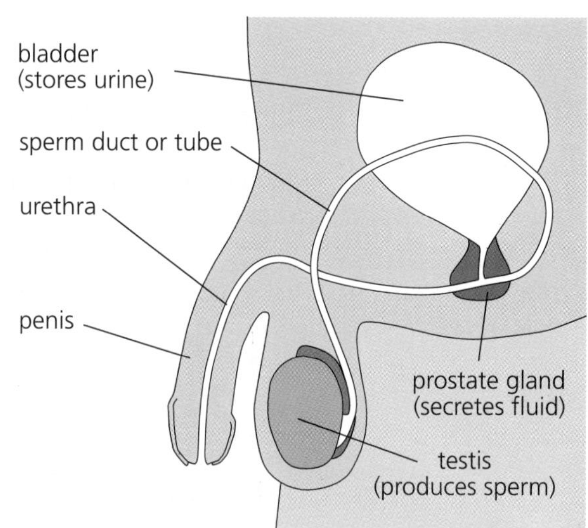

▲ ***Fig 2*** *Human male reproductive system.*

Q1 How does the body make sure sperm are made at the correct temperature?

Q2 What do you know about the role of male sex hormones?

The human female

The ova are made in two ovaries close to a pair of tubes that lead into the uterus. Ovaries also produce female sex hormones. When an egg is released it passes into the nearest **fallopian tube**. This is where it may meet a sperm cell and be fertilised. The egg travels on down the fallopian tube to the womb or **uterus**. If it has been fertilised by a sperm it stays here.

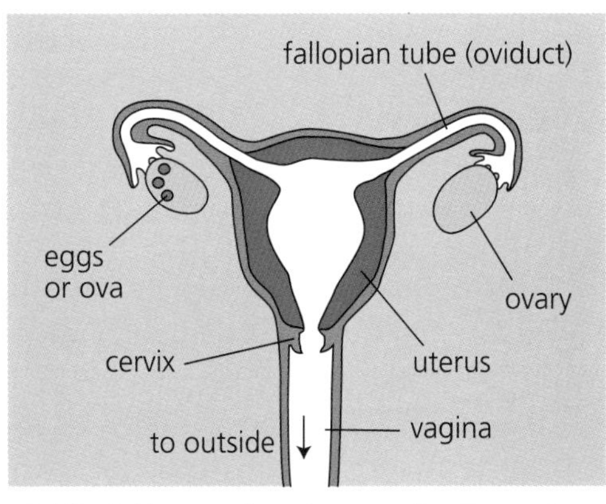

▲ *Fig 3 Human female reproductive system.*

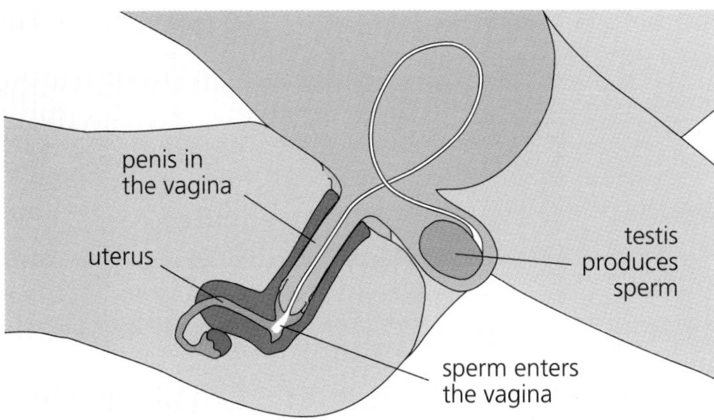

▲ *Fig 4*

Sexual intercourse

The vagina is a tube lined with muscle. It links the uterus with the outside of the body. When it is erect the male penis can enter the female vagina (Fig 4). This is how sperm cells enter the reproductive system of the female.

Q3 Why do human sperm and egg cells need to meet inside the female?

Q4 What two roles do the ovaries play in reproduction?

Q5 How do sperm cells enter the female reproductive system?

Q6 Where do sperm cells and egg cells meet?

Key Words

fallopian tube – tube carrying ovum to uterus
gamete – male or female sex cell (animal or plant)
ovary – part of the female reproductive system producing eggs
penis – part of the male reproductive system carrying sperm from the testes
scrotum – the bag of skin that holds the testes outside the body
sexual intercourse – the process that allows egg and sperm to meet in the female body
testis – the part of the male reproductive system that produces sperm
uterus – womb

SUMMARY

- Nearly all land animals are designed for sperms and eggs to meet inside the female's body.
- Testes make sperm cells which pass along the penis.
- Ovaries make eggs which pass along the fallopian tubes to the uterus.
- The testes and ovaries also make sex hormones.
- The erect male penis can carry sperm directly into the female vagina.

SUMMARY *Activity*

Explain why humans have sexual intercourse but fish do not.

17 Fertilisation

In this section of the book you will learn the following things:

- **how sperm cells and egg cells meet;**
- **what happens to the fertilised egg;**
- **how the menstrual cycle works and why it is important.**

During sexual intercourse more than 300 million sperm cells may enter the female at one time. Only about 100 will reach the egg. Only one can enter an egg.

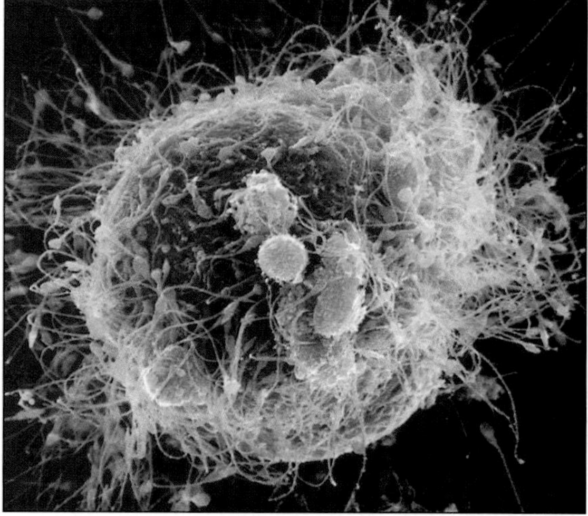

▲ ***Fig 1*** *Hundreds of sperm (yellow in the picture) are clustered on the surface of the egg.*

Fertilisation

When one sperm cell enters an egg, the surface of the egg changes to prevent any more sperm from entering. Each egg can only be fertilised by a single sperm. After the sperm enters, the genetic material from the male and the genetic material from the female combine. The fertilised egg now has a complete set of genetic material to make a new human.

The fertilised egg contains genetic material from two different people. This means that the new baby will have a mixture of characteristics from both parents. The mixture is different for each individual. It makes each person unique.

Q1 How do eggs make sure that they are fertilised by only one sperm cell?

Q2 How does sexual reproduction make each baby unique?

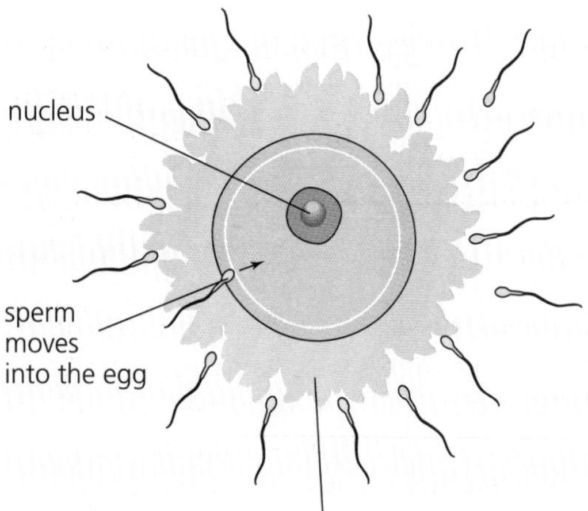

▲ ***Fig 2*** *Once the sperm has entered, the egg coating changes and seals off the egg.*

After it is fertilised the egg cell begins to divide and grow into a baby. For the first two months it is called an **embryo**. The embryo will grow and develop inside the uterus.

The menstrual cycle

An egg is normally released from one of the ovaries each month. Each time an egg cell is released from an ovary the uterus gets ready to grow a baby. A thick lining full of blood vessels slowly develops inside the uterus. If the egg is fertilised it will pass into the uterus and become attached to this layer (Unit 18).

The uterus grows a fresh new lining for each new egg. If the egg is not fertilised the lining breaks down and passes out of the vagina. The breakdown of the lining of the uterus is called **menstruation**. The whole cycle of making a new lining and a new egg is called the **menstrual cycle** (Fig 3).

Menstruation can sometimes be painful. Muscles in the uterus may cramp and cause stomach and back pains. Water can also collect in body tissues and make them swell. Menstruation may cause tiredness and depression, especially when the lining of the uterus begins to break down.

▼ *Fig 3*

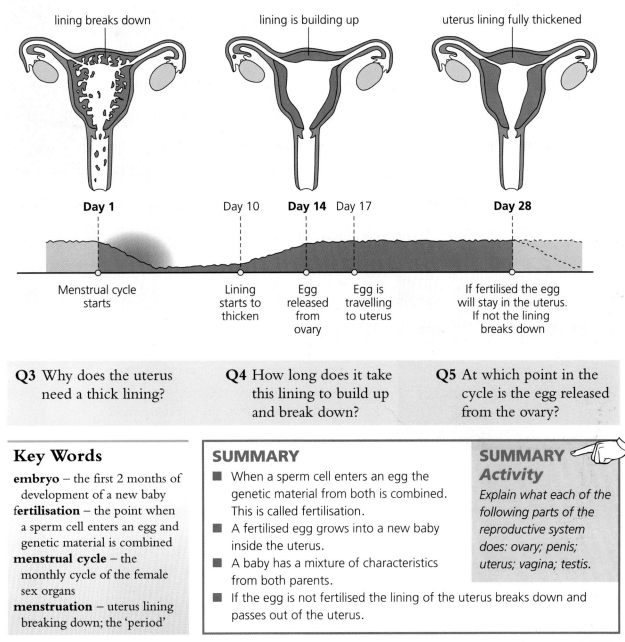

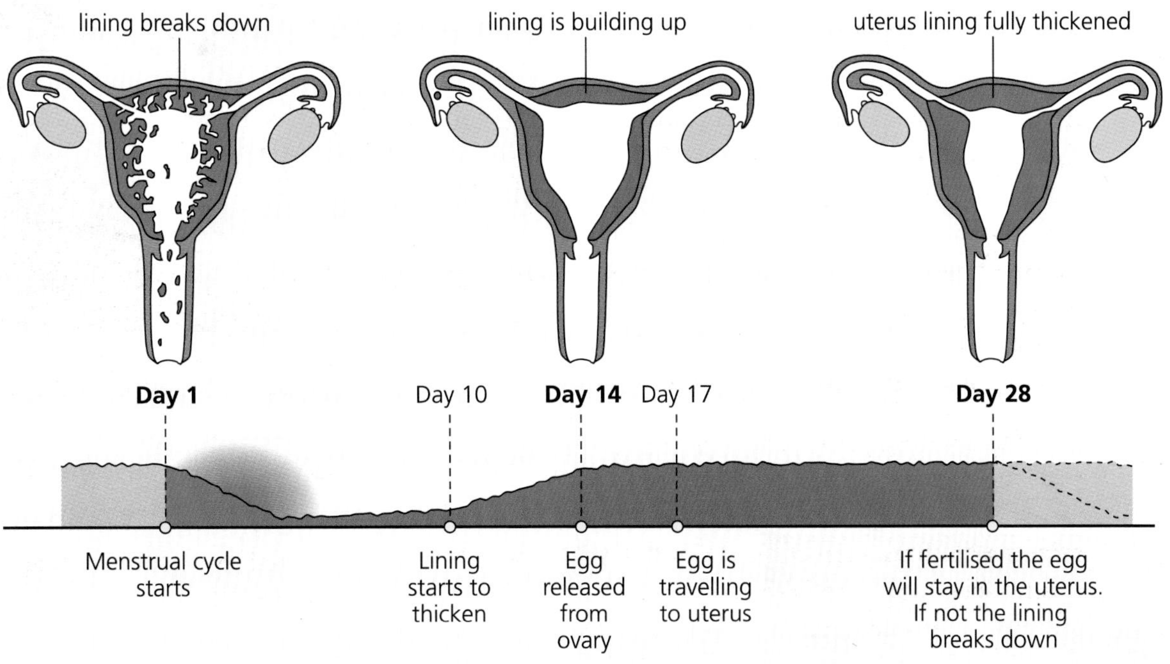

Q3 Why does the uterus need a thick lining?

Q4 How long does it take this lining to build up and break down?

Q5 At which point in the cycle is the egg released from the ovary?

Key Words

embryo – the first 2 months of development of a new baby

fertilisation – the point when a sperm cell enters an egg and genetic material is combined

menstrual cycle – the monthly cycle of the female sex organs

menstruation – uterus lining breaking down; the 'period'

SUMMARY

- When a sperm cell enters an egg the genetic material from both is combined. This is called fertilisation.
- A fertilised egg grows into a new baby inside the uterus.
- A baby has a mixture of characteristics from both parents.
- If the egg is not fertilised the lining of the uterus breaks down and passes out of the uterus.

SUMMARY 
Activity

Explain what each of the following parts of the reproductive system does: ovary; penis; uterus; vagina; testis.

18 Pregnancy

In this section of the book you will learn the following things:

- **what happens to an egg after fertilisation;**
- **how a baby develops in the uterus;**
- **the role of the placenta.**

In order to develop into a new human being the fertilised egg needs:

- food
- warmth
- oxygen
- room to grow

Growth of the baby

The uterus is already prepared to receive the egg (see Unit 17).

As the fertilised egg cell moves down the fallopian tube it starts to divide into more cells. When it reaches the uterus it is a ball of cells. The ball of cells buries itself in the soft wall of the uterus. The thick lining provides food and protection. Here, the developing ball of cells carries on growing into an **embryo**. When a woman is carrying an embryo she is **pregnant**. Her menstrual cycle stops. No new eggs are released and the uterus keeps its lining to protect her embryo. The uterus is not much bigger yet.

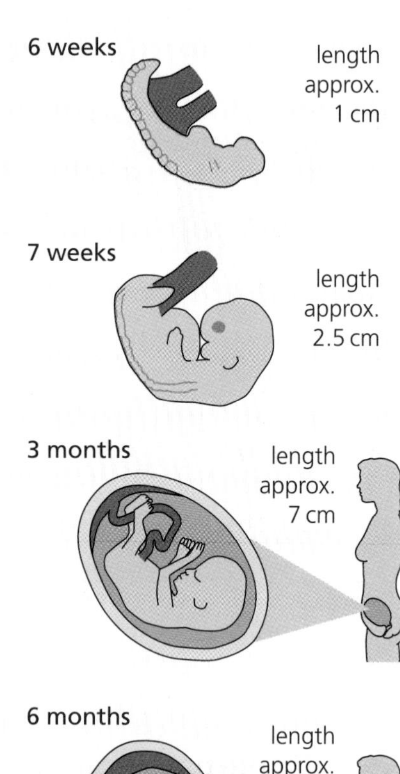

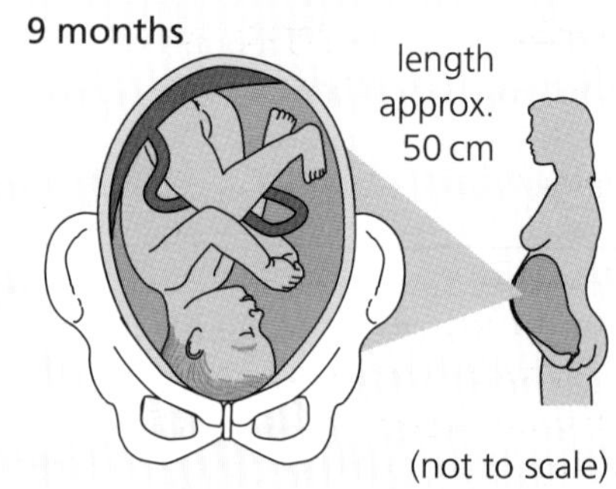

▶ ***Fig 1*** *Development of a human embryo.*

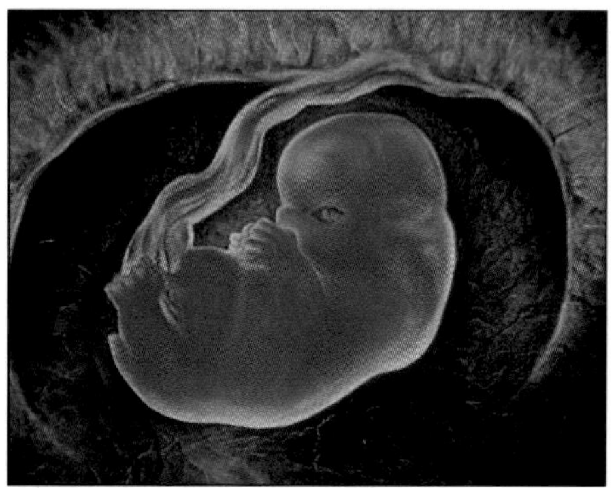

◀ ***Fig 2*** *The embryo floats safely inside the uterus.*

Q1 How does the uterus prepare for the fertilised egg?

The placenta

After six weeks the embryo is approximately 1cm long. It now has a brain and a beating heart and floats in a sac filled with fluid. A close link is formed between the embryo and the uterus to supply the embryo with food and oxygen. This is called the **placenta**. Here the mother's blood and the embryo's blood flow in capillaries side by side.

Food and oxygen can pass from the mother's blood into the embryo's blood. At the same time waste materials can pass in the other direction. The blood of the baby does not mix with the blood of its mother. Only food, oxygen, waste products and some other chemicals are exchanged.

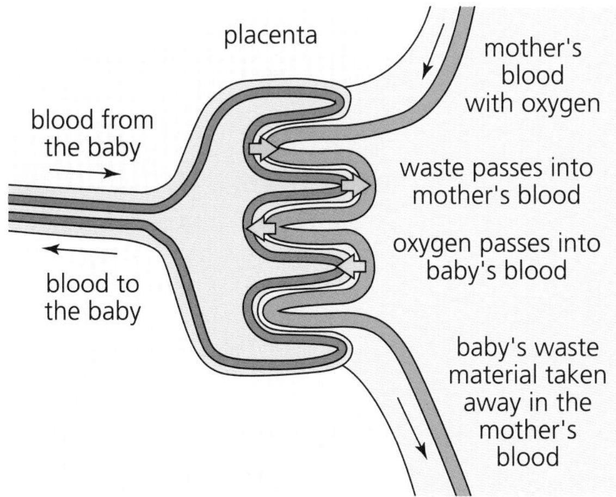
placenta
mother's blood with oxygen
blood from the baby
waste passes into mother's blood
oxygen passes into baby's blood
blood to the baby
baby's waste material taken away in the mother's blood

▲ ***Fig 3*** *Some drugs can enter the baby's blood together with food and oxygen.*

After two months the embryo becomes a **foetus**. It grows too big to stay buried in the uterus lining but is still connected to the placenta by a tube called the umbilical cord.

Q2 How does the uterus protect the embryo?

Q3 When does the embryo become a foetus?

Q4 Where does oxygen and food pass from the mother to the embryo?

Q5 Name two waste materials that pass from the embryo to the mother.

The birth

Approximately nine months after fertilisation the baby is ready to be born. It has usually turned round so that the head is ready to emerge first. First the opening of the uterus, called the **cervix**, relaxes. The bag of fluid around the baby may now burst. Gradually, powerful muscles in the uterus wall begin to contract to push the baby out. Eventually the baby is born through the vagina.

After it is born the baby's umbilical cord will be sealed and then cut to separate it from the placenta. The stub is pushed in to make the belly button or **navel**. The uterus pushes the placenta out a little while after the baby, which is why it is often called the 'afterbirth'.

Key Words

cervix – the neck of the uterus where it enters the vagina
embryo – a developing egg
foetus – a human embryo after 2 months
placenta – the structure made by an embryo to obtain food and oxygen from its mother
umbilical cord – the connection between embryo and placenta
womb – uterus

SUMMARY

- After fertilisation the egg grows into a ball of cells called an embryo.
- The uterus lining provides protection, food and oxygen for the growing embryo.
- After two months the embryo is called a foetus. The growing foetus is fed through the placenta. It is connected to the placenta by the umbilical cord.
- After about 38 weeks the baby is ready to be born.

SUMMARY *Activity*

Describe the life story of a fertilised egg, using the following words in the correct order: vagina; fallopian tube; placenta; foetus; embryo; uterus; cervix; umbilical cord.

19 Staying healthy

In this section of the book you will learn the following things:

- the names of some drugs and solvents;
- how drugs and solvents can damage your health;
- how alcohol affects your body.

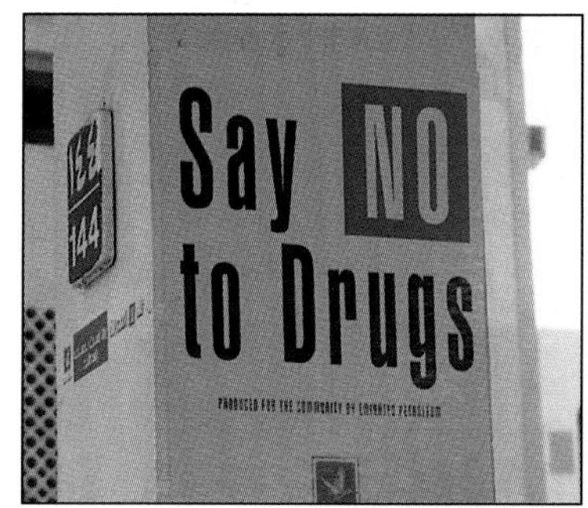

▲ ***Fig 1*** *Some people make a lot of money from selling drugs. They may try hard to persuade people to buy from them. People who know the health risks say 'no'.*

Effects of drugs on the body

The reason why the drugs you get from your doctor work is because they have an effect on your body. If you take them without medical advice you can damage your health. Some people take drugs in large doses because they enjoy one or two of the effects they have on their body. This is very dangerous because drugs have other effects that we do not notice. These are called **side-effects**. Side-effects can permananently damage your body. Side-effects can affect a person's personality and can cause brain damage. Side-effects can kill you.

Drug	Effects
Heroin	Sense of well being but is addictive and can lead to death.
Barbiturates	Can relax or slow people down. May cause death, especially if mixed with alcohol.
Cocaine	Feelings of excitement followed by depression. Can cause death.
Cannabis	Hallucinations and feelings of well being. May cause mental damage. Can lead to infertility in men (cannot produce sperm).
LSD	Hallucinations or 'trips' may cause serious mental derangement. The person may act in a wild manner.

▲ ***Table 1*** *Some drugs and their effects.*

Drug addiction

Many drugs are also addictive, which means that they start making you feel bad when your body wants them. At the same time they often stop making you feel good. When a person has become an addict it takes more and more of the drug to cause an effect. Many drug addicts, even young people, die before they can be given help. There are strict laws about the use of drugs. These laws are made to protect us from the danger of drug abuse.

The table shows some of the drugs that some people misuse.

Q1 Name two drugs that cause hallucinations.

Q2 How are people in danger during hallucinations?

Alcohol as a drug

Alcohol is very easy to buy and can be bought legally by people over 18 years of age. This does not mean it is safe. Alcohol can also damage health. It is sometimes difficult to work out how much alcohol some drinks contain. Table 2 shows how alcohol affects the way people behave.

Drinking a large amount of alcohol at one time can kill a person. People who drink too much alcohol may become addicted. A person addicted to alcohol is called an alcoholic.

Drinking too much alcohol can damage the brain and liver. Alcohol can also make some people aggressive. Even a small amount of alcohol can make people sleepy and slow down their reactions. It also causes them to make poor decisions. They may think they are capable of driving when they are not. This is why it is very dangerous for anyone to drive a car if they have been drinking alcohol. There are very strict drinking and driving laws to protect people from drink-drivers.

◀ ***Fig 2*** *Drinking and driving can kill friends or strangers.*

Units of alcohol	Effect on the body
up to 2	cheerful, self-confident
2	increased risk of having an accident
2–3	poor judgement
3–5	illegal for driving
8–10	slurred speech, loss of control
10–12	cannot walk straight, loss of memory
12–18	possible coma and death

▲ ***Table 2*** *Note: These figures are for an adult man. Women, and especially children, will show effects much sooner. One unit of alcohol is ½ pint of beer, a single measure of spirits, a glass of cider or a glass of wine.*

Q3 How many glasses of lager contain 8 units of alcohol?

Q4 What effect does drinking 8 units of alcohol have on the body?

Solvent abuse

Chemicals that dissolve other chemicals are called solvents. They have many uses in industry and the home. Our body uses water as a solvent. Solvents other than water can harm our body.

The vapour from a solvent can make a person light headed. This may feel funny but it means a person is not in control and may have an accident. Solvents can also cause damage to your body. Smelling, or 'sniffing' glues and solvents can damage your lungs and brain very badly. Even a small amount of solvent can kill. Some solvents can also be addictive. Once a person starts to abuse solvents it can be very difficult for them to stop.

▲ ***Fig 3*** ⚠ *Some household solvents.*

Key Words

addict – a person who needs a drug to feel normal
alcoholic – a person who is addicted to alcohol
side-effect – unwanted effect of a drug
solvent – a chemical that dissolves other chemicals

SUMMARY

- Drugs such as alcohol, heroin, cannabis and solvents damage health.
- The enjoyable effects of drugs soon wear off and the side-effects are very dangerous.
- Some drugs are addictive. They are very difficult to give up once they are used.
- Some drugs are illegal. There are also strict limits on drinking alcohol.
- Small amounts of some drugs, especially solvents, can kill.

SUMMARY *Activity*

Design a poster that aims to persuade young people to say no to drugs.

20 Health and micro-organisms

In this section of the book you will learn the following things:

- **how we catch some diseases;**
- **how we can avoid catching diseases;**
- **how bacteria can affect health;**
- **what viruses are and how they can make people ill.**

Micro-organisms are so small you need a microscope to see them. Two main types of micro-organisms that can cause disease are bacteria and viruses.

Bacteria

There are millions of bacteria everywhere you go. Your skin is covered in them and they are present in air, water and soil. Most are harmless and many are useful. Yoghurt is one good thing made by bacteria.

Some bacteria can cause diseases. If these bacteria enter our bodies and start to multiply we say we have an infection. Bacteria can enter your body in different ways:

- from the air you breathe;
- from the water you drink;
- from the food you eat;
- through cuts in your skin;
- from contact with infected people;
- from contact with some animals.

A person with a chest infection may cough and sneeze. This sprays tiny drops of water into the air (Fig 1). The water can contain the bacteria that caused the infection. Breathing in the bacteria can give the infection to somebody else.

▲ *Fig 1*

Bacteria can also get into drinking water. This may happen if sewage goes into rivers without being cleaned. Drinking infected water can make you ill. A disease called cholera (Unit 7) is spread in this way.

Bacteria can get into our mouth from our fingers. It is very important to wash our hands after visiting the toilet. This is especially true if we are going to handle food, because bacteria from a person's hands can infect other people who eat the food.

Cooking food kills many bacteria because they cannot survive high temperatures. But it is important to cook food thoroughly. Each year there are thousands of cases of food poisoning caused by undercooked food. It is important to know that bacteria like to grow in warm, moist places.

Your skin helps to keep bacteria out of your body. If bacteria can enter through a cut they may cause an infection. One serious infection that comes from soil is called tetanus. Washing cuts thoroughly and keeping them clean while they heal helps to prevent infections.

Q1 Why is it important to cover your mouth and nose when you cough or sneeze?

Q2 Why must we wash our hands after visiting the toilet?

Q3 How does cooking food help to prevent food poisoning?

Some animals such as flies and rats can carry bacteria that cause diseases in humans. These animals may pass the bacteria on by biting or by infecting food or water. An animal that passes on bacteria in this way is called a **vector**. Plague bacteria are carried from rats to humans by rat fleas.

A few diseases can only be caught by touching a person who is ill. These are called contagious diseases. Some diseases are passed on during sexual intercourse. These are called **sexually transmitted diseases** (STDs)

▲ ***Fig 2*** *Flies can carry bacteria from faeces to uncovered food.*

Q4 Why is it better to store cream cake in the refrigerator than on a shelf in the kitchen?

Q5 Name two animals that are vectors of disease.

Viruses

Viruses are much smaller than bacteria but can be spread in the same ways. Viruses multiply right inside a living cell. Eventually the virus takes over the cell and turns it into more viruses. Then the cell wall bursts open and the virus particles escape and infect other cells. Colds, influenza, mumps, chicken pox and smallpox are some of the diseases caused by viruses.

Key Words

host cell – a cell that has been infected by a virus particle
infection – the result of disease-causing bacteria entering the body
sexually transmitted disease – a disease passed on by sexual contact
vector – an animal that carries disease

SUMMARY

- Bacteria are everywhere. Most of them do not cause disease.
- Bacteria that cause disease can be spread in a number of ways.
- Personal hygiene and careful cooking and storage of food can prevent diseases from spreading.
- Viruses are much smaller than bacteria.

SUMMARY *Activity*

Look up the examples of diseases mentioned in these pages. Make a table that shows which are caused by bacteria and which are caused by viruses.

21 Defence against disease

In this section of the book you will learn the following things:

- **that the body has natural defences against disease;**
- **that immunisation and medicines can help the natural defences of your body.**

Your body's three main natural lines of defence are your skin, white blood cells and immune system.

Skin

Skin is a natural barrier against infection. Every normal opening in your body has special defences. Your nose contains hairs and mucus which help to trap micro-organisms. Your ears have hairs and wax and your eyes have eyelids and tears. Tears help to wash dust away and contain chemicals that kill bacteria. Your body has other lines of defence against bacteria and viruses that get past the skin.

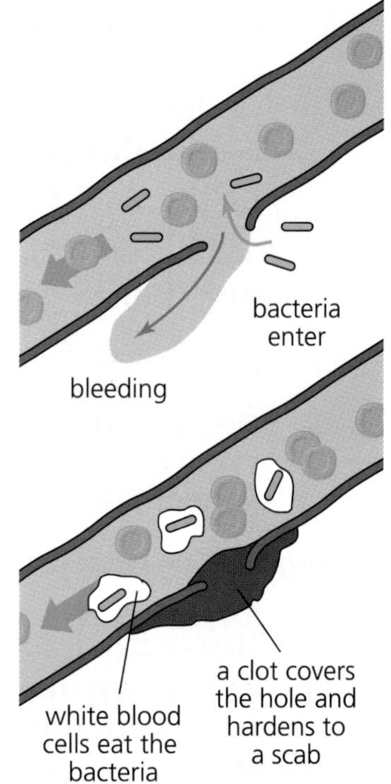
bacteria enter
bleeding
white blood cells eat the bacteria
a clot covers the hole and hardens to a scab

▲ *Fig 1*

Q1 List three methods your body uses to keep bacteria out.

White blood cells

When bacteria enter a cut in your skin, platelets (Unit 9) help to seal up the cut while white blood cells move to the site of the damage. Some white blood cells directly attack bacteria and destroy them (Fig 1). This may also kill the white blood cells. Dead white blood cells are part of the pus in an infected cut.

Q2 Why are white blood cells an important defence?

The immune system

Your body can recognise that bacteria and viruses are invaders. It produces special proteins called **antibodies** to fight them. Antibodies stick to bacteria or viruses and make it easier for your body to destroy them (Fig 2). Your body makes a special antibody for every bacterium and virus it meets.

The first time you are infected with a new micro-organism a new antibody has to be made. During this time you may feel unwell.

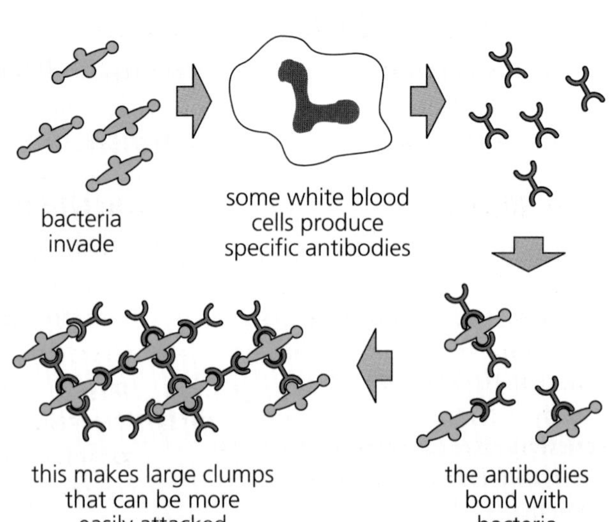
bacteria invade
some white blood cells produce specific antibodies
the antibodies bond with bacteria
this makes large clumps that can be more easily attacked

▲ *Fig 2*

If you are ever infected again with the same micro-organism the antibodies are made much quicker. This is why it is unusual to catch some diseases twice. Your body already has some **immunity**.

Q3 What are antibodies?

Q4 Why is it unusual to suffer from chicken-pox twice?

Helping your body's defences

Your immune system cannot protect you from a really dangerous disease that could kill you before you have time to make antibodies. Luckily, doctors and scientists have found a way of safely starting up your immune system before you catch a serious disease. This is called immunisation or **vaccination**.

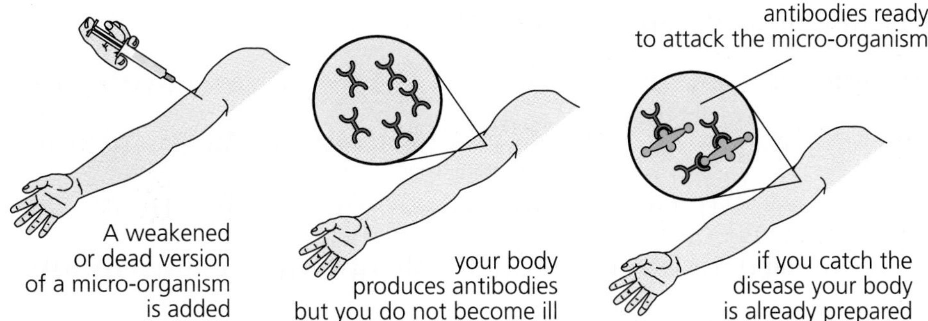

A weakened or dead version of a micro-organism is added
your body produces antibodies but you do not become ill
antibodies ready to attack the micro-organism
if you catch the disease your body is already prepared

▲ *Fig 3*

Q5 Why do you think some vaccines make you feel slightly ill after you have been vaccinated?

A weak or dead micro-organism can work on your immune system as well as a strong one can. Your body will make antibodies even if the micro-organism is too feeble to hurt you. Weakened or dead organisms can be used to make a **vaccine** which can be injected into your body (Fig 3) to protect you in the future. If you catch a serious disease after being vaccinated against it your body will be able to beat the disease. You may not even know that you caught it.

When we cannot prevent a disease we may need to use medicines to treat it. One group of medicines that have been very useful in treating diseases are the antibiotics. These chemicals kill bacteria but do not cause much damage to the cells of your body. They can work very quickly.

Key Words

antibody – a protein produced by your body to fight disease
antibiotic – a chemical that kills bacteria
immunity – being immune. Having antibodies against a disease
vaccination – an injection of a weak or dead micro-organism to create immunity
vaccine – a weak or dead micro-organism ready for injection

SUMMARY

- The skin is a natural barrier that prevents bacteria and viruses from entering your body.
- Micro-organisms can be attacked and destroyed by white blood cells.
- The immune system produces antibodies which help to destroy micro-organisms.
- Vaccinations and medicines can help your body to fight disease.

SUMMARY *Activity*

Ask for permission to collect some leaflets about vaccination from your doctor's surgery. Using the leaflets, make a list of the diseases that can be prevented by vaccination.

22 How plants make food

In this section of the book you will learn the following things:

- **that plants use energy from sunlight to make food;**
- **that this process is called photosynthesis;**
- **that oxygen is produced during photosynthesis.**

Animals get their food by eating plants or other animals. Plants make their own food by joining together simple molecules. They need energy from the Sun to do this.

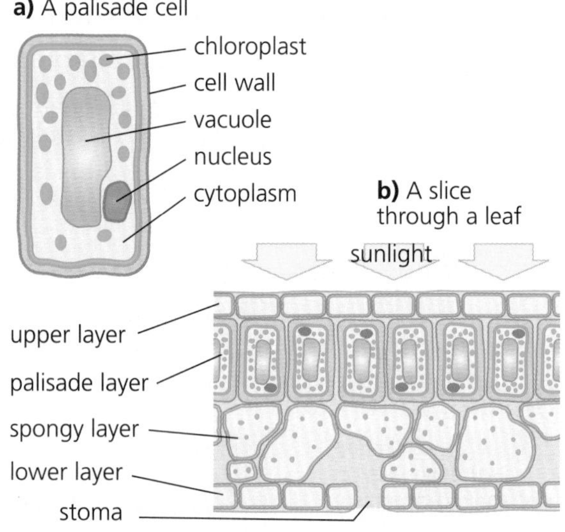

▲ ***Fig 1a** Plant cell showing chloroplasts.*
***b** Leaf showing leaf structure and cells.*

Energy from the Sun

During the day green plants use energy from the Sun to join together water and carbon dioxide molecules to make glucose. This is called **photosynthesis**. Photosynthesis takes place mainly in leaves and depends on a very important green pigment called **chlorophyll.** The chlorophyll is contained in **chloroplasts.**

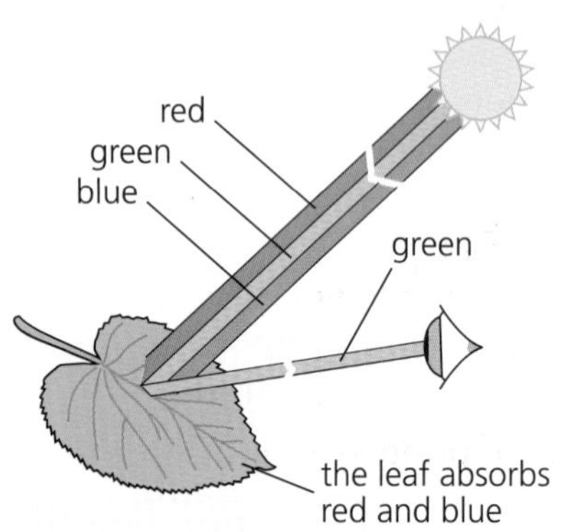

▲ ***Fig 2** The pigment in the leaf looks green because blue and red light energy is absorbed, leaving the green light to be reflected back to the eyes of the observer.*

Having a large surface helps a leaf to obtain as much sunlight as possible. Small holes called stomata allow gases to pass in and out of the leaf. Each leaf is thin and has a spongy structure of cells. This allows gases to reach all the cells.

Palisade cells (Unit 4) contain a large number of chloroplasts. The cells are lined up in the leaf like a small fence. This helps the energy entering the surface of the leaf to travel a long way through the palisade cells. This allows as much light as possible to reach the chlorophyll in the chloroplasts.

Q1 Why are most leaves thin and why are they spongy inside?

Q2 Why are palisade cells lined up at right angles to the surface of the leaf?

Biomass and photosynthesis

The glucose made by photosynthesis is sent around the plant to provide food. Cells in the root or stem can use the glucose to make energy. If the plant does not need to use all the glucose immediately then it has to be stored. Glucose is hard to store because it dissolves in water. Plants solve this problem by joining hundreds of glucose molecules together to make starch. Starch makes a better food store because it does not dissolve very well in water.

It is easy to test whether a plant has made some starch. Starch reacts with iodine solution by turning blue-black. Fig 3 shows some leaves that have been stained with iodine. Both plants were left in the Sun but one of them had part of a leaf covered up. You can see that this leaf only contains starch in the uncovered parts.

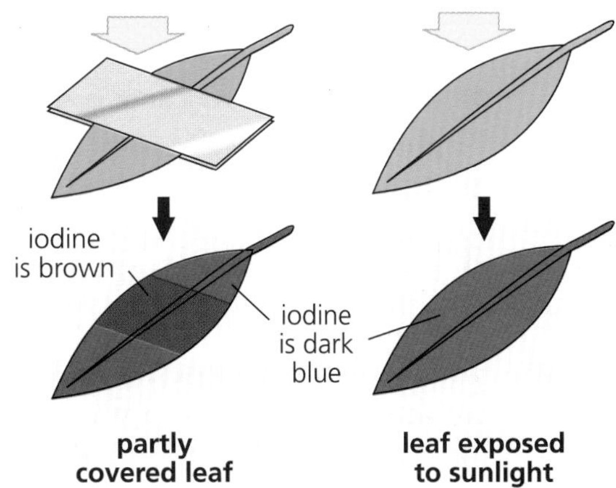

▲ *Fig 3*

Glucose can provide energy or carbon. Carbon can be used to manufacture other molecules in the plant. In this way plants use the energy of the Sun to create new living matter from non-living matter. We call this material **biomass**.

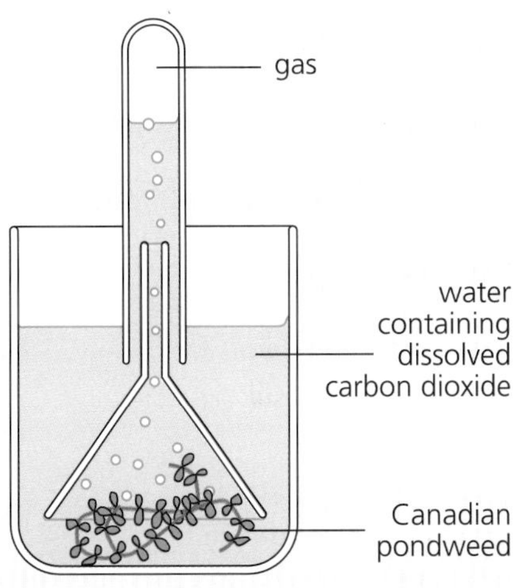

▲ ***Fig 4*** *The gas is collected in a test tube.*

Oxygen and photosynthesis

When glucose is made from water and carbon dioxide some oxygen is left over. It is easiest to test this on a submerged water-plant (Fig 4) because any gases the plant makes can easily be collected.

When a glowing piece of wood meets the gas from the water-weed it begins to burn with a flame again. This shows that the gas produced during photosynthesis is oxygen.

Q3 Name two products of photosynthesis.

Key Words

biomass – the total amount of living material in any object or area
chlorophyll – the green pigment in plants that traps the energy in sunlight
chloroplasts – small bodies in plant cells that contain chlorophyll
photosynthesis – the process of making glucose by using energy from the sun

SUMMARY

- The leaves of plants are specially adapted to trap sunlight and to let gases pass in and out.
- The energy in the sunlight is used by chlorophyll to make glucose.
- Glucose can be used for energy, stored as starch, or used to build new plant material.
- Oxygen gas is a waste product of photosynthesis.

SUMMARY *Activity*

How could you use the apparatus in Fig 4 to find out whether or not increasing the amount of light will increase photosynthesis?

23 Photosynthesis in detail

In this section of the book you will learn the following things:
- **that plants need carbon dioxide, water and light for photosynthesis;**
- **the word equation for photosynthesis.**

The raw materials

A plant growing in air is in contact with a mixture of gases. These gases are shown in Table 1. In water, a plant is still in contact with these gases because of the air that is dissolved in the water.

Gas	Percentage
nitrogen	78%
oxygen	21%
other gases (mainly carbon dioxide)	1%

▲ ***Table 1*** *Composition of air.*

If we try the iodine test (Unit 22) on a plant growing in air that has had all the carbon dioxide removed, nothing happens. The iodine does not turn blue-black so we know there is no starch in the leaf. This tells us that a plant needs carbon dioxide to make starch. Because we know that starch is made from glucose, we can guess that the plant needs carbon dioxide to make glucose.

Q1 How do we know that carbon dioxide is a raw material of photosynthesis?

Q2 Why do you suppose some plant growers try to increase the amount of carbon dioxide inside a greenhouse?

It is more difficult to test whether water is needed for photosynthesis because if you remove water from the plant it will die before your experiment is finished. Scientists have shown that water is a raw material for photosynthesis by watering a plant with **radioactive** water. Glucose from the plant is then tested for radioactivity. The test shows that the radioactive water does go into the glucose.

Building glucose

You now know that carbon dioxide, water and sunlight are needed for plants to make glucose. Next, we need to find out how they do this.

Glucose contains carbon, hydrogen and oxygen atoms. There are twice as many hydrogen atoms as oxygen atoms, as there are in water (Unit 46).

The atoms needed to make glucose come from carbon dioxide and water. These raw materials provide all the elements the plant needs to make glucose.

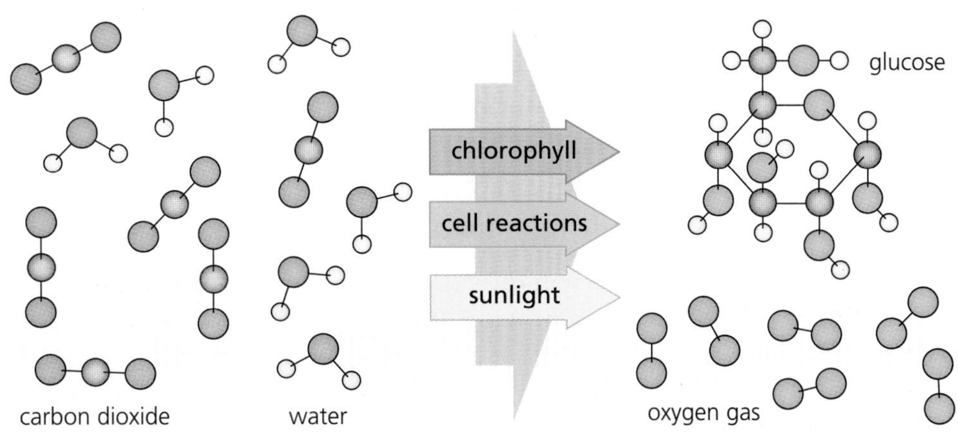

▲ ***Fig 1*** *Notice that the extra oxygen atoms are given off as a waste product.*

This chemical reaction can be written down as a word equation.

carbon dioxide + water --(light, chlorophyll)--> glucose + oxygen

This equation is exactly the reverse of the equation for **respiration**. Respiration (Unit 12) is the process of breaking glucose down to release the energy that once came from the sun. Photosynthesis and respiration are opposite reactions.

Q3 Why do green plants use both respiration and photosynthesis?

Q4 What is the name of the gas given out by a green plant at night?

Q5 Name the part of a leaf where gases pass in and out.

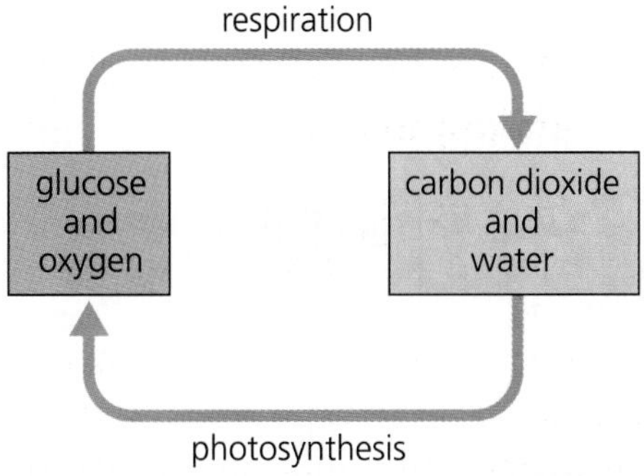

▲ ***Fig 2*** *Animals can only respire. Plants can make the equation go both ways. Remember that plants also respire.*

Key Words

carbohydrate – a high energy molecule containing carbon, hydrogen and oxygen

radioactive – the ability to give out radiation

respiration – the process of breaking down foods for energy

SUMMARY

- Green plants use sunlight energy to join together carbon dioxide and water molecules.
- Carbon dioxide enters through stomata in the leaf and water travels to the leaf from the roots.
- The oxygen atoms left over from making glucose in the leaf emerge through the stomata as oxygen gas.

SUMMARY *Activity*

Draw a diagram to show the path of an atom of carbon from carbon dioxide in the air to starch in a leaf.

24 Nutrients needed by plants

In this section of the book you will learn the following things:

- **that plants need more raw materials than carbon dioxide and water;**
- **what some of these raw materials are and where they come from;**
- **how scientists know that these raw materials are needed;**
- **how this knowledge can help farmers and gardeners.**

A plant makes glucose from carbon dioxide and water by photosynthesis. However, plant cells also contain protein. Protein contains nitrogen but glucose does not. The nitrogen must therefore come from somewhere else.

Essential elements

In addition to carbon, hydrogen and oxygen, plants also need other **essential elements**. One way to find out which elements are essential for healthy plant growth is to give them different diets and see how they grow.

This may sound easy but it is almost as difficult as working out an ideal diet for a person. A large number of plants must be grown in exactly the same conditions; the only difference is that one element is left out of the diet of half of them. This test has to be done all over again for each element tested, and then repeated many times to work out exactly how much of each element a plant needs. The same set of tests must be repeated for every different kind of plant a farmer or gardener wants to know about.

Growth medium with all essential elements

Growth medium with one essential element missing

▲ ***Fig 1*** *Why are so many plants used in the test?*

▼ ***Table 1***

Element	Symptoms if lacking
iron	poor leaves, no chlorophyll
sulphur	poor growth, proteins not made
nitrogen	poor growth, proteins not made
calcium	cells do not divide properly
potassium	poor growth, water lost
magnesium	pale leaves, no chlorophyll
phosphorus	poor growth, no energy molecules

Q1 Name three factors that must be kept the same during a fair test.

Nitrogen is needed to make proteins and enzymes. A plant cannot grow or repair itself without protein.

Sulphur is also essential for many proteins. Without sulphur these proteins could not be manufactured by the plant.

Phosphorus is needed for proteins and energy storage molecules. Plant cells could not survive for more than a few seconds without phosphorus.

Magnesium is a vital part of chlorophyll. A shortage of magnesium slows down photosynthesis. A lack of magnesium kills the plant.

Q2 Why is iron an essential element for plants?

Fertile ground

Most plants get their essential nutrients from the soil. They absorb the nutrients as minerals dissolved in water. Soil with a good supply of essential elements is called **fertile**. The trees in a forest first take nutrients out of the soil and then, when they die, the nutrients are returned to the soil. This how the soil of the forest remains fertile.

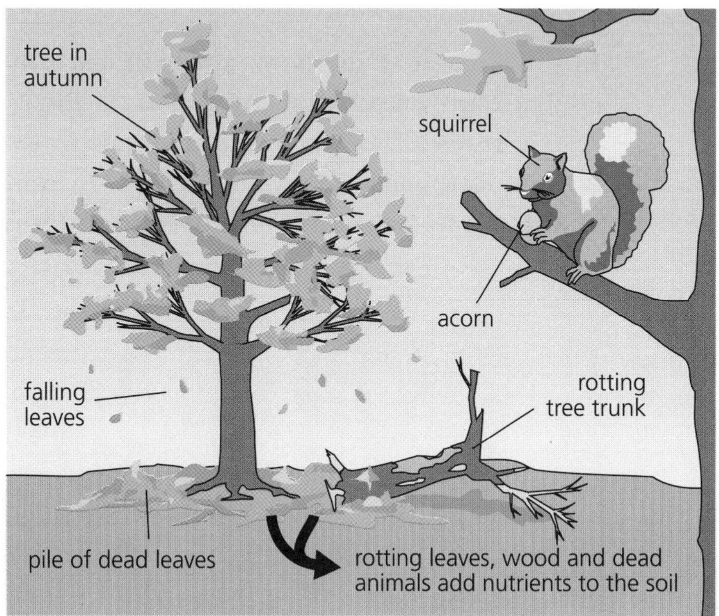

▲ ***Fig 2*** *The essential elements in a forest return naturally to the soil.*

The plants we eat are removed from the soil where they grew. The essential elements in the plants are also removed. When the same land is used over and over again the soil becomes infertile. Plants will not grow well there because essential elements are missing. The **yield** will fall. There are two main solutions for this problem:

1 Natural fertilisers can be added to the soil. Farmyard manure, compost or other **organic** material can restore essential nutrients. Natural fertilisers can be difficult to store and handle but they release essential elements slowly and well. They can also improve the physical texture of the soil.

2 Artificial fertilisers can be added to the soil. These are mixtures of chemicals made in factories. They work quickly and are easy to handle and store, but must be used carefully because rain can carry them into rivers and streams. Chemicals in water can make it bad to drink and damage the environment.

Q3 Why do you think chemical fertilisers contain nitrogen, phosphorus and potassium but not carbon?

Key Words

essential elements – elements necessary for healthy plant growth
organic – material that has been produced by living things
trace – a very tiny amount
yield – the edible amount of a plant produced from an area of land

SUMMARY

- Plants need essential elements such as nitrogen, sulphur and phosphorus.
- Most plants get these essential elements from the soil as compounds that are dissolved in water.
- When crops are removed from soil they take away essential elements and the soil becomes infertile.
- Essential elements can be returned to the soil by adding organic or commercially made fertilisers.

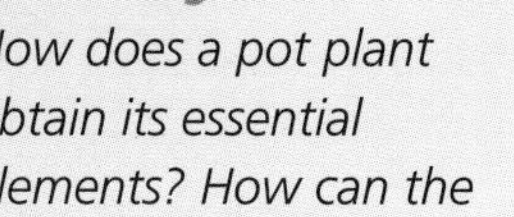

SUMMARY *Activity*

How does a pot plant obtain its essential elements? How can the owner of the plant help?

25 Those vital roots

In this section of the book you will learn the following things:

- that roots help to anchor a plant in the soil;
- that roots allow water and minerals to enter the plant;
- how root hairs are adapted to absorb water and minerals from the soil;
- that plants have a vascular system to transport materials.

The roots of a plant are normally under the soil. Roots fix a plant firmly in the soil so that it is not easily uprooted by animals or blown over by the wind. However, roots have other equally important jobs.

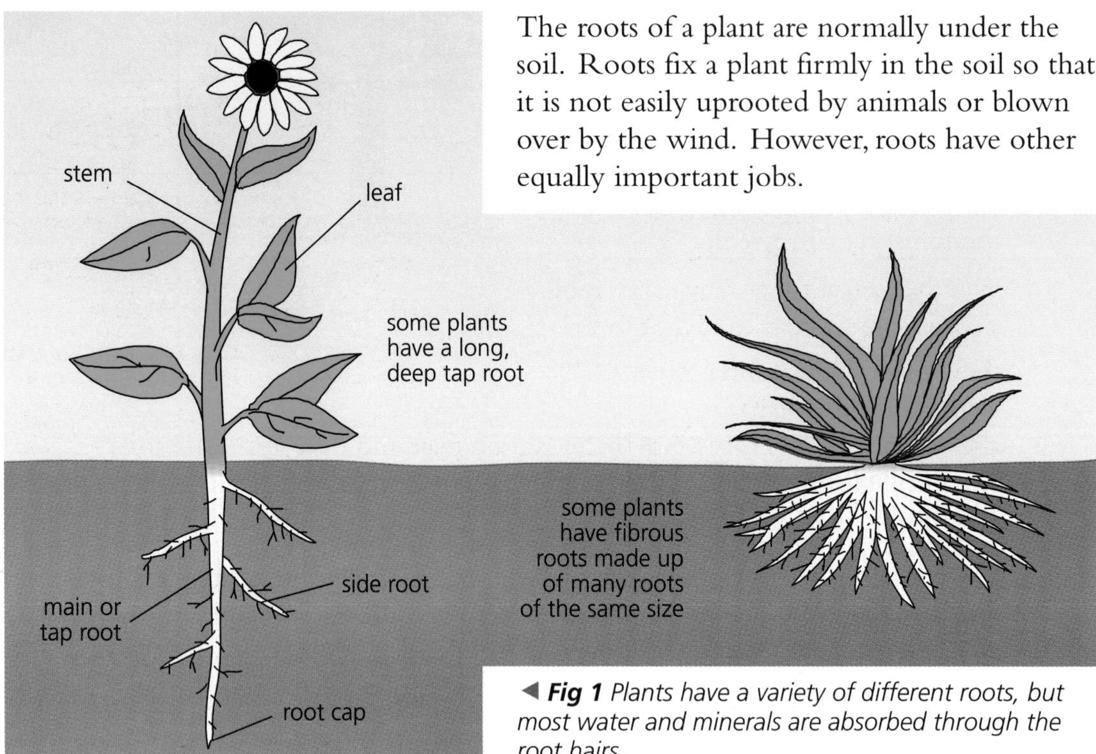

◀ ***Fig 1*** *Plants have a variety of different roots, but most water and minerals are absorbed through the root hairs.*

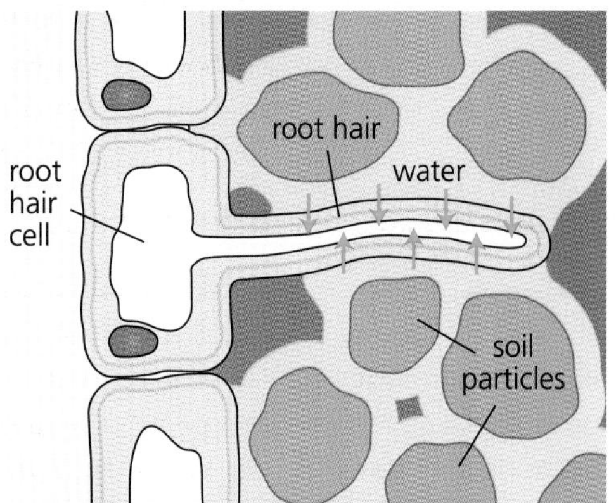

▲ ***Fig 2*** *A root hair can penetrate between soil particles.*

Root hairs

Root hairs are found on specially adapted cells on the outer surface of the root. These cells grow just behind the root tip. The **root hair cells** have special outgrowths that push between the soil particles into the water there. The walls of root hairs are very thin. This makes it easy for water to pass from the soil into the root. Root hairs also increase the surface area of the root. This increases the amount of water that the roots touch and increases the amount of water they can absorb.

Q1 Name two different types of root.

Q2 How are root hair cells specially adapted to absorb water from the soil?

Transport of water and minerals

Water and minerals that enter the roots must next be transported to where they are needed. Water may have to travel all the way up to the leaves. Water, food and minerals are carried in a plant's **vascular system**. This contains a series of long cells connected together to make tubes that run from the roots to every part of the plant. One set of tubes carries water and minerals upwards. Another set of tubes may carry food down from the leaves. The tubes can easily be seen in the roots, leaves and stems of many plants.

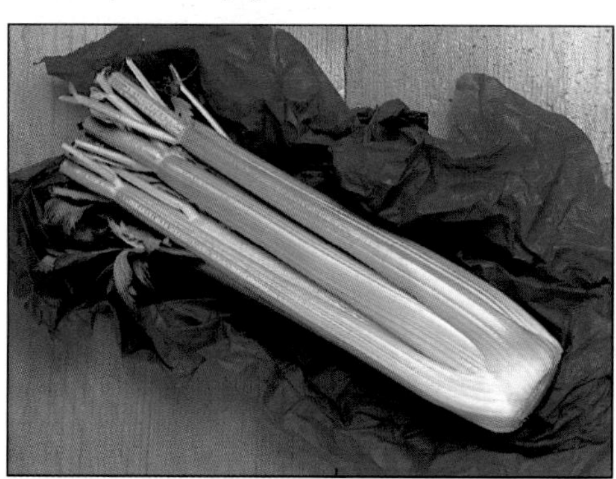

▲ ***Fig 3*** *The strings in a celery stem are part of its vascular system. Try leaving a celery stem in coloured water for an hour before cutting it into slices.*

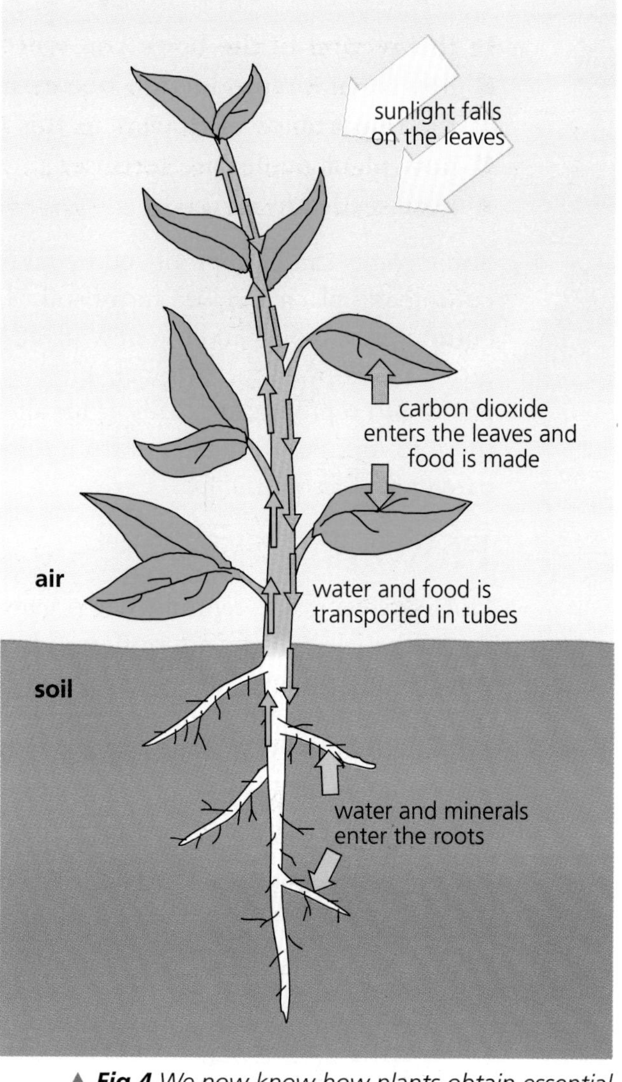
sunlight falls on the leaves
carbon dioxide enters the leaves and food is made
air
water and food is transported in tubes
soil
water and minerals enter the roots

▲ ***Fig 4*** *We now know how plants obtain essential elements, make food by photosynthesis, and transport substances from one part to another.*

Q3 Describe two ways in which roots and leaves are adapted to do their jobs.

Key Words

root – the part of a plant normally beneath the soil
root hair cells – root cells adapted to take in water
tap root – a plant's main deep root
vascular system – the plant's transport system

SUMMARY

- Roots anchor a plant and absorb water and minerals.
- Root hairs have thin walls to increase the uptake of water and minerals from soil. Root hairs also increase the surface area.
- Plants have a vascular system to carry water, minerals and food from where they enter or are made to where they are needed.

SUMMARY *Activity*

Make a list of the similarities between the vascular system of plants and the circulatory system of humans.

26 Sexual reproduction in plants

In this section of the book you will learn the following things:

- **how sexual reproduction occurs in plants;**
- **the importance of flowers in this process;**
- **how plant ovules are fertilised;**
- **how seeds are formed.**

Some plants can be reproduced by taking a cutting and placing it into moist soil. The cutting grows roots and the new plant that grows is a copy of the original. Flowering plants also reproduce sexually. This allows them to mix genetic material from different parents (see also Unit 17).

Flowers

Flowers are a plant's reproductive organs. A plant's male gametes are **pollen**. The female gametes are **ovules**. Flowers are designed so that pollen from one plant can fertilise ovules of another plant. Some plants produce separate male and female flowers but many contain both male and female reproductive parts (Fig 1).

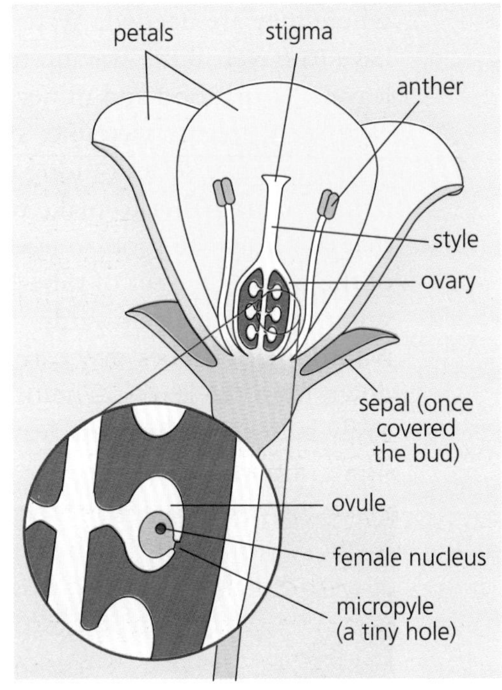

▲ *Fig 1*

Pollen is contained in the yellow **anther** at the top of each **stamen.** When the pollen grains are ripe, the swollen anther breaks open and releases them.

The plant's ovary is at the base of the petals. A stalk called the **style** carries a sticky tip called the **stigma**.

◀ ***Fig 2*** *Flowers are not colourful and sweet-smelling for our pleasure. They are designed to attract insects and other animals.*

Pollination

Pollination occurs when a pollen grain from a different plant of the same species lands on the sticky stigma.

Pollen may be carried to a flower by an insect. Some flowers attract insects by producing a sugary liquid called nectar. Many flowers have a brightly coloured landing pad to make it easy for insects to find them and reach inside for nectar.

Pollen can also be carried on the wind. Pollen grains in the air can be so numerous that they irritate people who are sensitive to them. 'Hay fever' gets its name from the fact that grasses are pollinated this way.

The whole point of sexual reproduction is to have two parents. Flowers are often cunningly made to prevent self-fertilisation. One of the simplest methods is to let the pollen and ova ripen at different times.

Q1 What are the male and female gametes of plants called?

Q2 Why is cross-pollination better than self-pollination?

Fertilisation

A pollen grain landing on a sticky stigma grows a long **pollen tube** down the style, which eventually reaches an ovule inside the ovary. The genetic material from the pollen grain passes down the tube and fertilises the ovule. After fertilisation the petals usually fall.

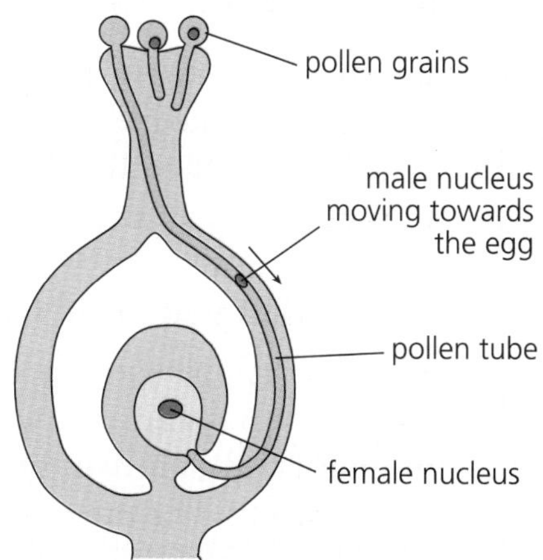

▶ ***Fig 3*** *An ovary containing a single seed may be called a carpel. A blackberry is a bunch of carpels.*

Seeds and fruits

Inside the ovary each fertilised ovule begins to divide into many cells. The final **seed** contains an **embryo** and a food store within a tough protective coat. A single ovary may contain just one seed or many seeds. An ovary filled with fertile seeds is called a **fruit**. This can mean a plum, a grape, an apple, a tomato, a marrow or a pea-pod.

Fruits and seeds can be spread by wind, water, heat or animals. It is important for a plant to scatter its seeds, so that they colonise new places and do not grow in the shadow of their parents.

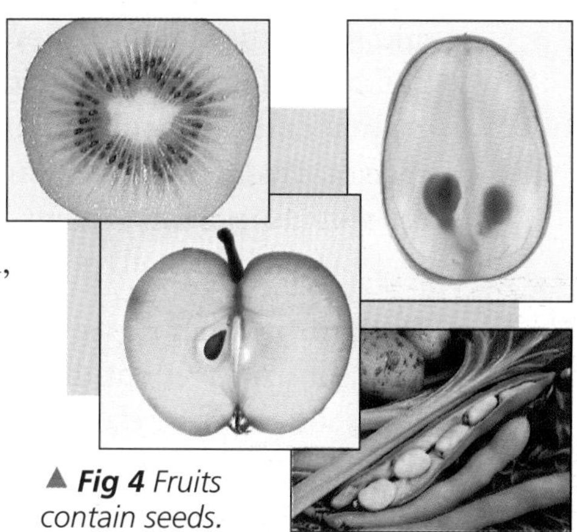

▲ ***Fig 4*** *Fruits contain seeds.*

Key Words

anther – the part of a flower where pollen is made
fruit – ovary plus fertile seed(s)
ovary – the female reproductive organ of flowering plants
pollen - the male sex cell of a flowering plant
pollination – the moment when pollen lands on a stigma
seed – an embryo plant and food store inside a protective coat
stamen – the male reproductive organ of a flowering plant

SUMMARY

- Flowering plants reproduce by sexual reproduction. Male gametes are pollen grains and female gametes are ovules.
- Flowers are pollinated by insects, water or the wind. Cross-pollination combines genetic material from two parents.
- After fertilisation the ovule develops into a seed. The ovary becomes a fruit.
- Seeds can be dispersed by wind, water, heat or animals.

SUMMARY *Activity*

Find some pictures of flowers in books and magazines. Copy the flowers and try to label the main parts. How are they adapted to make pollination easier?

27 Variety of life

In this section of the book you will learn the following things:

- **the meaning of the word species;**
- **that living things differ and that this is called variation;**
- **that animals and plants within one species vary;**
- **that there is even more variety between different species.**

Everyone you know is different. These differences make life more interesting and help us to identify friends. They are also vitally important to the course of evolution.

▲ ***Fig 1*** *These people are very different in many ways, but they are also very similar.*

What is a species?

Although the people you know are different in many ways, they are also very similar. They live in similar ways, move in similar ways and need similar foods. The most important similarity of all is that, even if they look quite different, male and female humans can reproduce and make children together. Animals that are as similar as this are called a **species**. Human beings are a single species. Budgerigars are a single species. House sparrows are a single species. Robins are a single species. They can mate among themselves but not with each other.

Q1 What is the main test of whether two organisms are in the same species?

Variation within a species usually has limits. All the people in your class will have different sized feet but there is a limit for the largest and the smallest shoe size. The shoe sizes of a class of 13 year old pupils are shown in Table 1 and Fig 2.

Shoe size	2	3	4	5	6	7	8	9
Number of people	1	1	4	7	8	4	2	2

◀ ***Table 1***

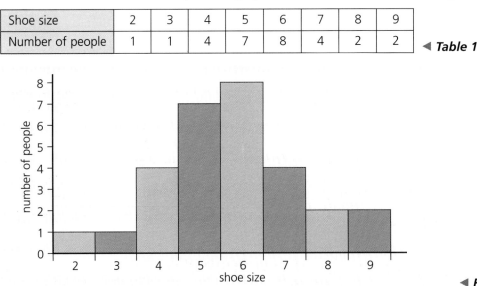

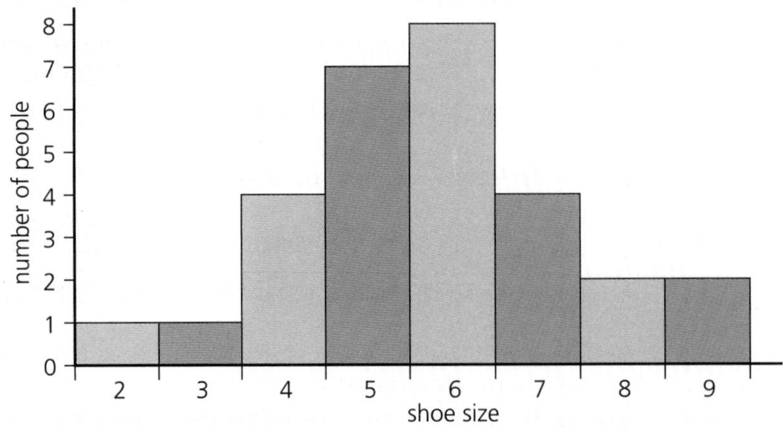

◀ ***Fig 2***

Some people may think they have large or small feet but their size will fall within the normal range for people of their age. This normal range is called the **normal distribution.** The same is true for height and other characteristics. The shoe sizes for an elephant or a mouse would fall off the chart. They would be outside the normal distribution.

Other species also show variation. People who study animals that may look alike at first are soon able to spot differences and use these to identify individuals. Lions all look like lions but each has particular facial features, body shapes and markings that set it apart from the rest. In other words, they show variation. Variations are vital for evolution.

Q2 What does the term normal distribution mean?

Variation between species

Animals and plants from different species show more variation than animals from the same species. Two people will have more in common than a person and a bear. A whale has more in common with another whale than with a wolf. However, some species are very similar and it is thought that they could be closely related. It is possible to make a chart that shows the relationships between species. Species with very little in common are far apart on the chart. Species that have a lot in common, such as humans and chimpanzees, are close together. Some examples are shown in the diagram.

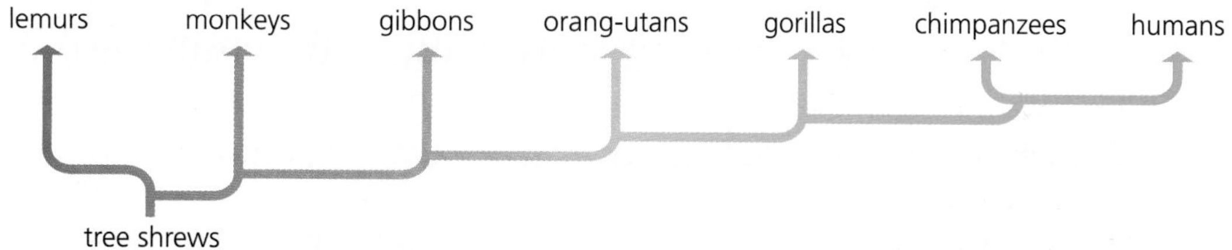

▲ *Fig 3 Some species are more closely related than others.*

Q3 List four characteristics that humans and chimpanzees have in common.

Key Words

normal distribution – a pattern on a graph that shows the normal range of differences within one species

species – an organism that is genetically distinct

variation – a small difference between members of the same species. A larger difference between members of different species

SUMMARY

- Males and females can reproduce sexually with others of the same species. Despite this, members of the same species show variation.
- The variation within a species is important.
- The variation between species is greater than the variation within a species.
- Closely related species resemble one another more closely than unrelated species.

SUMMARY *Activity*

Carry out a survey of hand span among your friends and family. Measure from the tip of the thumb to the tip of the little finger in each case. Use the results to produce a chart like Fig 2.

28 The causes of variety

In this section of the book you will learn the following things:

- **that the characteristics of an organism are inherited from its parents;**
- **that variations can come from a number of causes;**
- **that some variation is a result of the environment.**

When animals and plants reproduce sexually their offspring acquire a mixture of characteristics from both parents. New combinations of characteristics can be made. Mixing genetic material causes variation. If an organism survives long enough to reproduce, its characteristics can be **inherited**, or passed on to future generations. If a variation creates a weakness, the organism may not survive long enough to pass on its weakness.

Inherited characteristics do not always develop fully. A person who has inherited the ability to grow large may not get enough to eat to grow properly. This person will not become as large as possible. Factors such as food and lifestyle are called **environmental** factors.

▶ ***Fig 1*** *These players inherited the characteristics needed to grow tall, but they must also have eaten well and remained healthy.*

Inherited variation

The information for all the characteristics of an organism is copied and then passed to the next generation in large molecules called **genes.** Genes are the coded instructions that make up our genetic material. You received half of your genes from each parent. Your own personal characteristics are therefore a selection from both of your parents. You have two genes for every characteristic and one comes from each parent. One may be stronger than its partner. If you inherit one gene for brown eyes and one for blue eyes, for example, you will have brown eyes. This is because the brown eye gene is stronger or **dominant**. Family members often look alike but can sometimes look completely different.

Sometimes a mistake occurs when the genetic code is being copied. Information might be lost, changed or added. If this happens a gene may not work at all or it may work differently. A sudden change in a gene is called a **mutation**. This means there is always a chance of some completely new characteristic. Most mutations simply cause problems, but once in a while something different and useful arises this way. Mutations can occur naturally but the rate of mutation can be speeded up. Radiation and some chemicals can increase the chance of mutations.

Environmental variation

Identical twins come from a single fertilised egg that divided in half before each half grew into a new baby. Because their genetic material is identical you would expect them to be exactly the same in every way.

Studying identical twins that were separated at birth and brought up in different situations can give us some idea of how important environment might be. If one twin has a healthy home life with good food and exercise and the other is less fortunate there can be a visible difference in their adult size and shape.

Plants can also show how the environment can affect inherited characteristics. Identical plants are easy to create from cuttings. When they are grown in different areas they can produce different yields, depending on sunshine, rainfall and soil fertility.

▲ ***Fig 3*** *The pale green crops are growing in soil with low nitrogen levels.*

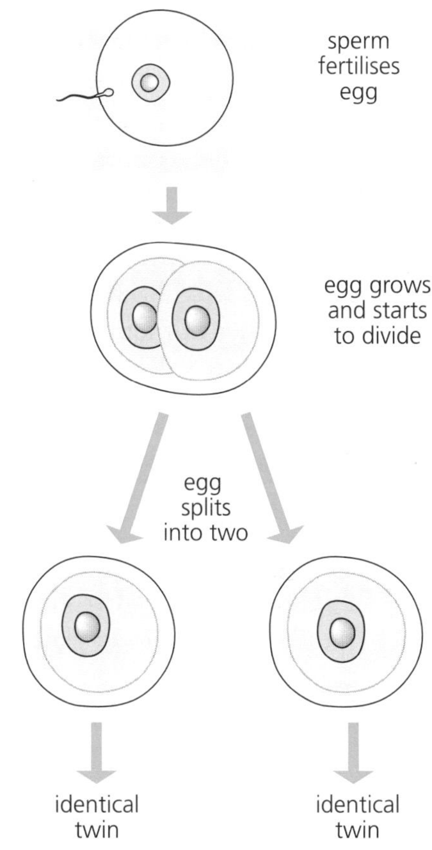
sperm fertilises egg
egg grows and starts to divide
egg splits into two
identical twin
identical twin

▲ ***Fig 2*** *Identical twins come from a single fertilised egg.*

Q1 Do you think that environmental variations can be passed on from parents to offspring?

Q2 Do you think that mutations can be passed on from parents to offspring?

Key Words

dominant gene – a gene that is stronger than its opposite number

gene – a very large molecule carrying a code for one characteristic

mutation – a sudden change in the structure of a gene

SUMMARY

- Combining genes by sexual reproduction causes variation.
- Genes can suddenly change, or mutate. Mutations occasionally create useful new characteristics.
- Environmental factors also cause variation.

SUMMARY *Activity*

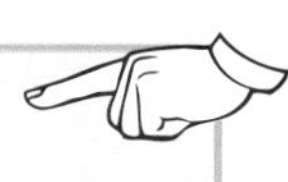

Design an experiment using one packet of seeds and two plant pots of compost that shows how environmental factors can create variation among members of the same species.

29 Selective breeding

In this section of the book you will learn the following things:

- **the meaning of the term selective breeding;**
- **that selective breeding can create new varieties of plants and animals;**
- **that this has commercial importance;**
- **that this can sometimes cause problems.**

Every new organism is unique. Characteristics inherited from both parents make it different from either of them. It is possible to mix characteristics deliberately to create special varieties of animals and plants.

▲ ***Fig 1*** *These trees have been selectively bred for generations. They are disease resistant, strong, and give a high yield.*

Selective breeding

One **variety** of plant may be very tall and strong but only produce small fruits. This plant might be very good at surviving wind and bad weather, but the food yield would be low.

Another variety of the same plant might be small and weak but produce very large fruits. This plant would be easily damaged but if it did survive it would give a good yield. The farmer would like to combine the good characteristics from both varieties to get a tall, strong plant with big fruits. If the farmer fertilises one plant with pollen from the other one the offspring will have a chance to combine some of the good characteristics. This is called **selective breeding**. Each step in selective breeding is called **cross breeding**.

Q1 Why do you think plant breeders try to prevent self-pollination?

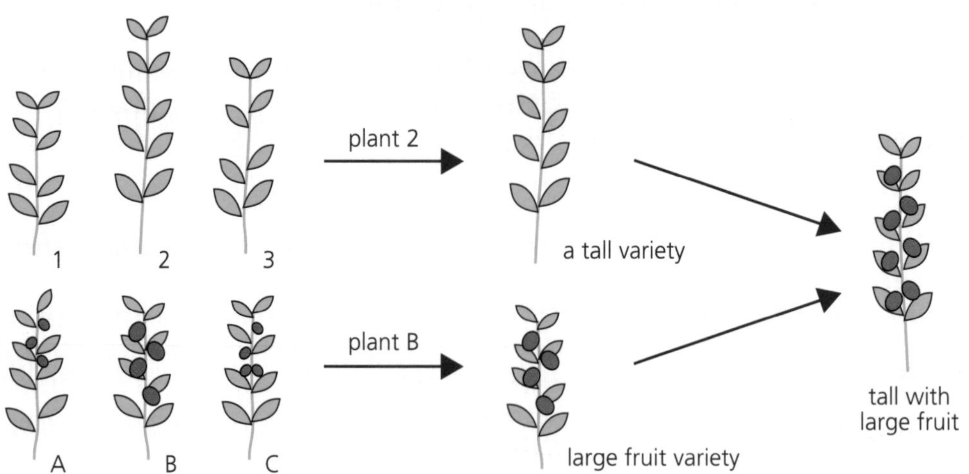

▲ ***Fig 2*** *Some variations can lead to useful characteristics.*

It is important to realise that the perfect mixture of characteristics will not show in the first generation of offspring. The ones that seem most promising then are used as parents for the next generation. It takes many generations of breeding to arrive at a variety that can be grown commercially.

▲ ***Fig 3*** *Selective breeding is not new. Ancient Egyptians began creating wheat from wild grasses three thousand years ago.*

Garden varieties

Many modern garden plants are the result of selective breeding. Flowers can be made bigger and even be created in unnatural colours. Plant breeders also select for characteristics that make a new plant easier to grow, sturdier and resistant to disease.

Q2 List two characteristics that plant breeders try to select for.

Animal breeding

Selective breeding is used for animals as well as plants. Poultry and cattle have been selectively bred for many generations. Chickens can be bred to gain weight quickly or lay brown eggs, and cattle can be bred to give more milk or meat. Some people believe that selective breeding can be cruel. Animals may become too heavy to move comfortably. Even some pets have been bred for characteristics that make them uncomfortable.

▲ ***Fig 4*** *Bulldogs have difficulty breathing and cannot have puppies normally.*

Q3 How has selective breeding improved farming and food production?

Q4 Do you think that selective breeding is a good thing?

Key Words

cross breeding – encouraging or forcing one variety of an organism to breed with a different variety

offspring – any organism created by reproduction

selective breeding – breeding to produce a combination of desired characteristics

variety – an organism of a single species that has distinctive features. In animals, often called a 'breed'

SUMMARY

- Cross breeding parents with special characteristics can produce offspring with a combination of these characteristics. This is selective breeding.
- Selective breeding takes many generations to create a 'perfect' plant or animal.
- Many animals and plants that we use today are the result of selective breeding.
- Selective breeding can cause health problems for animals.

SUMMARY *Activity*

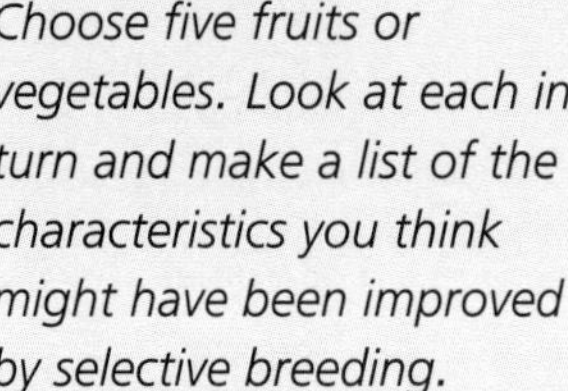

Choose five fruits or vegetables. Look at each in turn and make a list of the characteristics you think might have been improved by selective breeding.

30 Classifying animals and plants

In this section of the book you will learn the following things:

- **that living things can be named and classified;**
- **that this is done by placing them into groups according to their major characteristics;**
- **that this is called taxonomy.**

There are millions of different species of living things on Earth. Scientists have divided organisms into groups which make them easier to study and understand. The groups are organised according to the characteristics of the organisms they contain. First, all living things are placed in five main groups called **kingdoms**. Each kingdom is then divided into smaller and smaller groups. Placing an organism into a group is called **classification**. The process of describing, classifying and naming organisms is called **taxonomy**.

The five kingdoms

There are a lot of obvious differences between a horse and a tree. Horses and trees clearly belong to completely different kingdoms. One main kingdom is the animal kingdom and another is the plant kingdom (see Table 1).

The kingdoms can be further divided until each organism is classified to species level (see Fig 1). This is the smallest group in the classification of living things.

Kingdom	Types of organisms
prokaryotes 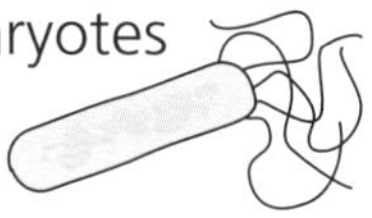	bacteria and some algae
protists 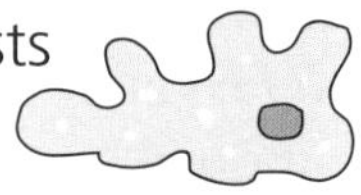	single-celled organisms
fungi 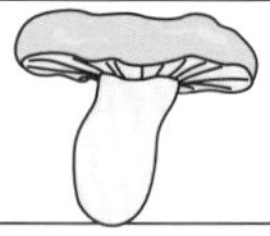	moulds, mushrooms and toadstools
plants 	plants such as ferns, mosses, conifers and flowering plants – all green plants
animals 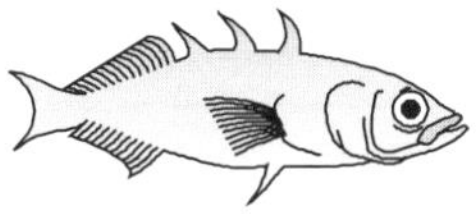	insects, worms, shellfish, birds, mammals – all multicelled animals

▲ ***Table 1***

▼ ***Fig 1***

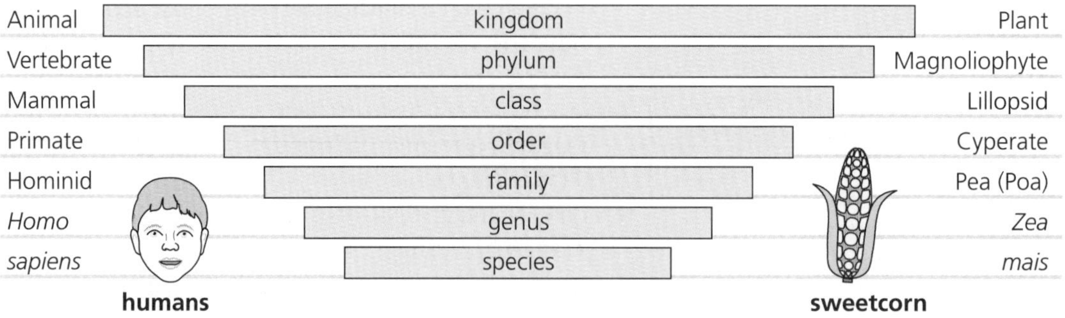

Vertebrate class	Characteristics
fish	backbone, gills, live in water, scales, fins, streamlined body
amphibians	backbone, eggs laid in water, soft and wet skin, adults have lungs, adults can live on land and in water
reptiles	backbone, lay eggs with a shell, lungs, skin covered in dry scales
birds	backbone, lay eggs with a hard shell, lungs, feathers, wings
mammals	backbone, young develop inside the mother, young fed on milk from the mother, lungs, hair or fur

▲ *Table2*

The animal kingdom

Some animals have a backbone and others do not. This helps us to divide the animal kingdom into two main groups. Animals with backbones are called **vertebrates**. Animals without backbones are called **invertebrates**. Vertebrates include fishes, snakes and people. Invertebrates include starfishes, snails, worms and insects.

Then vertebrates are divided into five smaller **classes**. The main characteristics of each class are shown in Table 2.

Q1 Why are slugs classified as invertebrates?

Q2 List two differences between amphibians and mammals.

Key Words

invertebrate – an animal without a backbone
genus – a group of organisms just above species level
kingdom – one of the five major divisions of living things
vertebrate – an animal with a backbone

SUMMARY

- All living things can be classified into groups according to their main characteristics. The process of describing, classifying and naming organisms is called taxonomy.
- The five major divisions are called kingdoms. Each kingdom is further divided until species level is reached.
- The two major divisions of the animal kingdom are vertebrates and invertebrates.
- Vertebrates are subdivided into five classes.

SUMMARY *Activity*

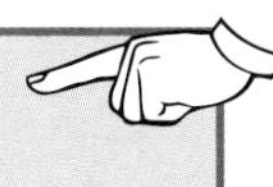

Find a picture of a horse and a picture of a rose. Study them carefully and try to classify them, step by step, as far as you can. Search carefully for clues.

31 Identifying animals and plants

In this section of the book you will learn the following things:

- **that the plant kingdom can also be divided into smaller groups;**
- **how to use a key to identify and name living things;**
- **that there are different types of keys.**

The plant kingdom

The plant kingdom can also be divided into smaller and smaller groups. One of the main divisions is made according to whether a plant has a vascular system or not (Unit 25). Some very simple plants do not need a vascular system because they are small enough for water, food and gases to move around easily.

Vascular plants are divided into those that produce flowers and those that do not. A simplified classification for plants is shown opposite. Only the larger groups are shown. Each can be further divided down to the species level, as animals are.

▼ ***Fig 2*** *Green plants.*

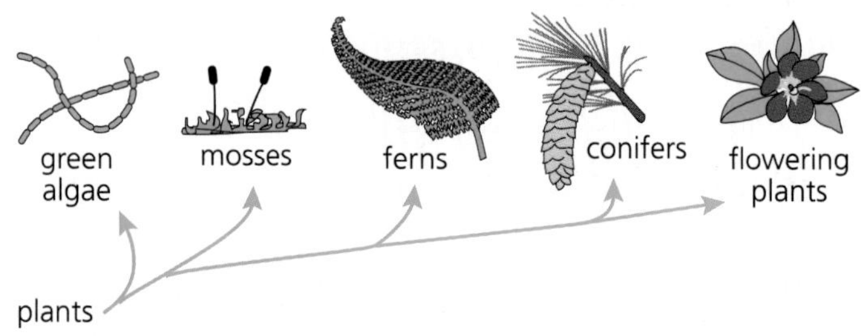

A warning about classification

The system of classification we use today has been made up and modified by scientists for generations. When new information is discovered the system is changed and improved. Small changes are regularly made. An organism placed in one **genus** can be moved to another genus, or even put into a completely new genus, when somebody notices something different about it.

Q1 Why might a key from 1866 not be very useful for identifying insects or plants?

Reviewing keys

There are far too many living things on Earth for any one person to learn all their names. It is impossible to memorise more than a small fraction of all the different insects or flowers. This can be a problem for scientists and other people interested in living things. It could take a long time just to memorise all the species that you might see during a short walk. Using a key is a short cut.

Identification keys

You do not have to memorise every hill and street in your area in case you get lost. A map will help you to find out where you are and where you need to go. To help us find our way through the variety of life and identify living things we have never seen before we do not have a map, but we have keys. A **key** is a special chart or table that helps us to identify living things.

As you will know from your previous study, there are different types of keys. Some are in the form of a list of questions about the living thing you are trying to identify.

Another type of key is set out as a diagram rather than a list of questions.

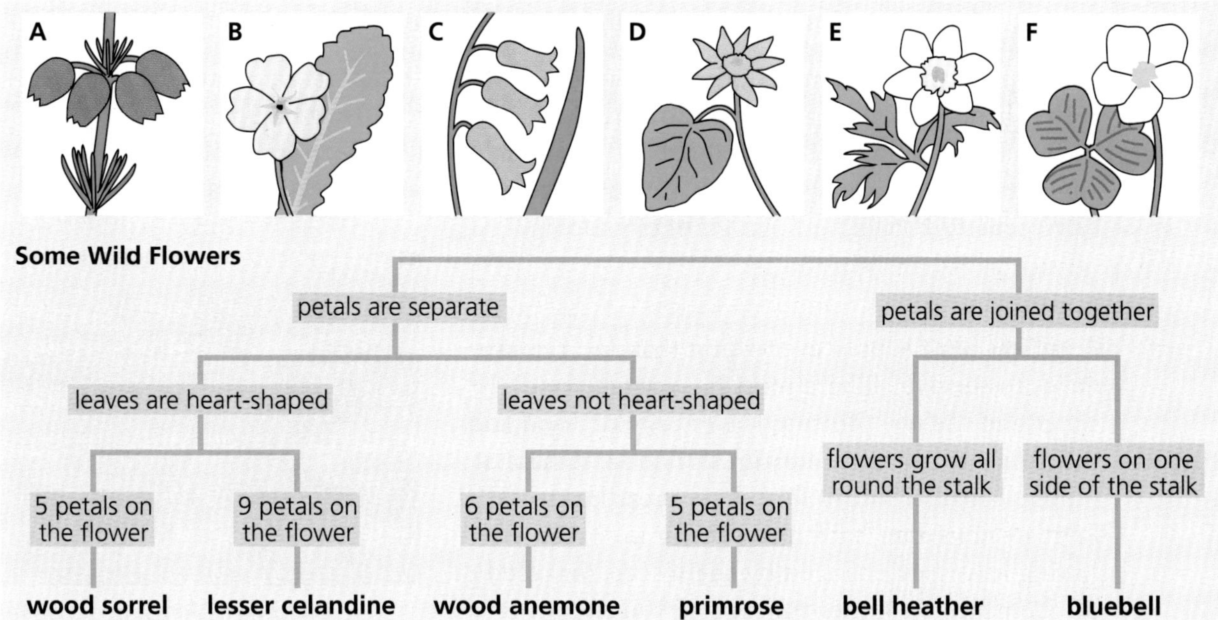

▲ *Fig 2*

The key in Fig 2 asks a question and gives you a choice of two branches to follow. You take each branch in turn until you reach the end. This is called a **dichotomous** key or a **spider** key. When using a key it is important to examine the organism carefully. Sometimes a detail can be vital. If you take a wrong turning you never get another chance to jump across to the correct branch.

Q2 Using a key to identify trees using their leaves can very useful. Why might this cause problems at certain times of the year?

Q3 Other than studying the organism itself, what other clues can be used to identify it?

Key Words

dichotomous – anything with two branches

key – a table or chart that helps you to identify living things

SUMMARY

- The plant kingdom can also be divided into smaller groups.
- A key can help you to identify and name almost any living thing.
- A dichotomous key asks questions in a series of steps.
- Some characteristics can only be seen at certain times of the year.
- Other clues such as environment can help with identification.

SUMMARY *Activity*

Collect some pictures of insects from a magazine and then design a key so that others can identify them.

32 Plant and animal habitats

In this section of the book you will learn the following things:

- **that the natural home for each living thing is called its habitat;**
- **that different habitats have different plants and animals living in them;**
- **that animals and plants are adapted to live in their own habitats;**
- **that a habitat includes the other living things there.**

The type of place where an organism normally lives is called its **habitat**. A tiny habitat is called a **microhabitat.** A crack in a rock may be a microhabitat within the general habitat of a beach. The collection of plants and animals in a habitat make up a **community**. A community and its **environment** together form an **ecosystem**.

Habitats

A habitat must supply everything that an organism needs to survive. There must be oxygen, food, water and shelter. Rotting leaves provide food and shelter for many small creatures. The same habitat supplies small creatures for bigger creatures to eat. Living things alter habitats by living in them. The rotting leaves are changed by the insects that feed on them and push them around. Even the rot is caused by micro-organisms that live there.

▲ ***Fig 1*** *The forest floor habitat contains hundreds of microhabitats.*

Ponds, rivers, beaches, rock pools and soil are all different habitats and there are hundreds more. Different habitats support different animals and plants. An animal that lives in a tree may not be able to live in a pond. Sometimes different habitats support the same animals at different stages of their lives. A dragonfly grows up in a pond but eventually comes out of the water to hunt in the air.

Q1 List five microhabitats that you may find in a garden habitat.

Competition

The different species of animals and plants in a habitat use it in different ways. Each one occupies a different **niche**. Two species fighting for the same niche would be in **competition**. When two species compete, one generally drives the other out. A beach may support many different birds. There may be curlews feeding on animals that burrow under the sand and plovers picking animals from the surface of the sand (Fig 2). Both species live within the same habitat but they do not compete for the same food.

Fig 2 a *Curlew* ▲
b *Grey plover* ▶

Adaptation

Q2 How are the grey plover and curlew adapted to different niches in their habitat?

Animals and plants are adapted to their habitat. A fish can breathe underwater. A limpet clings to a seashore rock. Conifers have thin shiny leaves so that heavy snow can slide off without breaking their branches. The leaves of a desert cactus have become sharp spines and the fat stem has a waxy coat to guard the water inside. Marram grass can grow on a beach because its long, deep roots can grip soft sand.

The lives of animals and plants in a habitat may be closely connected. Some animals eat plants, others eat smaller animals. Being adapted to a habitat may mean protecting yourself from being eaten at the same time as finding food for yourself.

The dog whelk (Fig 3) is a sea-snail that feeds on other shellfish. Dog whelks on exposed shores have thinner shells than ones on sheltered shores. This may seem mysterious until you also discover that crabs eat dog whelks. Crabs cannot survive on exposed shores with big waves. The thick shell of the dog whelk protects it from crabs rather than the environment. Even though the dog whelk is a **predator** itself, it needs to keep itself safe from other predators.

Q3 Describe how some plants are adapted to their habitat.

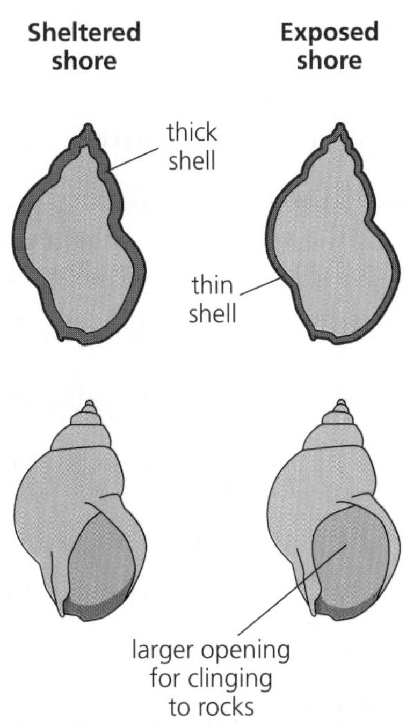

▲ ***Fig 3*** *Dog whelk.*

Key Words

competition – one or more living things requiring the same food, mate or shelter
community – the collection of animals and plants that share a habitat
ecosystem – a self-contained community interacting with the environment
habitat – the home for a living thing that provides everything it needs
microhabitat – a small area within a larger habitat, e.g. under a stone
niche – an exact lifestyle within a habitat
predator – an animal that eats other animals

SUMMARY

- A habitat is the place where a living thing normally lives.
- Living things are adapted to live in their habitats.
- The living things in a habitat are called a community. The community plus the environment forms an ecosystem.
- Many species can occupy different niches within the same habitat, even if they eat one another.

SUMMARY *Activity*

Identify five different habitats around your school or home. List some of the animals and plants that live there. How do these living things interact with one another and with their environment?

33 Adapting to change

In this section of the book you will learn the following things:

- **that organisms are adapted to survive daily changes in their habitat;**
- **that organisms are adapted to survive seasonal changes in their habitat;**
- **the importance of factors such as light intensity and temperature to the survival of organisms.**

Regular changes occur daily or seasonally in most habitats. Some habitats also suffer occasional changes, such as drought or forest fire. Organisms need adaptations to help them to survive both regular and occasional changes.

Daily changes

Each morning the sun rises and daylight begins. Every evening the level of light falls until it becomes dark. Living things adapt to the pattern of light and dark in many ways.

Most animals and plants are more active during the day. They are **diurnal**. Some are more active at night. They are **nocturnal**. Being nocturnal can keep small animals safe from predators that hunt in daylight. Some predators specialise in hunting at night. A bat uses sound to hunt nocturnal insects. An owl uses sensitive ears and large eyes.

▲ ***Fig 1*** *An owl is specially adapted to see a warm body moving in dim light.*

Q1 What is the advantage of being a nocturnal animal?

▲ ***Fig 2*** *Sunflowers are so sensitive to light that the flowerheads follow the Sun as it crosses the sky.*

Flowers attract insects for pollination (Unit 26). Many bee-pollinated flowers open in sunlight and close at night. Moth-pollinated flowers may only open at night. These flowers are often strongly scented to attract moths. Plants can also turn their leaves towards the sun to gather more light for photosynthesis.

Q2 How is a sunflower adapted for pollination?

Seasonal changes

▲ ***Fig 3*** *Oak trees can survive more than a hundred winters by losing their leaves and becoming dormant.*

Tropical regions of the world do not have seasons. The climate there is warm all the year round.

Northern or southern regions can be very cold in winter and very warm in summer. Plants and animals there must adapt to these seasonal changes or they would not survive.

Many plants survive the winter by becoming **dormant**. Annual plants die after making seeds to survive the winter. Biennial plants survive for two years by making an underground food store and allowing their green parts to wither. Next year, the root can grow new leaves and a flower to make seeds. Perennial plants such as bulbs and trees can survive for many years by losing their leaves each winter and growing new ones in the spring.

Animals also have different ways to survive through the winter. Some invertebrates die after laying eggs that can survive the cold, like annual plants. Some spend the winter as a dormant pupa, like biennial plants.

Mammals and birds can survive cold weather but they cannot survive without food, and food is scarce in winter. Many birds simply fly to a warmer region. This is called **migration**. Some mammals hide away and sleep when food is scarce. This is called **hibernation.** Before hibernating an animal builds up a store of body fat to provide food and warmth during the winter. Animals that remain active through the winter also need extra fat and thick fur to protect them from the cold.

Heat and drought

Desert plants are specialised for collecting and storing water. Snails keep moisture in by withdrawing into their shells and sealing the entrance. Many desert animals hide underground during the day and come out to feed at night.

Q3 List some of the ways in which animals and plants are adapted to cope with changes in light intensity and temperature.

Key Words

diurnal – belonging to the day
dormant – resting
hibernation – winter sleep
migration – regularly travelling to a different region
nocturnal – belonging to the night

SUMMARY

- Plants and animals are adapted to changes in light intensity.
- Plants and animals are adapted to survive seasonal or daily temperature changes.
- Plants and animals may be adapted to survive periods of drought.

SUMMARY *Activity*

Think about seashore animals. Twice every day they are covered by the tide. Make a list of the daily and seasonal changes they must be able to survive.

34 Food chains

In this section of the book you will learn the following things:

- **what a food chain is;**
- **how a food chain can be shown as a pyramid of numbers;**
- **what happens to the energy within a community of plants and animals.**

Energy for life comes from the sun. Green plants use sunlight to make food by photosynthesis. Animals cannot make their own food. They must feed on plants or other animals.

Food chains

Green plants building their own food are called **producers**. Animals eating plants or other animals are called **consumers**. Consumers fall into three groups. Animals that eat green plants directly are called **primary consumers** or **herbivores**. Animals that eat herbivores are called **secondary consumers**. Animals that eat secondary consumers are called **tertiary consumers**.

The relationship between producers and consumers can be drawn as a chain.

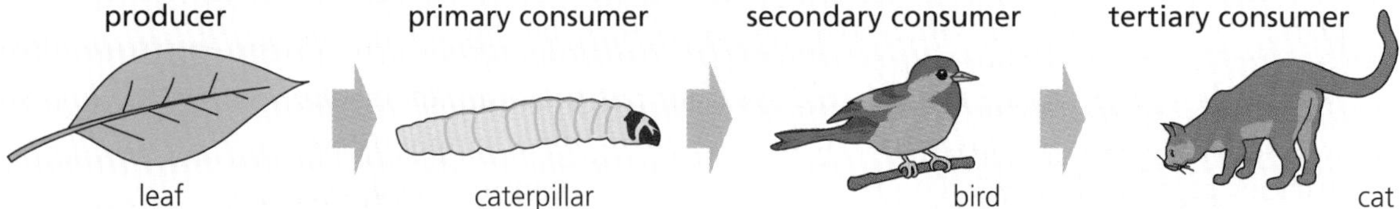

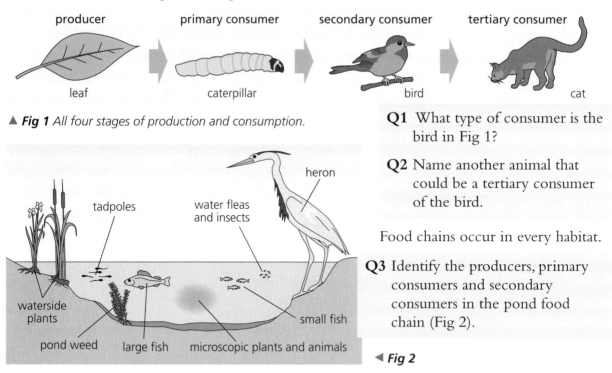

▲ ***Fig 1*** *All four stages of production and consumption.*

Q1 What type of consumer is the bird in Fig 1?

Q2 Name another animal that could be a tertiary consumer of the bird.

Food chains occur in every habitat.

Q3 Identify the producers, primary consumers and secondary consumers in the pond food chain (Fig 2).

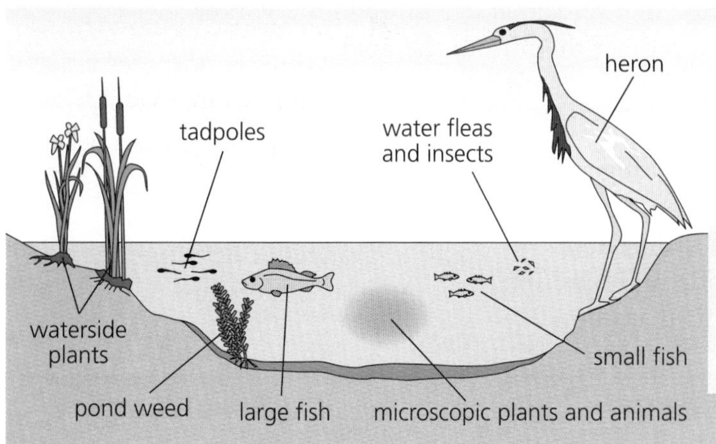

◄ ***Fig 2***

Energy flow

When an animal eats a plant it uses the food to provide energy and raw materials (Units 6, 7, 12). Some of the plant material is simply wasted. Some energy is given out as heat and some material is egested. Half of the grass a cow eats is used to provide energy. Less than half of the grass becomes part of the cow. Energy is lost or used up in this way at every stage in the food chain.

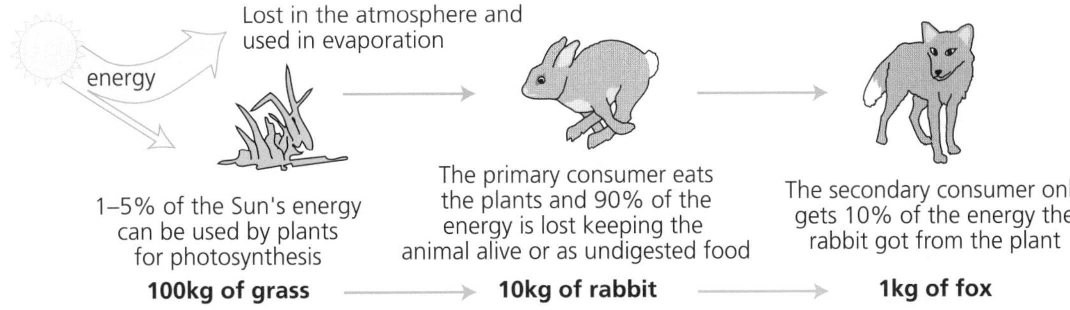
energy
Lost in the atmosphere and used in evaporation
1–5% of the Sun's energy can be used by plants for photosynthesis
The primary consumer eats the plants and 90% of the energy is lost keeping the animal alive or as undigested food
The secondary consumer only gets 10% of the energy the rabbit got from the plant
100kg of grass
10kg of rabbit
1kg of fox

▲ ***Fig 3*** *A lot of energy is lost as it passes down the food chain.*

Pyramids of numbers

Counting the numbers of organisms at each stage in a food chain gives us a **pyramid of numbers**.

The pyramid of numbers for the pond (Fig 4) is what you would expect. As energy is lost at each stage, the secondary and tertiary consumers must always eat larger amounts of food than the stage below.

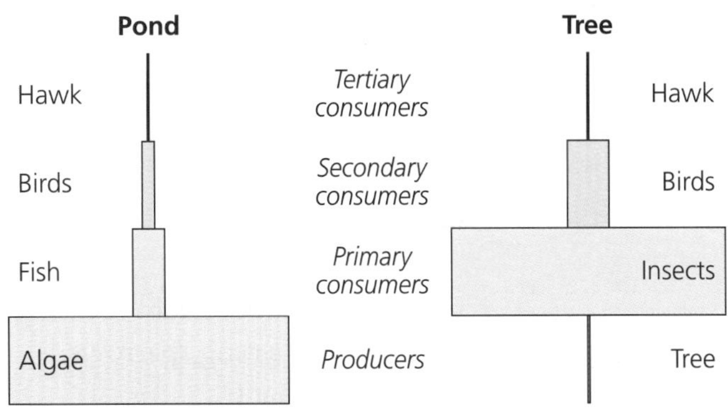
Pond
Hawk
Birds
Fish
Algae
Tertiary consumers
Secondary consumers
Primary consumers
Producers
Tree
Hawk
Birds
Insects
Tree

▲ ***Fig 4*** *Pyramids of numbers.*

However, the pyramid for the tree looks different. This is because one tree can produce lots of leaves for the caterpillars and other animals that eat them. If **mass** was measured instead of numbers, the pyramid would always be the right way up. This would be a **pyramid of biomass**.

Q4 Why does one sparrow hawk have to eat so many small birds in a week?

Key Words

consumer – an animal that feeds on plants or other animals
herbivore – an animal that only eats plants
producer – a green plant making food by photosynthesis
pyramid of numbers – a diagram showing the number of organisms at each stage of a food chain
pyramid of biomass – a diagram showing the mass of organisms at each stage of a food chain

SUMMARY

- Green plants are called producers because they produce their own food.
- Animals are called consumers because they feed on plants or other animals.
- The passage of food from producers to consumers can be shown as a food chain.
- Energy is lost at each stage of the chain.
- Organisms in a food chain can be counted and shown as a pyramid of numbers.
- Organisms in a food chain can be weighed and shown as a pyramid of biomass.

SUMMARY *Activity*

Choose three different foods you have eaten recently. Place the food and yourself into a food chain that shows how the energy in the food reached you and where it came from.

35 Food webs

In this section of the book you will learn the following things:

- **that food chains combine to form complex webs;**
- **that food webs provide a more accurate picture of feeding patterns within communities than simple chains;**
- **that food webs are critical for the survival of everything in a community.**

Each habitat has its own collection of food chains. Most habitats are very complex and some animals and plants play a part in more than one food chain. For example, a fish could either be eaten by a bird or by a larger fish. A more accurate way of showing these relationships is as a **food web**.

Food webs

The food web tells you more about a habitat than a food chain. The links between and across chains give a truer picture of the complex relationships between organisms in a habitat.

A food chain can only show a rabbit eating grass or a sparrowhawk eating sparrows. Rabbits also eat other plants. Sparrowhawks eat many other small birds.

Q1 Why do food webs show us more than food chains?

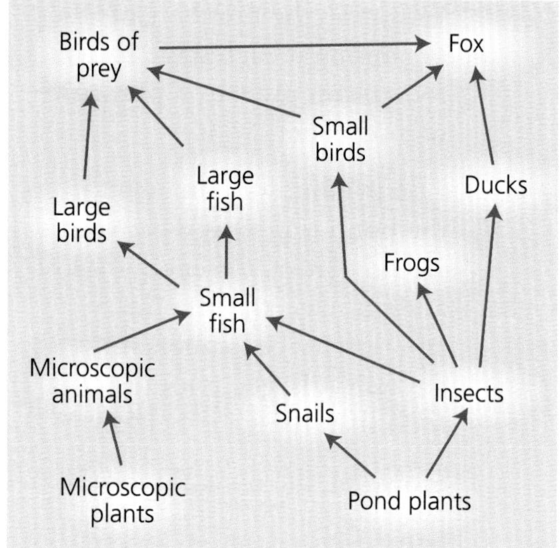

▲ ***Fig 1*** *How many different chains can you trace in this food web?*

Marine food webs

The **plankton** is a very important part of the marine food web (Fig 2) because many of the living things in plankton are green plants. They are the main producers of the ocean. Without plant plankton there would be little life there, because all life depends on producers locking the sun's energy into molecules that other living things can use for food.

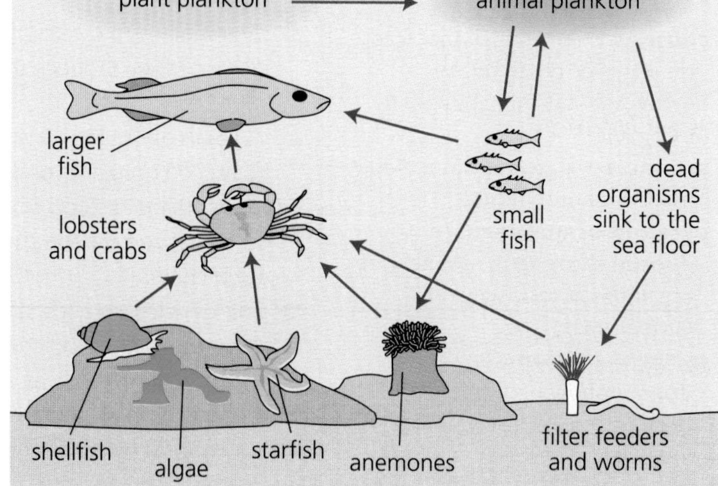

▶ ***Fig 2***

Q2 Why is plant plankton so important?

Q3 Name two consumers from the marine food web.

Dead animals and plants are also important, especially in the deep sea. Dead plankton can be eaten by marine worms and shellfish. Live plant plankton is normally eaten by animal plankton, which is eaten by slightly larger animals, which are then eaten by bigger creatures. One notable exception is the huge whales that live almost entirely on shrimp-sized plankton called **krill**. They are adapted to feed on krill by having a large mouth that can filter mouthful after mouthful of seawater, leaving the krill inside to be swallowed by a huge tongue.

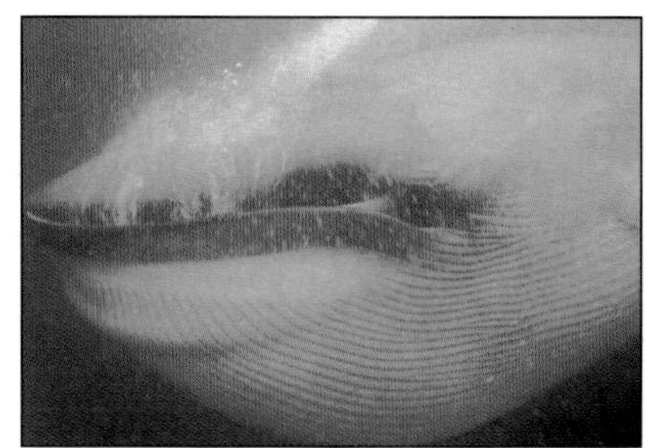

▲ ***Fig 3*** *The blue whale is the biggest animal on Earth. It lives on shrimp-like krill.*

Q4 What does the blue whale's diet tell you about plankton?

The balance of nature

All the animals and plants in a food web are linked together. Removing just one animal or plant can easily disrupt the whole web. The balance of nature is very delicate. We are constantly learning more about how food webs work but there is a lot left to learn. Until we understand the balance of nature perfectly, it could be disastrous to interfere.

If you were being annoyed by midges on holiday, for example, you might wish for them all to be destroyed. It is important to remember that the midges are part of a food web which includes animals and plants you may like or need. If we created a midge-free world many fishes and birds that feed on midges might die. Other animals that depend on these creatures would also be threatened.

Introducing a new creature into a food web can as dangerous as taking one away. Humans have introduced rats everywhere that ships have stopped to collect fresh water. The life of some beautiful tropical islands has been wrecked by introduced rats.

Key Words

balance of nature – the complex interaction between different species

food web – a network of food chains

plankton – tiny plants and animals found in surface waters of oceans

SUMMARY

- Food webs are made of intersecting food chains.
- Food webs are a more accurate way of showing feeding relationships within a community.
- Food webs demonstrate how animals and plants are dependent on others within the community. Damage to one organism will have an effect on the rest of the web.
- Microscopic plant plankton forms the producer level of marine food webs.
- The balance of nature is easily upset.

SUMMARY *Activity*

Work out and draw a food web to show some of the places where food chains in a garden habitat affect one another.

36 Food chains and toxic materials

In this section of the book you will learn the following things:

- **how toxic materials can enter food chains;**
- **how toxic materials can build up in food chains;**
- **some effects of toxins in food chains.**

Many chemicals have been sprayed onto soil, ponds and rivers to control the spread of diseases in humans, farm animals and crops. These chemicals are designed to kill the organisms that spread the diseases. They are therefore poisonous or **toxic.**

Toxins that kill pests are called **pesticides**.

Toxic substances and food webs

Pesticide sprayed on a crop will land on everything. It may slow poisoned insects down and make them easier to catch. If it does not kill the insects quickly they may be eaten by birds or other secondary consumers. Each secondary consumer eats many primary consumers (Unit 34). Each time a bird eats a poisoned insect it will collect some more pesticide. If the bird cannot excrete a pesticide it will become more and more concentrated in the bird's body. If the bird is eaten by a predator all this poison will enter the predator's body. A hawk eating many smaller birds can collect an immense dose of pesticide. This might be enough to kill the hawk. Even if it is not enough to kill, it can upset the hawk's behaviour or chemistry badly enough to prevent it breeding.

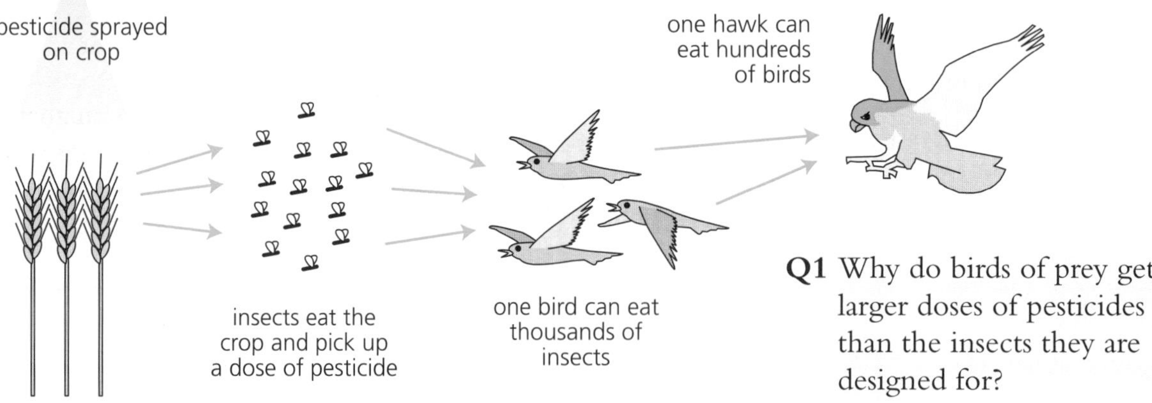
pesticide sprayed on crop
insects eat the crop and pick up a dose of pesticide
one bird can eat thousands of insects
one hawk can eat hundreds of birds

Q1 Why do birds of prey get larger doses of pesticides than the insects they are designed for?

▲ ***Fig 1*** *A pesticide can be concentrated at each step until a lethal dose accumulates.*

DDT was once used to poison all kinds of insects. As well as protecting crops, it worked very well on mosquitoes and helped to control the disease called malaria. DDT does not harm people but it is very toxic to many other animals. Eventually the damage to animals along the food chain became so serious that the use of DDT was banned in most countries.

Reversing the effects

Evidence is sometimes hard to collect and to understand. It took a long time to discover that a particular type of pesticide caused some birds to lay eggs that were not fertile. Pesticides can also make eggshells so thin that the eggs break easily. These side effects caused a decrease in the population of birds of prey. Since the pesticides responsible for these and other side effects were banned, the bird populations have increased.

Q2 Why did the numbers of birds of prey fall when DDT and similar pesticides were widely used?

Other toxic chemicals

Many other toxins can enter the environment accidentally. Some of the waste products of industry can spill into rivers. When a **polluted** river enters the sea the toxins get into the food webs there. Some toxins, such as oil spilled from tankers or chemical cargoes washed overboard, enter the sea directly.

▲ ***Fig 2*** *Waste water containing mercury being discharged into Minamata bay.*

Heavy metals

Toxins can be simple chemical elements. **Lead** is toxic to people, and so is **mercury**. Mercury from a plastics factory by the sea in Japan poisoned cats and people in the nearby town of Minamata. First the cats became very ill and died. A few months later people in the town began to suffer from the same illness. By the time the disease was identified as mercury poisoning more than 40 people had died and 60 were permanently disabled. Many of the fish and birds near Minamata were also dead. Scientists found 20 to 60 times the normal amount of mercury in the shellfish from the sea there. Because the cats and people were the tertiary consumers they had received very large doses of mercury.

Q3 How did the cats and people in Minamata receive high doses of mercury?

Key Words

DDT – a pesticide that is now banned in most countries

mercury – a toxic metal used in many industrial processes

pesticide – a poison intended to kill an annoying animal

toxic – poisonous

toxin – a poison

SUMMARY

- Toxic chemicals such as pesticides can enter the food chain.
- Toxic chemicals that do not break down quickly can become concentrated in the bodies of animals.
- Tertiary consumers get very large doses of toxins because they eat many secondary and primary consumers.
- Mercury and DDT are examples of toxic substances that are known to have caused problems in food chains.

SUMMARY *Activity*

Make a list of some pesticides that can be bought at garden centres. Why is it important to follow the instructions and handle them carefully?

37 Populations

In this section of the book you will learn the following things:

- what affects the size of a population;
- how crowding and disease can affect the size of a population;
- how competition can limit the size of a population;
- how predation can limit the size of a population.

A **population** is the number of organisms of the same species living in the same area at the same time. The total number of dandelions in a field is the dandelion population at the time they are counted. Populations change with time. One year later there may be a different number of dandelions in the same field.

Changes in population

Whether a population grows, shrinks or stays the same depends on the rate of arrival and the rate of departure. If more organisms arrive than leave the population will increase.

Rate of arrival = organisms being born + those moving into the area.
Rate of leaving = organisms dying + those moving out of the area.

The most important factors are the **birth rate** and **death rate**.

Disease and population growth

When a population increases, the organisms become more crowded. They may meet more frequently. This makes it easier for diseases to spread. A disease spreading through a population may kill some of the organisms and make the population smaller. As the space between organisms increases the disease spreads more slowly. If the disease does not kill too many organisms at once the population may remain fairly constant. If the disease is serious, the population may swing from one extreme to the other.

Q1 How does the spread of disease limit the size of a population?

Competition and population growth

When a population increases each organism has a smaller share of space and food. There is more **competition**. About 100 years ago a few moose walked across a frozen lake to an island in Lake Superior. At first they had plenty of space and plenty of food. After 30 years the population had grown to 3000.

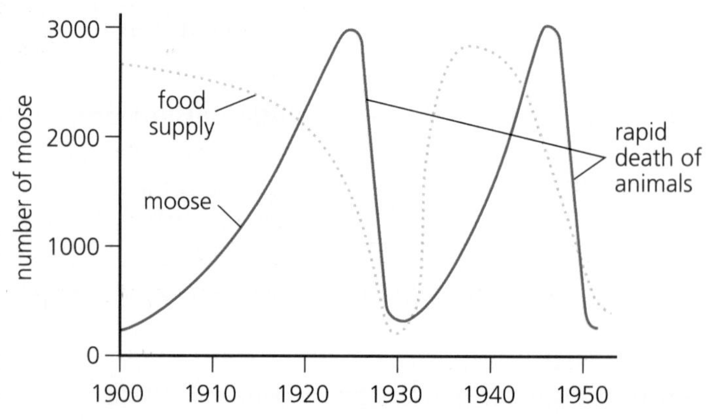

Fig 1 The moose population falls when competition for food increases.

Soon after this 90% of the moose died of starvation. Then the plants grew back and the moose population started to grow again. Within 20 years the population had grown back to 3000 again, and again most of the moose starved.

Competition for food is one reason why larger animals normally defend a territory. The size of the territory will depend on how much food they need and how much is available. If there is plenty of food the territory can be small. If there is very little food they need a larger territory to supply enough to eat.

Q2 List some of the resources that animals in a habitat may be competing for?

Predation and population growth

A major cause of death for many animals is being eaten by other animals. A population of small animals such as mice in an area with no predators will increase dramatically. Soon there will be thousands of mice. A predator such as a cat can help to control the population. There is a complex relationship between predators and **prey**. If a predator eats all the prey it will eventually die of starvation itself. Prey and predator populations are linked.

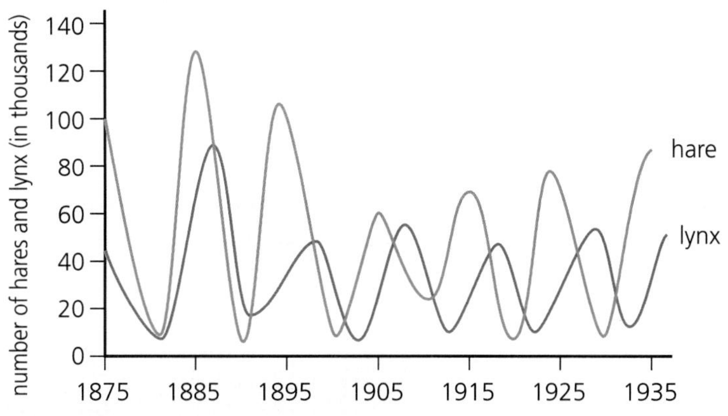

▲ *Fig 3 As the population of hares falls, so does the population of lynx. This is a typical example of a prey/predator relationship.*

▲ ***Fig 2** A Canada lynx chasing a snowshoe hare.*

Q3 Describe some of the factors that control plankton populations in the sea.

Key Words

birth rate – the number of animals born or seeds germinating at one time

death rate – the number of animals or plants dying at one time

prey – a specific animal eaten by a predator

population – the number of individuals of one species in one area at one time

SUMMARY

- A population is the total number of individuals of one species in one area at one time.
- Crowding can help the spread of disease. Disease can reduce the population.
- Organisms compete for space and food. A population can be reduced by competition.
- Predators control prey populations. A predator's population is closely related to its prey's population.

SUMMARY *Activity*

Fox populations are supposed to be higher in some cities than in the countryside. Can you think of some reasons why this might be true?

38 Adaptation and survival

In this section of the book you will learn the following things:

- **that some organisms can compete better than others;**
- **that these organisms contribute more offspring to the next generation.**

Variation and survival

Every organism is slightly different from others of its species (Units 15, 27). Variation plays an important part in survival. A big, strong piglet will get more milk than a small, weak one. The biggest piglet will grow but the smallest one might not survive.

▲ ***Fig 1*** *Some piglets are already stronger. They will be more successful in the struggle for milk than the weaker ones.*

Q1 What other variations might help a piglet to survive?

Other useful variations

Antelopes escape from predators by running fast. Natural variation will mean that some antelopes run faster than others. Even a small difference in speed might mean that another antelope is eaten instead.

Some animals hide instead of running away. They may be disguised to look like leaves or sticks. This is called **camouflage**. Many butterflies have wing markings that startle a predator by looking like a pair of large eyes. If some of the offspring of these animals look even more like a stick or have slightly better wing markings they will have a better chance of surviving.

▲ ***Fig 2*** *Peppered moths.*

There are two different varieties of a species of moth that normally sit on the bark of trees during the day. One variety is very dark and the other is very pale (Fig 2). Both varieties occur in polluted and unpolluted areas, but the dark variety is more common in polluted areas and the light one is more common in unpolluted areas. The dark variety has better camouflage on sooty, polluted bark where a pale moth is easy to spot. In unpolluted areas the opposite happens. Dark moths are easier to see on clean bark and more of them are eaten by birds. Keeping both varieties going means that some moths always survive, even when the level of pollution changes.

Q2 What do you think would happen to a brightly coloured stick insect?

Plants also vary. A plant that grows slightly taller than the rest can get more light. This will help it to grow even taller and collect even more light. The variation in height that gives the plant an advantage over other plants may be a disadvantage in a windy place, so plants also benefit from staying variable.

Natural selection

Characteristics that help a living thing to survive also help it to reproduce. The most **successful** organisms have most offspring. Their genetic material will be passed on to the next generation, which will also contain some individuals that are more successful than others. In this way a species becomes better adaptated to its habitat. Living things that fail to adapt become **extinct**. Instead of selective breeding (Unit 29) nature selects the survivors. This is called **natural selection**. Natural selection is sometimes known as the 'survival of the fittest'.

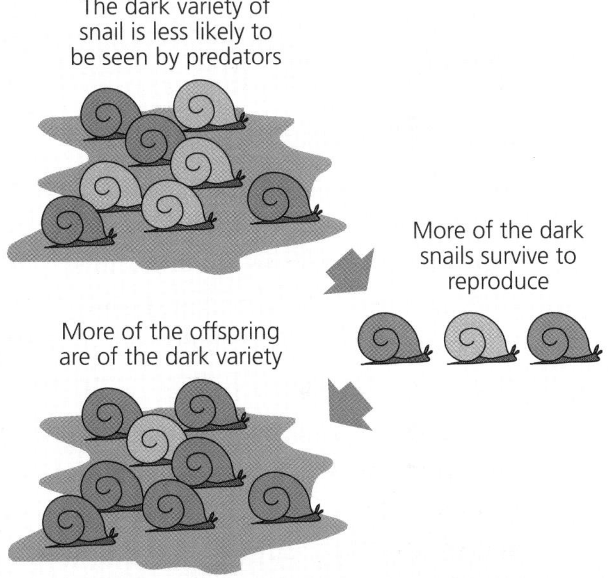
The dark variety of snail is less likely to be seen by predators
More of the dark snails survive to reproduce
More of the offspring are of the dark variety

▲ ***Fig 3*** *Organisms better adapted to their habitat will reproduce and have more offspring than less well adapted individuals.*

Q3 What are the similarities between natural selection and selective breeding? What are the differences?

Key Words

camouflaged – blending into the background or looking like something else
extinction – the death of an entire species
natural selection – survival of well-adapted organisms and death of badly adapted ones

SUMMARY

- Individuals in a species vary naturally.
- Some variation results in individuals that are better adapted to their environment.
- Organisms that are better adapted to a habitat contribute more offspring to the next generation.
- The number of individuals with useful characteristics will naturally increase. This helps a species to adapt and be successful.

SUMMARY *Activity*

Study this list of plants and animals. Name three characteristics of each that help it to survive in its environment: polar bear; fir tree; mole; pike; whale; coconut palm; person.

Summary – Life processes and living things

After studying this part of the book you should have learned about life processes and living things.

Life processes and cell activity

You should know the basic processes carried out by all living things. Five of these are respiration, feeding, excretion, growth and reproduction.

- What other basic functions are necessary for life?

You should know that both plant and animal cells have a cell membrane and contain cytoplasm and a nucleus. Plant cells also have a cell wall and contain chloroplasts. Cells become specialised to carry out specific jobs. You will also have studied how cells are organised into tissues, organs and organ systems.

- List two differences between plant and animal cells.
- How are red blood cells and nerve cells adapted to do their job?
- Name two organs in your body.

Humans as organisms

You should understand the importance of a healthy diet and know about essential nutrients such as proteins and fats. You should also know why vitamins and minerals are important.

- Name the six essential nutrients.
- Name two minerals and write down why we need them.
- List five foods that are rich in protein.

You will understand how food is digested, absorbed and transported around your body. You will know that blood also carries waste materials away. You should understand how our lungs work and be familiar with their structure.

- What are villi and why are they important?
- Draw a diagram of the digestive system and label it.
- Which gas passes from the blood into the lungs as a waste product?
- How can smoking damage your lungs?

After learning about the skeleton and muscles you should understand how your body moves and know the names and functions of some important bones. This section of the book also gave you information about some important health issues. You should know about bacteria and viruses and how your body's defence mechanisms work. You should also know why abuse of some substances is very dangerous.

- Which bones protect the heart and lungs from damage?
- Describe three different types of joint.
- Explain why most muscles have to work in pairs.
- How can bacteria be spread from person to person?

Green plants as organisms

This section of the book will have shown you how plants make food. You will have learned about the structure of leaves and the roles of sunlight and chlorophyll in plant nutrition. You should also know how a plant's roots obtain other nutrients from the soil. You will have studied plant structure and reproduction. You will also understand why cross-pollination is important.

- Write a word equation for photosynthesis.
- How do gases move in and out of the leaves of a plant?
- What are the three main functions of roots?
- Draw a diagram of a root hair and explain why root hairs are important.
- What does cross-pollination mean? Name two ways in which pollen travels.

Variation, classification and inheritance

After studying this section you will know that there are many differences between living things. You should understand the terms 'species' and 'variation'. You should know that variations can be inherited and how this fact helps species to evolve and makes it possible for us to improve crops. Finally, you should understand the importance of being able to classify and identify living things. You should also know how to use an identification key.

- Describe some of the differences between a worm and a bird.
- How can selective breeding lead to better crops?
- Name the five kingdoms of living things.
- What is the main difference between vertebrates and non-vertebrates?

Living things in their environment

You should have learned how and why different habitats support different plants and animals. You should also know that animals and plants adapt to daily and seasonal changes. You should be able to explain what food chains, food webs and pyramids of numbers mean. You should also be able to explain how toxic materials, such as pesticides, build up in food chains and how energy is transferred through food chains. You should know about the relationships between predator and prey animals, and why animals and plants that are well adapted to their environment can breed more successfully than those that are less well adapted. Finally, you should be able to explain what the terms 'population' and 'competition' mean.

- List five examples of habitats in your area.
- How are fish adapted to their habitat?
- What is meant by a 'pyramid of numbers'?
- Draw an example of a food chain and explain what happens to the energy available at each stage.
- What do the terms 'predator' and 'prey' mean? Give two examples of each.

Materials and their properties

This part of the book looks at the way different substances can be classified, changed and used. The units will build on your growing knowledge of different chemicals and help you to understand the science of particles (atomic science). Understanding the way particles behave helps you to understand how chemicals react. You will also be shown how to detect patterns in what you study, especially patterns in chemical reactions. This part of the book has three sections.

Classifying materials

You will begin by considering the differences between the three states of matter. Each state is then discussed in more detail. Separate units explain the properties of solids, liquids and gases in terms of their particle structure. You will also learn about other properties, such as diffusion and gas pressure. The next units introduce atomic structure. You will now begin to understand why different chemical elements behave differently, and what they are. At this stage you meet the chemist's shorthand symbols for the elements. Next, you will learn how to distinguish between mixtures, elements and compounds. Some of the compounds you will learn more about include water, carbon dioxide and sodium chloride. You will also find out how to separate mixtures. This section ends with several units that will help you to understand physical and chemical differences between metals and non-metals and why these differences are important in chemistry and life.

Changing materials

The second section begins with physical changes. These include changes of state and the formation of solutions. You will discover that different substances change state at different temperatures. Physical changes are closely linked to energy changes. You may wish to jump to

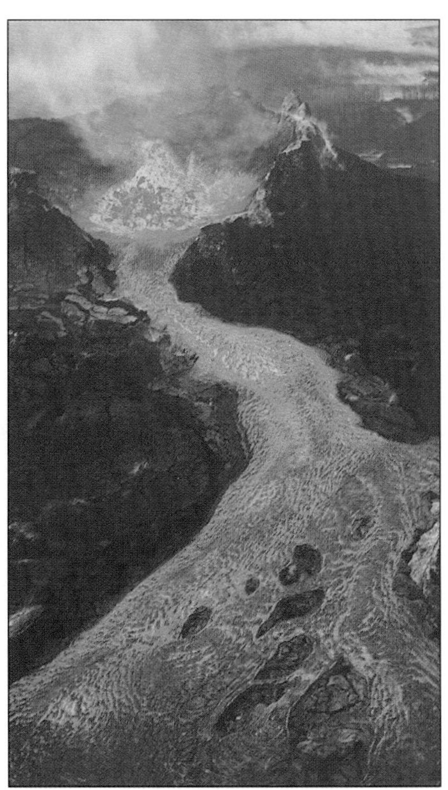

the pages about energy transfer in the final part of the book at this point. This section continues with a unit that explains expansion and contraction. You will learn how expansion and contraction are part of geological change, and how geological changes shape the Earth. The formation of different types of rocks – sedimentary, igneous and metamorphic – and how they are weathered comes next. These units account for the rock cycle. The final units of this section come back to chemistry in the laboratory. You will learn the law of conservation of mass and study different types of chemical reactions. You will also learn how to write chemical reactions as word and symbol equations. When you reach the end of this section you will have learned enough to understand how burning some fuels can affect the environment.

Patterns of behaviour

This section of the book concentrates on the way chemical reactions fall into patterns. The first few units examine how metals react with air, water and acids. You will find out that there is a reactivity series that can be used to predict chemical reactions. It also helps to explain why some metals are found as native or pure metal and others are only found as compounds. The next units discuss the reactions of acids and bases. You will learn what pH means and how it is measured. Then you will look at specific reactions of acids and how they react with metals, bases and carbonates to make salts. You will learn about neutralisation and how it occurs in everyday life. Finally, this section of the book will show you how acids in the environment can corrode metals and weather rocks, taking you back to physical and geological changes.

39 Solids, liquids and gases

In this section of the book you will learn the following things:

- that there are three states of matter;
- that these three states are solids, liquids and gases;
- how we tell the difference between solids, liquids and gases.

The chair you sit on, the water you drink and the air you breathe are all made of different substances. A chair is **solid**, water is **liquid**, and air is a mixture of **gases**. Many substances occur naturally. Air, wood, rubber and rock are examples of **natural** substances. Plastic is not a natural substance. It is a **synthetic** substance made by people. Every substance, natural or synthetic, is either a solid, a liquid or a gas.

Q1 Name three natural liquids.

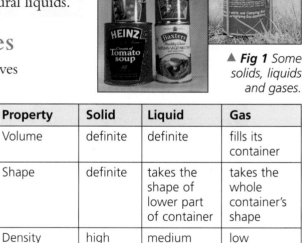

▲ *Fig 1* Some solids, liquids and gases.

Properties of substances

The way a substance looks, feels or behaves is called a **property** of that substance. The properties of a substance show whether it is a solid, a liquid or a gas (see Table 1). Some properties that we can test are:

- hardness
- compressibility
- shape
- density
- ease of flow
- volume

Q2 Describe two of the physical properties of iron and of petrol.

Property	Solid	Liquid	Gas
Volume	definite	definite	fills its container
Shape	definite	takes the shape of lower part of container	takes the whole container's shape
Density	high	medium	low
Ease of compression	very low	low	high
Ease of flow	nil	easy	easy

▲ ***Table 1***

Solids

Solids keep their shape. They are not easily compressed or squashed. Even a soft solid has the same volume when it is squashed. If a rubber ball is squashed it spreads out to cover a bigger area. A solid never flows unless it has been ground up into powder. The physical properties of solids make many of them useful for building furniture, houses, and other solid structures.

Liquids

Liquids have a definite volume but no fixed shape. A liquid takes the same shape as its container. Liquids are difficult to compress but they do flow easily. You can see these properties when you pour milk from a bottle into a glass. As the milk flows, its shape changes from the shape of the bottle to the shape of the glass.

Gases

Gases have no fixed shape or volume. A gas spreads out to fill its container and also flows very well. The reason why you can smell a person's scent soon after they come into a room is because the gases of the scent spread out to fill the room. A draught can blow the scent away because gases flow easily. Gases are also easy to compress (Fig 2).

▼ *Fig 2*

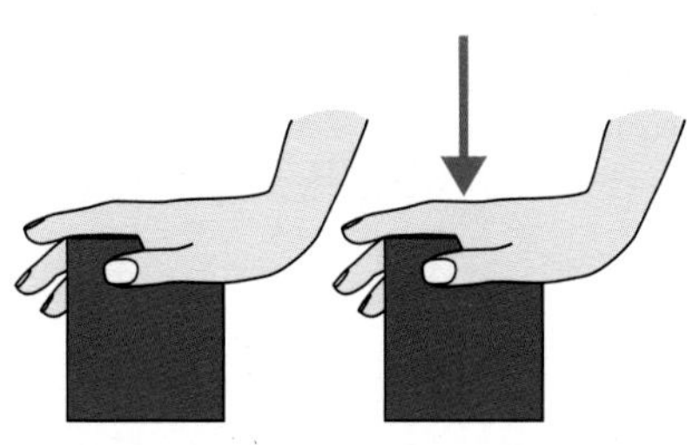

Solids have a fixed shape and are hard to compress.

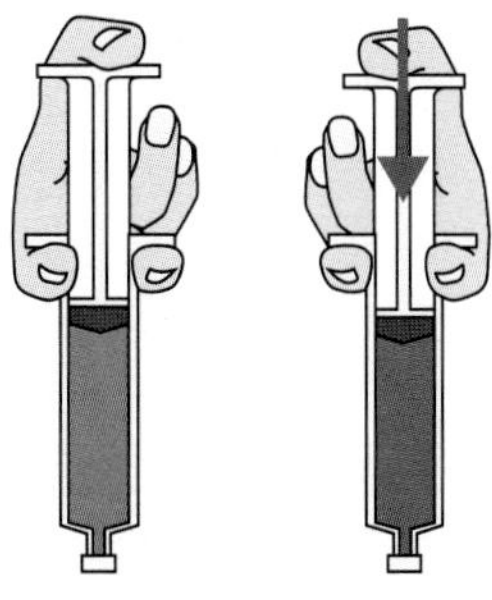

Liquids take on the shape of their container and are hard to compress.

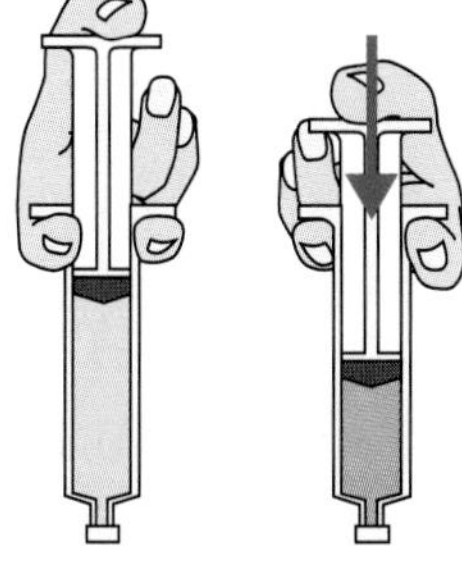

Gases take on the shape of their container and are easy to compress.

Changes of state

Substances do not always stay in the same state (Fig 4). The liquid water in a pond can freeze into a solid called ice when it becomes very cold (Fig 3). Liquid water boiled in a kettle can become a gas called steam. These physical changes are called **changes of state**. Different substances change state at different temperatures. For example, water boils at 100°C and alcohol boils at 78°C.

▲ *Fig 3*

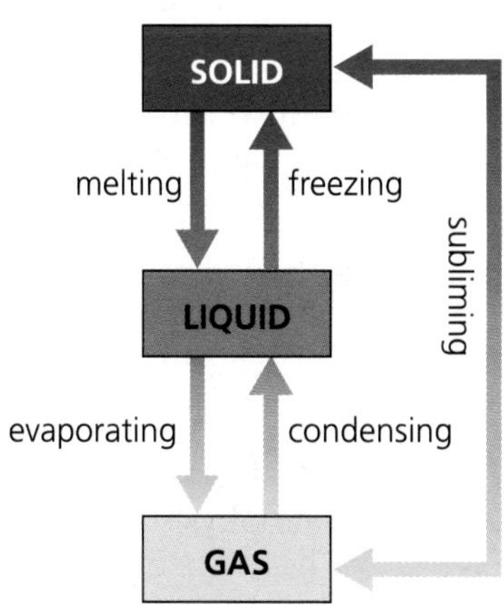

▲ *Fig 4*

Q3 What do we call the physical change of state from liquid to solid?

Key Words

change of state – a change between a solid, liquid or gas state; a direct change of state from solid to gas without passing through the liquid state is known as sublimation

property – any characteristic of a substance, such as colour or shape

synthetic – manufactured, not natural

SUMMARY

- The three states of matter are solids, liquids and gases.
- Materials are either natural or synthetic.
- The physical properties of a substance tell us its state.
- Substances can change from one physical state to another.

SUMMARY *Activity*

Draw up a table with three columns marked solids, liquids and gases. Think of some of the substances you use at home and place them into the table under the correct heading. Try to find at least three for each column.

40 Particles and states of matter

In this section of the book you will learn the following things:

- that substances are made up of tiny particles;
- that the way particles behave explains the differences between solids, liquids and gases;
- that the way particles behave explains changes in state.

States of matter

Substances can exist in three different states (Unit 39). These states are solid, liquid and gas.

The particle theory

To explain how substances can exist in these three very different forms we must first look at what substances are made of. According to the **particle theory**, all substances are made up of very small **particles**.

The particles in a solid are arranged in regular patterns. They are very close together with little space between them. This is what gives a solid its fixed shape. The particles can vibrate but they cannot move far. This is why solids are dense. When a solid is heated the particles hold on to each other very firmly and do not move very far apart.

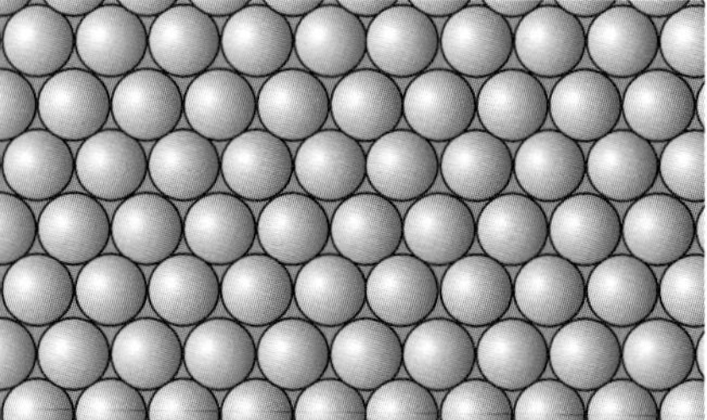

▲ ***Fig 1*** *Particles in a solid.*

The particles in a liquid are less tightly packed than particles in a solid. Because they are not arranged in a regular pattern they can move more easily. This is why liquids can flow and why they take the shape of any container they are poured into. When a liquid is heated it can expand more easily than a solid because the particles are not held together as firmly. At a particular temperature, however, a liquid occupies the same amount of space no matter what shape it is.

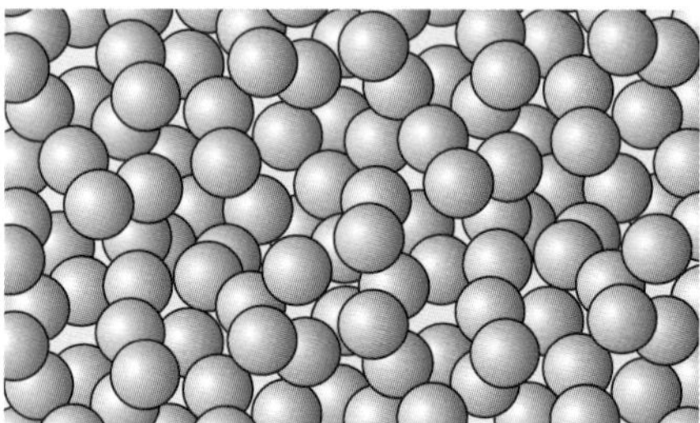

▲ ***Fig 2*** *Particles in a liquid.*

The particles in a gas are not regularly arranged. They are widely spaced and move at great speeds in all directions. Gas particles are said to be in **random motion**. This is why gases have a low density and can flow easily. Gas particles do not hold on to each other very much. When you heat a gas it expands a great deal.

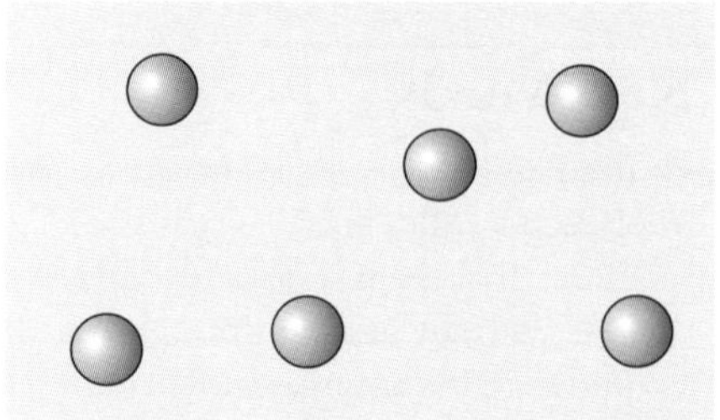

▲ ***Fig 3*** *Particles in a gas.*

Q1 How does the particle theory explain why solids expand less than gases?

Particles and changes of state

When you heat a solid, the particles in it start to vibrate faster. The closely packed particles start to break free from each other. This makes the solid melt into a liquid. If the substance is heated even more the particles move even faster until they are in random motion. Now the liquid has become a gas. This is called **evaporation**.

If you cool a gas down you force the particles to slow down. Eventually they are moving slowly enough and packed closely enough to be a liquid. This is called **condensing**. You can sometimes see invisible steam condense to visible water on a cold window pane.

If the liquid is cooled even more the particles slow down even more. Eventually the liquid will become a solid. This is called freezing. Water can do this in water-pipes on very cold days.

Changes of state therefore depend on how close the particles are in a substance and how quickly they are moving (see Fig 4).

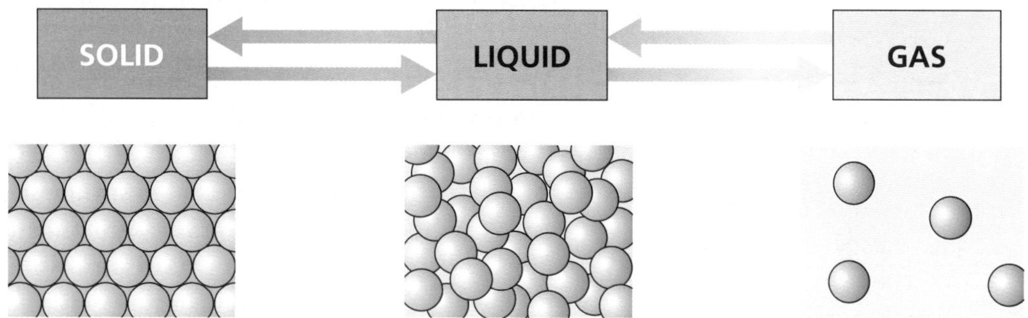

▲ *Fig 4*

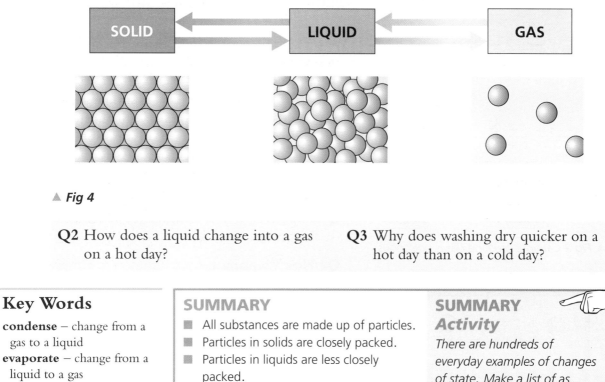

Q2 How does a liquid change into a gas on a hot day?

Q3 Why does washing dry quicker on a hot day than on a cold day?

Key Words

condense – change from a gas to a liquid
evaporate – change from a liquid to a gas
particle – a very small part of a substance
random motion – movement of particles with no regular pattern

SUMMARY

- All substances are made up of particles.
- Particles in solids are closely packed.
- Particles in liquids are less closely packed.
- Particles in gases are far apart, and in random motion.
- Changes in state occur when substances are heated or cooled.

SUMMARY *Activity*

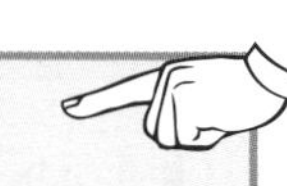

There are hundreds of everyday examples of changes of state. Make a list of as many examples as you can. Explain one of your examples by drawing a diagram of what happens to the particles.

41 Moving molecules

In this section of the book you will learn the following things:

- **that the movement or diffusion of gases can also be explained by particle theory;**
- **that particle theory can be used to explain gas pressure.**

Diffusion

If a drop of ink falls into a glass of water some of the ink particles will begin to spread out. Eventually all the water will be coloured. The spread of ink particles is called **diffusion**. Movement of particles is called diffusion.

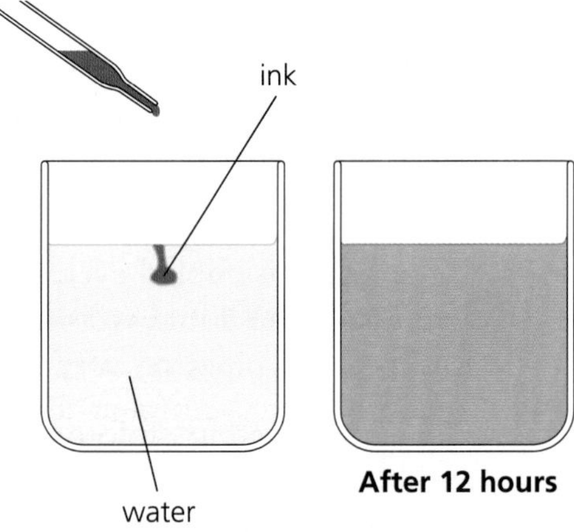

▲ ***Fig 1*** *Ink particles gradually spread out into the water. This is diffusion.*

Gases or **vapours** diffuse very easily because their particles are not fixed together and can move quickly in all directions. It is possible to watch a coloured gas diffusing. Bromine is a brown liquid at normal room temperature but becomes a brown gas if it is warmed up.

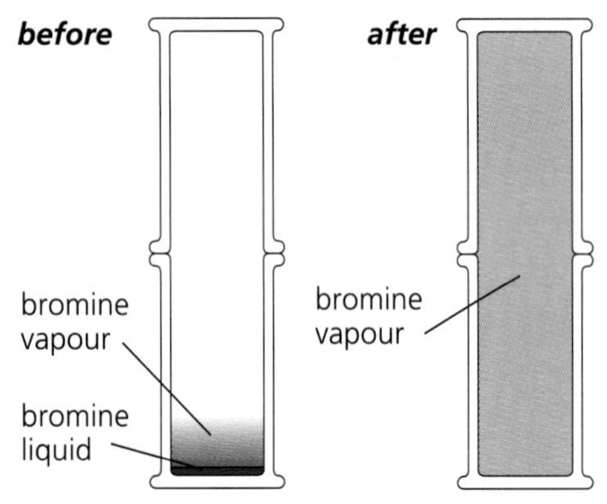

▲ ***Fig 2*** *Caution: bromine gas is poisonous.*

We can also detect the movement of scented gases. You can smell the scent of a flower from a distance because the particles of scent diffuse through the air from the flower to your nose. The scent is strongest near the flower, where the particles are most concentrated. Flower scents are important to moths. Some moths can catch the scent of just one particle and follow it back to the flower.

Q1 Explain how you can smell food being cooked a long way away.

Q2 How do plants use gas diffusion to attract moths?

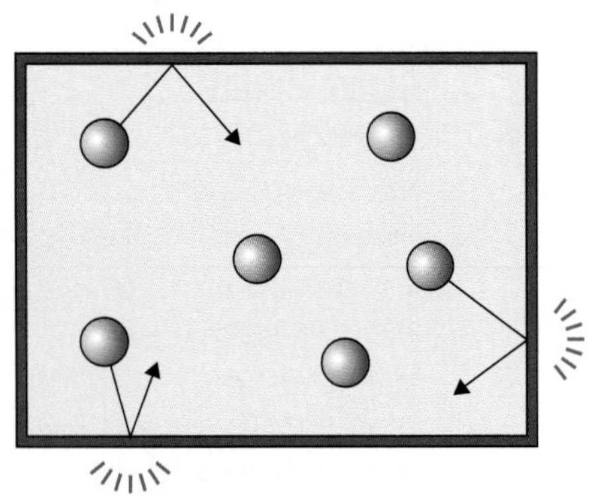

Gas pressure

Particles of a gas are moving around very quickly. When a gas is put into a container the moving particles constantly crash against the sides (Fig 3). The force of all these collisions creates pressure inside the container. If more gas is added then there will be more particles hitting the sides. The **gas pressure** will increase.

◀ ***Fig 3***

You can feel gas pressure when you blow up a balloon (Fig 4). As you begin to blow into the balloon some air particles are forced inside. The particles begin to hit the inside of the balloon. The rubber of the balloon can stretch. When the air pressure inside the balloon is greater than the air pressure outside, the balloon is stretched by the force of the collisions. More pressure is created by adding more gas particles.

▶ *Fig 4*

Pressure can also be increased by heating particles up or squashing them into a smaller space. This is what happens inside a bicycle pump. The more you squash the air, the higher the pressure becomes. Eventually the air particles are squashed so tightly that they can be forced into a hard rubber tyre.

Gases are often stored by being squashed into small containers. The pressure inside these containers is very high because they hold so many gas particles.

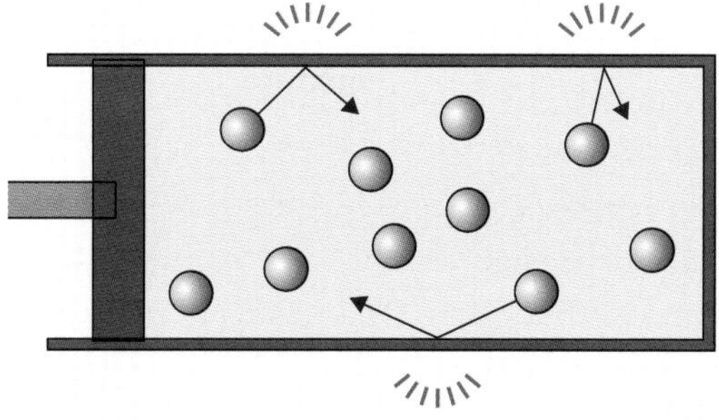

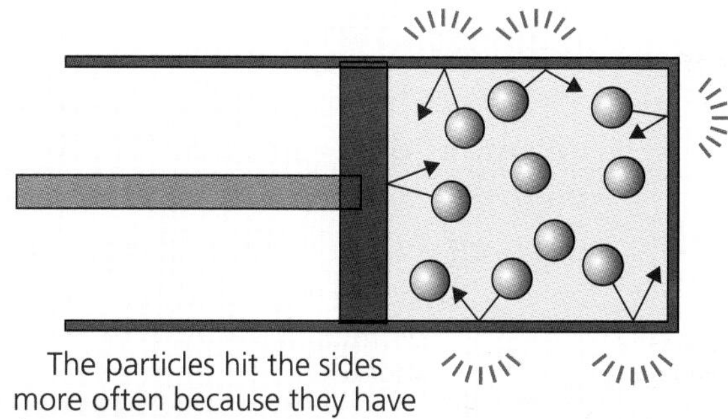

The particles hit the sides more often because they have less space to move around in.

▲ ***Fig 5*** *Adding more particles or squashing particles into a smaller space will increase the gas pressure.*

Q3 Why is it dangerous to puncture an aerosol can?

Q4 Why is it dangerous to heat an aerosol can or throw it onto a fire?

Key Words

diffusion – the movement of one substance through another substance

vapour – a gas at the same temperature as its liquid state

SUMMARY

- Substances diffuse slowly in liquids.
- Gases diffuse quickly and easily in other gases.
- Gas pressure is caused by particles of gas hitting the sides of a container.
- Gas pressure can be increased by adding more gas particles, by heating them, or by squashing them into a smaller space.

SUMMARY *Activity*

Where do you find examples of (a) diffusion and (b) gas pressure in everyday life? Which of them do you find most useful? Which can be potentially harmful, and why?

42 Atoms apart and together

In this section of the book you will learn the following things:

- **that substances can be mixtures, compounds or elements;**
- **that elements consist of specific atoms.**

▲ ***Fig 1*** *A cup of tea is a mixture of different substances.*

Mixtures

A **mixture** is a collection of different substances that are not connected in any special way. A cup of tea is a mixture of hot water and chemicals from the tea leaves, perhaps with milk and sugar added. The water, tea, sugar and milk do not change one another. You can feel the water, you can see and taste the tea, you can see and taste the milk and you can taste the sugar. If you could separate the different parts of a cup of tea you would end up with the same collection of substances that went into it.

Compounds

The water in your tea is not a mixture. Water is a **compound**. It cannot be 'unmixed'. The only way to divide water into its separate parts is by a chemical reaction. When water is divided chemically it breaks up into hydrogen gas and oxygen gas. The water you drink is obviously not a mixture of two gases. Once water has been split into oxygen and hydrogen it is no longer water.

Atoms

If we could look at the hydrogen gas from the water, we would find that it is made up of many tiny particles. All the particles are exactly the same. They are called **atoms**.

It is almost impossible to see atoms because they are so small. You would need to line up at least 2 billion atoms to span one metre. Each atom is made up of an exact number of even smaller parts. Every different type of atom has its own exact number of parts. Atoms with more parts are heavier than atoms with fewer parts.

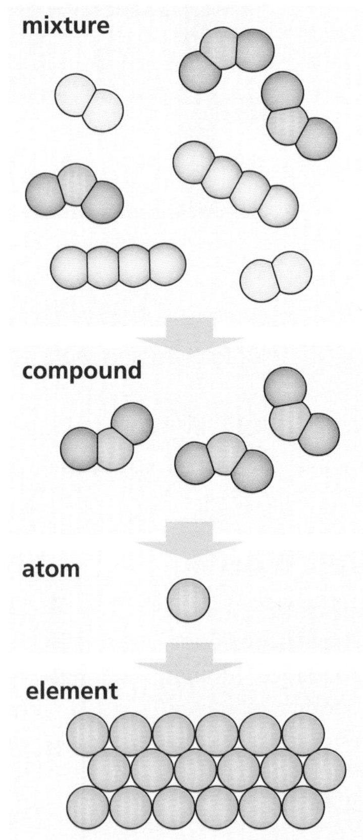

▶ ***Fig 2*** *Particles in different substances.*

Elements

A substance that is made up of only one type of atom is called an **element**. There are over 100 different atoms which means there are over 100 different types of element. Aluminium is an element. It is made up of nothing but aluminium atoms. These will all act in the same way. They are different from the atoms in other elements. For example, lead atoms are heavier and larger than aluminium atoms. This is why lead is a heavier metal than aluminium.

Element	Type	Uses
Oxygen	gas	Respiration; burning
Silicon	non-metal	Electronic components; glass
Iron	metal	In steel for buildings and cars
Aluminium	metal	Aircraft; cooking foil; cans
Sulphur	non-metal	fertilisers; dyes; paper-making
Carbon	non-metal	May be diamond (very hard) or graphite (very soft) in pencil 'lead'
Hydrogen	gas	Fertilisers; margarine; plastics

▲ ***Table 1*** *Some elements and a few of their uses.*

Q1 What is the difference between an element and a compound?

Q2 List 5 examples of mixtures and 5 examples of elements or compounds.

Molecules

The atoms of most elements are normally linked together. Oxygen atoms in the air are normally linked in pairs. Each pair is called an oxygen **molecule**. Hydrogen and nitrogen also join up into pairs. Molecules do not have to be pure elements. Any group of atoms chemically linked together (e.g. water) is called a molecule. A molecule is a single particle of a compound.

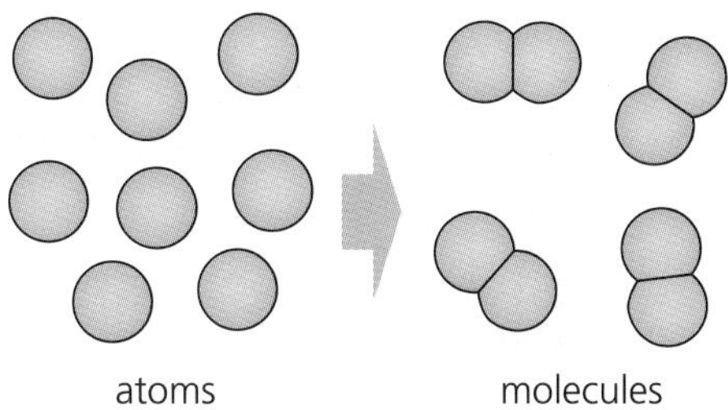

▲ ***Fig 3*** *Oxygen atoms in the air join up into pairs to form oxygen molecules.*

Key Words

atom – the smallest particle of an element
compound – a chemical substance made of different elements
element – a substance made of one type of atom
mixture – substances mixed but not chemically joined
molecule – a group of atoms chemically joined

SUMMARY

- Substances may exist as mixtures, compounds or elements.
- All substances are made from small particles called atoms.
- Elements are made up of only one type of atom.
- Elements can form molecules with themselves.
- Elements can form molecules with other elements.
- Molecules made of different elements are called compounds.

SUMMARY *Activity*

Which of the following substances do you think are mixtures, which are chemical compounds, and which are elements? Air; iron; lemonade; sugar; soil. How could you test your answers to see if they are correct?

43 Inside the atom

In this section of the book you will learn the following things:

- **that atoms are made up of smaller particles called electrons, protons and neutrons;**
- **that atoms are never split during chemical reactions;**
- **that atoms of the same element have the same number of protons.**

An atom is the smallest unit of an element. Each atom is made up of even smaller components called **sub-atomic particles**. These particles cannot be separated by chemical reactions.

A model of an atom

We now believe that each atom contains a dense **nucleus** surrounded by **electrons**. The electrons are very small and fly around the nucleus at high speed. Most of the atom is empty space.

Electrons carry a negative electrical charge. The **nucleus** consists of two different types of particles called **protons** and **neutrons**. Protons carry a positive electrical charge. Neutrons carry no charge; they are neutral.

A single proton has the same mass as a single neutron. Electrons are much smaller than protons and neutrons. It takes 1850 electrons to make up the mass of one proton or neutron. Most of the mass of an atom is therefore in the nucleus where the protons and neutrons are clustered together.

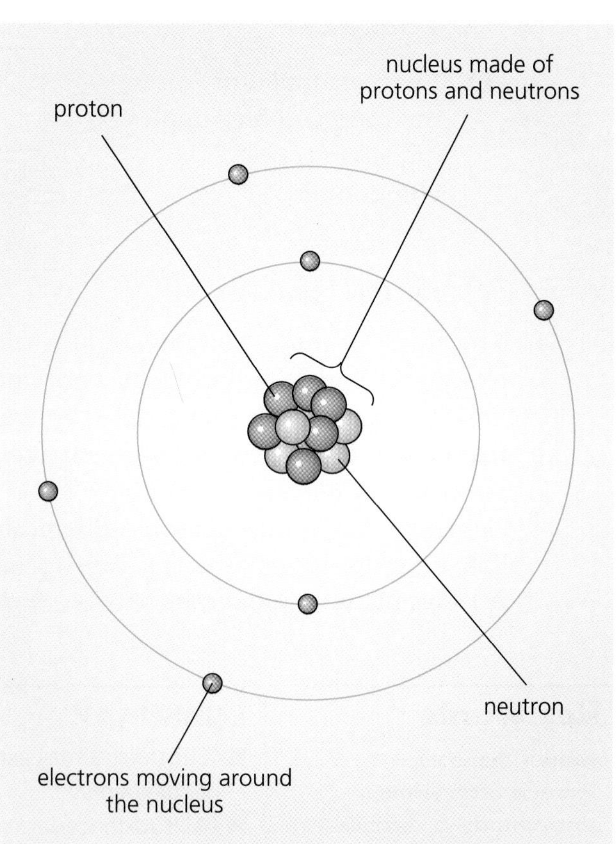

▲ ***Fig 1*** *A simplified drawing of a single carbon atom. Electrons were discovered in the early 20th century. The protons and neutrons in the atom's nucleus were discovered later. None of them can be seen: scientists worked out atomic structure by deduction.*

sub-atomic particle	relative mass	electrical charge
proton	1	+1
neutron	1	neutral
electron	$\frac{1}{1850}$	−1

◀ ***Table 1*** *The charges and masses of sub-atomic particles.*

Atomic number

The electrical charge on a proton is exactly opposite to the electrical charge on an electron. Each atom of an element contains the same number of electrons as protons. The whole atom therefore has no electrical charge even though it contains positive protons and negative electrons. The number of protons or electrons in an atom is called its **atomic number**. Each element has its own unique atomic number.

Q1 Name the three sub-atomic particles.

Q2 How do we know that the number of protons and electrons in an atom are the same?

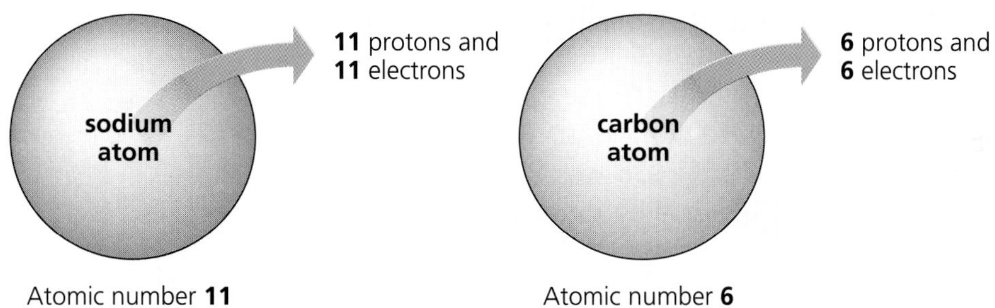

▲ ***Fig 2*** *The atomic number for sodium is 11. This means that it has 11 protons and 11 electrons. The 11 positive charges cancel out the 11 negative charges.*

The atomic number for carbon is 6. This means that it has 6 protons and 6 electrons. The 6 positive charges cancel out the 6 negative charges.

Q3 The atomic number for potassium is 19. How many protons does each potassium atom have? How many electrons does it have?

Key Words

atomic number – the number of protons in an atom

electron – a small negatively charged sub-atomic particle

neutron – a sub-atomic particle with no electrical charge

nucleus – the central core of an atom

proton – a positively charged sub-atomic particle

SUMMARY

- An atom contains protons and neutrons surrounded by electrons.
- Protons have a positive electrical charge. Electrons have a negative electrical charge. Neutrons have no charge.
- The number of protons or electrons in an atom is its atomic number.
- Each element has a unique atomic number.

SUMMARY *Activity*

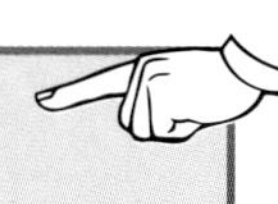

How many protons and electrons are in one atom of each of the following elements? Lead (atomic number = 82); magnesium (atomic number = 12); chlorine (atomic number = 17); iodine (atomic number = 53). Which do you think has the heaviest atoms? Which has the lightest ones?

44 The Periodic Table

In this section of the book you will learn the following things:

- **that the names of elements can be written as symbols;**
- **that elements can be listed in order according to their atomic numbers;**
- **that the Periodic Table is a very useful way to arrange elements.**

There are more than 100 different elements. Scientists often have to write their names down many times. To make this easier, each of the elements is given a short **symbol**.

▲ ***Fig 1*** *The old Latin word for lead was plumbum. We still use this word to name the person who mends water-pipes as well as in the chemical symbol for lead.*

The symbols for elements

The symbol for an element usually comes from the first one or two letters of its full name. The symbol for carbon is C, which is easy to understand. Some elements have symbols that are more difficult to work out. This is because ancient scientists preferred to use Latin words. The Latin word for lead is plumbum, which is why the symbol for lead is still Pb.

Some simple rules for chemical symbols

- The symbol is usually the first one or two letters of the name.
- Sometimes the old name is used.
- The first letter of a symbol is always a capital letter.
- The second letter of a symbol is always a small letter.
- Every element has a different symbol.

The symbols for some common elements are shown in the table below. Notice how calcium, carbon, copper and chlorine have been given different symbols because they all begin with the same letter of the alphabet.

Q1 Why would it be a problem if the symbol for sodium was S?

Q2 The symbol for boron is B. What would be the most obvious symbol to use for the element barium?

Q3 Why do you suppose the symbol for gold is Au? What other words might give you a clue?

Element	Symbol
Aluminium	Al
Bromine	Br
Calcium	Ca
Carbon	C
Chlorine	Cl
Copper	Cu
Gold	Au
Hydrogen	H
Iodine	I
Iron	Fe
Lead	Pb

Element	Symbol
Magnesium	Mg
Nitrogen	N
Oxygen	O
Phosphorus	P
Potassium	K
Silicon	Si
Silver	Ag
Sodium	Na
Sulphur	S
Tin	Sn
Zinc	Zn

▲ ***Table 1*** *Some common elements with their symbols.*

The Periodic Table

It is not especially helpful to list elements alphabetically, like names in a phone book. The atomic number of an element is much more important than its name. Scientists normally set out the elements in order of atomic number. They are also arranged according to the natural groups that they fall into. This arrangement is called the **Periodic Table**. An outline of the Periodic Table is shown in Fig 1. Notice that atomic numbers go across from left to right.

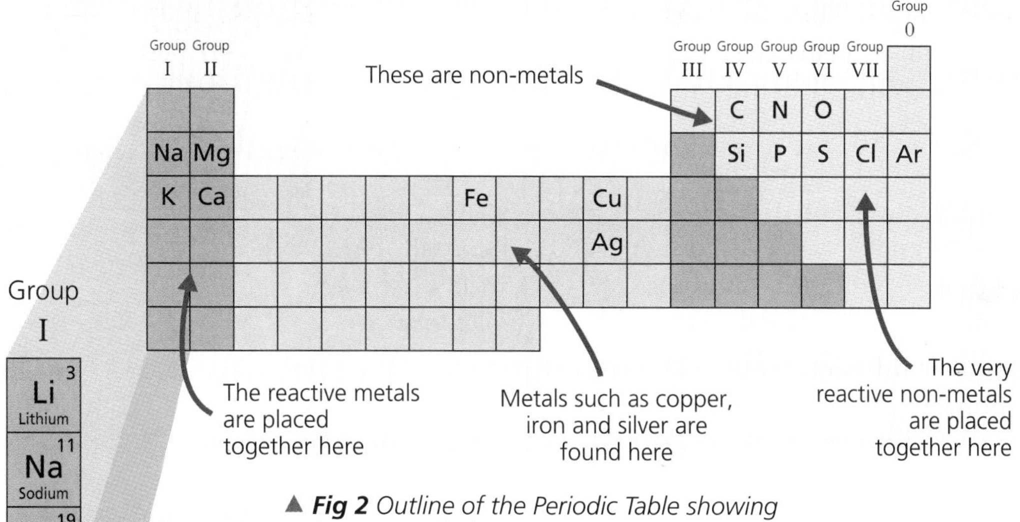

▲ ***Fig 2*** *Outline of the Periodic Table showing main groups of elements.*

▲ ***Fig 3*** *The reactive metals are all placed on the same side of the Periodic Table.*

The Periodic Table groups similar elements together in vertical rows. All the elements in Group I react with water in a similar way, for example, and all the elements in Group 0 are very unreactive gases. The Periodic Table is especially useful when we need to understand an element that we know very little about. Looking at where they come in the table can also help us to predict how two elements may react together when they meet.

Q4 Why is the Periodic Table so useful?

Key Words

Periodic Table – a useful chart of elements

symbol – the short version of an element's name

SUMMARY

- Each element has its own unique shorthand symbol.
- This symbol is often the first one or two letters of an element's modern or Latin name.
- Elements can be arranged in a useful chart called the Periodic Table.
- The Periodic Table arranges elements in order of atomic number. It also groups similar elements together.

SUMMARY *Activity*

Caesium has an atomic number of 55. It is a very reactive metal. Where in the Periodic Table might it fit?

45 Making compounds

In this section of the book you will learn the following things:

- **that compounds are made when elements join together;**
- **that elements join together during chemical reactions;**
- **that not all elements combine to make compounds.**

A compound is made when two or more elements join together. Not all elements will combine easily with others. Some, such as neon and argon, will not combine at all. They are **inert**. Elements such as sodium and chlorine combine very easily. They are highly **reactive**. When elements do combine they follow certain rules.

▲ ***Fig 1*** *Potassium is very reactive. It combines with other elements so quickly that it is hardly ever seen as a pure element.*

Metals and non-metals

Elements can be divided into metals and non-metals (Fig 2). Metals never combine with other metals to make chemical compounds. Compounds can only be formed between:

1 metals and non-metals;

2 non-metals and other non-metals.

Q1 Why is there no such compound as sodium magnesium?

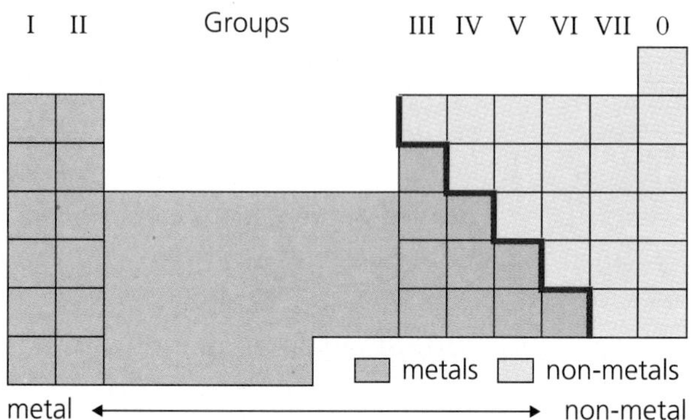

▲ ***Fig 2*** *The Periodic Table divided into metals and non-metals.*

A compound gets its name from the elements in it. If one of the elements is a metal then this comes first in the name. The names of the other elements in the compound are changed slightly so that we know the substance is a compound and not a mixture. Oxygen in a compound often becomes oxide.

Chemical reactions

When carbon is burned in air it joins with the oxygen and makes carbon dioxide. This is a **chemical reaction**. Carbon and oxygen are elements but carbon dioxide is a compound. Carbon dioxide is a totally new substance. It does not behave like carbon or like oxygen. It does not behave like a mixture of carbon and oxygen. It has its own unique properties.

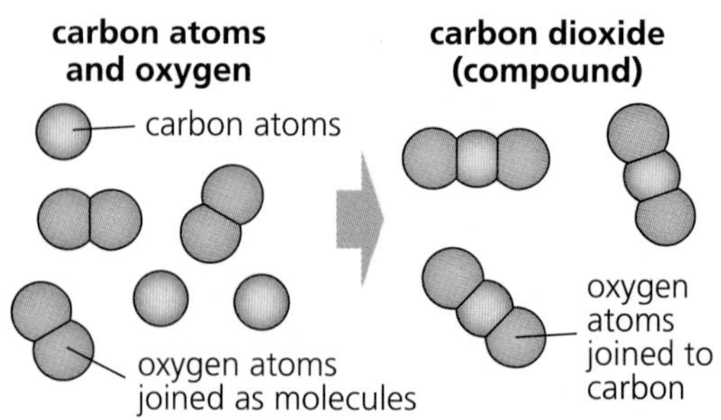

▲ ***Fig 3a*** *One carbon atom combines with two oxygen atoms to make one molecule of carbon dioxide.*

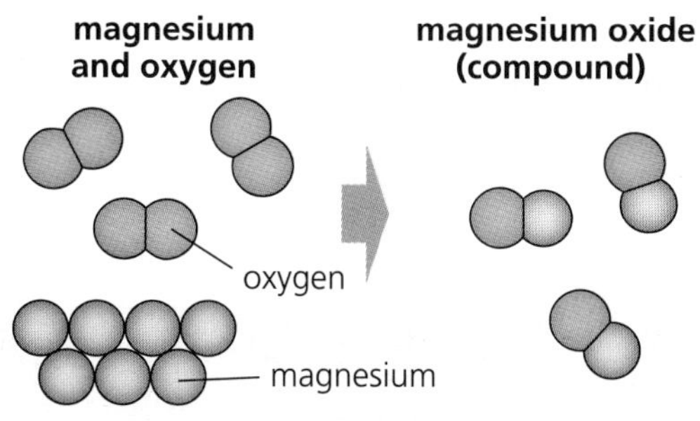

◄ ***Fig 3b*** *One magnesium atom combines with one oxygen atom to make one molecule of magnesium oxide.*

When iron and sulphur are heated in a test tube they react to make a new compound. This compound is called iron sulphide. Notice that the name sulphur has been changed to sulphide. This reminds us that we are talking about a compound and not a mixture. Iron is a magnetic substance. It is attracted to a magnet. Iron sulphide is a new and different substance. It is not attracted to a magnet.

An even more dramatic change between the elements and the compound they form is seen in sodium chloride (Fig 4).

▼ ***Fig 4***

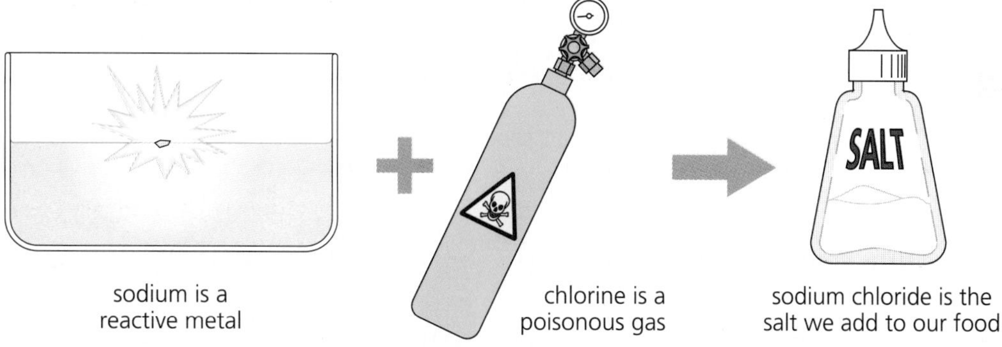

sodium is a reactive metal

chlorine is a poisonous gas

sodium chloride is the salt we add to our food

Q2 What evidence proves that sodium chloride is not just a mixture of sodium and chlorine?

Q3 Why is the ending of the word chlorine changed to chloride in compounds?

Water is a compound that contains the elements hydrogen and oxygen. If you put a flame into a mixture of hydrogen and oxygen you will hear a loud pop. You will see droplets of water on the container. The gases have joined together to form water.

Key Words

chemical reaction – substances joining together to make new substances

inert – does not react with other substances

reactive – readily reacts with other substances

SUMMARY

- Elements combine to make new chemicals called compounds.
- Compounds have different properties from the elements they are made from.
- Compounds are usually named after the elements they are made from.
- Metals never combine together into chemical compounds.
- Some examples of compounds are carbon dioxide, water, sodium chloride and magnesium oxide.

SUMMARY *Activity*

Identify the elements contained in each of the following compounds: iron oxide; lead sulphide; magnesium chloride. Which of the elements are metals?

46 Compounds and formulae

In this section of the book you will learn the following things:

- **that compounds have a definite composition;**
- **that we can use symbols to write down formulae for compounds.**

▲ ***Fig 1*** *Water molecules always have the same composition.*

Atoms are not split in chemical reactions. They simply combine in new patterns. Whole numbers of atoms are always found in each new pattern. The patterns are called compounds. Every time the same compound is made it always has the same **composition**. Each molecule of a compound has the same composition as all its other molecules.

Composition of compounds

Water is made up of hydrogen atoms and oxygen atoms joined together. There are two atoms of hydrogen for every atom of oxygen. This is true for every molecule of water.

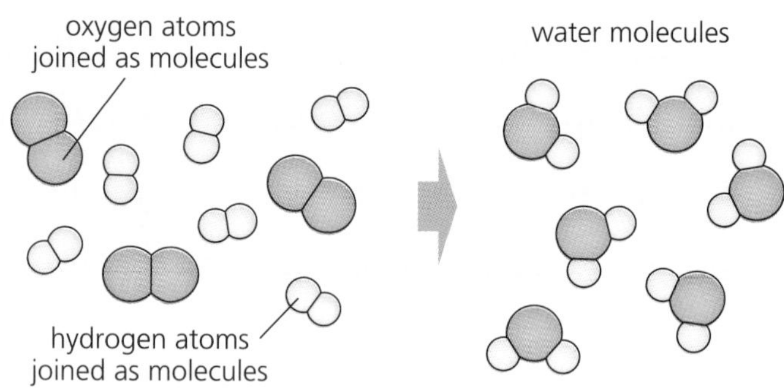

► ***Fig 2*** *The ratio of hydrogen to oxygen in water is 2 to 1. Each water molecule has one atom of oxygen and two atoms of hydrogen.*

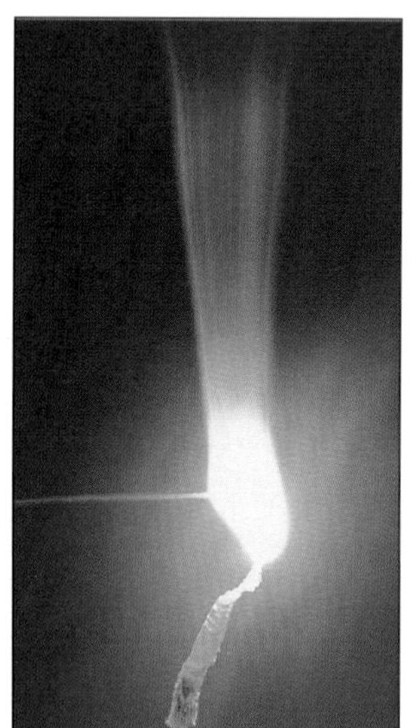

Carbon dioxide contains two oxygen atoms for each carbon atom. Every molecule of carbon dioxide has exactly the same ratio of oxygen to carbon atoms. The ratio is very important. A different gas, called carbon **mon**oxide, has only one atom of oxygen for every carbon atom. Carbon **dioxide** and carbon **monoxide** are different compounds with different properties.

In magnesium oxide, each magnesium atom is joined to one oxygen atom. This is true for every magnesium oxide molecule. It is not possible for magnesium oxide to contain any other number of magnesium or oxygen atoms.

◄ ***Fig 3*** *Each magnesium atom is joining up with one oxygen atom to make magnesium oxide.* ⚠ ***Caution:*** *Magnesium burns with a brilliant light; never look at it directly. Always wear goggles when you heat chemicals.*

Q1 What is the difference in composition between carbon monoxide and carbon dioxide?

Formulae of compounds

The shorthand names of elements can be used to write out the exact composition of a chemical compound. When a compound is written down as a set of symbols we call it a **formula**. A formula shows the elements in a compound. It also shows the ratio of those elements. Water is made of two atoms of hydrogen joined to one atom of oxygen. The formula for water is H_2O. The small number 2 after the H tells us that there are two hydrogen atoms. We do not write a number 1 after the O because a single atom needs no number.

▼ ***Table 1*** *Some common compounds and their formulae.*

Compound	Formula
water	H_2O
copper oxide	CuO
ammonia	NH_3
carbon dioxide	CO_2

The formula for a compound shows us a lot more than its name does. As you can see in Table 1, the formula quickly tells us which elements the compound contains. It also tells us exactly how many atoms of each element are contained in a single molecule of the compound.

The name of the compound aluminium oxide tells us that the compound is made up of the elements aluminium and oxygen. The formula for aluminium oxide is Al_2O_3. This tells us that there are two atoms of aluminium and three atoms of oxygen in every molecule of aluminium oxide. This information can be very useful. One way a scientist can use this information is to work out exactly how much of each element is needed to make a particular compound.

Q2 The formula for methane gas is CH_4. How many atoms of hydrogen does each molecule of methane contain?

Q3 Sodium oxide has two atoms of sodium for every atom of oxygen. What is the formula for sodium oxide?

Key Words

composition – all the different atoms in a compound

formula – the shorthand name of a compound

SUMMARY

- Every compound has its own special composition.
- The number of atoms in a compound is always a whole number.
- Compounds can be written with symbols. This gives a formula.
- A formula shows the number and type of atoms in a compound.
- A small number after the symbol for each element in a compound shows how many atoms each molecule contains.

SUMMARY *Activity*

Using the formulae given, work out the number of different atoms in the following compounds. Copper oxide (CuO); Lead chloride ($PbCl_2$); Sulphuric acid (H_2SO_4).

47 Mixtures

In this section of the book you will learn the following things:

- **that mixtures contain substances that are not chemically combined;**
- **that mixtures can contain solids, liquids and gases;**
- **that some mixtures of solids and liquids can be separated by filtration.**

Mixtures contain more than one substance. A mixture can contain solids, liquids or gases but these substances are not chemically joined. This means that the materials in a mixture can be separated without using chemical reactions.

Types of mixtures

Solids can be mixed with solids. A mixture of two metals is called an **alloy**. Brass is one example of an alloy. It is a mixture of copper and zinc. The alloy has a mixture of the properties of both metals. An alloy is not a new substance.

	gas	liquid	solid
gas	The air		
liquid	Foams and sprays	Emulsions such as hair oil. Solutions such as beer.	
solid	Smoke	Solutions such as salty water.	Alloys such as brass.

▲ ***Table 1*** *Some different kinds of mixtures.*

Solids can be mixed with liquids. If the solid dissolves, the mixture is called a solution. Sea water is a solution. One of the main chemicals dissolved in sea water is sodium chloride.

Liquids can be mixed with other liquids. Wine and beer are mixtures of water and alcohol. They also contain other substances that give them flavour.

Q1 Give another example of a solid dissolved in a liquid.

Solids can be mixed with gases. This happens when smoke rises into the air or when dust blows from the ground.

Liquids can be mixed with gases. A mixture of a liquid in a gas is called an **aerosol**. A mixture of a gas in a liquid is a **foam**. Deodorant sprays and shaving foams (Fig 1) are mixtures of gases and liquids.

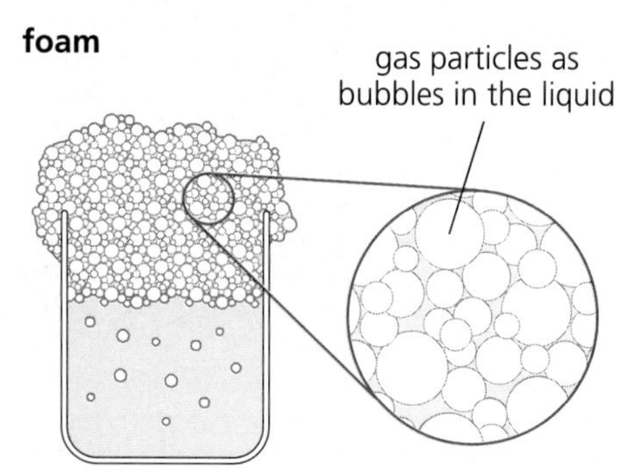

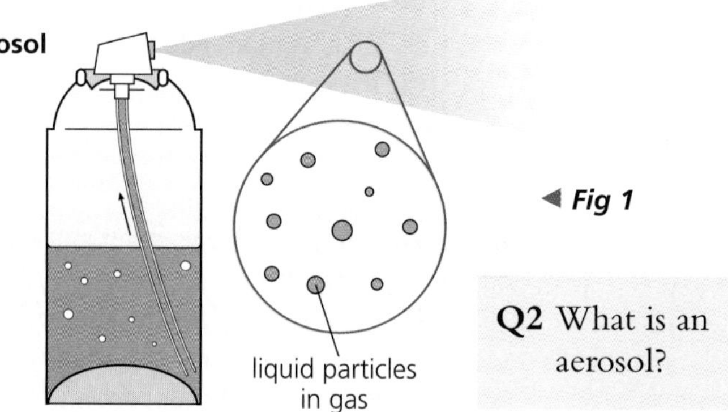

◀ ***Fig 1***

Q2 What is an aerosol?

Gases can be mixed with gases. The air is a mixture of gases. Air contains oxygen, carbon dioxide and nitrogen and some other gases (Unit 10). We know that the gases in air are not combined because we can easily remove oxygen from the air we breathe.

◀ ***Fig 2*** *Foam is a mixture of air and water. Sea water is also a mixture. It has solids and gases dissolved in it.*

Separating mixtures

There are many different types of mixtures. They cannot all be separated by the same method. Different mixtures are separated in different ways. In the next few pages we will look at some ways of separating mixtures.

Filtration

Large particles can be separated from smaller particles by filtering the mixture. A mixture of stones and soil can be separated with a sieve, which is a kind of filter. Filters can also separate solids from a gas. Vacuum cleaners and breathing masks have filters inside.

In a mixture of a solid and a liquid, the solid is not always dissolved. This kind of mixture could be separated by **filtration**. A liquid can pass through the tiny holes in a filter but the particles of a solid cannot. It is very easy to separate sand from water by filtration.

The solid part of a mixture that is trapped in a filter is called the **residue**. The liquid that passes through is called the **filtrate**.

Q3 Why is it not possible to separate salt from sea water by filtration?

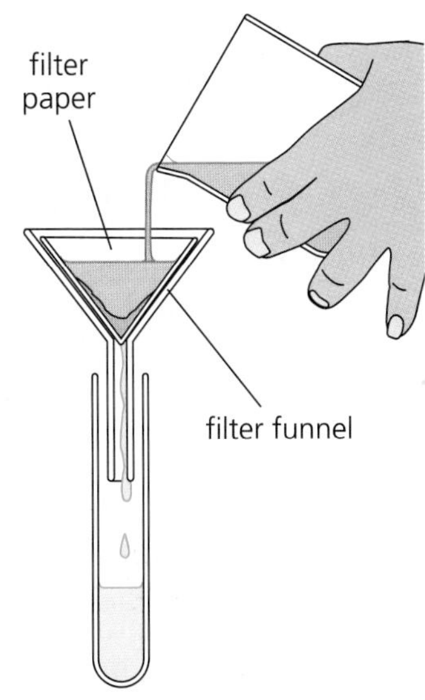

▲ ***Fig 3*** *The small water particles can pass through the filter paper but the large sand particles are held back.*

Key Words

aerosol – a mixture of a liquid in a gas
alloy – a mixture of metals
filtrate – the part of a mixture that passes through a filter
filtration – separating a mixture by passing it through a filter
foam – a mixture of a gas in a liquid
residue – the part of a mixture that is trapped by a filter

SUMMARY

- The substances in a mixture are not chemically joined together.
- A mixture can contain solids, liquids and gases.
- There are many different ways of separating mixtures.
- Filtration is one method of separating solids from mixtures. It depends on differences in the size of particles in the mixture.

SUMMARY *Activity*

Make a list of some of the mixtures you can find at home. Try to classify them into groups, e.g. gas in gas, gas in liquid, solid in liquid.

48 More separation methods

In this section of the book you will learn the following things:

- that mixtures can be separated by a variety of methods;
- that the best separation method to choose depends on the type of mixture;
- how distillation and chromatography can be used to separate mixtures.

Imagine that you have three different mixtures. One contains salt, water and sand. The second contains alcohol and water. The third contains blue, red and green ink mixed with water. How could you separate each one into its component parts? One method will not work for all of the mixtures. You need to consider a number of different methods and then choose the best one for each mixture.

Decanting

Filtering is only one way to separate a solid from water. You could wait until the solid settles to the bottom of the container and then carefully pour off the liquid. This is called **decanting** (Fig 1).

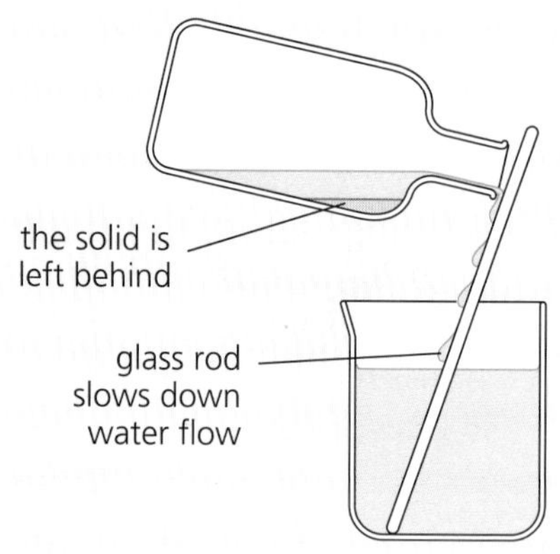

▲ *Fig 1*

Q1 Why is decanting a less effective way of separating mixtures than filtration?

Distillation

Liquids can be separated from mixtures by heating them. If a mixture of salt and water is boiled, the water will turn to steam. This rises out of the mixture and leaves the salt behind. If we want to save the liquid we need to cool it until it becomes a liquid again. One way to do this is shown in Fig 2.

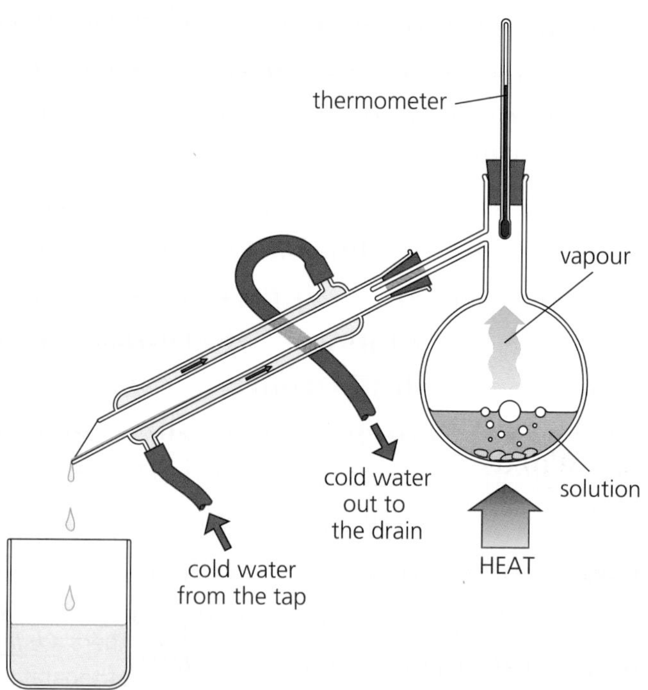

▲ ***Fig 2*** *The salt remains in the flask as the water boils away. The water vapour condenses back to liquid water as it passes through the cold tube.*

Different liquids turn to vapour (Unit 41) at different temperatures. This means that liquids can also be separated from other liquids by heating them. Separating liquids by heating them is called **fractional distillation**.

Separating liquids by distillation depends on getting the temperature exactly right. When strong alcoholic drinks are made this way, great care is taken to make sure that the alcohol is separated from some other poisonous liquids that vaporise at nearly the same temperature. Another reason for being careful is that alcohol can catch fire.

Q2 Why do you think a place where whisky or gin is made is called a distillery?

▲ ***Fig 3*** *A place where whisky is made is called a distillery.*

Chromatography

Chromatography is another way of separating mixtures. You can see how it works by using it to separate a mixture of coloured inks. First a spot of the mixture is placed near the bottom of a piece of filter paper and allowed to dry. When the bottom edge of the paper is dipped into a liquid that can dissolve ink, the liquid slowly rises up the paper and carries some of the ink with it. Because the different colours move at different speeds they will eventually be spaced out along the path of the solvent.

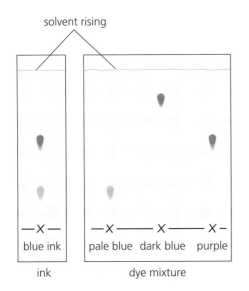

▲ ***Fig 4*** *The colours move apart as the solvent soaks upwards.*

Q3 How could you use chromatography to detect whether the ink used to write a letter came from a particular pen?

Key Words

chromatography – a method of separation using a solvent
distillation – a method of separation using evaporation
fractional distillation – a method of separating liquid mixtures by evaporation
suspension – a mixture of very small solid particles in a liquid

SUMMARY

- Decanting can separate a liquid from an insoluble solid.
- Distillation can be used to separate a liquid from a soluble solid.
- Fractional distillation can separate liquids with different boiling points.
- Chromatography can separate a tiny amount of a mixture by using a solvent to spread the different parts out.

SUMMARY *Activity*

How would you separate a mixture of sand, salt, water and alcohol into its constituents?
Hint: You may need to use more than one method.

49 Metals

In this section of the book you will learn the following things:

- **that most metals are shiny solids at room temperature;**
- **that many metals are malleable, ductile and sonorous;**
- **that most metals are good conductors of heat and electricity;**
- **that some metals are magnetic.**

Metals have many uses in everyday life. Buildings and cars contain a great deal of metal. Metals are also used in electrical wires, radiators, water pipes and jewellery. All these things are made with metal because of the special properties that metals possess. However, metals do not all behave in exactly the same way.

▲ ***Fig 1*** *Some properties of metals make these bridges possible.*

Malleable, ductile and sonorous

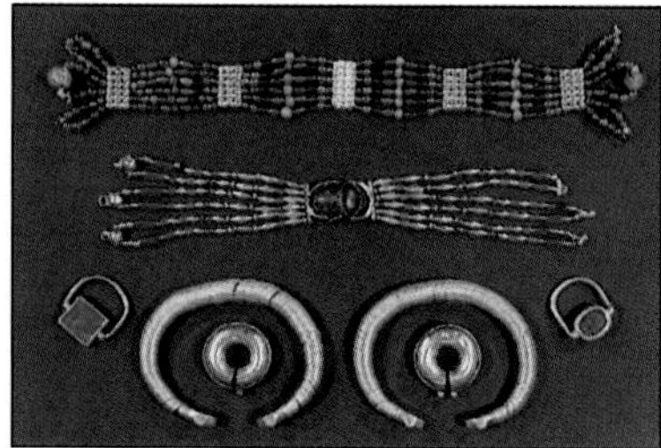

▲ ***Fig 2*** *Some metal shapes.*

Q1 Which three properties of metals make them useful for creating decorative bowls?

Most metals can be hammered into shapes. They are **malleable**. Malleable metals have been shaped into cooking pots and tools for thousands of years. Many metals are bright and shiny. Shiny and malleable metals such as gold and silver have been used to make ornaments and jewellery for thousands of years.

Not all metals are solid at room temperature, however. Mercury is a metal that is a shimmering liquid at room temperature.

Many metals can also be drawn out into long wires. They are **ductile**. This is a useful property for turning copper into electrical wires.

Some metals make a ringing sound when hit. They are **sonorous**. Church bells and temple gongs make use of this property.

Thermal conductivity

If you have ever poured boiling water into a metal container you will know that the outside of the container gets hot very quickly. This property is called **thermal conductivity.** Most metals are very good thermal conductors. This is why we use metal to make radiators and saucepans. When you put a metal spoon into a hot cup of tea, the handle that is not in contact with the hot tea soon becomes warm.

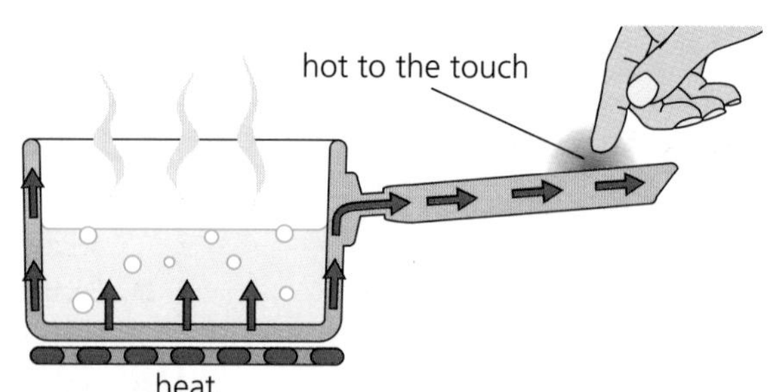

▲ ***Fig 3*** *Thermal energy travels through the base of the pan to the contents. It also spreads into the handle.*

Q2 Why do some metal saucepans have plastic or wooden handles?

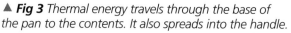

Electrical conductivity

Q3 Why are light switches not made of metal?

All metals conduct electricity. Some metals conduct electricity better than others. Copper is commonly used in electrical wires. It is ductile and is a good electrical conductor.

An electrical circuit can be used to find out which substances conduct electricity. A test circuit is shown in the next unit. The circuit needs a complete ring of metal wires. Only substances that can conduct electricity will light up the test bulb. All metals make the bulb light up.

Magnets

Some metals are magnetic. Most metals are not. You can test to see whether a metal is magnetic by using a magnetic compass. A magnetic metal will make the compass needle move. The only common magnetic materials are iron, nickel and cobalt. Steel is an alloy containing a lot of iron.

Q4 Is steel magnetic? Is steel an element?

▼ ***Fig 4*** *Metals, their properties and uses.*

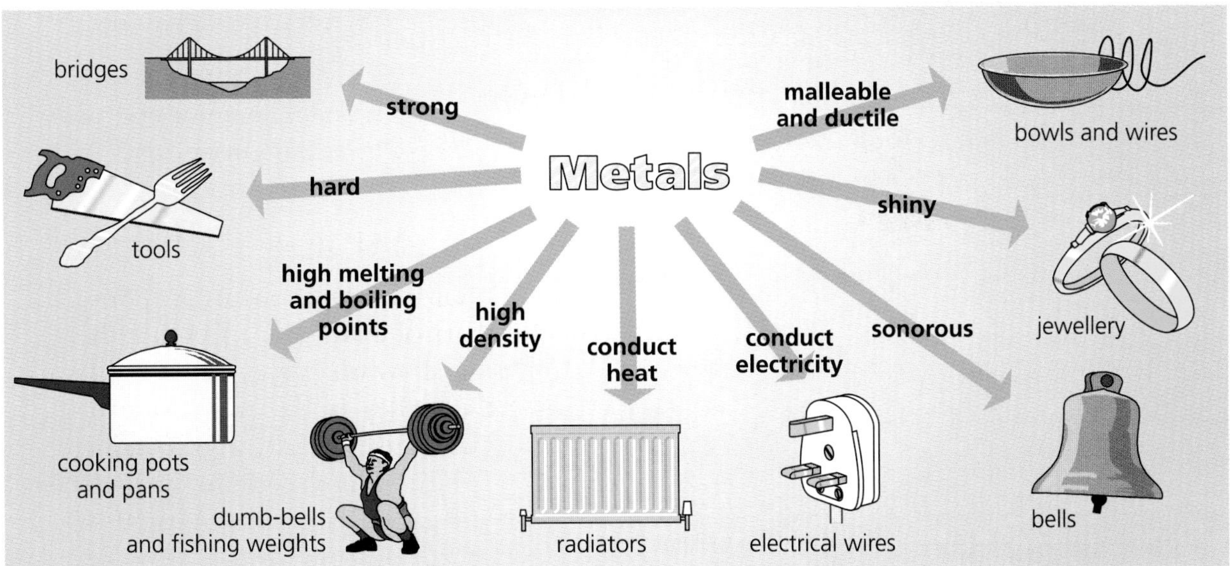

Key Words

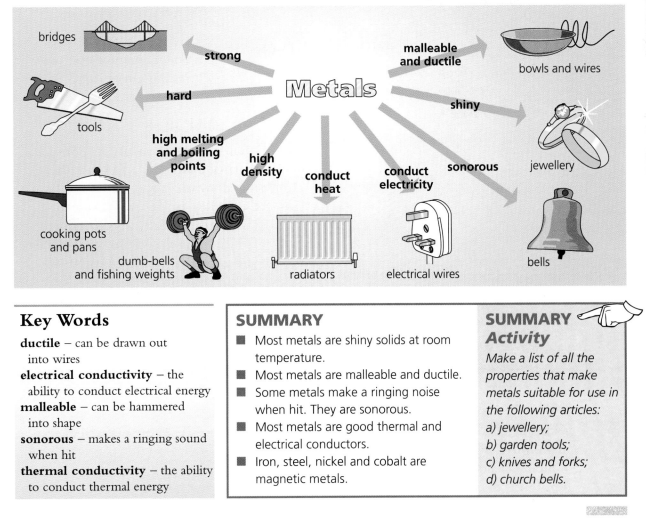

ductile – can be drawn out into wires
electrical conductivity – the ability to conduct electrical energy
malleable – can be hammered into shape
sonorous – makes a ringing sound when hit
thermal conductivity – the ability to conduct thermal energy

SUMMARY

- Most metals are shiny solids at room temperature.
- Most metals are malleable and ductile.
- Some metals make a ringing noise when hit. They are sonorous.
- Most metals are good thermal and electrical conductors.
- Iron, steel, nickel and cobalt are magnetic metals.

SUMMARY *Activity*

Make a list of all the properties that make metals suitable for use in the following articles:
a) jewellery;
b) garden tools;
c) knives and forks;
d) church bells.

50 Non-metallic elements

In this section of the book you will learn the following things:

- **that non-metallic elements vary widely in their physical properties;**
- **that many non-metallic elements are gases at room temperature;**
- **that most non-metallic elements are poor thermal and electrical conductors.**

The non-metallic elements are placed towards the right-hand side of the Periodic Table. There are many more metallic elements than non-metallic elements. Non-metals vary a great deal in their physical appearance and in many respects are the opposite of metals. Nearly half of the 20 or so non-metallic elements are gases.

▲ *Fig 1 These cylinders contain oxygen and nitrogen.*

Physical appearance

All gases are non-metals. Only one non-metallic element – bromine – is a liquid. Solid non-metals melt easily and most are very **brittle**. They are never ductile or malleable. Some well known non-metallic solids are carbon, sulphur and silicon. Some well known gases are oxygen, nitrogen and neon.

Q1 Which non-metallic element is a liquid?

Q2 Give two reasons why sulphur is not used for making jewellery.

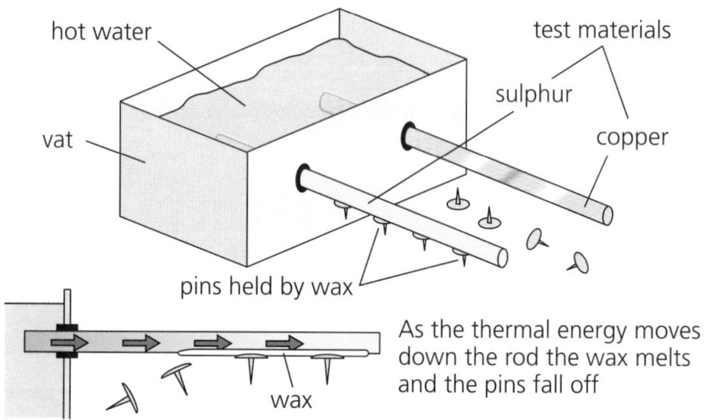

◄ *Fig 2 Copper conducts heat five hundred times faster than sulphur.*

Thermal conductivity

Non-metallic elements are poor thermal conductors. Because they do not allow thermal heat to pass through them, they are thermal **insulators**. Gases are especially poor conductors of heat. This is because the molecules of a gas are far apart (Units 39–41).

Q3 Explain why oxygen and nitrogen are poor thermal conductors.

Q4 Why does air trapped in your clothes help to keep you warm?

Electrical conductivity

Non-metallic elements are very poor electrical conductors. They are **electrical insulators**. Fig 3 shows a circuit for testing different substances to find out which can conduct electricity. If the substance is an electrical conductor then the bulb will light up. If it is not an electrical conductor then the bulb will not light up.

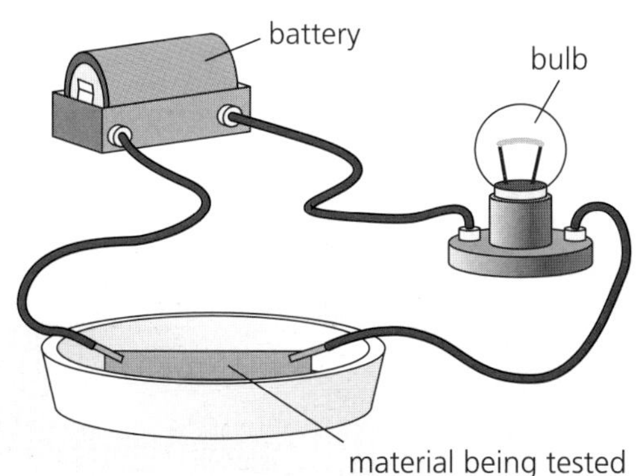

▲ *Fig 3 A simple circuit to test electrical conductivity of different substances.*

The results for some substances are shown in Table 1. Notice that one of the non-metallic elements, **graphite**, will conduct electricity. This is a special form of carbon.

▶ ***Table 1***

Material	Conduct electricity
copper	yes
iron	yes
lead	yes
sulphur	no
graphite	yes
coke (carbon)	no

Q5 Which of the elements in Table 1 are metals and which are non-metals?

Comparing metals with non-metals

It is usually fairly easy to decide whether an element is a metal or a non-metal. Metals and non-metals normally have opposite properties. Metals are good conductors but non-metals are good insulators. Metals are malleable and ductile but non-metals are not. Metals make a ringing sound when they are hit but non-metals sound flat and dull. The general properties of metals and non-metals are shown in Table 2.

It is important to look at more than one property because some metals and non-metals do not follow the rules. Most metals are solids but mercury is liquid at room temperature. Most solid non-metals are brittle, but the hardest natural substance in the world is the diamond crystal made of pure carbon.

▼ ***Table 2***

Metal	Non-metal
malleable and ductile	brittle or soft
rings when hit	does not ring when hit
good heat conductor	insulator (bad conductor)
good electrical conductor	insulator (bad conductor)
clean surface is shiny	surface is dull
usually high density	low density

Q6 Which non-metallic element is not an electrical insulator?

Key Words

brittle – easily broken, not malleable or ductile
graphite – a form of carbon that conducts electricity
insulator – a substance that does not easily conduct energy
material – substance

SUMMARY

- There are about 20 non-metallic elements. Approximately half are gases and one is a liquid.
- Non-metallic solids are not malleable or ductile.
- Most non-metallic elements are poor conductors.
- Graphite is a non-metallic element which conducts electricity.

SUMMARY *Activity*

Divide the following into metallic and non-metallic elements:
a) a shiny solid that conducts electricity and heat; b) a brittle solid that is a good insulator; c) a brittle solid that conducts electricity.

51 Physical changes

In this section of the book you will learn the following things:

- **some of the differences between physical changes and chemical changes;**
- **that a physical change does not produce any new substances;**
- **that a physical change does not change the mass of a substance;**
- **that chemical changes always produce new substances.**

You see **physical changes** every day. All changes of state are physical changes. Dissolving sugar in a cup of tea is a physical change. A physical change happens when one or more of the physical properties of a substance is changed. This means a substance may look and behave differently and be in a different form but it will still be the same chemical. When liquid water changes to ice its hardness, density, volume and appearance all become different but it is still the same chemical with the same chemical formula.

▲ *Fig 1 Very cold water becomes solid ice.*

Q1 List three examples of physical changes you have seen today.

Physical and chemical change

Physical changes are temporary and can easily be reversed. Water can easily be turned into ice and back again. If we add salt to water we can evaporate the water and get the salt back. These are physical changes.

When paper burns we see a total change. The paper gets very hot and turns to ash. What happens if we cool the ash? Does it change back into paper? Obviously the answer to that is no. The paper no longer exists. It has changed into new chemicals. This is an example of a **chemical change**.

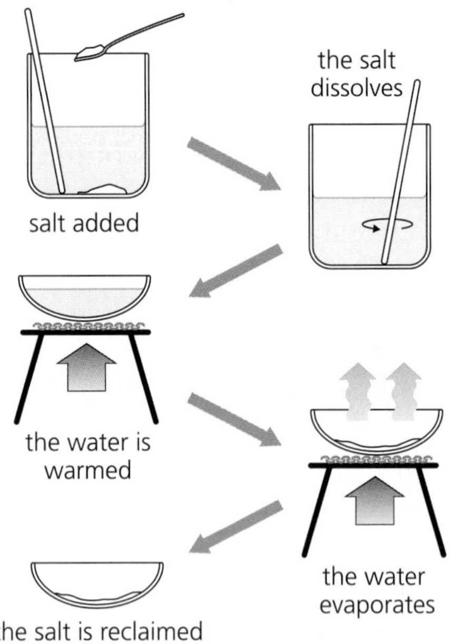
salt added
the salt dissolves
the water is warmed
the water evaporates
the salt is reclaimed

▲ *Fig 2 The salt has simply dissolved. It still exists as salt in the water.*

▲ *Fig 3 The paper is changing into new chemicals.*

Q2 What is the difference between a chemical change and a physical change?

Conservation of mass

If you add 10 grams of salt to a glass of water and give it a stir it will dissolve and become invisible. You can get it back by evaporating the water (Fig 4). If you weigh the salt at the end, you will find that there are still 10 grams. None of it will have gone missing. When something stays the same we say that it is conserved. The mass of the salt was conserved through two physical changes. This is called **conservation of mass**.

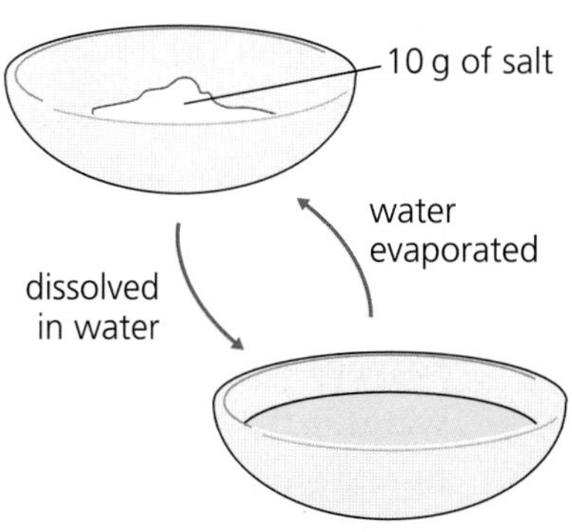

▲ ***Fig 4***

Do substances alter in mass when they change state? You can try this out for yourself with plain water. You could measure an exact weight of water, then freeze it and weigh it again, then thaw it out and weigh it again. An easier method is shown in Fig 5. No matter which method you use, you will find that the change of state has no effect on the mass of the water. Conservation of mass applies to all physical changes of state.

Q3 How could you prove that evaporation of alcohol is a physical change and not a chemical one?

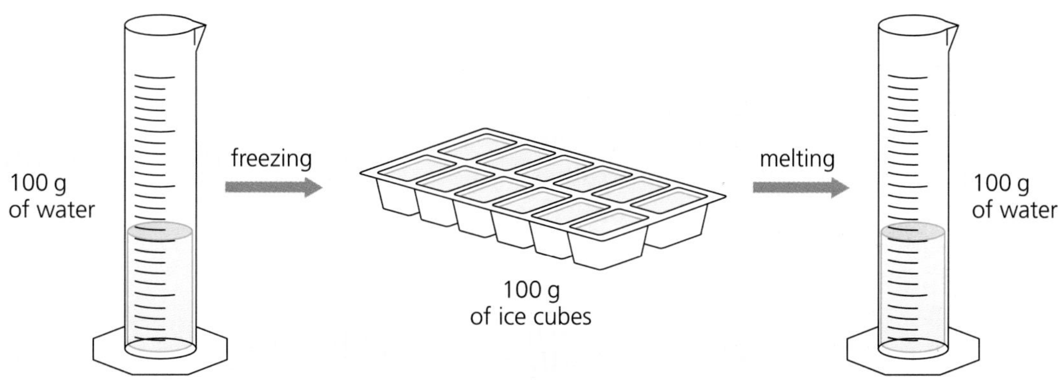

▲ ***Fig 5*** *There is no change in mass during a change of state.*

Key Words

chemical change – a change into a new substance not easily reversed

conservation of mass – no alteration in mass during a change

physical change – a change affecting the appearance of a substance but not its chemistry

SUMMARY

- Changes of state and dissolving are examples of physical changes.
- During a physical change a substance remains the same chemical.
- Physical changes are temporary and can easily be reversed.
- Chemical changes are permanent and difficult to reverse. New chemicals are made.
- The mass of a substance is conserved during a physical change.

SUMMARY *Activity*

Which of the following are physical changes and which are chemical changes: a) steam condensing on a mirror; b) petrol burning; c) bread being toasted; d) sugar dissolving in tea; e) mincing meat?

52 Dissolving substances

In this section of the book you will learn the following things:

- **that some substances dissolve in water and others do not;**
- **that water is not the only liquid that can be used to dissolve things;**
- **that temperature can affect the way a substance dissolves.**

If a solid will dissolve in a liquid we say that it is **soluble**. The liquid is called the **solvent** and the solid is called the **solute**. So if salt is dissolved in water, the water is the solvent and the salt is the solute. When a solute and a solvent are mixed they make a **solution** (see Fig 1) There are many different solvents and many different solutes.

▼ *Fig 1*

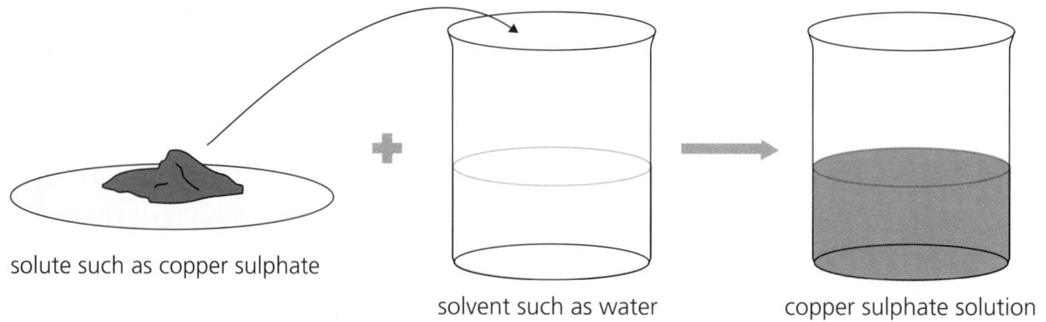

Water as a solvent

Water is a very good solvent. It can dissolve many things. However, some things do not dissolve in water and others only dissolve slightly. They have different solubilities. The **solubility** of a substance is a measure of how well it will dissolve in a solvent. If it dissolves well it has a high solubility. Substances that do not dissolve in a solvent are called **insoluble**.

Q1 Are any of the chemicals in the table insoluble in water?

Chemical	How many grams dissolve in 100 grams of water at 20°C
sodium chloride (salt)	36
sodium carbonate	22
calcium sulphate	0.2
sugar	211
sand	0

▲ ***Table 1*** *Different chemicals have different solubilities.*

Temperature and solubility

You have probably noticed that sugar dissolves more quickly in hot water than in cold water. This is true for most solvents and solutes. The warmer the solvent is, the easier it is to dissolve the solute. It does not only dissolve more quickly. More solute dissolves in a warm solvent than in a cold solvent. This can be tested by trying to dissolve as much solute as possible in 100 grams of water at different temperatures. The results of this experiment are shown in Fig 2. You can see that more and more solute dissolves as the solvent's temperature rises.

Salt is extracted from layers under the ground by pumping water down into it. The salty water (brine) rises to the surface and can be collected. Then the salt is removed by letting the water evaporate.

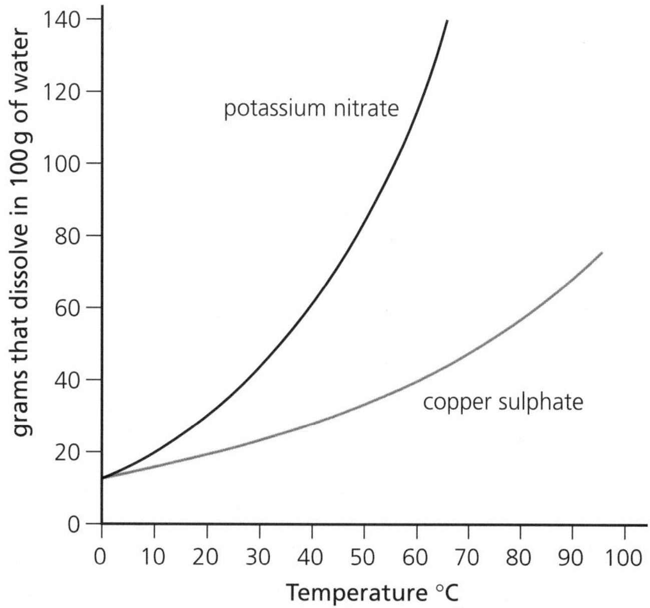

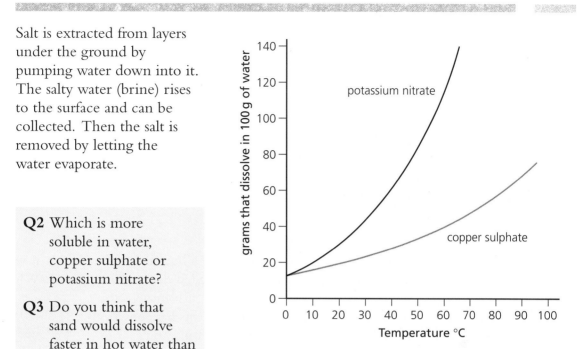

▲ *Fig 2 As the solvent's temperature rises, more of a solute will dissolve in it.*

Q2 Which is more soluble in water, copper sulphate or potassium nitrate?

Q3 Do you think that sand would dissolve faster in hot water than cold water?

Solvents other than water

Whether or not a substance will dissolve can depend on the solvent. Salt dissolves easily in water but it does not dissolve very well in alcohol. Candle wax does not dissolve in water but it will dissolve in some other solvents. Different solvents are used to dissolve different solutes. Solvents have many uses. Some are used to remove stains that water will not wash out. Others are used in nail varnish, glues, paints and correcting fluid. Many solvents are harmful and must not be breathed in or spilt on your skin.

▶ ***Fig 3*** *Many of the old-fashioned solvents in paints and varnishes can make people ill. Some modern paints and varnishes use water as a solvent.*

Key Words

insoluble – unable to dissolve in a liquid
solubility – how well a substance dissolves
soluble – able to dissolve in a liquid
solute – the substance that dissolves in a liquid
solution – a mixture of a solute in a solvent
solvent – the liquid that dissolves a solute

SUMMARY

- Some substances are soluble in water and others are insoluble.
- Soluble substances dissolve better in hot liquids than in cold.
- There are many different solvents. Substances that do not dissolve in water may dissolve in other solvents.
- Many of the products we use contain solvents.

SUMMARY *Activity*

Make a list of some of the solutions you have seen this week. Try to name the solvent and solute in each solution.

53 Melting and freezing

In this section of the book you will learn the following things:
- **that different solids melt at different temperatures;**
- **what the terms boiling point and freezing point mean;**
- **that different liquids have their different boiling and freezing points;**
- **that different materials change state at different temperatures.**

Materials can exist as solids, liquids or gases. When materials change between these states their particles either get closer together or move further apart. This usually happens when the substance is heated or cooled.

Melting and freezing points

When a solid is heated it will eventually turn into a liquid. In other words, it will melt. The temperature at which this happens is called the **melting point**. When a liquid is cooled it will eventually turn into a solid. The temperature at which this happens is called the **freezing point**. Melting and freezing points are the same. Each substance has its own melting and freezing point. This is why melting point or freezing point can be used to identify chemicals.

Substance	Melting point (°C)
water	0
wax	50
iodine	114
lead	327
mercury	–39
sulphur	113–119
phosphorus	44

Q1 Why is the melting point of a particular substance always the same as its freezing point?

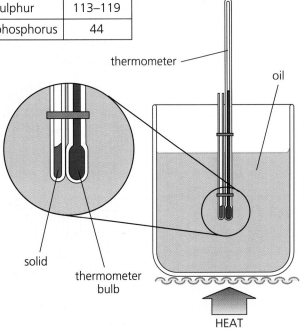

thermometer
oil
solid
thermometer bulb
HEAT

▲ ***Fig 1*** *Every pure substance has its own special melting point, which is the same as its freezing point. This is one way to test how pure a solid substance is.*

The freezing point of pure water is 0°C. Adding a substance such as sodium chloride (table salt) changes the freezing point. Salty water freezes at a much lower temperature. This is why salt is sometimes spread on roads in winter (Fig 2).

▲ ***Fig 2***

Q2 Why does putting salt on the roads in winter make driving safer?

Boiling point

Substance	Boiling point (°C)
butane	0
alcohol	78
water	100
sulphur	444
phosphorus	280

When a liquid is heated it changes state from liquid to gas. As the temperature rises, bubbles of gas begin to form in the liquid. This happens at the **boiling point** of the substance. Every pure substance has its own unique boiling point, just as every pure substance has its own unique melting/freezing point.

The boiling point of a liquid can be changed by adding another substance. It is also affected by air pressure. As you go up a mountain the air gets thinner and the air pressure falls. At sea level, water boils at 100°C. Up a mountain it may boil at 80°C.

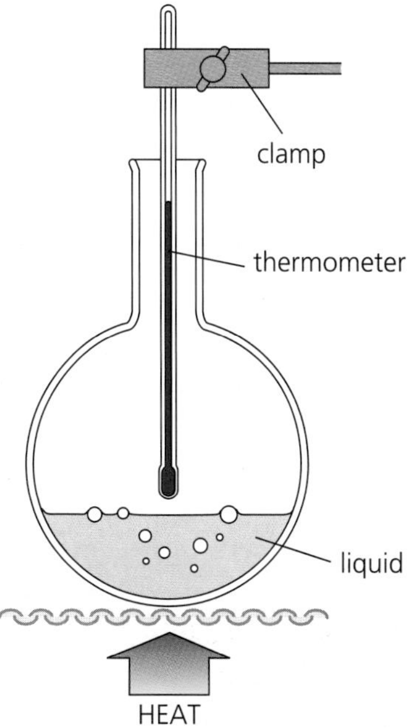

▲ ***Fig 3*** *Every pure substance has its own special boiling point. This is one way to test how pure a liquid substance is.*

Q3 Why does the water in an aluminium pan boil but the pan not melt?

Room temperature and state

We usually think of water as a liquid, iron as a solid and oxygen as a gas. This is the state they are in at room temperature, which is about 25°C. It only seems normal to us because this is our normal temperature. Room temperature on Mars and Venus would be totally different. Water, oxygen and iron would be in different states there.

Temperature	–218°C	*25°C*	200°C	2000°C
Oxygen state	solid	*gas*	gas	gas
Water state	solid	*liquid*	gas	gas
Iron state	solid	*solid*	solid	liquid

Q4 If a sample of water was found to have a freezing point of –5°C what would this tell you about the water?

Key Words

boiling point – the temperature at which gas bubbles form in a liquid
freezing point – the temperature at which a liquid becomes a solid
melting point – the temperature at which a solid becomes a liquid

SUMMARY

- Melting point is the same temperature as freezing point for any particular substance.
- Each substance has its own boiling point and melting point.
- Anything added to a pure substance can change its freezing and boiling point.
- The purity of a substance can be checked by testing its melting or boiling point.
- The state of a substance depends on temperature.

SUMMARY *Activity*

Decide which of the following would be a liquid, a solid or a gas at 500°C and at –200°C: a) nitrogen; b) lead; c) iodine.

54 Energy on the move

In this section of the book you will learn the following things:

- **that energy is transferred during changes of state;**
- **that materials lose energy when they condense or freeze;**
- **that materials gain energy when they evaporate, melt or boil.**

Energy transfer

If you wet your finger and then blow on it you will notice that it feels cool. It will eventually become dry as the liquid evaporates away. The liquid is changing state into a gas. When a liquid changes to a gas its particles start to move much faster (Unit 40). When anything moves faster it needs more energy. Liquid evaporating from your skin takes heat energy from your body. Your finger feels cool because it really is losing heat. Every change of state gives or takes energy. This is called **energy transfer**.

▲ ***Fig 1*** *As water evaporates from wet clothes, heat energy is taken from a person's body. This happens more quickly when the wind is blowing. The extra heat loss due to wind is called wind chill.*

Our body uses this principle to keep itself cool. When perspiration evaporates it draws heat energy from our skin. The reason why we perspire more in hot weather is because our body is releasing more liquid to speed up the cooling effect.

Evaporation and surface area

Spreading a liquid out speeds up evaporation by making the surface bigger. Bubbling air through a liquid also increases the surface area. Air moving across the surface blows away vapour particles and makes room for more particles to escape.

▼ ***Fig 2*** *Speeding up evaporation.*

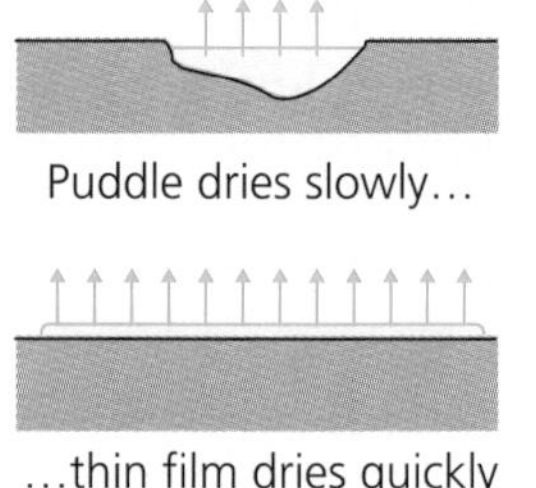

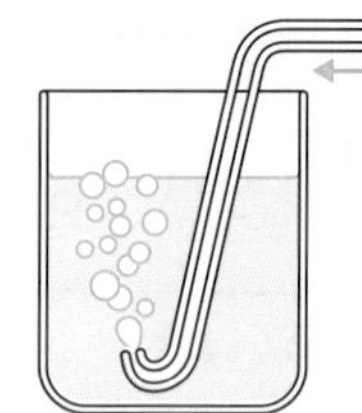

Puddle dries slowly...
...thin film dries quickly

The hot air drier blows warm air across your hands

Blowing air through the liquid will increase surface area

Evaporation and heat

A liquid needs energy to change state to a gas. Heat energy comes naturally from the sun. Liquids evaporate more quickly in the sun. In a kitchen, heat energy may come from a cooker or a kettle. Water evaporates more quickly when it is boiled. However, liquids will evaporate even if they are not heated. A liquid can take heat energy from anything it touches.

Q1 Why does washing dry faster on a windy day than on a calm day?

Q2 Why does washing dry faster in the sun than in the shade?

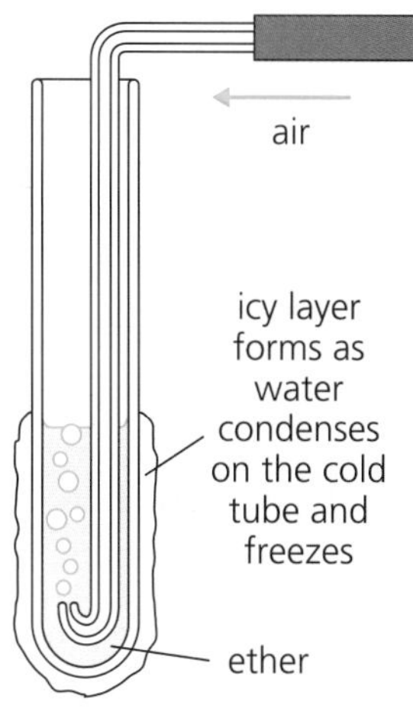

▲ ***Fig 3*** ⚠ *Ether is dangerously inflammable.*

Ether evaporates very easily. If air is bubbled through ether in a test-tube (Fig 3), the ether will evaporate and the test-tube will become very cold. Water vapour from the air will condense on the outside. It may even turn into ice. Evaporating ether can cool a test-tube below the freezing point of water.

A refrigerator works by using a gas called a **coolant** that evaporates and compresses easily. The coolant is pumped around in a series of tubes. Tubes in the refrigerator walls are wide and tubes on the outside are narrow. Coolant evaporates in the wide tubes and takes heat energy from the inside of the refrigerator. This makes the inside colder. The coolant is then compressed into a liquid in the narrow tubes. This releases the heat energy it took from the refrigerator into the air outside.

Q3 Why does the air around a refrigerator become warm?

Energy and particles

The particles in a solid are close together and not moving very much. The particles in a liquid are further apart and can move around. The particles in a gas are very far apart and moving very fast.

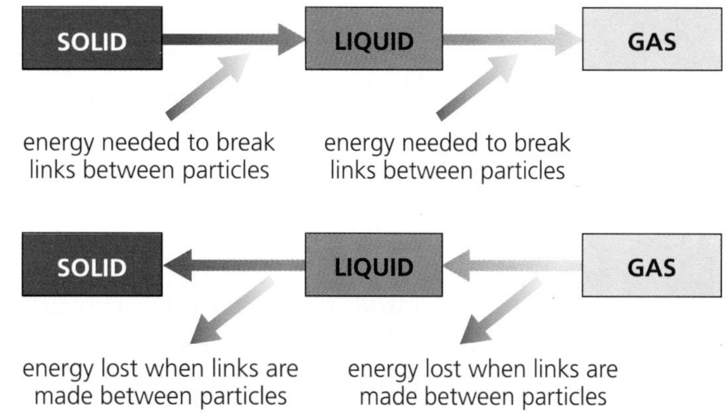

▲ ***Fig 4*** *Changes of state involve loss or gain of energy.*

Q4 When ice melts in your hand, where does it get the energy to change from a solid to a liquid?

Key Words

coolant– a substance used for refrigeration

energy transfer – the movement of energy from one place to another

SUMMARY

- When substances change state there is a transfer of energy.
- Changing a solid into a liquid or a liquid into a gas requires heat energy.
- Changing a gas into a liquid or a liquid into a solid releases heat energy.
- Refrigeration and sweating are two useful examples of energy transfer.

SUMMARY *Activity*

Explain how placing a damp cloth on your forehead can reduce your body temperature.

55 Expansion and contraction

In this section of the book you will learn the following things:

- that materials expand when they are heated;
- that materials contract when they are cooled;
- that expansion and contraction can create powerful forces;
- that expansion and contraction can be useful.

When particles are heated they move faster and further apart. A substance therefore grows bigger when it is heated. This is called **expansion**. When the substance cools down the particles slow down and move closer together. The substance becomes smaller. This is called **contraction**.

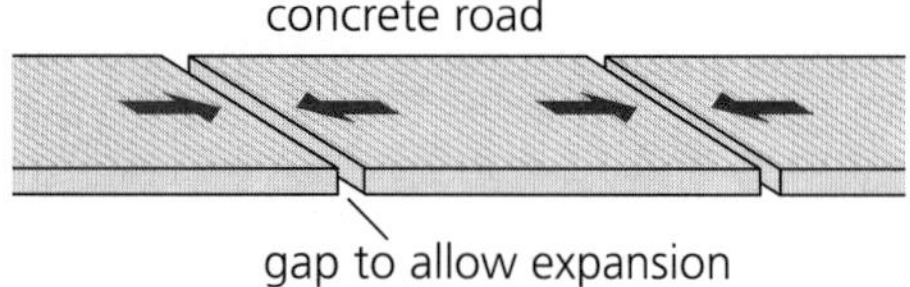

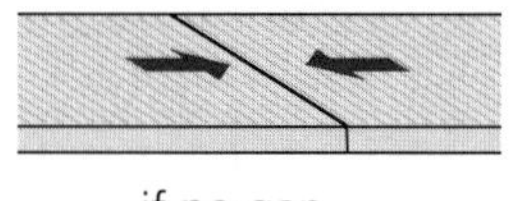

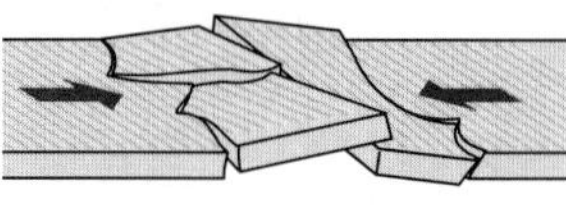

▲ ***Fig 1*** *Expansion can create enough force to damage a road or a bridge.*

Expansion in different substances

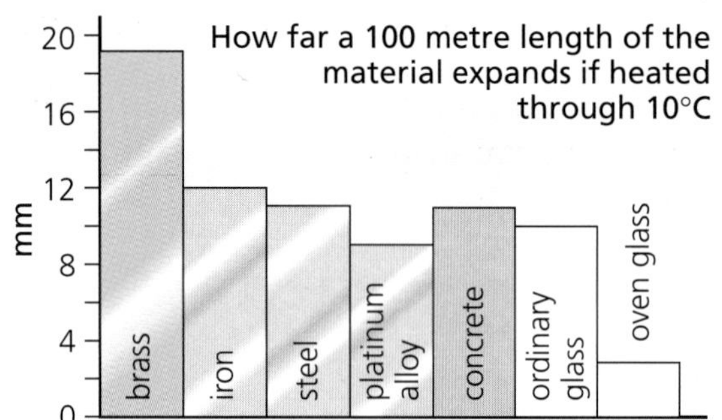

▲ ***Fig 2***

Different states affect the way substances expand.

- Particles in solids are held tightly together. Solids do not expand very far.
- Particles in liquids are loosely arranged. Liquids expand more than solids.
- Gas particles move very freely. Gases expand most of all.

Some solids expand more than others. It is important to know how much a solid will expand when choosing materials for a special job. Fig 2 shows how much some different solids expand when heated.

The fact that steel and concrete expand the same amount means that steel can be safely combined with concrete. Steel rods are used to make concrete beams stronger. If the steel and concrete expanded differently they would damage each other.

When you pour hot water into a glass container, the inside of the container heats up a moment before the outside. While the hot inside is pushing against the cold outside, the glass can crack. Thick glass cracks more easily this way than thin glass.

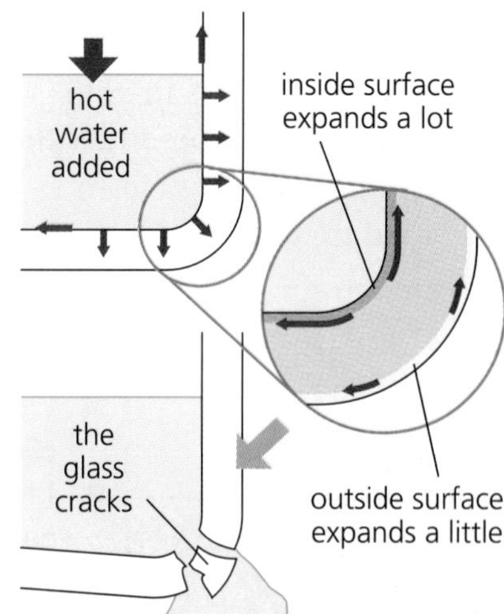

▲ ***Fig 3*** *The forces created by pouring hot water into a thick glass container can break it.*

Q1 Why is it sensible to put a metal spoon into a glass before pouring hot liquid in?

Q2 Why is oven-proof glass (e.g. Pyrex) more useful in the kitchen than normal glass?

Q3 Could pouring cold water into a hot glass make the glass crack?

Uses of expansion

Expansion and contraction are not always bad. They are also used for many everyday jobs.

When a steel tyre is fitted onto a train wheel, it is first heated until it expands. The expanded tyre slips easily onto the wheel. After it cools and contracts it grips the wheel very tightly. This method has been used for hundreds of years to fit metal tyres onto wooden cartwheels and metal hoops around wooden barrels.

Expansion of metals is also used very cleverly in the **bimetal strip** (Fig 4) This is made from a strip of brass and a strip of iron joined together. When it is heated, the brass expands more than the iron. This makes the strip bend. The hotter the strip gets the more it bends. Some thermometers contain a coiled bimetal strip which turns a needle as it expands or contracts. Bimetal strips are most commonly found in heat alarms and **thermostats**.

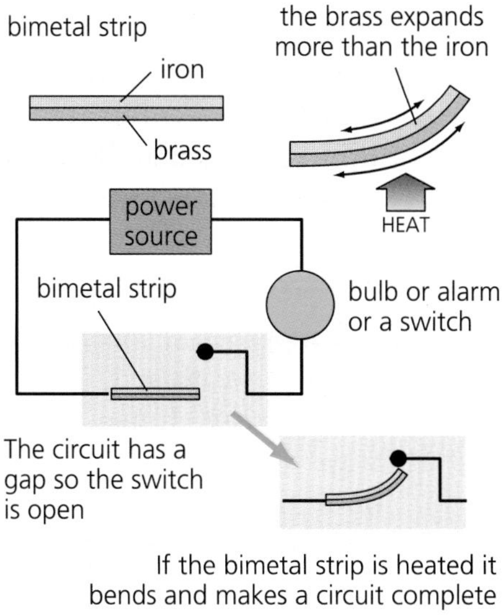

bimetal strip

iron

brass

the brass expands more than the iron

HEAT

power source

bimetal strip

bulb or alarm or a switch

The circuit has a gap so the switch is open

If the bimetal strip is heated it bends and makes a circuit complete

▲ *Fig 4*

The expansion of liquids also makes thermometers work.
A measured amount of alcohol or mercury expands and moves up a narrow tube marked with the corresponding temperature.

Q4 Why does a thermometer have a thin-walled bulb and a thick-walled tube?

Q5 An inflatable boat taken from hot sand and placed in the cold sea becomes soft. Can you think of an explanation?

Key Words

bimetal strip – a strip made from two metals joined together

contraction – shrinkage caused by cooling

expansion – growth caused by heating

thermostat – equipment to keep temperature constant

SUMMARY

- Materials expand when they are heated.
- Materials contract when they are cooled.
- Expansion and contraction can be powerful enough to cause damage.
- Different materials expand at different rates.
- Expansion and contraction can be used to make thermometers, thermostats and heat alarms.

SUMMARY *Activity*

Explain why a gap is always left at the point where a roadway joins a bridge. What might happen in summer if there was no gap? What might happen in winter?

56 Changing rocks

In this section of the book you will learn the following things:

- **that the rocks of the Earth are constantly breaking down;**
- **that the forces of expansion and contraction can break rocks down;**
- **that freezing water also breaks rocks.**

You only need to look at old gravestones to see that rock does not last forever. Many old gravestones are difficult to read. Their surfaces may be broken and peeling. Our world is constantly being changed by the weather.

▼ *Fig 1*

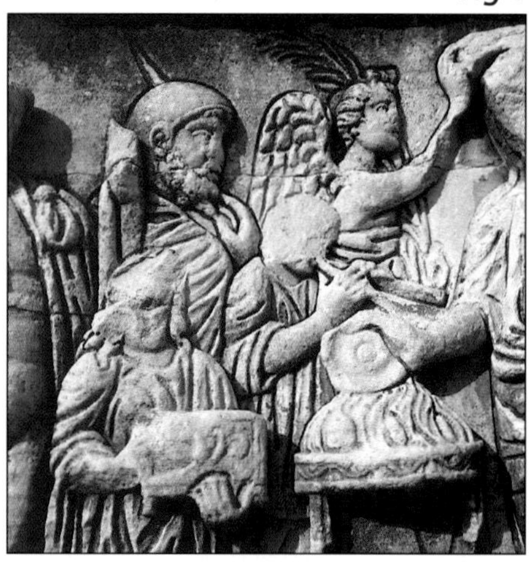

Weathering of rocks

When a rock is changed by natural forces we say that it is weathered. This process is called **weathering**. It may happen in one or more ways. The acid in rain can start to attack the rock. This can be seen in Fig 1. The statues have also been exposed to the wind, rain and sun for centuries. Even plants can help to break down rocks. When they push their roots into tiny cracks in the rock, this makes the cracks a little bigger.

Q1 List four ways in which rocks can be weathered.

The heat of the day and the cool of the night

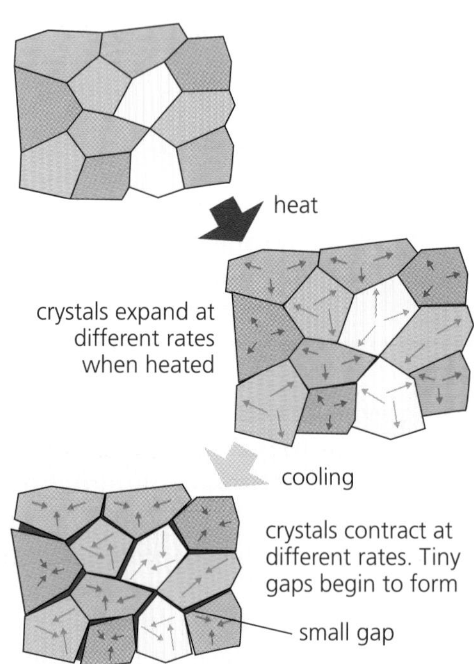
heat
crystals expand at different rates when heated
cooling
crystals contract at different rates. Tiny gaps begin to form
small gap

Rocks are a mixture of different substances. Rock expands when it is heated by the sun. The different substances in the rock expand in different ways. This creates forces inside the rock. When the rock cools again, it will contract. Again, the different substances inside the rock will contract in different ways and at different speeds. After months and years of heating and cooling, the forces in the rock may eventually break it down. Heating and cooling can be very extreme in deserts or high up in the mountains. The days may be very hot and the nights can be very cold. The rock expands and contracts most at the surface, where the weather and sun can easily reach it. Sometimes the whole surface can peel away.

◀ ***Fig 2*** *The substances in rock expand and contract according to the temperature.*

Q2 Can you think of a reason why early miners used to light fires near rocks and then throw cold water onto them?

Ice power

Many rocks contain tiny cracks. These cracks can fill with water every time it rains. Water can slowly wear away a rock or dissolve some of the substances in it but it will not damage the rock very quickly. Freezing water can damage rock very quickly (see Fig 3). Unlike other liquids, water expands when it freezes. This can create pressure inside tiny cracks. When water in the cracks freezes and thaws over and over again, the cracks become wider and wider until the rock breaks down. This **freeze-thaw** action is very common in mountains. It is the reason why so many mountains are covered with sharp, broken rocks. A mass of ice-broken rock is called **scree**.

Pieces of broken rock may be moved away by ice or rivers. They can be transported many kilometres. This is all part of a larger cycle called the rock cycle. You can find out more about the rock cycle in Unit 59.

Q3 Why do mountains have sharp, broken rocks on them?

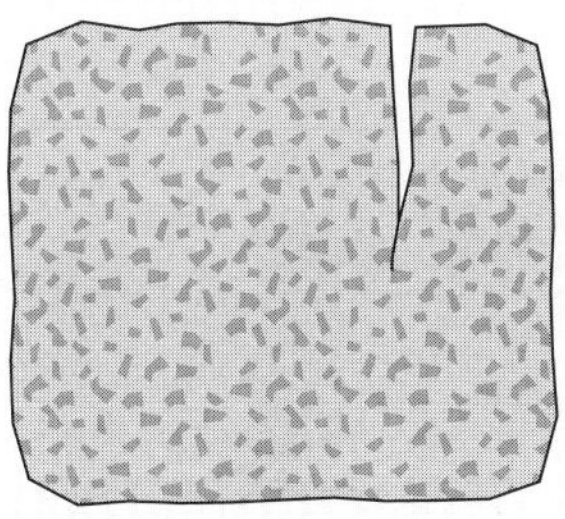

A rock with a small crack

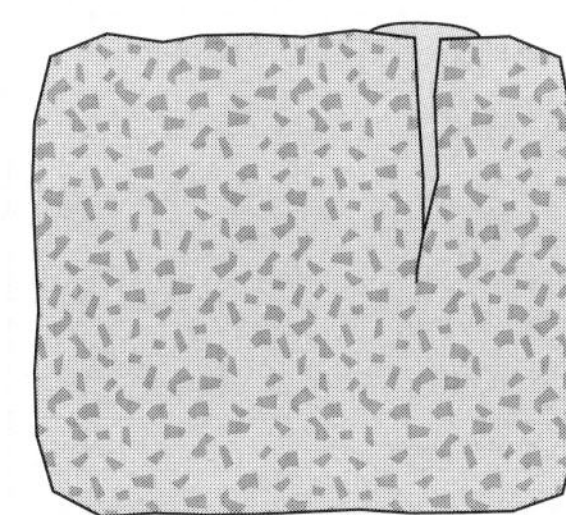

The crack fills with water

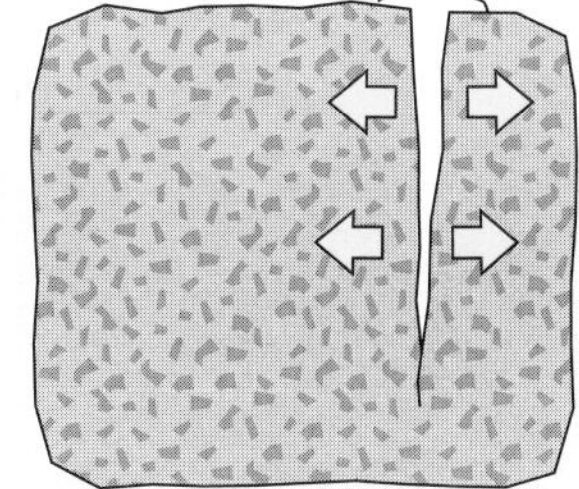

The water freezes and expands. This widens the crack

▲ *Fig 3*

Key Words

freeze-thaw – repeated freezing and thawing of water

scree – sharp fragments of loose rock on mountain slopes

weathering – physical and chemical breakdown of rocks

SUMMARY

- Weathering is caused by weather and other natural forces weakening rocks until they break.
- Expansion and contraction can weather rocks.
- Freezing and thawing rainwater can weather rocks.
- The weathering of rocks is part of the rock cycle.

SUMMARY *Activity*

Carry out a survey in your area. Look at some of the rocks used for buildings and make a note of any that are weathered. What do you think caused the weathering?

57 Rocks from fire

In this section of the book you will learn the following things:

- that rocks deep within the Earth are liquid;
- how some rocks are made from liquid rock;
- that these rocks are called igneous rocks;
- how to recognise igneous rocks.

Granite is a very hard type of rock. It does not weather easily. This is why it is often used for building. The reason why granite is so hard is that it is made up of **crystals** that are locked tightly together. The way a rock appears and feels is called its **texture**. The texture of granite tell us a lot about how it was made.

▲ ***Fig 1*** *Granite is a tough rock that resists weathering.*

Molten rocks

The crystals in granite were made when hot liquid rock called **magma** cooled down, millions of years ago. Magma comes from deep inside the Earth where it is very hot. Great pressures inside the Earth can force liquid magma upwards through weak parts of the Earth's crust (Figs 2 and 3). When magma reaches the surface it cools down and becomes a solid. Rocks formed in this way are called **igneous** – from ignis, an ancient word for fire.

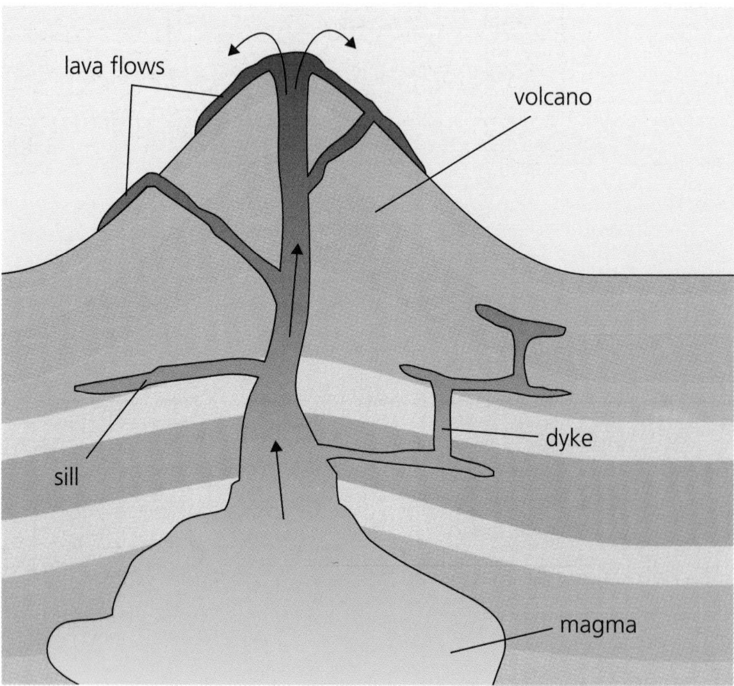

▲ ***Fig 2*** *Magma can reach the surface when a volcano erupts. It cools and forms solid rock.*

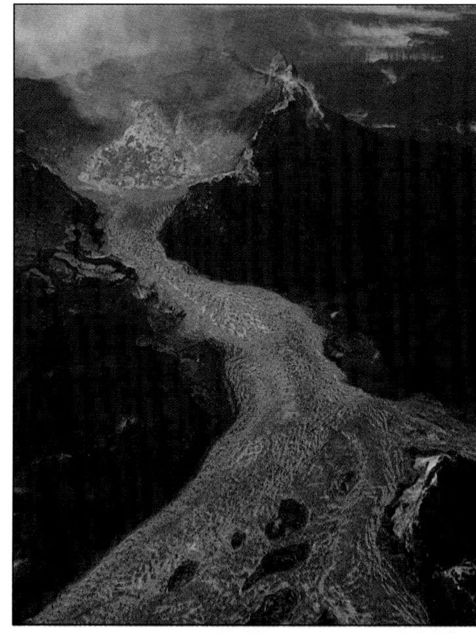

▲ ***Fig 3***

Q1 How are volcanoes formed?

Q2 Can you think of another word that comes from the same old word as igneous?

Magma that reaches the surface cools very quickly and becomes lava. Magma that does not reach the surface cools more slowly. Deep underground, a pool of magma can remain hot for a long time. Small vertical **dykes** and horizontal **sills** may make and fill cracks in the surrounding rock. These cool down more slowly than lava but more quickly than big pools of magma.

Q3 What is the difference between a sill and a dyke?

When magma cools slowly there is a lot of time for crystals to grow. Slowly forming crystals grow close together and interlock. This makes a hard and strong rock. Rocks that cool very slowly deep underground form very large crystals. Some of the crystals in granite are more than 3 centimetres long. The rocks in sills and dykes have smaller crystals but you can still see them quite easily. Magma that cools quickly at the surface forms very small crystals. You would need a hand lens to see them clearly.

Interlocking crystals make many igneous rocks very strong and resistant to weathering. Igneous rocks with large crystals have cooled more slowly and were formed deep underground. The smaller the crystals are in an igneous rock the more likely it is that the rock was at or near the surface of the Earth when it cooled.

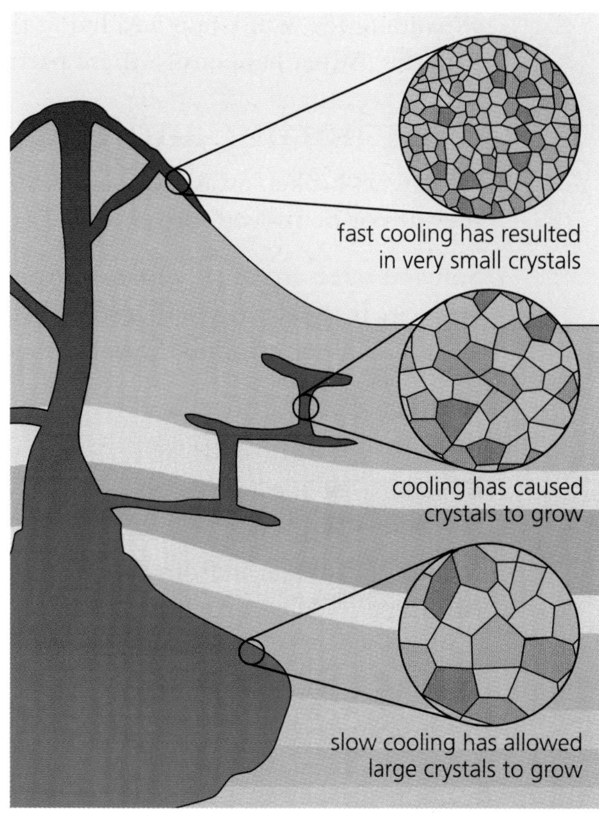
fast cooling has resulted in very small crystals
cooling has caused crystals to grow
slow cooling has allowed large crystals to grow

▲ ***Fig 4*** *The largest crystals grow where magma cools most slowly.*

Q4 Why are many igneous rocks resistant to weathering?

Key Words

dyke – a vertical crack filled with magma
igneous – rock formed when magma cools
magma – hot liquid rock
sill – a horizontal crack filled with magma
texture – the appearance and feel of a substance

SUMMARY

- The Earth's core is hot and liquid (molten).
- Igneous rocks are made when molten rock cools down.
- Igneous rocks are made of interlocking crystals.
- Large crystals grow when molten rock cools slowly.
- Small crystals grow when molten rock cools quickly.

SUMMARY *Activity*

Describe how a rock with large interlocking crystals could have formed. Look for some examples on buildings. Hint: They are often polished to show the crytals.

58 Sedimentary rocks

In this section of the book you will learn the following things:

- **what sedimentary rocks look like;**
- **how sedimentary rocks are made;**
- **that this process can take a very long time.**

The rocks at the surface of the Earth are attacked by heat and cold, expanding ice, wind, rain and living things. They break down into smaller particles. What happens to these particles?

Weathering and transport

Fragments broken away from large masses of rock can either remain where they are or be moved somewhere else.

Soil and scree are usually formed from rock fragments that have not moved very far. It is easy to see that scree is the same as the bigger rocks. You may need a hand lens to find the rock fragments in soil.

Weathered rock can be carried away by:

- water
- ice and snow
- wind
- gravity

Removal of material from the landscape is called **erosion**.

Water transport

Rivers can carry rock fragments away. As they bounce along in a fast flowing river the fragments rub against each other and the sides of the river. They become rounder and smaller as they go along.

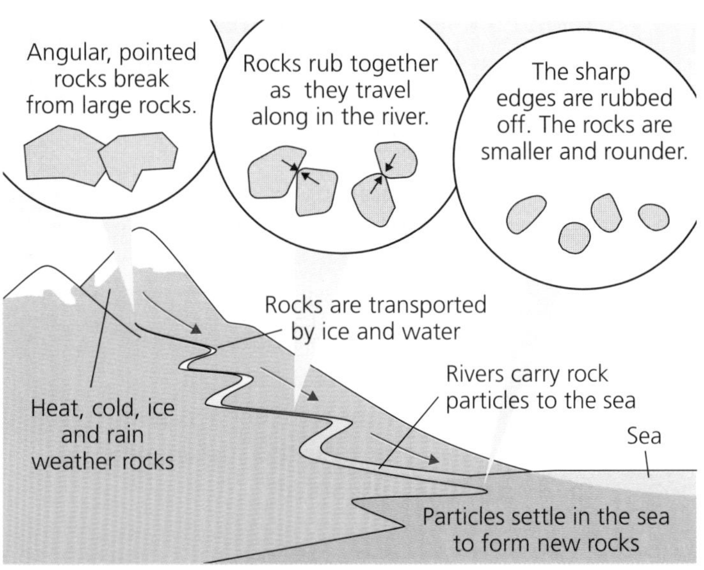
Angular, pointed rocks break from large rocks.
Rocks rub together as they travel along in the river.
The sharp edges are rubbed off. The rocks are smaller and rounder.
Rocks are transported by ice and water
Rivers carry rock particles to the sea
Heat, cold, ice and rain weather rocks
Sea
Particles settle in the sea to form new rocks

▲ ***Fig 1*** *In their journey down a river to the sea, large sharp rocks gradually become small smooth pebbles.*

Tiny particles worn away from rocks in a river are called **sediment**. When the water arrives at a slow part of the river – or a lake or the sea – the sediment sinks to the bottom. Sediment can build up for millions of years until the weight of all the layers on top squashes the bottom layers into solid rock. Rock formed in this way is called **sedimentary** rock. Sedimentary rock often contains rounded particles. Rounded particles do not lock together as crystals do. They are held together by a weak cement made of smaller rounded particles mixed with chemicals. Because of the way they form, sedimentary rocks are usually found in layers.

Q1 Why do rock fragments become smaller and rounded as they travel along in a river?

As the particles enter the sea the biggest and heaviest ones sink first. Smaller particles move further away from the shore. The very smallest may be washed far out to sea and eventually sink to the bottom of the deepest oceans. This means that the size of the particles or grains in a sedimentary rock can give us a clue where it was formed.

Q2 How can the size of grains in a sedimentary rock help us to work out where it was formed?

Sandstones are made from small grains of sand. They usually form near the coast or in a desert.

Mudstones are made from tiny particles of mud. They usually form in deep water far away from the shore.

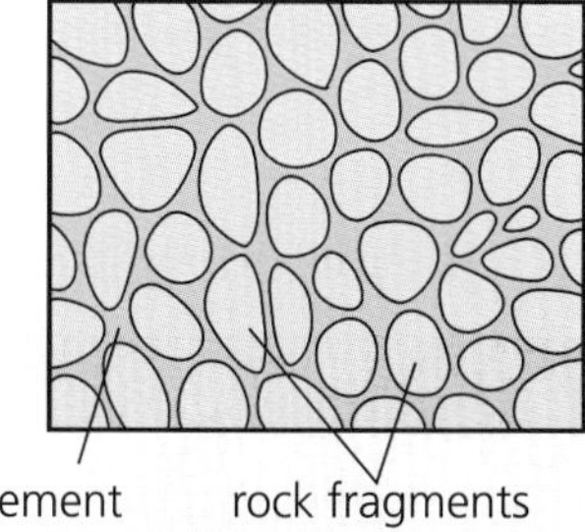

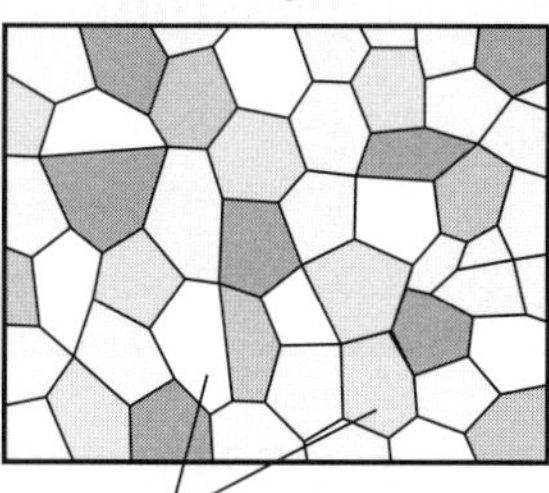

▲ **Fig 2** *Sedimentary rock has rounded grains. Igneous rock has interlocking crystals.*

Shells and rocks

Chalk and limestone are also sedimentary rocks. They are not made of rock grains but the skeletons of long-dead water animals. When the animals died, their skeletons sank to the sea-bed for millions of years and turned into rock in the same way as other sediments do. These rocks are made from the chemicals that the animals used to make their skeletons. They are easily attacked by acids and are often weathered by water to form tunnels and caves. The shells can be seen as **fossils** and these fossils tell us a lot about conditions in the past.

▲ **Fig 3** *Chalk cliffs on the Eastbourne coast.*

Q3 Why are fossils sometimes found in sedimentary rocks but never in igneous rocks?

Key Words

erosion – the movement of weathered rock
fossil – evidence of living things preserved in rocks
sediment – small particles of rock
sedimentary – rock formed from sediment

SUMMARY

- Rock fragments can be transported by water, wind and ice.
- Sedimentary rocks are formed from layers of rock fragments.
- Sedimentary rocks contain rounded fragments.
- The grain size of sedimentary rocks can tell us where they were formed.
- Some sedimentary rocks are made from the shells and skeletons of dead animals.

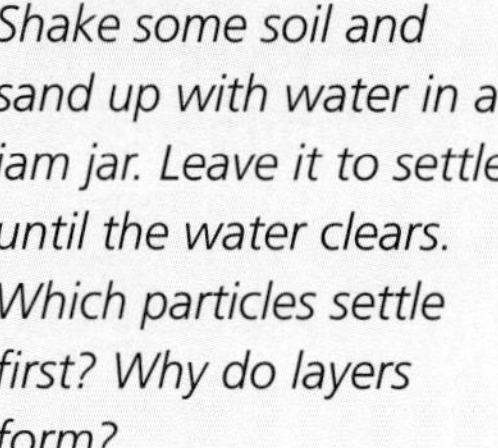

SUMMARY *Activity*

Shake some soil and sand up with water in a jam jar. Leave it to settle until the water clears. Which particles settle first? Why do layers form?

59 New rocks from old

In this section of the book you will learn the following things:

- **the meaning of the term metamorphic rock;**
- **how metamorphic rocks are formed;**
- **the names and properties of some metamorphic rocks;**
- **how metamorphic rocks fit into the rock cycle.**

When magma erupts through the Earth's crust it comes into contact with rocks that are already formed. It makes these rocks very hot and may also create tremendous pressure. The heat and pressure can change the rocks. It may change them so much that they become a different type of rock.

◀ ***Fig 1*** *The powerful forces that folded these rocks also changed their properties.*

Metamorphic rocks

Rocks that have been altered by heat and pressure are called **metamorphic** rocks. 'Meta' means change and 'morph' means shape.

Limestone becomes marble when it is heated and squeezed by magma. Marble is a white rock with interlocking crystals. It is chemically the same and fizzes with acid like limestone does but it has a new structure. Marble is used to make statues and decorative buildings.

Q1 How is marble different from limestone?

Sandstone contains a lot of the **mineral** called quartz. When heated and squeezed by magma, its grains melt and turn into crystals called quartzite. Quartzite is a very hard rock.

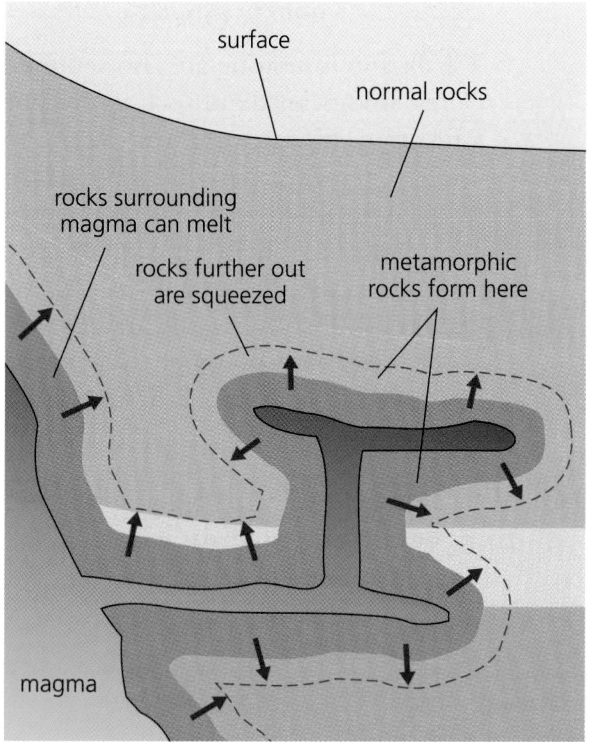

▲ ***Fig 2*** *Some areas where molten magma can alter normal rocks.*

Rocks a long way away from the magma may be only slightly changed by the heat. They may not look very different from the way they were before. A layer of coal might become a little harder and change to coke. This is something we can also do to coal, so it does not involve great heat or force.

High pressure alone can create metamorphic rocks. Mudstone becomes slate when it is compressed. This involves tremendous pressure, such as when the surface of the Earth is folded to make new mountains. Slate is still made of layers, as the mudstone was, but they are thin and hard. This is why slate is good for making roof tiles.

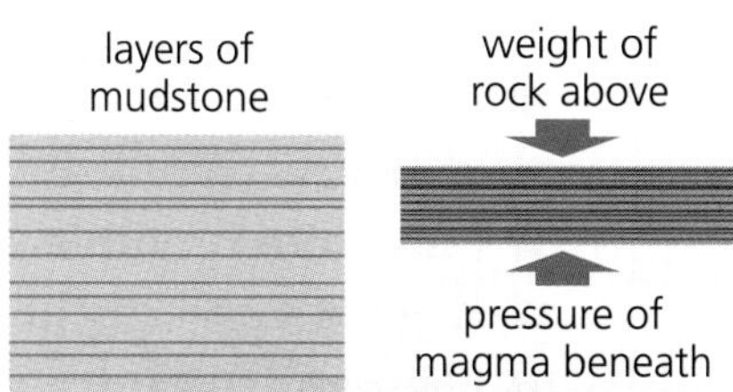

▲ ***Fig 3*** *Layers of mudstone in a great upheaval like Fig 1 may be compressed into slate.*

Q2 Give four examples of metamorphic rocks.

Q3 Which metamorphic rock comes from sandstone?

The rock cycle

Igneous, sedimentary and metamorphic rocks are all connected together in the **rock cycle**. Sedimentary rocks may take millions of years to form. Igneous rocks can form quickly, especially if they erupt out of a volcano. Metamorphic rocks are made wherever and whenever igneous rocks are forming. The whole cycle takes millions of years. The solid rocks that miners cut through to get our coal were fragments floating in a shallow sea more than 300 million years ago.

Why is it called a cycle? Igneous, metamorphic and sedimentary rocks are forming and being weathered all the time. New mountains are made and then eroded, sending new sediments into the sea. These sediments are hardening into rock that may be pushed up to create new mountain chains. Sea shells are often found in desert rocks, which isn't very surprising. But they are also found in the rocks at the top of Mount Everest. All these rocks were once beneath the sea.

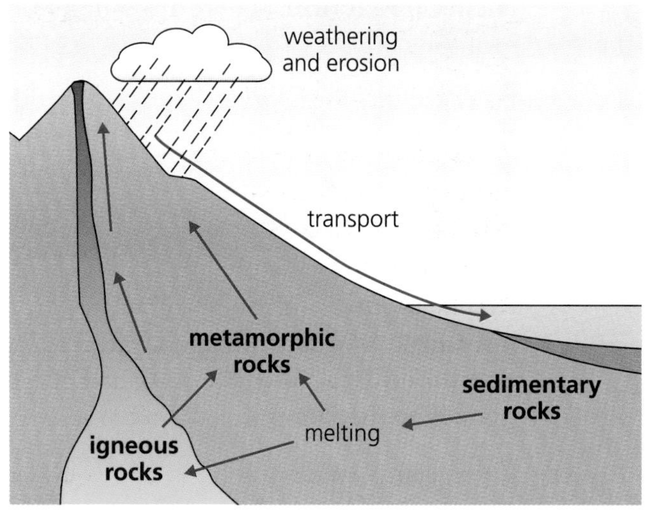

▲ ***Fig 4*** *The rock cycle.*

Key Words

metamorphic rock – rock changed by heat or pressure

rock cycle – the repeated breaking and building of rocks

SUMMARY

- Heat and pressure can change one type of rock into another.
- Rocks changed by heat and/or pressure are called metamorphic rocks.
- Marble and quartzite are formed by great heat.
- Slate is formed by great pressure.
- All rocks are connected. They form the rock cycle.

SUMMARY *Activity*

Write a short story to describe how a particle of granite from a mountain becomes a grain of sand in the sea and then a quartzite slab in a quarry.

60 Chemical changes

In this section of the book you will learn the following things:

- **that new chemicals are made when chemical reactions happen;**
- **that atoms combine in new arrangements when reactions happen;**
- **that no matter is lost or gained during chemical reactions.**

The change from water to ice is a physical change. It can easily be reversed. Many everyday changes cannot easily be reversed. Burned paper cannot be unburned. This is a permanant change. New substances have been made. This is an example of a chemical change.

▶ ***Fig 1*** *The match will not reappear after it has cooled down. Burning is a chemical reaction.*

Chemical reactions

A chemical change is a permanent change. New substances are made by a chemical **reaction**. There are different types of chemical reaction. Some examples are:

- iron and steel rusting;
- sulphur burning in air;
- limestone fizzing in acid.

Q1 Name two examples of chemical changes not given here.

Chemicals that react together in a reaction are called **reactants**. The new chemicals created are called the **products**.

All chemicals are made up of atoms. In a chemical reaction, atoms are rearranged into new patterns. Atoms are never broken down during chemical reactions (Unit 43). If we look at what happens when sulphur burns we can see where the atoms go.

If you start out with 100 grams of sulphur and then burn half of it you will have 50 grams of sulphur left. Where does the other half go? It may seem that the chemical reaction made half of the sulphur disappear. If this was possible then you would have performed a magic trick.

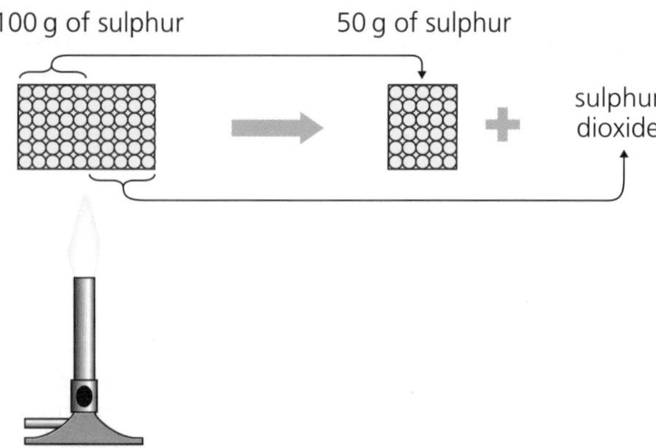

▲ ***Fig 2*** *The sulphur seems to disappear as it burns.*

Conservation of mass

Atoms cannot be destroyed by a chemical reaction. The missing sulphur must therefore still exist somewhere.

Before the experiment began all the sulphur atoms were packed together into a solid. When the sulphur burned, it reacted with oxygen in the air. A new chemical called sulphur dioxide was made. Each atom of sulphur joined with two atoms of oxygen from the air to make a gas called sulphur dioxide. Because sulphur dioxide is a gas, it spread into the air. If you could collect all the sulphur dioxide gas you would find that it contained exactly 50 grams of sulphur.

Sulphur atoms cannot be destroyed. The mass of sulphur stays the same throughout the experiment. It simply goes somewhere else.

Q2 Where are the missing sulphur atoms?

Magnesium metal burns with a very bright flame. If we burn the magnesium inside a covered pot then we can measure any change in mass during the experiment. This experiment is shown in Fig 3.

If we start with 24 grams of magnesium we end up with 40 grams of powder. The mass of magnesium is not reduced by burning. On the contrary, it is increased. Have we done a magic trick? No, we cannot create or destroy atoms. The increase in mass occurred because the magnesium atoms joined with oxygen atoms from the air. The extra mass is the mass of the oxygen atoms that were added to the magnesium.

During chemical reactions matter is not created or destroyed. The atoms are rearranged to make new substances.

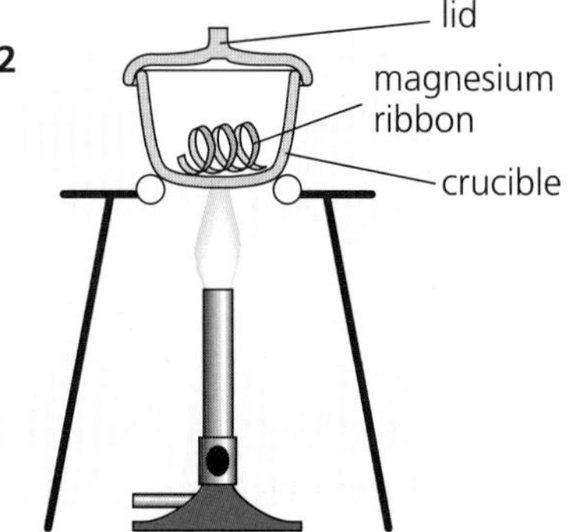

▲ ***Fig 3*** *⚠ Never watch magnesium burning. The bright light can damage your eyes.*

Q3 Why does charcoal have a smaller mass than the wood it is made from?

Key Words

product – a substance produced by a chemical reaction

reactant – a substance changed by a chemical reaction

reaction – the point when a chemical change occurs

SUMMARY

- Chemical reactions cause permanent changes.
- Chemical reactions create new chemicals.
- Matter is neither created nor destroyed during chemical reactions.
- Some chemical reactions create gases which diffuse into the air.
- Some chemical reactions combine gases into solids.
- The mass of the products is the sum of the mass of the reactants.

SUMMARY *Activity*

Explain where all the atoms go when a match burns.

61 Important new chemicals

In this section of the book you will learn the following things:

- **that many important chemicals are made by chemical reactions;**
- **that many industries depend on chemical reactions;**
- **that chemical reactions also take place in living things.**

There are fewer than 100 natural chemical elements. There are more than a million known chemical compounds. Chemical compounds are made by combining atoms of elements. Most of the chemicals that we find and use on Earth must be created by chemical reactions.

Ammonia

Fertilisers are often added to soils to make them more fertile. They may come from natural sources such as animals or plants or be made in factories. One chemical that is important for making fertilisers is a gas called ammonia. This gas occurs naturally. It is also made in very large amounts by chemical reaction in a factory. As well as helping to make fertilisers, ammonia is used to make cleaning materials, plastics and nitric acid.

Ammonia molecules are made of nitrogen atoms and hydrogen atoms. In a factory, these elements are mixed together and heated under high pressure. Each nitrogen atom combines with three hydrogen atoms (Fig 1). This is called a **synthesis** reaction because a new chemical is made by joining other chemicals together.

Q1 Name as many uses for ammonia as you can.

Q2 Look at Fig 1 and try to write down the chemical formula for ammonia. *Hint:* check back to Unit 46.

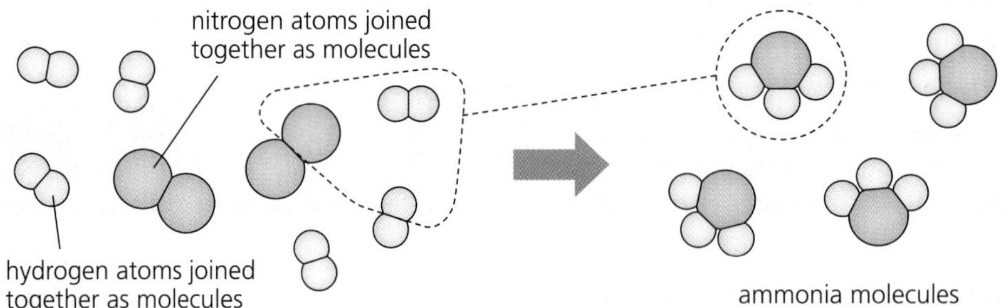

▲ *Fig 1*

Lime

Lime is the common name for the chemical called calcium oxide. This chemical is needed to make cement. It also helps to make water or soil less acid. Lime is made from limestone. The chemical name for limestone is calcium carbonate. Limestone (calcium carbonate) is turned into lime (calcium oxide) by heating it in an oven or kiln until the molecules split into smaller ones. The smaller molecules are calcium oxide (lime) and carbon dioxide gas. This type of reaction is called a **decomposition** reaction because new chemicals are made by breaking another chemical down.

▶ ***Fig 2*** *Millions of tonnes of limestone are quarried for roads and to make lime.*

Q3 What is the difference between a synthesis reaction and a decomposition reaction?

Living things and chemical reactions

Your body is a giant factory carrying out hundreds of chemical reactions. Chemical reactions are essential to life. Plants use energy from the Sun to **synthesise** glucose from water and carbon dioxide (Unit 23). Animals and plants get that energy back by respiration.

Industry can use very high temperatures to make reactions go faster. These high temperatures would kill living things. Living things use enzymes instead of heat to speed up chemical reactions so that they do not need high temperatures. Enzymes are **catalysts**. Industry also uses catalysts to help chemical reactions. The production of ammonia (Fig 1) is speeded up by having iron as a catalyst.

Q4 When your body breaks down food to get energy is this a synthesis or a decomposition reaction?

▶ ***Fig 3*** *Everything in this picture – all the plants, animals, buildings and vehicles – came from chemical reactions.*

Key Words

catalyst – a substance that helps a chemical reaction without becoming a product

decomposition – breaking down

synthesis – building up

synthesise – make or build

SUMMARY

- Everything on Earth is made by combining 92 natural elements.
- Two main types of reaction are synthesis and decomposition.
- Ammonia is made by a synthesis reaction.
- Lime is made by a decomposition reaction.
- Chemical reactions make all living things survive and grow.

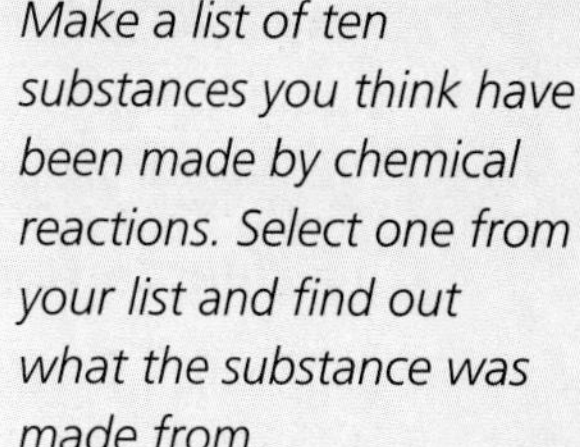

SUMMARY *Activity*

Make a list of ten substances you think have been made by chemical reactions. Select one from your list and find out what the substance was made from.

62 Word equations

In this section of the book you will learn the following things:

- **that chemical reactions can be written down in a shorthand form called an equation;**
- **that there are rules for writing down equations;**
- **some more examples of important reactants and products.**

The names of elements and compounds can be written in a shorthand way (Units 44 and 46). This is also true for chemical reactions. The shorthand way of writing down a chemical reaction is called an **equation**. We shall begin by using the full names of the chemicals. This is called a word equation.

Word equations

A word equation is like a short sentence that summarises a chemical reaction. Some of the words from the sentence are changed into symbols to save space. Fig 1 shows the main symbols used and what they mean.

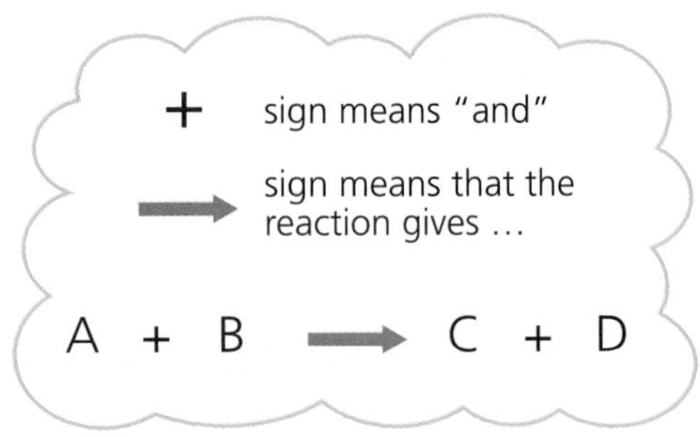

+ sign means "and"
sign means that the reaction gives ...
A + B → C + D

▶ ***Fig 1*** *Chemicals A and B were added together and a reaction happened. The reaction gave two new chemicals, C and D.*

Q1 Which chemicals in Fig 1 were the reactants and which were the products?

Some real reactions

Marble is made of calcium carbonate. This reacts with hydrochloric acid to give off carbon dioxide. Carbon dioxide makes the reaction fizzy. The reaction also produces calcium chloride and water. The word equation for this is:

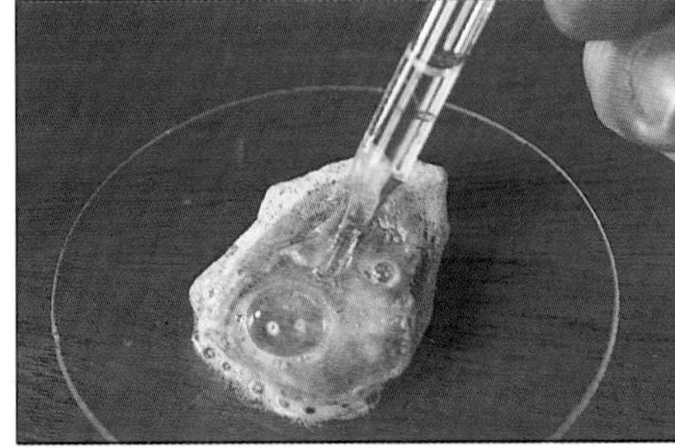

◀ ***Fig 2*** *Acid fizzing on marble.*

calcium carbonate + hydrochloric acid → calcium chloride + water + carbon dioxide

Q2 Hydrochloric acid reacts with magnesium to give magnesium chloride and hydrogen. Write the word equation for this reaction.

The decomposition of limestone was described in Unit 61. The word equation for this reaction would be:

calcium carbonate → calcium oxide + carbon dioxide

This tells us about the reactant and the two products. It does not tell us that the limestone was heated. We can add this information above the arrow. This is where we write information about the **conditions** that are needed to make a reaction happen.

calcium carbonate $\xrightarrow{\text{heat}}$ calcium oxide + carbon dioxide

The word equation for photosynthesis was given in Unit 23. Now we can look at it again and understand what it means.

carbon dioxide + water $\xrightarrow[\text{chlorophyll}]{\text{light}}$ glucose + oxygen

Ammonia is manufactured by combining nitrogen and hydrogen. High temperature, high pressure and a catalyst are needed to make this happen. Refer back to Unit 61 for the name of the catalyst.

Q3 Write down a word equation that shows how ammonia is made from nitrogen and hydrogen.

Reversible

You may see a double arrow in a chemical equation. It looks like this: $\rightleftharpoons$

The double arrow means that a reaction can go either way depending on the conditions. The reaction is **reversible**. In the right conditions the products can react together and change back into the reactants. When ammonium chloride is heated it breaks up into ammonia gas and hydrogen chloride gas. If the mixture of ammonia and hydrogen chloride cool together they combine to make ammonium chloride again.

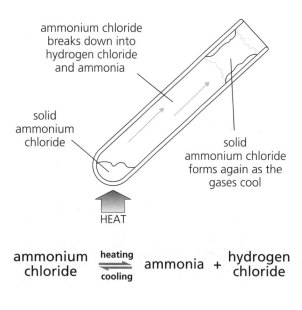

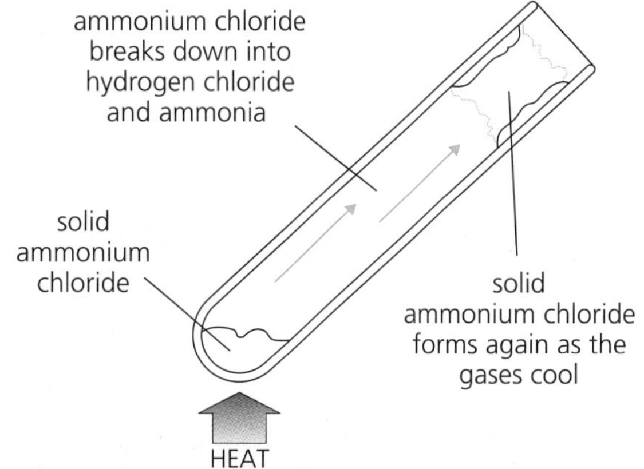
ammonium chloride breaks down into hydrogen chloride and ammonia
solid ammonium chloride
solid ammonium chloride forms again as the gases cool
HEAT

▶ ***Fig 3*** *Ammonium chloride can be made to split into ammonia and hydrogen chloride. This reaction can also go backwards if the mixture cools before the gases fly away.*

ammonium chloride $\underset{\text{cooling}}{\overset{\text{heating}}{\rightleftharpoons}}$ ammonia + hydrogen chloride

Key Words

conditions – extra requirements
equation – a shorthand description for a chemical reaction
reversible – able to go both ways

SUMMARY

- A chemical reaction can be written down as a word equation.
- Word equations show the reactants, the products and the conditions of the reaction.
- Word equations use arrows to show the direction of a reaction.
- An equation with double arrows shows a reversible reaction.

SUMMARY *Activity*

Try to write down a word equation for iron rusting in oxygen to give iron oxide. Use your experience to work out what the necessary conditions might be.

63 Symbol equations

In this section of the book you will learn the following things:

- **that chemical compounds can be represented by symbols;**
- **that the symbols of formulae can be combined into symbol equations.**

Word equations (Unit 62) are a useful shorthand for writing down what happens in a chemical reaction, but they only go so far. To get more useful information we must use **symbol equations**.

Formulae of compounds

When atoms combine or join together they do so in very strict ways. Each atom has the ability to **bond** or join on to a specific number of other atoms. This is called its **valency** or combining power. Some common valencies are given below in Table 1.

Positive ions		Negative ions	
Name	**Symbol and charge**	**Name**	**Symbol and charge**
ammonium	NH_4^+	chloride	Cl^-
sodium	Na^+	hydroxide	OH^-
copper	Cu^{2+}	nitrate	NO_3^-
magnesium	Mg^{2+}	carbonate	CO_3^{2-}
zinc	Zn^{2+}	oxide	O^{2-}
aluminium	Al^{3+}	sulphate	SO_4^{2-}

◀ ***Table 1*** *Valencies.*

There are important rules to follow when writing the formula of a compound.

- Write down the name of the compound. Be careful, some names are very similar.
- Look up the symbols for the chemicals. Use a table of valencies like the one above. Try to remember the most common ones.
- Count the number of positive charges and the number of negative charges on the ions. Compounds do not have an electrical charge so these must eventually balance.
- If you have too many positive charges, you must add more of the negative ions. If you have too many negative ions you must add more of the positive ions.
- Once the charges are balanced you can write down the formula.

Let us see an example worked out for us. The compound is zinc chloride.

Name	zinc	chloride
Symbols	Zn^{2+}	Cl^-

There are more positive charges than negative so we add extra chloride.

$$\begin{array}{ll} Zn^{2+} & Cl^- \\ & Cl^- \\ \hline Zn\,Cl_2 & \end{array}$$

Notice that a small 2 is used to show that there are two chloride atoms for every zinc atom.

Symbol equations

Once you have worked out the formula of each compound NEVER alter it. You can add more or less of the substance in order to balance the equation.

In a chemical reaction matter is not created and it is not destroyed. Therefore, every atom on one side of the equation must be found on the other. So, to write symbol equations you:

- Write down the correct word equation.
- Find the symbol for each atom and work out the formula for each compound.
- Write the formulae and symbols underneath the word equation.
- Balance the equation by making sure that every atom on one side can be found on the other.

For example, if zinc metal is added to hydrochloric acid (hydrogen chloride) it reacts. The products of the reaction are zinc chloride and hydrogen gas. The word equation is:

zinc + hydrochloric acid → zinc chloride + hydrogen

$Zn + HCl \rightarrow ZnCl_2 + H_2$

$Zn + 2HCl \rightarrow ZnCl_2 + H_2$

To balance the equation we needed to make sure we had exactly the same number of atoms on both sides. Notice there are two chlorides in the products but each compound of acid contributes only one. Therefore, we needed to add extra hydrochloric acid. This also helped us to balance the hydrogen, as hydrogen gas is two hydrogen atoms joined together into a molecule.

Q1 Why are brackets sometimes useful in the formulae of compounds?

Q2 Why are symbol equations more useful than word equations?

Q3 Explain what each of the numbers represent in the following compounds.

$3NaOH$ $\quad$ $2FeCl_2$

Al_2O_3 $\quad$ $4H_2SO_4$

Key Words

bond – the link between one atom and another

symbol equations – a shorthand way of writing a chemical reaction that shows the symbols of elements and formulae of compounds involved

valency – the maximum number of bonds an atom can form with other atoms

SUMMARY

- Chemical compounds can be represented by symbols. This is called a formula.
- The symbols of formulae can be used to write symbol equations.
- Symbol equations are specially useful because they tell us how much of each chemical takes part in a reaction.

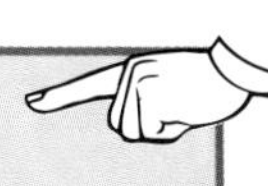

SUMMARY *Activity*

Write word and symbol equations for the following reaction: sodium metal reacting with water to give sodium hydroxide and hydrogen gas.

64 Extracting metals from ores

In this section of the book you will learn the following things:

- that most metals are too reactive to exist naturally on their own;
- that many metals occur naturally as ores;
- that many metal ores are oxides;
- that many pure metals can be separated from from metal oxides by chemical reactions but some cannot.

A few metals do not react easily with oxygen. Gold and silver are unreactive metals. They can be found in the ground as pure metal. This is not true for most other metals. Metals are normally found as **ores**. Ores are metals combined with other elements. If we want to get a pure metal, we need to dig its ore out of the ground and separate it from other elements in the ore.

▲ ***Fig 1*** *Iron comes from iron ore dug out of a quarry.*

Metal ores

Metal	Common name of the ore	Chemical name of the ore	Method of extraction
copper	copper pyrites	copper iron sulphide	chemical reaction
aluminium	bauxite	aluminium oxide	electricity
iron	haematite	iron oxide	chemical reaction
tin	cassiterite	tin oxide	chemical reaction

Many metal ores are oxides. Some common ores are shown in Table 1.

◄ ***Table 1*** *Some metals and their ores.*

Many metals are extracted from their ores by reduction (see Unit 65). When carbon powder is heated with lead oxide, the carbon takes the oxygen and becomes carbon dioxide. The lead oxide is reduced to pure lead metal. This can be done in the laboratory. *Caution*: Lead and all its compounds are poisonous. Never experiment with lead at home.

Q1 Why do you think gold and silver were two of the first metals used by humans?

Q2 Write the word equation for the reduction of lead oxide by carbon.

Iron from iron oxide

The iron ore called haematite is rusty red because it contains iron oxide. Pure iron is obtained from crushed haematite by reduction. Many metals react more strongly with oxygen than iron does. Aluminium or magnesium, for example, could be used to take oxygen from iron. These metals are not used because they are too expensive to extract.

Fortunately, carbon can also be used to reduce iron oxide. This reaction requires heat, but the heat can come from the same source as the carbon. This source is coke.

The reduction of iron oxide to iron is done in a **blast furnace**. The burning coke gives off carbon monoxide, and the carbon monoxide reacts with the iron oxide to make iron and carbon dioxide. The word equation for this is:

iron oxide + carbon monoxide → iron + carbon dioxide

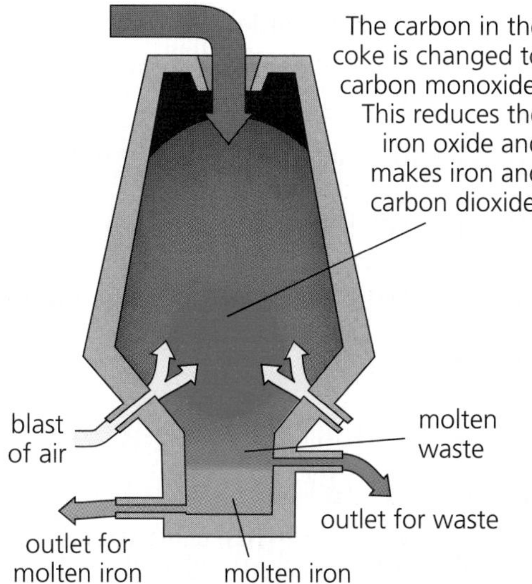

▲ ***Fig 2*** *In a blast furnace, carbon monoxide from burning coke reduces iron oxide to pure iron.*

Aluminium from bauxite

Some metals cling to oxygen very firmly. They cannot be extracted from their ores by simple chemical reactions. Ores containing these metal ores require a great deal of energy to break them down. Electricity can provide this energy. Splitting a chemical with electricity is called **electrolysis**. Aluminium is extracted from its oxide, called bauxite, by electrolysis. It is a very expensive process.

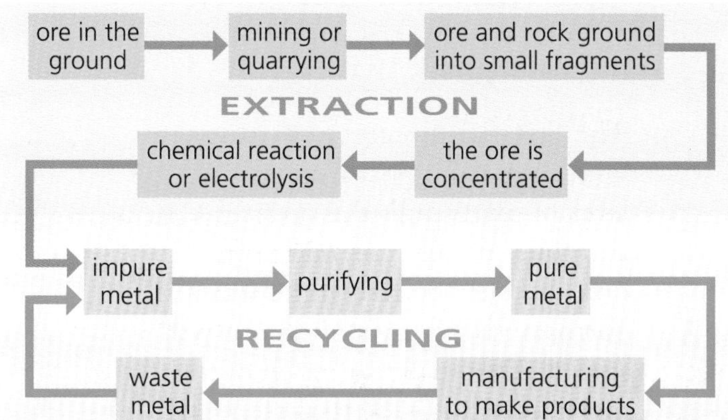

▲ ***Fig 3***

Q3 Name two metals that are extracted by heating them with carbon.

Q4 What do you think would happen if you tried to use carbon to extract magnesium from magnesium oxide? Why?

Q5 Why does it make sense to recycle aluminium cans?

Key Words

blast furnace – a furnace for extracting iron from iron ore

electrolysis – splitting chemicals with electricity

ore – a natural metal compound

SUMMARY

- Most metals are found combined with other elements.
- The less reactive metals can be extracted by chemical reactions.
- Metals are extracted from their oxides by reduction.
- Iron is reduced from iron ore in a blast furnace.
- Very reactive metals are extracted with electricity. This is called electrolysis.

SUMMARY *Activity*

Chromium metal is obtained by heating chromium oxide with aluminium. Write a word equation for this reaction and say which chemicals are oxidised and which are reduced.

65 Corrosion and spoilage

In this section of the book you will learn the following things:

- that some chemical reactions can cause problems;
- that corrosion can damage metals;
- that rusting is an example of oxidation;
- that food spoilage is often due to chemical reactions.

Chemical reactions keep living things alive and help us to extract useful metals from ores. We find these chemical reactions convenient. Some chemical reactions are less convenient.

▲ ***Fig 1*** *The chemical reactions inside a battery make it work. They can also destroy it.*

Corrosion

We know that most metals react easily with oxygen (Unit 64). After a metal has been extracted and purified it gradually reacts with oxygen in the air to become an oxide again. This is called **corrosion**. Metal corrosion is destructive. It costs people and industries in the UK around 6 billion pounds per year. Water speeds up the rate of metal corrosion, especially in the presence of heat, acid or salt. Rust is a perfect example. Rust is iron oxide (see Fig 2). Iron rusts when it gets wet. This happens more quickly in warm weather, and most quickly of all when the water is also salty or acid.

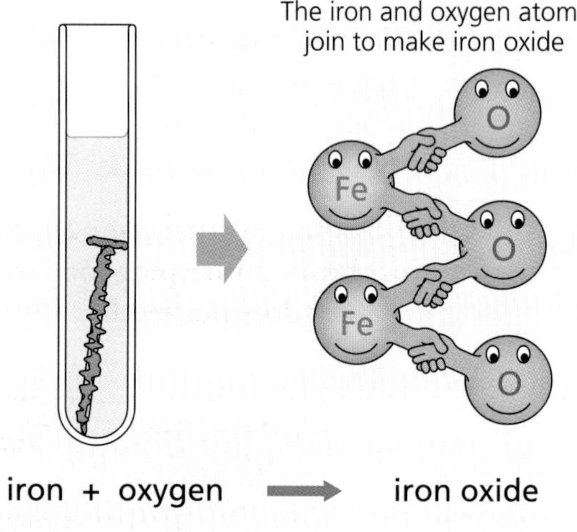
The iron and oxygen atoms join to make iron oxide
O
Fe
O
Fe
O
iron + oxygen → iron oxide

▲ ***Fig 2***

Q1 Why is corrosion a bigger problem now than it was in the Stone Age?

Q2 Why do cars last longer in hot, dry countries than cold, wet ones?

The first visible sign of corrosion is when a metal object loses its shine. A layer of oxide dulls the surface. Cracks and holes usually corrode more quickly than the rest of the metal. If corrosion is not treated then it will spread. Eventually so much of the metal turns to oxide that the metal object may break.

▲ ***Fig 3*** *Rust has been allowed to spread and weaken the metal. Holes are appearing.*

Preventing rust

Many different methods are used to protect iron from rusting.

- Covering the iron with paint or oil can prevent air and water from reaching it.
- Coating the iron with a more reactive metal can protect the surface in a different way. The reactive metal forms a very stable oxide which protects it from further attack. Zinc is often used to coat iron. Iron covered with zinc is called **galvanised** iron.
- Mixing the iron with another metal can make an alloy that does not rust as easily as pure iron. Stainless steel is made by adding chromium to iron.

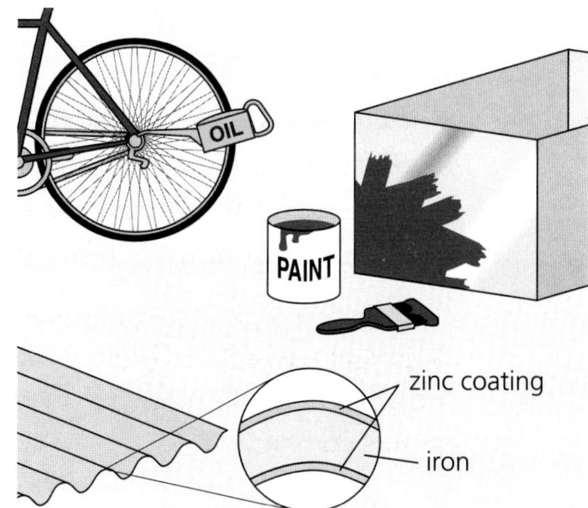

▲ ***Fig 4*** *These are some of the ways in which rusting can be prevented.*

Q3 Why could corrosion also be called oxidation?

Oxidation and reduction

When a chemical joins with oxygen during a chemical reaction we say that it has been **oxidised.** If a chemical loses oxygen during a chemical reaction we say that it is **reduced**.

- When a chemical gains oxygen it is oxidised.
- When a chemical loses oxygen it is reduced.

Food spoilage

Bacteria or other micro-organisms can make food unpleasant or poisonous to eat. The poisons are often waste products excreted by micro-organisms when they feed. Food spoilage is not always due to micro-organisms. The enzymes in animal and plant cells also cause them to break down. When the chemicals in dead animals and plants go on working without the organisation of life the chemical reactions go wrong. Food spoilage is an example of chemical changes in food that we do not welcome.

Q4 How many methods can you think of for keeping food so that it does not spoil?

Key Words

corrosion – destruction of a metal due to oxidation
galvanised – iron coated with a thin layer of zinc
oxidised – combined with oxygen
reduced – having oxygen taken away

SUMMARY

- Some chemical reactions cause problems.
- Metals corrode by reacting with oxygen from the air.
- When a chemical gains oxygen it is oxidised.
- When a chemical loses oxygen it is reduced.
- Corrosion can be prevented by preventing oxygen and water from reaching the metal.
- Food spoilage is caused by chemical reactions, some created by micro-organisms.

SUMMARY *Activity*

Describe some of the ways in which a bicycle can be prevented from rusting.

66 Energy from reactions

In this section of the book you will learn the following things:

- that energy is transferred during chemical reactions;
- that this energy can be controlled and used;
- that burning fuels gives us energy we can use.

When methane gas burns we can see a number of changes. The gas flame is hot and blue. This means that when methane burns it gives out heat and light. We use the heat to cook food or keep us warm. The chemical reaction also changes methane gas into carbon dioxide and water. Chemicals that react with oxygen to give out heat are called **fuels**.

◀ ***Fig 1*** *Fuels give out heat and light when they burn.*

Energy in and energy out

The word equation for burning methane is:

methane + oxygen ⟶ carbon dioxide + water

There is a lot of energy stored in a methane molecule. Molecules of carbon dioxide and water contain less energy than methane molecules. This means that methane contains more energy than it needs to make carbon dioxide and water. The extra energy is released when a molecule of methane breaks down. This is why it burns. This is true for all fuels. Chemical reactions that give out heat are called **exothermic** reactions. We can show this as a chart.

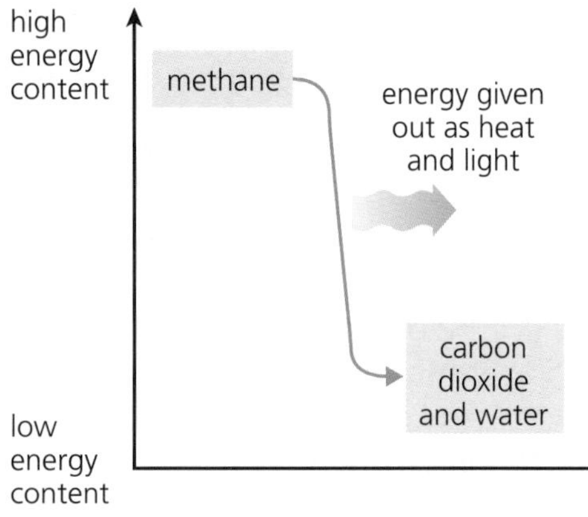

▲ ***Fig 2*** *Energy is released when methane burns. This is an exothermic reaction.*

Other fuels we use are coal, wood, butane, propane, paraffin, petrol and diesel. They provide energy for heating, transport and industry. Energy does not have to be heat or light. It can also be sound, movement and electricity. The chemical reactions in a battery produce electrical energy.

▶ ***Fig 3*** *The massive release of energy from a forest fire can be uncontrollable.*

Q1 Why is the energy contained in fuels so important to us?

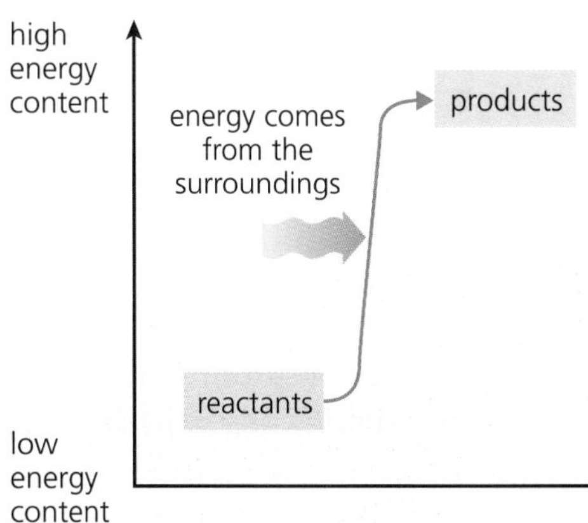

▶ ***Fig 4*** *Fizzing sherbet takes in energy. This is an endothermic reaction.*

A sherbet sweet is fizzy because of a chemical reaction that begins when it mixes with moisture. Sherbet is a mixture of citric acid and sodium hydrogencarbonate. When water is added to this mixture, the two chemicals react to release carbon dioxide. You may also notice that fizzing sherbet makes your mouth feel cold. This because the chemical reaction needs heat. It takes the heat from your mouth. Reactions that require heat are called **endothermic** reactions.

citric acid + sodium hydrogencarbonate ➡ sodium citrate + carbon dioxide + water

Q2 Give an example of an exothermic reaction from Unit 63.

Q3 Why does fizzing sherbet make your mouth feel cold?

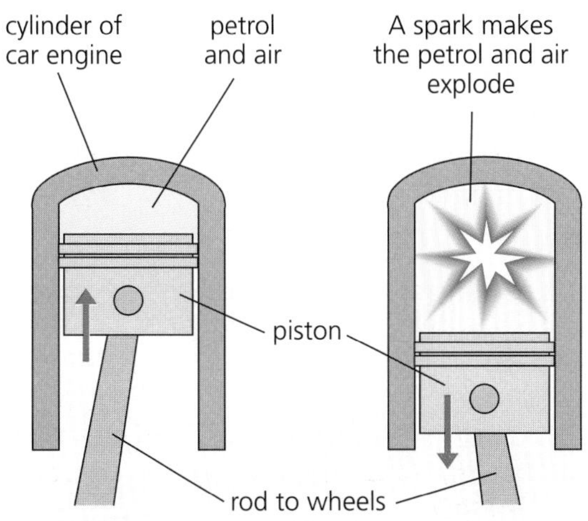

▲ ***Fig 5*** *Chemical energy harnessed in a car engine to drive the wheels.*

Fuels and engines

If we want to use energy for any kind of work we need to be able to control the way it is released. Petrol burns in air very quickly. The energy is rapidly lost as heat, light and sound. If we trap some petrol and air in a cylinder and then add a spark, there will be an explosion. In a petrol engine, this explosion moves a piston. The moving piston turns a rod which eventually turns a wheel. In this way, the chemical energy in the petrol is changed to movement energy.

Key Words

endothermic – taking in heat
exothermic – giving out heat
fuel – a substance that combines with oxygen to give out heat in a way we can use

SUMMARY

- A chemical reaction that gives out heat is called an exothermic reaction.
- A chemical reaction that takes in heat is called an endothermic reaction.
- Energy is not always released as heat. It may be sound, light, movement or electricity.
- Fuels must be burned under control. Controlled energy release is seen in car engines and central heating.

SUMMARY *Activity*

Make a list of all the different fuels mentioned above. Describe how you have seen them used.

67 Fuels and the environment

In this section of the book you will learn the following things:

- **what the greenhouse effect is;**
- **what global warming means;**
- **what causes acid rain;**
- **how burning fossil fuels can damage the environment.**

▲ ***Fig 1*** *Burning fossil fuels releases five thousand million tonnes of carbon dioxide into the atmosphere every year. This could double by the year 2020.*

Coal comes from prehistoric plants that have been buried for millions of years. Oil comes from dead animals that have also been buried for millions of years. They are called **fossil fuels** because they are the remains of ancient life.

Burning fossil fuels

Burning is a chemical reaction. Burning fuel gives out energy and creates new chemicals.

Fossil fuels contain carbon, hydrogen, nitrogen and sulphur. When fuel is burned, these elements combine with oxygen to make oxides. Carbon oxidises to carbon dioxide and carbon monoxide. Hydrogen oxidises to water. Nitrogen oxidises to nitrogen dioxide. Sulphur oxidises to sulphur dioxide.

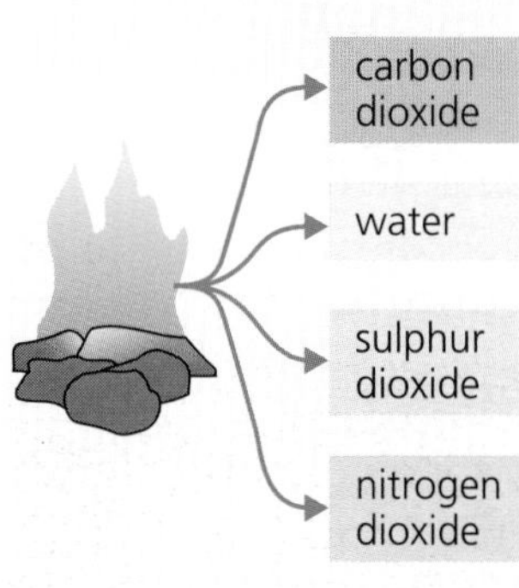

▲ ***Fig 2*** *Some of the gases created when coal burns.*

The greenhouse effect

The sunny side of the Moon is baking hot. The dark side is freezing cold. This is because the Moon has no atmosphere. Carbon dioxide in the Earth's atmosphere helps to keep the Earth warm. Some of the daytime heat from the Sun is kept in at night by a blanket of carbon dioxide. This is the **greenhouse effect**.

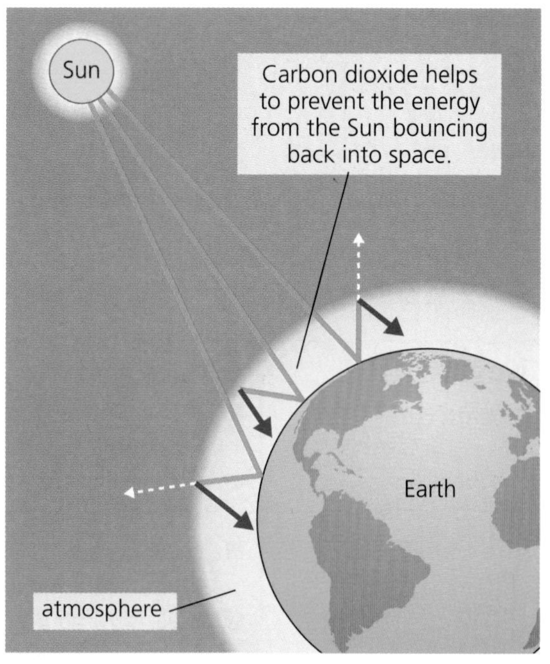

▲ ***Fig 3*** *The greenhouse effect.*

Global warming

Burning a tree that grew recently releases carbon dioxide it removed from the air recently. Burning fossil fuels releases carbon dioxide that has been locked in the ground for millions of years. This extra carbon dioxide increases the greenhouse effect. It makes the Earth warmer.

The Earth has become 2°C warmer in the last 100 years. This is evidence for the theory of **global warming**. Burning fossil fuels has also increased during this time. It is increasing all the time. If the temperature rises higher the Polar ice could melt and make sea levels rise. There will be less dry land to live on and grow food on.

Acid rain

The oxides produced when fuels burn include some acid gases. Two of them are sulphur dioxide and nitrogen dioxide. An acid gas mixed with water is an acid. Clouds and rain are water. When acid gases from chimneys and exhaust pipes enter clouds they make acid. When it rains, acid gas falls from acid clouds. Carbon dioxide is a normal part of the air. It is also an acid gas so rainwater is normally slightly acid.

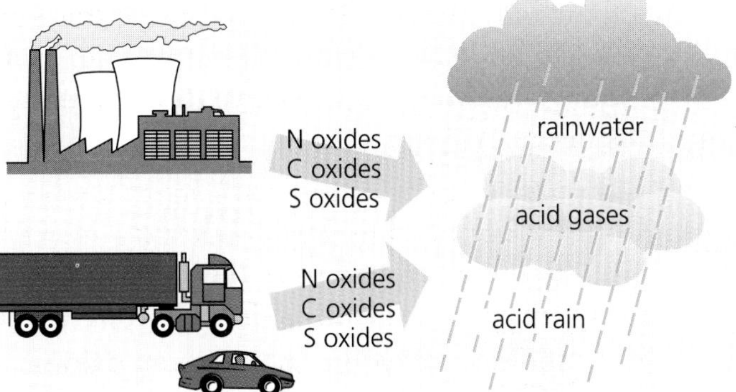

▲ ***Fig 4*** *Acid rain damages buildings, pollutes water and poisons forest trees.*

Q1 Name three chemicals produced when oil burns.

Q2 How does carbon dioxide help to cause global warming?

Q3 Why is acid rain an international problem?

Acid rainwater falls on the soil and runs into streams, lakes and the sea. Some lakes in Sweden now contain so much acid that nothing can live there. Some of the acid that rains on Sweden comes from factories and cars in the UK. Air pollution and **acid rain** are international problems.

► ***Fig 5*** *Nobody knows exactly how acid rain damages trees. All we know is that trees die where strongly acid rain falls.*

Key Words

acid rain – rainwater that is more acid than normal

global warming – an increase in the Earth's average temperature

greenhouse effect – how carbon dioxide keeps the Earth warm

pollute – spoil by adding a damaging substance

SUMMARY

- The gases produced by burning fossil fuels damage our environment.
- Extra carbon dioxide from burning fossil fuels can raise the Earth's temperature.
- Gases made by burning fossil fuels increase the normal acidity of rainwater.
- Acid rain can damage buildings, **pollute** water and kill wildlife.
- Gases produced by burning fossil fuels spread around the world.

SUMMARY *Activity*

Describe some ways in which people might be able to change their lifestyles to burn less fossil fuel. Remember that many industrial processes burn fossil fuels and that many of the things we use are made this way.

68 The reactions of metals

In this section of the book you will learn the following things:

- **how metals react with oxygen;**
- **how metals react with water and acids.**

Some metals are very unreactive. Gold stays shiny for thousands of years. If all metals were this unreactive we would not have to worry about rusting. This is not the case. Most metals are reactive. Some are very reactive indeed.

▲ ***Fig 1*** *Zinc reacts slowly with oxygen at room temperature but quickly forms zinc oxide when it is heated.*

Metals and oxygen

Oxygen is all around us in the air. Most metals react with oxygen to form metal oxides. Here are two examples:

sodium + oxygen ➡ sodium oxide

copper + oxygen ➡ copper oxide

Some metals react with oxygen more quickly than others. Sodium reacts with oxygen as soon as it is exposed to the air. Pure sodium metal is stored under oil to prevent it from oxidising. Some other metals such as zinc, iron and copper react quickly with oxygen when they are heated but only oxidise slowly at room temperature.

The oxides of reactive metals are called **bases**. If a base is soluble in water it makes an **alkaline** solution.

Metals and water

Water is a compound made of the elements hydrogen and oxygen. If a reactive metal is added to water the metal will 'steal' the oxygen. This leaves the hydrogen alone. Hydrogen atoms join up into pairs and fly away as a gas. The word equation for the reaction between magnesium and water is:

magnesium + water ➡ magnesium oxide + hydrogen

Magnesium reacts very slowly with cold water. Only a few bubbles of hydrogen gas would be produced in several days. It reacts very quickly with steam.

Sodium reacts very quickly with water. The sodium is pushed around on the surface of the water by the hydrogen gas released in the reaction. The other product is sodium hydroxide. This makes an alkaline solution. The word equation for this reaction is:

sodium + water ➡ sodium hydroxide + hydrogen

Metals such as gold, copper and silver will not react with water, even if it is heated into steam.

Q1 Write a word equation for zinc reacting with steam.

Metals and acids

Acids contain hydrogen. When a metal reacts with an acid it replaces the hydrogen. This makes a **salt**. The hydrogen is given off as a gas. Not all metals react with acids. We can place metals into a table of reactivity (see Unit 70).

Here are some word equations for metals reacting with acids:

magnesium + hydrochloric acid ⟶ magnesium chloride + hydrogen

zinc + sulphuric acid ⟶ zinc sulphate + hydrogen

calcium + nitric acid ⟶ calcium nitrate + hydrogen

The acids in the examples above are commonly used in laboratories. Notice that each forms a special type of salt.

- Hydrochloric acid forms chlorides.
- Sulphuric acid forms sulphates.
- Nitric acid forms nitrates.

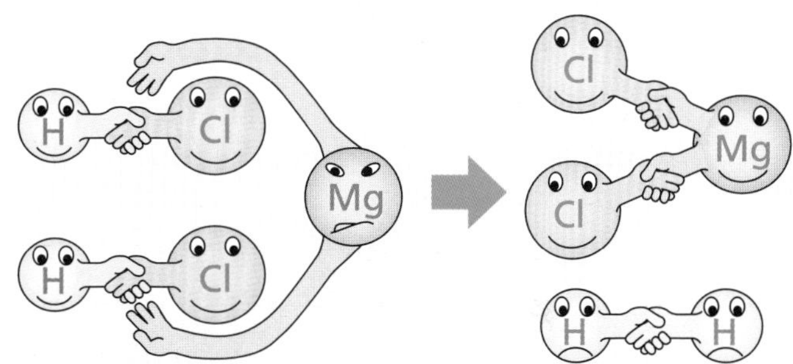

▲ ***Fig 2*** *Magnesium takes the hydrogen from hydrochloric acid to form the salt called magnesium chloride. Hydrogen gas is given off.*

<table>
<tr><th>Metal</th><th>Reaction with oxygen</th><th>Reaction with water</th><th>Reaction with dilute acid</th></tr>
<tr><td>sodium</td><td rowspan="4">burns quickly to form an oxide</td><td rowspan="3">reacts with cold water to give off hydrogen</td><td rowspan="3">reacts quickly with acids to give off hydrogen</td></tr>
<tr><td>calcium</td></tr>
<tr><td>magnesium</td></tr>
<tr><td>aluminium</td><td rowspan="3">reacts with steam to give off hydrogen</td><td rowspan="3">reacts slowly with acids to give off hydrogen</td></tr>
<tr><td>zinc</td><td rowspan="2">burns less quickly to form an oxide</td></tr>
<tr><td>iron</td></tr>
<tr><td>lead</td><td rowspan="2">reacts slowly to form a layer of oxide</td><td rowspan="4">no reaction</td><td>reacts very slowly to give off hydrogen</td></tr>
<tr><td>copper</td><td rowspan="3">no reaction</td></tr>
<tr><td>silver</td><td rowspan="2">no reaction</td></tr>
<tr><td>gold</td></tr>
</table>

Q2 Why is it unsafe to add sodium to an acid?

Q3 How could you make zinc nitrate from zinc metal?

Key Words

alkali – a solution made by dissolving a metal oxide in water

base – oxide or hydroxide of a reactive metal

salt – a compound formed from a metal and an acid

SUMMARY

- Metals react with oxygen to form metal oxides.
- Some metals react with cold or warm water.
- Some metals react with hot steam.
- Metals react with acids to give salts and hydrogen.
- A few metals, such as gold, do not react with oxygen, water or acids.

SUMMARY *Activity*

How could you safely make a pure sample of magnesium chloride from magnesium metal and an acid? Include a word equation.

69 Competition between metals

In this section of the book you will learn the following things:

- **that metals can replace other metals in salts;**
- **that these reactions can be used to make new salts;**
- **that these reactions depend on some metals being more reactive than others.**

Some different chemical reactions have been described in Units 61-68. A displacement reaction is a chemical reaction in which one metal replaces another. Metals displace one another in a regular order.

Metals and solutions

Crystals of copper sulphate are blue. They dissolve in water to make a blue solution. Zinc metal is bluish-grey.

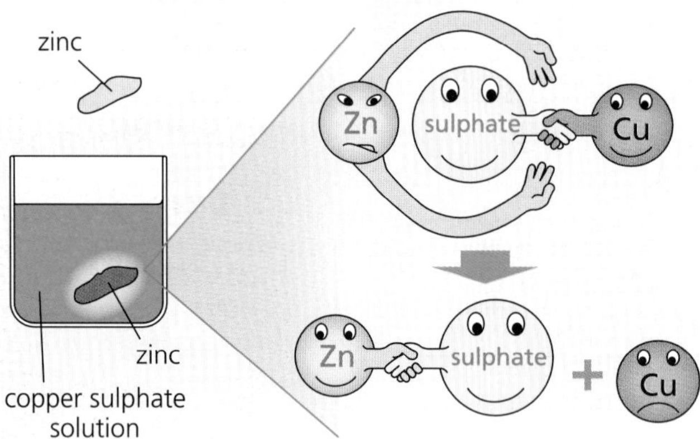

▲ *Fig 1 Zinc displaces copper from copper sulphate.*
⚠ ***Caution:** copper sulphate is poisonous.*

When a lump of zinc is added to copper sulphate solution the blue colour of the solution fades and the zinc becomes darker. This is what we see. We cannot see the chemical reaction between the copper sulphate and the zinc but we can see the result. Zinc has **displaced** the copper. The solution becomes paler because zinc sulphate is not blue. The zinc looks darker because a thin layer of copper forms on its surface.

Q1 What **evidence** is there that zinc has displaced copper in the reaction above?

The word equation for this reaction is

zinc + copper sulphate ➡ zinc sulphate + copper

We can use displacement reactions to make salts we want from salts we already have. If we want some magnesium chloride and we already have some lead chloride and some magnesium, we can make magnesium chloride by putting them together in water. The magnesium will displace the lead and magnesium chloride will be formed.

magnesium + lead chloride ➡ magnesium chloride + lead

Q2 Why is this type of reaction called a displacement reaction?

Competing metals

We cannot make copper from zinc sulphate and zinc, or magnesium from magnesium chloride and lead. A displacement reaction is the result of a competition between two metals. The most **reactive** metal always wins.

Zinc is more reactive than copper and magnesium is more reactive than lead. Zinc holds onto chloride more firmly than copper does. Magnesium holds onto chloride more firmly than lead does.

We can arrange metals into an order of reactivity by comparing them, one by one, to find out which ones displace others from their salts.

Table 1 shows the reactivity for the four metals we have already mentioned. You can see that not all the mixtures result in reactions.

Metal	Solution			
	copper sulphate	zinc chloride	lead chloride	magnesium chloride
copper		no reaction	no reaction	no reaction
zinc	zinc sulphate forms		zinc chloride forms	no reaction
lead	lead sulphate forms	no reaction		no reaction
magnesium	magnesium sulphate forms	magnesium chloride forms	magnesium chloride forms	

▲ *Table 1*

Q3 Which is the most reactive metal, magnesium or zinc?

Q4 Why have we not tested sodium in this way?

Extracting silver

Silver does not oxidise easily, but it reacts with sulphur to make black silver sulphide. Pure silver is extracted from a silver sulphide ore called argentite by replacing it with zinc. Silver sulphide is not soluble in water so it has to be dissolved in cyanide solution first. Then zinc is added to force pure silver out.

▲ ***Fig 2*** *Silver is purified by displacement reactions.*

Table 1 shows that some metals are more reactive than others. This is one way to put them in order. Another way to list metals in order is by finding out how quickly and violently each one reacts with oxygen, water and acids. This league table is called the **Reactivity Series** and it is described in Unit 70.

Key Words

displace – take the place of another element in a chemical compound

evidence – visible sign

reactive – ready to react

Reactivity Series – metals arranged in order of reactivity

SUMMARY

- Reactive metals displace less reactive metals from their salts.
- Displacement reactions can be used to make new salts or to purify metals.
- A league table of reactivity can be based on displacement reactions.
- A similar league table can be based on the way different metals react with oxygen, water and acids.

SUMMARY *Activity*

Draw a diagram to show what happens to molecules of copper chloride in water when pure magnesium is added. Write a word equation underneath.

70 The Reactivity Series of metals

In this section of the book you will learn the following things:

- how the reactions of metals show that some are more reactive than others;
- how metals can be arranged in a league table of reactivity;
- how this table is connected with the methods used to extract or purify some metals.

Copper and gold do not react with water. Water flows into the bath through copper pipes and we can safely wear gold jewellery in the bath. Sodium reacts violently with water. Sodium is more reactive than copper or gold.

▶ ***Fig 1*** *Copper does not react with water. It can safely be used for water pipes and hot-water cylinders.*

The Reactivity Series

Table 1 shows the way some metals react with water. The list of metals is arranged in alphabetical order.

▼ ***Table 1***

Metal	Reactivity in water
aluminium	reacts with steam to give hydrogen
copper	no reaction
gold	no reaction
iron	slowly reacts to give hydrogen in steam
lead	no reaction
potassium	reacts violently with cold water
silver	no reaction
sodium	reacts violently with cold water

most reactive
potassium
sodium
calcium
magnesium
aluminium
zinc
iron
lead
copper
silver
gold
least reactive

▲ ***Fig 2***

Another way of organising the list in Table 1 is to put the most reactive metal at the top and the least reactive at the bottom. The ones in between are arranged by comparing them with one another. This arrangement is shown in Fig 2. Gold is at the bottom and potassium is at the top. This is the **Reactivity Series** of metals.

Q1 Which metals are more reactive than aluminium?

The order of reaction of these metals with oxygen and acids (Table 1 in Unit 68) is exactly the same. Potassium reacts violently with water, oxygen and acids. Gold is the least reactive metal of all.

Reactivity and displacement

The Reactivity Series explains displacement reactions. In Unit 69 you can see that magnesium displaces lead from lead chloride. The reactivity table shows that magnesium is more reactive than lead. This means that it clings to chloride more powerfully than lead does. This also shows why lead cannot displace magnesium from magnesium chloride.

Q2 Can zinc displace sodium from sodium chloride solution?

Hydrogen and carbon

Hydrogen and carbon are not metals but they can also be placed in the Reactivity Series. These elements play an important part in some reactions with metals. It is therefore useful to know where they fit.

- Hydrogen is found in water and all acids. Metals that are more reactive than hydrogen can displace it from water and acids to make **oxides** or **salts**. Metals that are less reactive than hydrogen do not react with water, steam or dilute acids.
- Carbon is used to extract some metals from their ores. Carbon can only displace metals that are less reactive than carbon itself. Iron can be extracted from iron ore with carbon but metals above zinc cannot be extracted with carbon.

<table>
<tr><td>potassium</td><td rowspan="5">metals above carbon cannot be extracted from ores by heating with carbon or carbon monoxide</td><td rowspan="9">metals above hydrogen will displace it from water, steam or dilute acids</td></tr>
<tr><td>sodium</td></tr>
<tr><td>calcium</td></tr>
<tr><td>magnesium</td></tr>
<tr><td>aluminium</td></tr>
<tr><td>carbon</td><td></td></tr>
<tr><td>zinc</td><td rowspan="7">metals below carbon can be extracted from ores by heating with carbon or carbon monoxide</td></tr>
<tr><td>iron</td></tr>
<tr><td>lead</td></tr>
<tr><td>hydrogen</td><td></td></tr>
<tr><td>copper</td><td rowspan="3">metals below hydrogen will not displace it from water, steam or dilute acids</td></tr>
<tr><td>silver</td></tr>
<tr><td>gold</td></tr>
</table>

▶ ***Table 2*** *Hydrogen and carbon are not metals. They are placed in the reactivity series to make it more useful.*

Metals from potassium down to aluminium are more reactive than carbon. They cannot be displaced from their ores by carbon. Metals that can be displaced by carbon include iron, zinc, lead and copper. They are less reactive than carbon itself. This is obviously very important to industry.

Q3 What will happen if silver is added to hydrochloric acid?

Q4 Can carbon be used to extract magnesium from magnesium oxide?

Q5 Why is aluminium more expensive to extract from its ore than iron is?

Key Words

oxide – an element chemically combined with oxygen

Reactivity Series – the league table of metals that shows how reactive each one is

salt – a compound formed when a metal replaces hydrogen in an acid

SUMMARY

- Metals can be arranged into a league table of reactivity called the Reactivity Series.
- The Reactivity Series places the most reactive metals at the top and the least reactive at the bottom.
- In chemical reactions, metals higher in the Reactivity Series displace all the metals below them.
- Hydrogen and carbon are not metals. They are added to the Reactivity Series for reference.

SUMMARY *Activity*

Tin is a metal that belongs between iron and lead in the Reactivity Series. How do you think it would react with dilute acids? Could carbon displace tin from tin oxide?

71 Predicting chemical reactions

In this section of the book you will learn the following things:

- **that the Reactivity Series can be used to predict whether a chemical reaction will occur;**
- **that the Reactivity Series can be used to predict the speed of a chemical reaction.**

The Reactivity Series shows that potassium is a very reactive metal. If we add potassium to water we know there will be a violent reaction. The Reactivity Series is already helping us to **predict** what is going to happen. We can also use it to predict the way other reactions will go.

Predicting reactions

Carbon powder and lead oxide react together when they are mixed up and heated. Look at the Reactivity Series in Unit 70 to find out what the reaction will be. Carbon comes above lead in the Reactivity Series. It should therefore displace lead. This is exactly what happens.

$$\text{Lead oxide + carbon} \xrightarrow{\text{heat}} \text{lead + carbon dioxide}$$

▲ ***Fig 1*** *Lead oxide and carbon heated together produce lead and carbon dioxide.* ⚠ ***Caution:*** *Lead is poisonous to swallow or inhale.*

Q1 What type of chemical reaction (apart from displacement) occurs when carbon displaces lead?

Predicting speed

▲ ***Fig 2*** *Potassium reacts violently with water. It is useful to know in advance when an experiment might be violent.*

Calcium fizzes or **effervesces** gently in water as hydrogen gas is produced. The water becomes warm. Potassium comes above calcium in the Reactivity Series. It should therefore react more violently with water. Potassium reacts so violently with water that the hydrogen bursts into flames.

The distance between two metals in the series gives us another way of predicting the result of an experiment. Lead is only slightly more reactive than copper. Reactions between copper and lead compounds do not go very fast.

When copper oxide and powdered lead are heated together the lead displaces the copper and takes the oxygen to produce lead oxide. Because there is not much difference in reactivity between these two metals the reaction is slow and very gentle.

When magnesium powder is heated with copper oxide the reaction is violent. Magnesium is much more reactive than copper. It snatches the oxygen very quickly. Once this reaction starts it goes like a firework.

Q2 Write the word equation for the reaction between copper oxide and lead.

Q3 Write a word equation for a more violent reaction between a metal and a metal oxide than magnesium reacting with copper oxide.

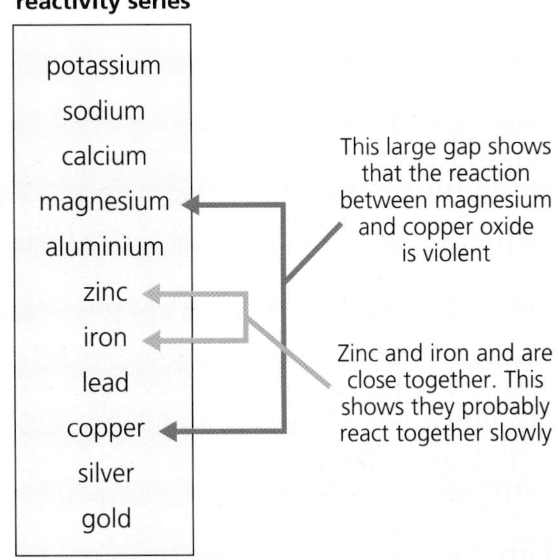
reactivity series
potassium
sodium
calcium
magnesium
aluminium
zinc
iron
lead
copper
silver
gold
This large gap shows that the reaction between magnesium and copper oxide is violent
Zinc and iron and are close together. This shows they probably react together slowly

▲ ***Fig 3*** *A small gap between metals gives a slow reaction between their compounds. A large gap can give a violent reaction.*

The Reactivity Series can also tell us how **stable** a chemical is likely to be. Metals higher in the Reactivity Series form compounds very easily because they hold onto other chemicals very firmly. Once they are part of a compound they are very difficult to remove. The compound is hard to **decompose**.

Copper carbonate breaks down into copper oxide and carbon dioxide very easily when it is heated. Potassium is higher in the Reactivity Series. Potassium carbonate cannot be decomposed even by very high temperatures.

$$\text{potassium carbonate} \xrightarrow{\text{heat}} \text{no reaction}$$

$$\text{copper carbonate} \xrightarrow{\text{heat}} \text{copper oxide + carbon dioxide}$$

Q4 Why does the process for making lime from calcium carbonate (Unit 61) need a lot of heat?

Key Words

decompose – to break down into smaller parts
effervesce – fizz with gas bubbles
predict – to know or guess in advance
stable – not easily changed or broken

SUMMARY

- The Reactivity Series can help us to predict whether a reaction will take place.
- The Reactivity Series can helps us to predict how easy or violent a reaction will be.
- The higher up the series a metal is the more reactive it is.
- Metals far apart in the series displace one another more violently than metals closer together.
- The Reactivity Series can also help to predict how stable the compounds of a metal may be.

SUMMARY *Activity*

Why do metals that react violently form stable compounds? Think of as many examples as you can, including food and biology.

72 Acids around us

In this section of the book you will learn the following things:

- that acids are important to all living things;
- the names of some common acids;
- that there are strong acids and weak acids.

▲ *Fig 1 Ants use acid to defend themselves.*

Natural acids

Ants make an acid called formic acid. Its name comes from *Formica*, which is the Latin name for ant. They squirt this acid at their enemies. Some ants can also bite, which allows the acid to get under your skin. Formic acid can be used to remove **scale** from kettles and pans.

◄ *Fig 2 Pickling was once a very important way to preserve vegetables.*

Vinegar contains a natural acid called ethanoic acid. Before refrigeration was invented pickling was one of the most important methods of preserving food, especially vegetables. Living things are sensitive to acids. Pickling food in vinegar helps to **preserve** it by destroying micro-organisms. It also helps to prevent chemicals in the food combining with oxygen, which might spoil the food. We also **pickle** vegetables and add vinegar to foods such as chips because we enjoy the flavour.

Q1 What is the name of the acid that ants make?

Q2 How does pickling food help to preserve it?

The hydrochloric acid in your stomach helps enzymes to digest proteins (see Unit 7). Citric acid in fruit helps to prevent oxidation. Many fruits contain acids. These acids are often named after the fruit. You may find ascorbic acid named on food labels. This is Vitamin C. It is mainly added to food as a preservative. Preservatives that prevent oxidation are called **antioxidants**.

Acid	Where found	uses
citric acid	lemons, oranges and other citrus fruits	cooking and drinks
formic acid	ants and nettles	cleaning pans
ethanoic acid	vinegar	cooking and preserving food
hydrochloric acid	stomach	digestion and many uses in industry
nitric acid	manufactured from nitrogen gas; in acid rain	in fertilisers and explosives
sulphuric acid	manufactured using nitric acid; in acid rain	fertilisers, batteries, plastics and paints
carbonic acid	rainwater	fizzy drinks

▲ *Fig 3 Some common acids.*

Laboratory acids

The three common laboratory acids are hydrochloric acid, nitric acid and sulphuric acid. They are used for many experiments. They are strong acids that must be handled carefully.

Q3 Write down five safety rules for using acids in the laboratory.

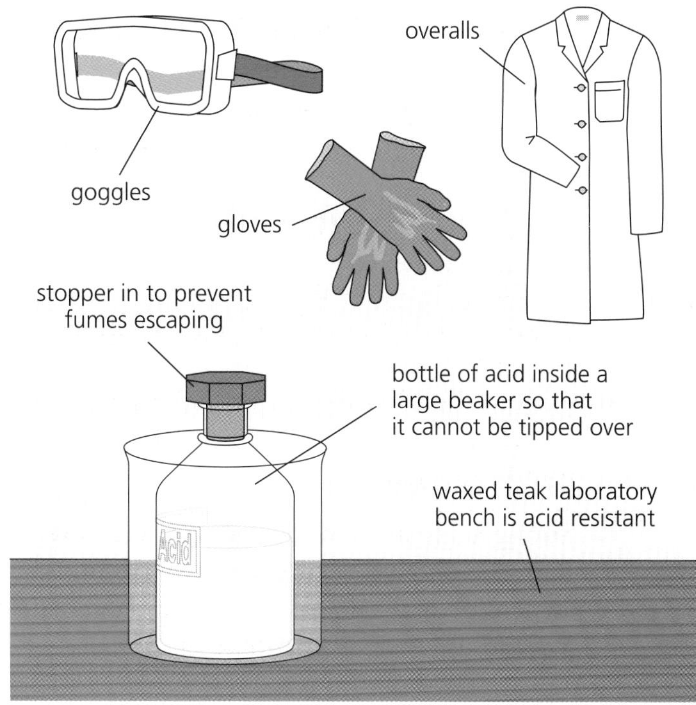

▶ ***Fig 4*** ⚠ *Acids must always be handled with great care.*

Strong and weak acids

The difference between a strong acid and a weak acid is not how **dilute** it is. A strong acid is strongly acid because the hydrogen it contains combines easily with other substances. This is a chemical property. Dilution is a physical property. Strong acids are **corrosive**. Sulphuric acid and nitric acid can corrode metal very quickly. Formic acid can take the scale off a kettle but it does not corrode the kettle.

Q4 How useful would citric acid be for cleaning rusty metal?

Key Words

antioxidant – preventing oxidation
corrosive – able to attack other materials
dilute – mixed with water
preserve – to keep a food in edible condition
pickle – to preserve a food in vinegar
scale – solid calcium carbonate from 'hard' water

SUMMARY

- Some plants and animals make acids for self-defence.
- Acids have many uses, including preserving foods.
- Pickling food in acid helps to preserve the food by killing micro-organisms and preventing oxidation.
- Some acids are strongly acid. Other acids are less strong.
- Strong acids in the laboratory must be handled with care.

SUMMARY *Activity*

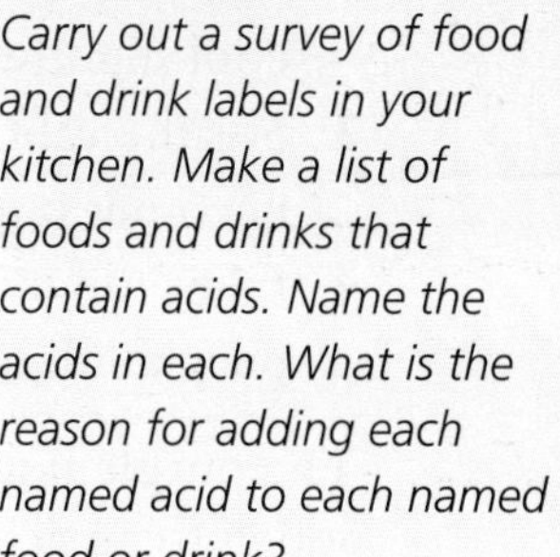

Carry out a survey of food and drink labels in your kitchen. Make a list of foods and drinks that contain acids. Name the acids in each. What is the reason for adding each named acid to each named food or drink?

73 Testing for acids

In this section of the book you will learn the following things:

- **how pH indicators can help us to detect acids;**
- **what the pH number tells us;**
- **how pH indicators can be made from plants.**

Acids and alkalis

Adding oxygen to a metal makes a metal oxide. Many metal oxides will not dissolve in water. They are insoluble. An **alkali** is a solution of a metal oxide in water. An insoluble metal oxide cannot become an alkali. Just as there are strong acids, there are also strong alkalis. Oxides of more reactive metals make stronger alkalis than oxides of less reactive metals.

Indicators

Strong acids and strong alkalis are corrosive. How can we test them without harming ourelves? Luckily there is a simple way to test whether a solution is an acid or an alkali. Some plant juices change colour in different solutions. We can use them as **indicators**.

pH number

Indicators measure acid or alkali on a scale called pH. The full range of pH runs from 1 to 14. Numbers under 7 are acid and numbers above 7 are alkaline. The neutral point is at 7, in the middle.

It is very easy to make a simple pH indicator from red cabbage following the instructions given here.

1. Remove some leaves from a red cabbage and tear them up into small pieces.
2. Add the torn leaves to some water that has been boiled and allowed to cool slightly.
3. Stir the cabbage and water until the water becomes purple with sap from the leaves.
4. Filter the mixture and collect the purple liquid.

The purple liquid is the indicator. If it is added to an acid it will become redder. If it is added to an alkali it will become bluer.

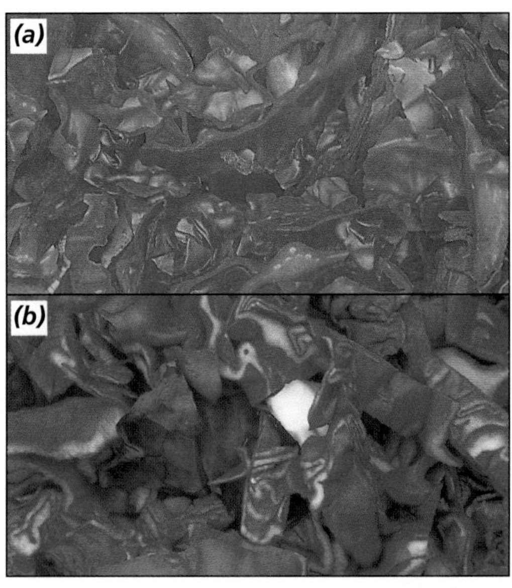

▲ ***Fig 1*** *Red cabbage becomes redder in acid vinegar **(a)** and bluer in alkaline tapwater **(b)**.*

Q1 Why is it dangerous to test acids by tasting them?

Q2 What is a pH indicator and why is it useful?

Red cabbage juice can only tell you whether a solution is an acid or an alkali. Some indicators can tell you how acid or how alkaline a solution is. Some indicators may only work for a small range of pH but can show very tiny differences. These are useful where great accuracy is important.

One very useful indicator is called universal indicator. This is a mixture of indicators that change colour at different points on the pH scale. Universal indicator can show whether something is an alkali or an acid *and* how strong it is.

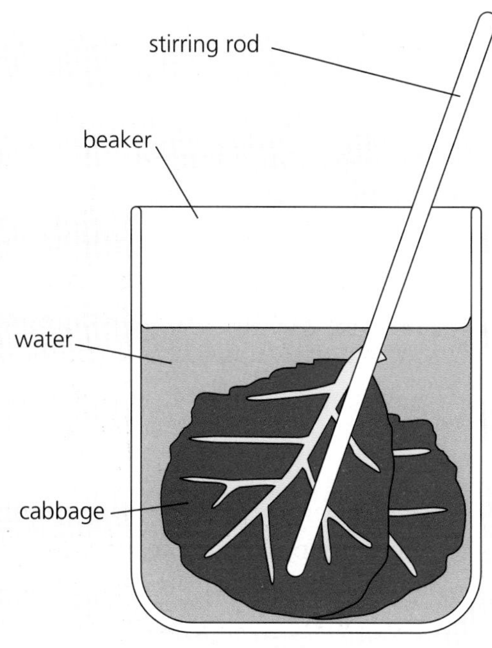

▶ ***Fig 2*** *You can do this at home. The only problem you may have is 'hard' tapwater. Hard water is alkaline so your indicator may start out blue. Boiling the water first can help.*

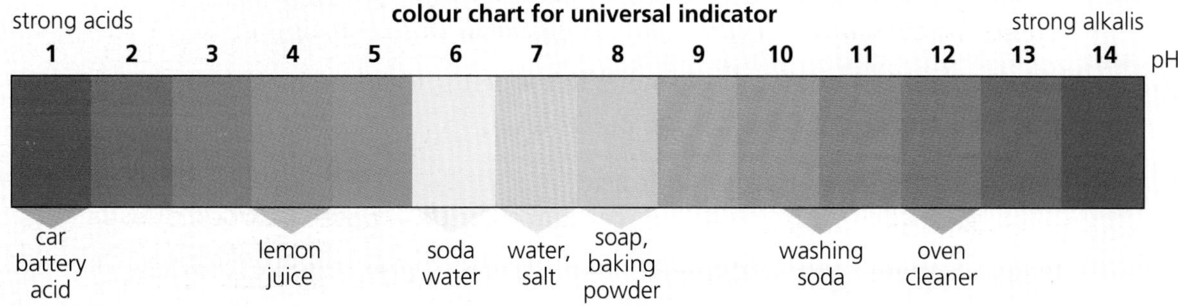

▲ ***Fig 3*** *Using universal indicator is an easy way to measure the pH of any solution.*

Q3 Give the names of two weak acids and two weak alkalis.

Key Words

alkali – a metal oxide dissolved in water

indicator – a chemical that indicates pH

neutral – a solution that is neither acid nor alkaline

pH number – a measurement of acidity or alkalinity

SUMMARY

- An alkali is a solution of a metal oxide in water.
- Alkalis vary in strength.
- The strength of an acid or alkaline solution is measured on a scale called pH.
- Plant juices can be used to test approximate pH.
- A chemical that changes colour in an acid or alkaline solution is called an indicator.
- Universal indicator is a mixture of indicators .
- Each colour of universal indicator corresponds to one number on the pH scale.

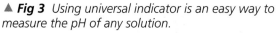

SUMMARY *Activity*

Describe exactly how you would test the pH of the soil in your local park. Would this test be any use to
(a) a gardener;
(b) a forester;
(c) the owner of a nearby factory?

74 Acid reactions

In this section of the book you will learn the following things:

- **that acids react with many things including metals;**
- **how acids react with carbonates;**
- **how caves are made.**

The walls and roof of the cave in Fig 1 are made of limestone. Acids in rainwater have been reacting with the limestone for millions of years. Acidic rain has turned small cracks into large caves. This is a natural example of an acid reaction.

▲ ***Fig 1*** *Acid made this underground cavern.*

Acids and carbonates

Limestone is a chemical compound called calcium carbonate. Other carbonates include copper carbonate and magnesium carbonate. These are called **metal carbonates** because they contain a metal as well as the carbonate. An acid reacts with a carbonate by breaking it down into a salt, water and carbon dioxide gas. The carbon dioxide makes the reaction fizz. This is one way to find out if a substance is a carbonate. The general word equation is:

acid + metal carbonate ➡ metal salt + water + carbon dioxide

Here are some real word equations for acids reacting with metal carbonates:

calcium carbonate + hydrochloric acid
➡ calcium chloride + water + carbon dioxide

lead carbonate + nitric acid ➡ lead nitrate + water + carbon dioxide

Q1 Write a word equation for sulphuric acid reacting with copper carbonate.

The acids in rainwater are very weak. They work very slowly to break limestone down. However, in time the limestone will be attacked. Statues and buildings made of limestone are exposed to extra acid from traffic fumes. Marble is another form of calcium carbonate. It is also slowly broken down by acid rain water. Extra acids in rain make limestone rocks weather more quickly.

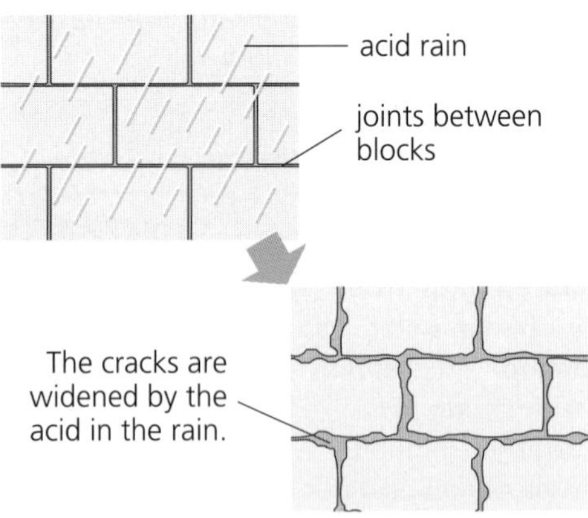
acid rain
joints between blocks
The cracks are widened by the acid in the rain.

▲ ***Fig 2*** *Limestone buildings are vulnerable to attack from acid rain.*

Q2 Why do you think there are there no large caves in sandstone rocks?

An acid will react with a carbonate very well if a soluble salt is produced. Marble chips react with hydrochloric acid to make calcium chloride. Calcium chloride is a soluble salt. It dissolves away and allows the reaction to continue.

If you try the same experiment with sulphuric acid instead of hydrochloric acid the reaction begins in the same way but then it stops. This is because calcium sulphate is insoluble. Instead of dissolving and going away, it stays and makes a protective layer around each chip. This separates the acid from the marble and stops the reaction.

Acids and metal oxides

We have seen how acids react with metals to make salts and hydrogen gas. How do acids react with metal oxides? They do not always react, but when they do react they also make salts. The oxygen in the oxide joins up with the hydrogen in the acid to make water. So instead of visible bubbles of hydrogen we get a little extra water quietly added to the solution.

metal oxide (**base**) + acid → salt + water

copper oxide + sulphuric acid → copper sulphate + water

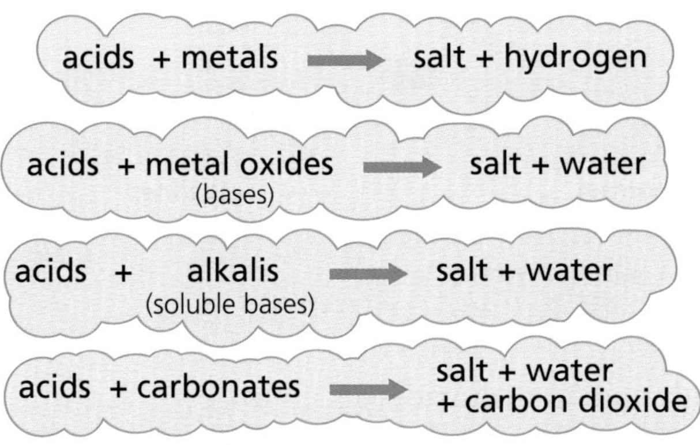

acids + metals → salt + hydrogen
acids + metal oxides (bases) → salt + water
acids + alkalis (soluble bases) → salt + water
acids + carbonates → salt + water + carbon dioxide

▲ ***Fig 3*** *How acids react with four main groups of chemicals. Notice that salts are formed every time. Acid reactions are a very good way to make salts.*

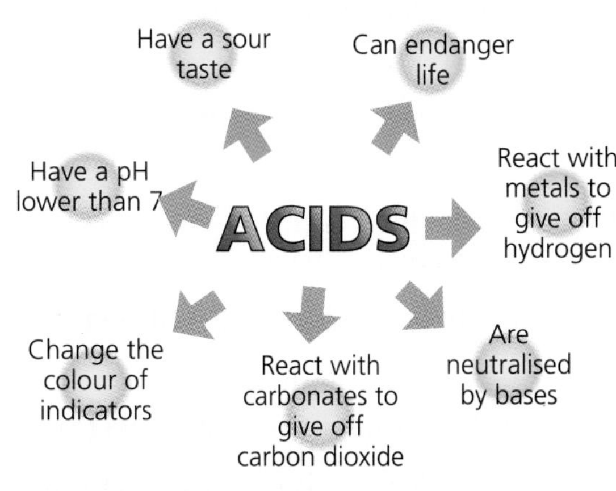

Have a sour taste
Can endanger life

Have a pH lower than 7

▲ ***Fig 4*** *General properties of acids.*

Q3 Why is acid kept in glass bottles and not metal containers?

Q4 What is another name for a metal oxide?

Key Words

base – a metal oxide

metal carbonate – a compound of a metal and a carbonate

SUMMARY

- All metal carbonates react with acids to give a salt, water and carbon dioxide.
- Limestone and marble are calcium carbonate. These rocks react with acids in rain water.
- Acids react with metals and metal oxides to give salts.
- Acids taste sour and have a pH of less than 7.

SUMMARY *Activity*

Use your knowledge of acid reactions to help you to work out three different ways of making copper sulphate.

75 Acids and neutralisation

In this section of the book you will learn the following things:

- **what neutralisation means;**
- **how neutralisation can treat indigestion;**
- **how acid soils can be neutralised.**

If you have been attacked by an angry ant you can take some of the pain away by rubbing calamine lotion or baking soda solution onto the sting. These are weak alkalis. They work by neutralising the acid.

Neutralisation

Adding an alkali to an acid (Fig 1) changes the pH. Testing the solution with an indicator before and afterwards shows that the pH has been raised. If we do this carefully we can stop adding alkali at the exact point when the pH is 7. The solution is then neutral. This is **neutralisation**.

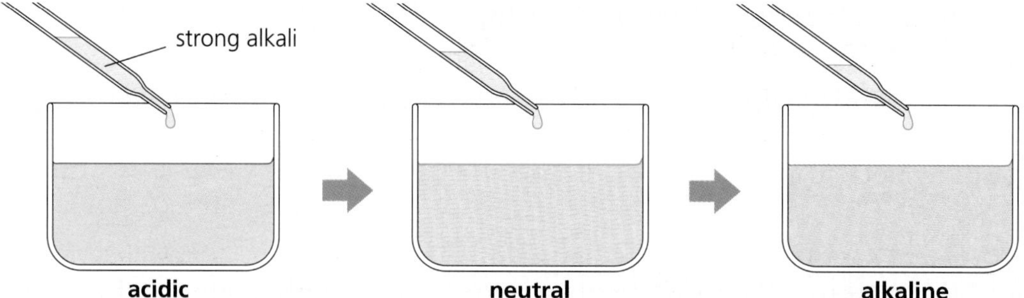

▲ *Fig 1*

The chemistry of neutralisation produces a salt and water.

acid + alkali ➡ salt + water

For example, hydrochloric acid reacts with sodium hydroxide (alkali) to make sodium chloride (table salt) and water:

hydrochloric acid + sodium hydroxide ➡ sodium chloride + water

Q1 Nettle-stings contain formic acid. What would you rub on a nettle-sting to stop it hurting?

Acid indigestion

Your stomach contains hydrochloric acid. This helps you to digest your food. Hydrochloric acid is a strong acid. Your stomach wall is designed to cope with a normal amount but if more acid than usual is produced you may feel a burning pain. This is called **acid indigestion**. The acid can be neutralised with a weak alkali such as bicarbonate of soda. This is how many types of indigestion tablets work.

Q2 Some acid indigestion tablets contain calcium carbonate. Why do they help to make indigestion go away? Why does the effect often wear off after a while?

Treating soils

Plants are adapted to grow wherever there is a space. Soils are different all over the world and plants grow all over the world. Some plants prefer acidic soil and others prefer alkaline soil. Soil with a pH just on the acid side of neutral is good for growing many garden plants.

An extremely acidic soil is not an easy place for plants to live. The reason why carnivorous plants exist is because it is difficult for plant roots to extract nutrients from strongly acidic soils. Carnivorous plants get nutrients such as nitrates and phosphates from the bodies of insects they trap.

▲ ***Fig 2*** *Rhododendrons flourish where crops are hard to grow.*

▲ ***Fig 3*** *Neutralising an acid soil can make it better for growing food crops.*

Many food plants do not grow well enough in moderately acid soil to satisfy farmers. They cannot extract enough nutrients to produce a profitable crop. Farmers often add **lime** to acidic soil to neutralise it. Calcium oxide is called quicklime, from the old word for 'alive'. It fizzes when it meets water. Calcium hydroxide is called slaked lime. Its name comes from an old word meaning not thirsty.

Q3 Lakes can be very acidic. How could you treat a lake to neutralise the acid?

Key Words

acid indigestion – pain due to too much acid in the stomach

lime – calcium oxide or hydroxide

neutral – pH 7, neither acidic nor alkaline

SUMMARY

- Acids and alkalis react together to produce a salt and water.
- The reaction between an acid and an alkali also changes the pH of the solution.
- If exactly the right amount of acid and alkali are mixed, they neutralise each other.
- Acid indigestion and nettle stings can also be neutralised.
- Acid soil is neutralised with quicklime or slaked lime.

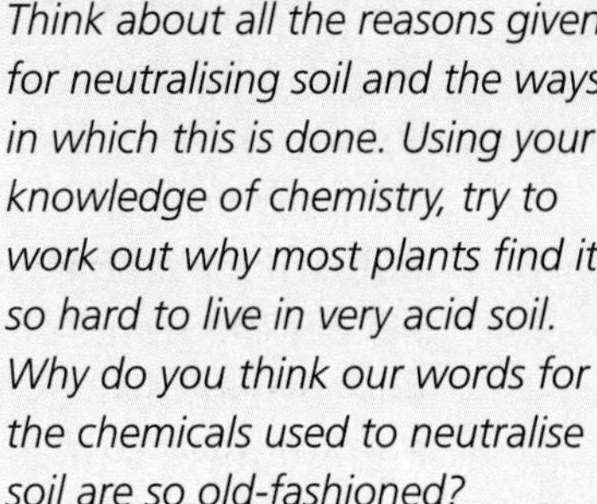

SUMMARY *Activity*

Think about all the reasons given for neutralising soil and the ways in which this is done. Using your knowledge of chemistry, try to work out why most plants find it so hard to live in very acid soil. Why do you think our words for the chemicals used to neutralise soil are so old-fashioned?

76 Acids and corrosion

In this section of the book you will learn the following things:

- **how acids in the atmosphere can cause damage;**
- **that these acids can corrode metals;**
- **that acids in the atmosphere make rocks weather more quickly.**

Rain water normally has a pH of 6. This means that the rain water is slightly acidic. This is because there is carbon dioxide in the atmosphere.

water + carbon dioxide ⟶ carbonic acid

The **carbonic acid** is very weak but it can eventually damage rocks such as limestone (see Unit 74).

▶ ***Fig 1*** *Marble reacts with hydrochloric acid (**a**) much more quickly than weak carbonic acid (**b**).*

Q1 How is carbonic acid formed?

Acid gases

As we saw in Unit 67, fuels produce gases such as nitrogen dioxide and sulphur dioxide when they burn. These acids can dissolve in water to form nitric acid and sulphuric acid. This can increase the acidity of rain to pH3, which is strongly acidic. Gases that dissolve in water to make acids are called **acid gases**.

Acids react with metals. They also react with metal oxides and carbonates. This means that acid rain falling on these chemicals will react with them.

Remember:

metal + acid ⟶ salt + hydrogen

metal oxide + acid ⟶ salt + water

metal carbonate + acid ⟶ salt + water + carbon dioxide

Metals at risk

Many important materials and structures are made from metals. Oxide on the surface of a metal can protect the metal. It can form a coating that prevents air from reaching the metal and turning any more into oxide. This is how the zinc coating on the surface of iron helps to protect the iron. Zinc is very reactive so its oxide is very stable. This is also the reason why we can use aluminium pots for cooking even though aluminium is a much more reactive metal than iron. Aluminium oxide is much stronger than rust.

Acid rain can destroy oxides that protect metal surfaces. The metal can then be attacked by the acid, too. If it makes another oxide skin, this will be removed by more acid rain. These are some of the reasons why acid rain makes metals corrode so quickly.

Q2 Which two acid gases are important in causing acid rain?

▲ ***Fig 2*** *The steel that strengthens concrete can be weakened by acid rain.*

Buildings at risk

Concrete is strong but it is brittle. Concrete often has steel rods added to strengthen it. This is called **reinforced concrete**. If acid rain soaks between the joints in reinforced concrete it can reach the steel rods inside. The steel can slowly corrode until it is too weak to support the concrete. The concrete may look good on the outside, but it can break suddenly when the rods become too weak to work. Buildings and bridges made of reinforced concrete have to be regularly inspected for corrosion.

Q3 Why are copper lightning rods on buildings not easily corroded by acid rain?

Rocks at risk

Limestone, chalk and marble all contain calcium carbonate. This substance is easily attacked by acids. Acids in rain can help to keep the surface of these rocks very clean. This is because the surface is constantly washed away by acid in the rain. It is not washed but weathered.

Key Words

acid gas – a gas that dissolves in water to form an acid

carbonic acid – a weak acid made from carbon dioxide and water

reinforced concrete – concrete with steel rods inside

SUMMARY

- Carbon dioxide dissolves in rain water to make it slightly acidic.
- Acid gases such as sulphur dioxide dissolve in rain to make acid rain.
- Acid rain can react with metals, metal oxides and carbonates.
- Metals corrode much more quickly in acid rain.
- Reinforced concrete contains metal rods that can be corroded by acid rain.
- Rocks such as limestone are easily attacked by acid rain.

SUMMARY *Activity*

There has been a great increase in the damage that acid rain has done to buildings and metal bridges in the last 100 years. Why do you think that this has happened? How do you think acid rain could be reduced?

Summary – Materials and their properties

In this part of the book you will have learned a great deal about different substances. You will know that many substances have important properties and uses and be able to describe some important chemical reactions.

Classifying materials

You should know the differences between the three states of matter and be able to describe the properties of solids, liquids and gases. You will be able to explain how particles are arranged in solids, liquids and gases. You should also know why particles are important in diffusion and gas pressure.

- Describe how the particles are arranged in a solid and a gas.
- What do we call the change from a liquid to a gas?
- Write down three differences between solids and liquids.
- How do the air particles inside a balloon make it inflate?

You should be able to describe the structure of an atom and know the symbols for some common elements. You will also know what the term 'atomic number' means and understand the importance of the Periodic Table.

- What are the symbols for copper, oxygen, potassium and lead?
- Name the three sub-atomic particles.
- Where would you find the reactive metals in the Periodic Table?

You should understand the differences between mixtures, elements and compounds. You will also be able to describe some methods for separating mixtures into their constituents. You should be able to list the properties of metals and non-metals.

- Describe how you would separate sand from water.
- Draw the apparatus you would use to separate alcohol from water.
- List four differences between metals and non-metals.

Changing materials

You should now know the difference between a physical and a chemical change. You should know about changes of state and how substances dissolve to make solutions. You will also know that mass is conserved during a physical change.

- What is the difference between a solute and a solvent?
- How does temperature affect solubility?
- How would you show that the mass of water is conserved when it freezes?

You should be able to make a connection between changes of state and tranference of energy. You should also understand how and why materials expand or contract when they change temperature.

- Describe some of the uses and problems of expansion.
- Why do liquids expand more than solids?

Geological changes are very important in shaping the Earth. You should now be able to explain these changes and understand how sedimentary, igneous and metamorphic rocks are formed and weathered.

- Draw and label a diagram that shows the rock cycle.
- Name two igneous rocks and two sedimentary rocks.
- Name a rock that is made from the remains of living creatures.
- How are metamorphic rocks made?

You should understand the importance of chemical reactions and know that mass is conserved when reactions take place. You will know about different types of reaction and be able to write chemical reactions as word equations. You will also know how burning fuels can affect the environment.

- Write a word equation for magnesium being burned in oxygen.
- List two different types of chemical reaction and give an example of each.
- What is meant by the term 'corrosion'?
- Describe how burning fuels can be useful but can also cause problems.

Patterns of behaviour

After studying this section of the book you should know how metals react with air, water and acids. You will know that some metals react violently with water and acids while others do not react at all. The results of these reactions can be used to place the metals into a reactivity series. You should now be able to use the reactivity series to make predictions about how a metal will react.

- Describe how potassium, magnesium and copper react with water.
- What is the least reactive metal in the reactivity series?
- Use the reactivity series to predict what happens when aluminium powder is heated with copper oxide powder.

You should also understand the difference between acids and bases, and the meaning of pH. You will know how acids react with metals, bases and carbonates. You should understand that acids can be neutralised.

- Write a word equation for hydrochloric acid reacting with copper carbonate.
- Name the salt made when sulphuric acid reacts with lead oxide.
- What is the pH of a neutral solution?
- Why are indicators so useful?
- List two strong acids and two strong alkalis.
- How can acid soils be neutralised?

Finally, this section of the book should help you to understand that acids can corrode metals and weather rocks.

- How is acid rain formed?
- Why does acid rain cause damage? Give some examples.

Physical processes

This part of the book is about the forces and processes of the physical world that affect our daily lives. There are five sections that are linked together. Electricity and magnetism are linked to forces and motion, for example. Other links exist between light, sound and electricity, and these are also connected with energy transfer. You will also learn that understanding the Solar System depends on knowing about forces, motion and light.

Forces and motion

This section of the book looks at the way objects move and the forces that can act upon them. You will study speed, distance and time. You will then learn how forces can be balanced and unbalanced, and how this can affect an object's shape, speed and direction. The next units show you how frictional forces can affect movement. You will discover many ways in which friction affects our lives. Forces can also make things turn, and these forces are important in everyday life. Finally, this section will show you why pressure is important and how forces can be concentrated or spread out.

The Earth and beyond

This section of the book takes us out into the Solar System. You will find out about night and day, and how the movement of the Earth creates different seasons. Next, you will learn more about other planets in the Solar System, such as their size and temperature. Gravity is an important force in Space. As well as introducing gravity this section will help you to understand more about forces and movement. The section ends with a discussion of natural and artificial satellites and the many ways in which we use orbiting satellites in our work and play.

Sound and light

Sound and hearing are important in our everyday life. This section explores the science of sound. You will first learn about vibration and sound waves and then go on to discover what causes differences in volume, frequency and pitch. You will also learn how to protect your own sense of hearing. This section of the book goes on to introduce some new properties of light. You may already have studied light and shadows but you will now begin to find out more. You will find out how light is reflected and how it moves through some substances. There are many examples in our daily life, and you will learn how to study what you see. You will move on to colour and explore the colours contained in white light. You will learn about the colours of the spectrum and how coloured filters create different effects.

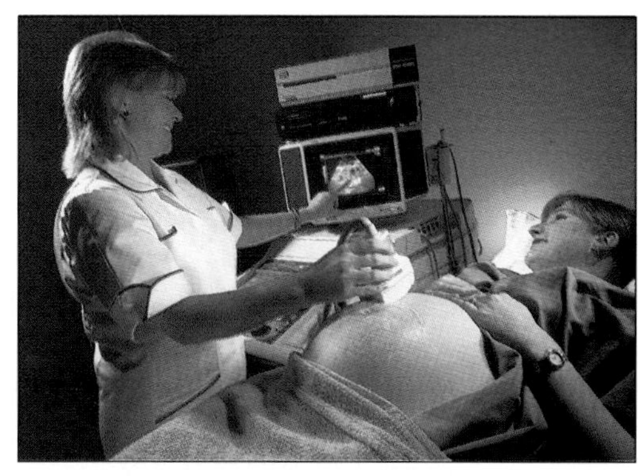

Electricity and magnetism

This section opens with static electricity. You will learn about some important examples, including lightning. The next units describe how electricity can flow in electric circuits and how we use circuits in everyday life. You will be able to look at conductors and insulators again, which you first met in the middle part of the book. After this you will learn more about electricity and magnetism. New subjects, such as the shape of a field around a magnet, will help you to understand more about how an electric current flows. Finally, you will find out about the properties and uses of electromagnets.

Energy resources and energy transfer

This section of the book will challenge you to think hard about energy and where it comes from. There are links here to the units on light, sound and electricity. You will learn how electricity is generated by burning fossil fuels and some ways in which we can harness other forces, such as wind and waves, to give us energy for living. You then move on to study the distinction between temperature and the energy that a substance contains. You will learn about energy transfer, in which one form of energy can change into another form. You will see that energy is never created or destroyed. You will also learn that all living things depend on stored energy, which brings you back to the first part of the book. Finally, this section will invite you to use the knowledge you have gained to suggest better ways of using energy in the future.

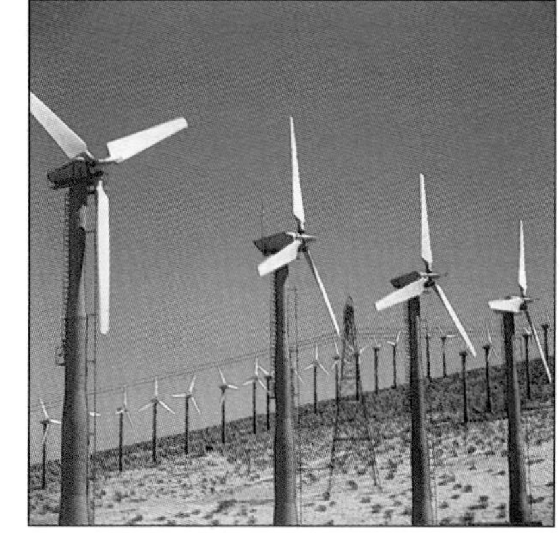

77 Speed

In this section of the book you will learn the following things:

- **how to work out the speed of a moving object;**
- **the units used for measuring speed;**
- **the relationship between speed, distance and time.**

Some people run faster than others. The fastest person in a race will get to the end of the track before the rest. How quickly he/she gets there depends on his/her **speed**. You could just say that a person is a fast, medium fast or slow runner but this is not much help if you want to compare a person with a train.

Units of speed

The exact speed of any moving thing is the exact distance it travels in an exact length of time. You can work out your own speed by using a watch to check how far you walk or run in one minute.

The fastest person in the chart (Table 1) managed to walk 60 metres in one minute. Another way of putting this is to say that her speed was 60 metres per minute. It is a good idea to pick units that are the right size for measuring speed. This is one reason why the speed of cars is normally measured in miles or kilometres per hour. The most common unit for measuring speed is metres per second. This is written as m/s.

Pupil	Distance in 60 seconds (metres)
Anita	35
Brenda	40
Colin	38
Diana	60
Vikram	51
Fiona	42
Guy	55

▲ ***Table 1***

Q1 What was the speed of the fastest person in the class in metres per second?

Q2 Why did everyone have to walk exactly the same route to make the test fair?

Calculating speed

Before we can work out the speed of anything we need to know exactly how far it moved and exactly how long it took. There are different ways of finding these out.

▶ ***Fig 1*** *The speed of this attempt to break the world land speed record was calculated by timing the car over a set distance.*

A car can easily be timed between fixed start and finish lines with a stop clock. The clock is started when the car crosses the start line. It is stopped when the car crosses the finish line. Calculating the speed then involves one easy equation:

Average speed = distance travelled ÷ time taken

We can make it shorter by using *d* for distance, *t* for time, and *v* for speed (**velocity**). The shorthand equation is:

$$v = \frac{d}{t}$$

This equation only gives us the average speed of the object. It does not tell us exactly how fast the car was going at every single moment along the way.

So if an object takes 10 seconds to travel a distance of 100 metres:

$$v = \frac{d}{t}$$

v = 100 metres ÷ 10 seconds

v = 10 metres per second or 10 m/s

Q3 If an object takes 30 seconds to travel a distance of 90 metres, what is its average speed?

Average speeds can be measured very accurately using a computer. In Fig 2, instead of a person with a stop clock, a light beam across the track is broken when a car goes past. The computer can measure the exact length of time that the beam is broken. If we know the exact length of the car we can calculate its exact speed at that spot.

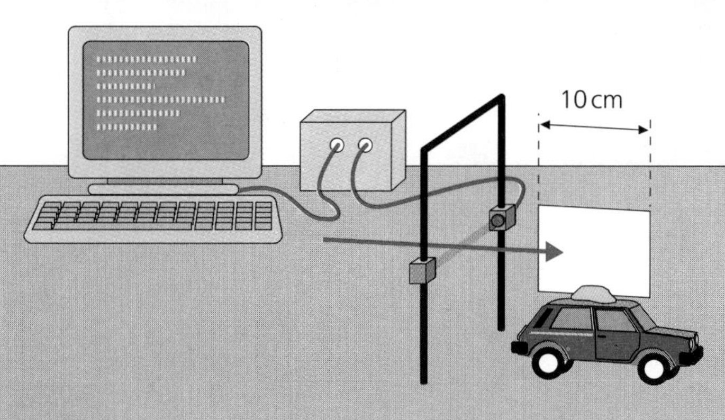

Run	Time (seconds)	Length (cm)
1	0.3	10
2	0.28	10
3	0.31	10

▲ *Fig 2*

Q4 Calculate the average speed of the car shown in the diagram.

Key Words

speed – distance divided by time

velocity – speed

SUMMARY

- The speed of a moving object is the time it takes to cover a measured distance.
- Speed can be measured in metres per second or kilometres per hour.
- The equation for calculating speed is speed = distance travelled ÷ time taken.
- A stop clock or computer timer can be used to calculate speed.

SUMMARY *Activity*

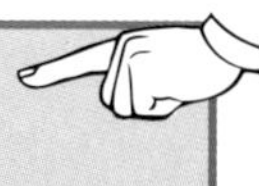

If the street lights along a road are 50 metres apart, how could you use this fact to check the speed of cars driving along the road? Describe your plan in detail so that anybody could do it.

78 Distance and time

In this section of the book you will learn the following things:

- **how to calculate distance from speed and time;**
- **how to use speed and distance to predict how long a journey will take;**
- **how to draw and use distance/time graphs.**

The Smiths are going on holiday abroad. Their ferry sails at 4:30 in the afternoon and they need to decide the best time to leave home. Luckily, they know about the relationship between speed, time and distance. They can calculate how long their journey will take.

The Smith family used a map to measure the distance between their home and the ferry port and chose a safe average speed. This gave them all the information they needed for their calculation (Fig 1).

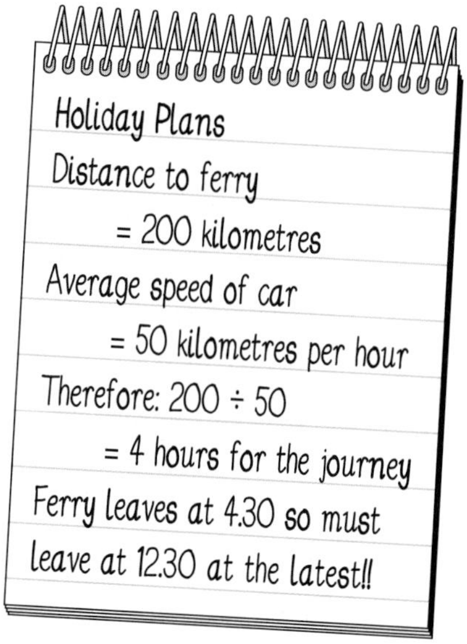

Holiday Plans
Distance to ferry
= 200 kilometres
Average speed of car
= 50 kilometres per hour
Therefore: 200 ÷ 50
= 4 hours for the journey
Ferry leaves at 4.30 so must
leave at 12.30 at the latest!!

▲ *Fig 1*

Remember the equation for calculating average speed:

average speed = distance travelled ÷ time taken $v = d/t$

Cover up the one you are trying to find

The Smith family simply changed this equation round to work out how long their journey would take:

time taken = distance travelled ÷ average speed $t = d/v$

If they wanted to see how far they have come at any time on their journey they could change the same equation round another way:

distance travelled = average speed × time taken $d = t \times v$

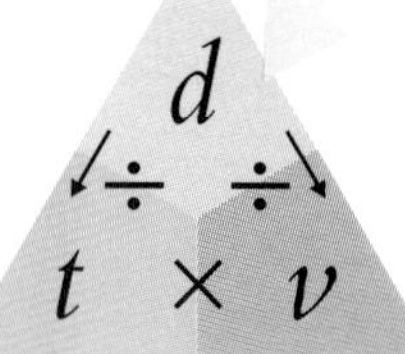

▲ *Fig 2*

Example 1
The distance travelled by a car moving at an average speed of 100 km/hour for 3 hours is:

distance = average speed × time
= 100 × 3 = 300 km

The car travels 300 km in 3 hours.

Q1 How far would you get in 2 hours if you cycled at an average speed of 30 km/hour?

Example 2
The average speed of a person walking slowly is 3 kilometres per hour. If someone walks 15 kilometres at this speed, the time they will take is:

time taken = distance travelled ÷ average speed
= 15 ÷ 3 = 5

The walk takes 5 hours.

Q2 The distance from London to Sheffield is 240 kilometres. How long would it take a bus going at an average speed of 80 km/hour to get from London to Sheffield?

Distance/time graphs

The relationship between distance and time can be drawn on a graph. This is called a **distance/time graph**. The graph is made by plotting how much distance is covered during each stage or leg of the journey.

The diagram (Fig 3) shows the distance/time graph for a girl walking to school. A steep line shows where she was walking quickly and went a long way in a short time. A flat line shows where she was standing still. We can use the graph to find out her speed at any time during the walk.

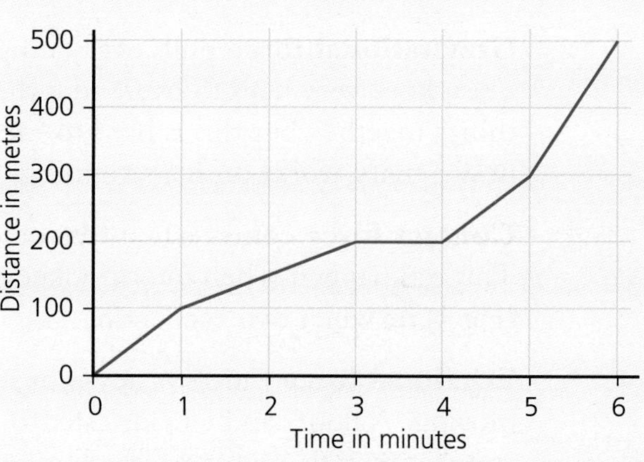

▲ ***Fig 3*** *A distance/time graph.*

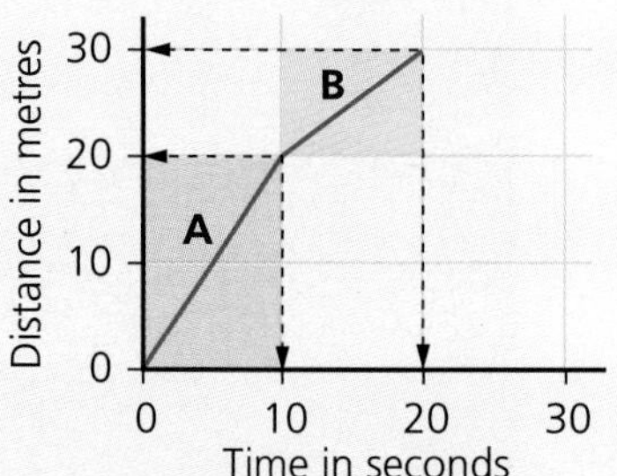

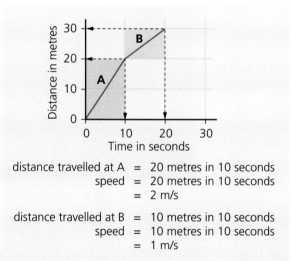

distance travelled at A = 20 metres in 10 seconds
speed = 20 metres in 10 seconds
= 2 m/s

distance travelled at B = 10 metres in 10 seconds
speed = 10 metres in 10 seconds
= 1 m/s

▲ ***Fig 4*** *How to calculate speed from distance and time on a graph.*

Q3 Study the graph in Fig 3 and then answer the questions below:

a) How long did the total journey take?
b) When did the girl stop to wait for a friend?
c) Where do you think she may have been walking downhill?
d) Where do you think she might have been walking up a steep hill?

Key Words

d – distance in km or m
h – time in hours
t – time in seconds
v – velocity (speed) in km/h or m/s

SUMMARY

- There is a fixed relationship between speed, time and distance.
- The distance travelled is average speed multiplied by time taken.
- The time taken is distance travelled divided by average speed.
- A journey can also be drawn as a distance/time graph.

SUMMARY *Activity*

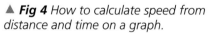

Draw a distance/time graph for your journey to school.
a) Where and when are the fastest and slowest parts of the journey? b) What is your average speed during the journey?

79 Forces

In this section of the book you will learn the following things:

- **that a force can change the speed of an object;**
- **that a force can change the direction of an object;**
- **that balanced forces do not change the movement of an object.**
- **that the force between the Earth and an object is called the weight of the object.**

A force is a push or a pull. Pushing or pulling forces can be caused by different things.

Gravitational force pulls everything down towards the Earth. A climber must work very hard to overcome the force of **gravity**. Gravity pulls most things together, but this is hard to measure with small things. It is easier to see how gravity works on massive things like planets in Space (see Unit 85).

Contact force comes when two objects collide. This can happen when one snooker ball hits another (Fig 1) or when two cars crash.

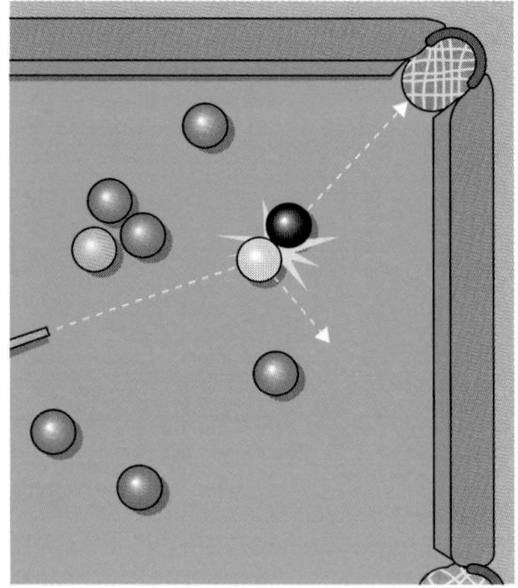

▲ ***Fig 1*** *Contact forces.*

Frictional force can slow down or stop a thing that is moving. A floor can be made safer to walk on by covering it with a substance such as rubber that adds to the **friction**. Friction can also help something to move. Car tyres use friction to grip the road so that they can move the car forward when they spin.

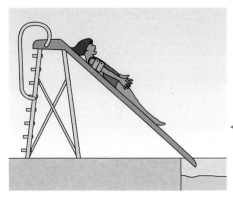

◄ ***Fig 2***

> **Q1** How many forces are working on the child playing on the slide (Fig 2)? What are they?

Electric forces and magnetic forces are described in Units 99–106.

Force and movement

Contact force can change the shape of an object. If you squeeze a lump of modelling clay it changes shape. Metal needs a much larger force to make it change shape. A crushing machine at a scrap yard is strong enough to force a whole car to change shape (Fig 3).

▼ ***Fig 3***

Forces therefore vary in size.

We need a way to measure forces accurately. The unit of measurement we use for measuring force is called a newton (N). Your mass plus gravity makes a force of about 500 newtons. If you stood on a car bonnet you would hardly dent it. A car crushing machine can make a force of many thousands of newtons.

Q2 What is the unit of force called?

Changing the balance

Forces can change the direction and speed of an object. A shopping trolley standing on a level surface (Fig 4) does not move by itself. It has equal forces all around it. The forces are balanced.

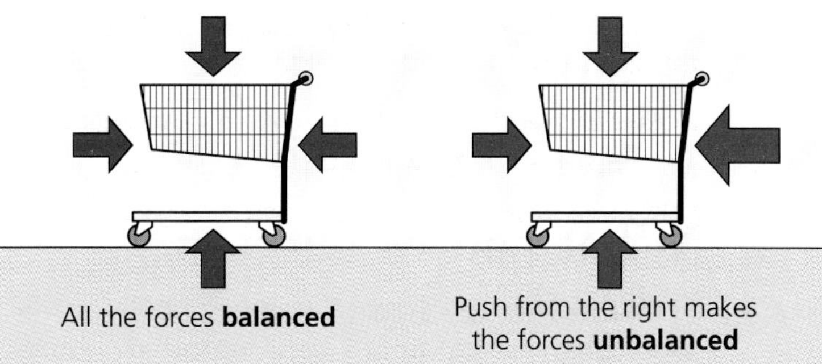
All the forces **balanced**
Push from the right makes the forces **unbalanced**

▶ ***Fig 4***

When you push the trolley you add extra force in one direction. The other forces are not as strong. You make the trolley move.

Q3 Imagine your trolley is hit by another trolley from the left-hand side. Why does your trolley move to the right?

Q4 List some examples of forces used in sport.

Weight and mass

The words **weight** and **mass** are often used wrongly. The mass of an object is a measure of how much matter there is in it. This depends on what the object is made of and its size. Mass is measured in kilograms.

Weight is the force of gravity pulling the object down towards the Earth or other body. A big body has a greater gravitational pull on an object than a small body. Weight is measured in newtons. On Earth a mass of 1kg has a weight of 10N.

Q5 Why is the weight of a 1 kg object only 2N on the Moon?

Key Words

contact force – the force between colliding objects
frictional force – force between objects sliding past each other
gravitational force – the force of the Earth's pull
mass – a measure of how much matter is in an object
weight – the force of gravity pulling an object down

SUMMARY

- A force is a push or a pull.
- Forces can come from gravity, friction, contact, magnetism and electricity.
- Unequal forces can change the shape, speed and/or direction of an object.
- An object stays still when the forces all round it are balanced.
- Weight is the force of gravity pulling an object down.

SUMMARY *Activity*

Try rolling a ball in as many different places as you can. Roll it downhill and uphill, down the stairs and up the stairs. Try to roll it around a corner. Write down how far the ball went each time, and how far it travelled. What were the forces involved?

80 Friction

In this section of the book you will learn the following things:

- **how friction affects the movement of an object;**
- **that the force of friction can be helpful or unhelpful;**
- **that air resistance is a form of friction.**

You can warm your hands up on a cold day by rubbing them together. The heat is real. It is made by friction.

▶ ***Fig 1*** *A slippery surface has very little friction.*

Q1 How is the wet floor around your local swimming-pool made safer to walk on?

What causes friction?

When surfaces get very close together their molecules touch. Even if the surfaces are smooth, rubbing their molecules together produces heat. If the surfaces are rough it is very difficult for them to slide past one another.

Friction has three effects:

- it produces heat when two surfaces rub against each other;
- it prevents objects from sliding or slows them down;
- it wears surfaces down as they rub together.

▼ ***Fig 2*** *Friction produces heat, slows down movement and causes wear and tear.*

brakes become hot as they wear out

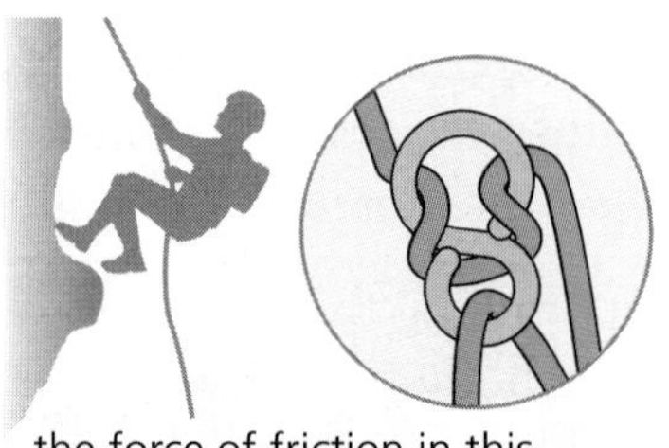

the force of friction in this arrangement helps a climber to control the speed of sliding down a rope

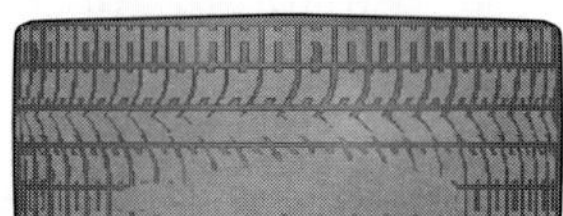

tyres wear out

Using friction to go and to stop

Car tyres grip best on a dry road. It is more difficult to steer on a wet or icy road and very hard to stop. Grooves and ridges, or **tread**, on the tyre can help to push water away when the tyre touches the ground. This improves friction and makes the tyres safer in wet weather. The same name is used for the ridges on the soles of trainers or walking boots. They help your feet to grip more firmly, especially on wet or muddy ground.

Brakes also work by friction. Brakes get hot when they are used. Some of the rough surface also rubs off. Brakes and tyres gradually wear out as they are used. This is why they need to be checked regularly.

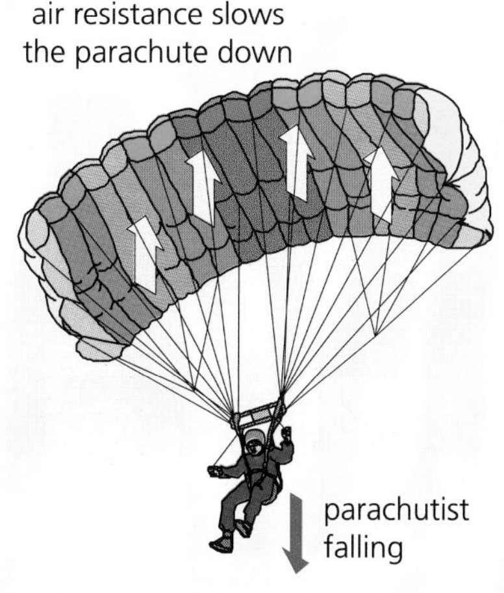

▲ ***Fig 3*** *Using air friction.*

Even air causes friction. When you move through the air you have to push past millions of gas molecules. This is why it is hard to walk into the wind, when all the gas molecules are rushing towards you. It is even harder if you are wearing loose clothes. This is how a parachute works. The wind is caused by a person rushing through the air towards the ground. The parachute's large surface hits many more air molecules than a person's body. This **air resistance** makes the parachutist fall very slowly.

Q2 Name three useful examples of friction.

Q3 Name two problems caused by friction.

Overcoming friction

One way to reduce friction is to **lubricate** smooth surfaces with oil. This helps them to slide past each other more easily. It also reduces heat and wear.

Air resistance can be reduced by changing the shape of a vehicle or a building. Cars are designed to cut into the air in front and help it to flow smoothly past as they go along. A vehicle designed to reduce air resistance is said to be **streamlined**. Water is even more difficult to cut through than air. Machines such as boats and animals such as fish that can move quickly through water are also streamlined.

▲ ***Fig 4***

Q4 Which of these cars has the least air resistance?

Key Words

air resistance – friction caused by air molecules
lubricate – cover a surface with a slippery substance
streamlined – shaped to reduce air or water resistance

SUMMARY

- Friction occurs between surfaces sliding across each other.
- Friction can be useful. Shoes, tyres and parachutes are designed to increase friction.
- Friction produces heat and causes wear and tear.
- Friction can be reduced by lubrication and design.

SUMMARY *Activity*

Describe some of the ways in which friction has been useful or a problem for you recently.

81 Turning forces

In this section of the book you will learn the following things:

- **that forces can make objects turn;**
- **that objects turn around a pivot;**
- **some of the principles of moments.**

Car wheels are attached firmly by tight nuts that cannot be loosened by hand. We need a wheel spanner to turn them. The nuts on the wheel turn around a point in the middle called the **pivot**. Many other tools also work by increasing the turning force a person can produce.

▲ ***Fig 1*** *Turning force comes from the handle of the spanner.*

Q1 Name two other tools that help to create a large turning force.

Q2 Why is it easier to undo a nut with a long spanner rather than a short spanner?

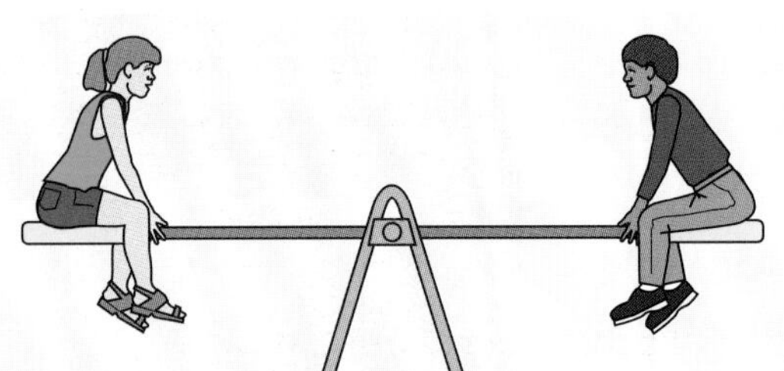

▲ ***Fig 2*** *When two people the same weight sit on a seesaw it is balanced.*

Moment of force

Both people on the seesaw in Fig 2 are pushing down with the same force. Each person is also the same distance from the pivot point. The force around a pivot is called the **moment**. The moment is a combination of the length of a lever and the force on it. A seesaw is balanced when the moment is the same on both sides of the pivot.

We can show this as a calculation.

moment of force
= force × distance from the pivot

Each child is sitting two metres (m) from the pivot and pressing down with a force of 300 newtons (N) so the moment on each side is:

300 N × 2m = 600 N m (newton metres)

This means that both sides cancel each other out.

The child in Fig 3 still pushes down with a force of 300 newtons but the adult is twice as big and pushes down with twice the force. The seesaw can still be balanced if the moments are made the same on both sides. We cannot make the adult smaller but we can adjust the distance. Halving the length of the adult's end of the seesaw can make up for the adult weighing twice as much.

child = 300 N × 2 m = 600 N m
adult = 600 N × 1 m = 600 N m

▲ ***Fig 3*** *An adult and a child need to allow for their difference in weight.*

Q3 What would be the moment created by a force of 200 N placed 0.5 metres from the pivot of a seesaw?

Q4 A child on a seesaw exerts a force of 200 N m. How far away from the pivot would an adult exerting a force of 600 N have to sit to balance the seesaw ?

Levers

The child on the seesaw lifts the heavy adult by being further away from the pivot. This is how levers work. A long lever can move a boulder more easily than a short one. A longer lever has a larger moment. The lever can also be made to lift larger objects by using more force. This means pushing down on the lever with more effort.

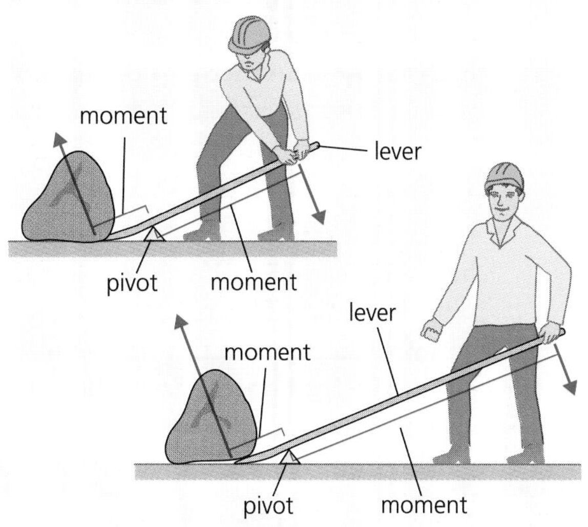

▶ ***Fig 4*** *Increasing the length of a lever between pivot and downward force increases the upward force on the boulder.*

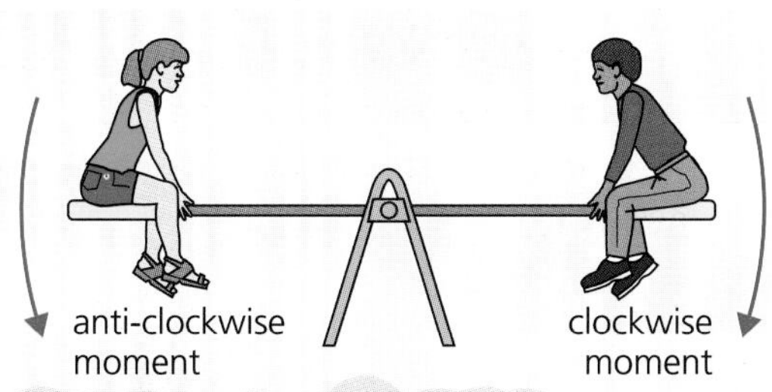

Two ways of producing more leverage, turning effect or **moment** are:

- to have a longer handle or lever;
- to increase the force on the handle or lever.

◀ ***Fig 5*** *A seesaw rocks easily when the moments are balanced.*

Key Words

lever – a rod used with a pivot to increase force
moment – the turning effect produced by a force
pivot – the point around which an object turns

SUMMARY

- Forces can make objects turn around a pivot.
- The turning effect is called the moment.
- Moments are calculated by multiplying the force by the distance from the pivot.
- Moments can be changed by altering the force, the distance or both.
- When the clockwise moment is the same as the anticlockwise moment an object does not turn.

SUMMARY *Activity*

Using a ruler with a pivot made from a pencil and some 2p coins work out 3 different ways of balancing the seesaw if:
a) 3 coins are placed 6 centimetres away from one side of the pivot;
b) 4 coins are placed 2 centimetres away from one side of the pivot.

82 Forces and pressure

In this section of the book you will learn the following things:

- **how pressure can be reduced;**
- **how pressure can be increased;**
- **the relationship between force and pressure.**

You can easily sink into soft mud because all your weight is on the small area covered by your feet. Walking on boards spreads the weight. The **pressure** on each square centimetre of the ground is much smaller. Boards are often used to protect busy paths from being damaged by people walking on them.

Reducing pressure

Caterpillar tracks spread the weight of a heavy vehicle (Fig 1) over a larger area than wheels would. This reduces the pressure and helps to prevent the vehicle from getting bogged down. Snowshoes (Fig 4) also help to reduce pressure and prevent a person from sinking into soft snow.

Many animals have feet designed to spread pressure. A camel's large flat feet help it to walk across soft sand. Birds that live in muddy places often have webbed feet.

▲ *Fig 1*

Q1 Why do beach buggies have very large, wide wheels?

Q2 Why do wading birds have large webbed feet?

Increasing pressure

A drawing pin can be pushed into wood quite easily. Your finger will not go into the wood even if you press down with enough force to make a drawing-pin go in. The force of the drawing pin is concentrated in one small area. Pressure describes how concentrated a force is. Nails, drawing pins and sharp knives are the opposite of snowshoes and webbed feet. They concentrate force in a small area. This is why they can pierce or cut hard materials.

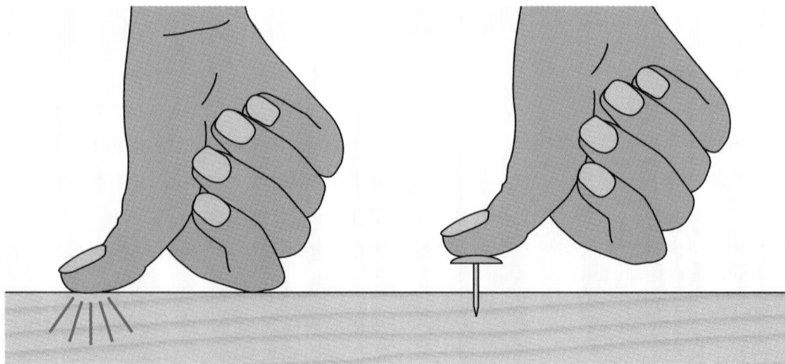

▲ ***Fig 2*** *If the force spreads out over a large area the pressure is low. If the force is concentrated on a small area the pressure is high.*

Calculating pressure

Pressure is defined as the force per unit area. It can be calculated by using this equation:

Pressure = force ÷ area

Fig 3 shows an easy way to remember the equation as a triangle.

F
÷ ÷
P × A

▶ ***Fig 3***

If you press on wood with a force of 100 N, the force is spread over one square centimetre. If you press on a drawing pin the force is concentrated on an area one hundred times smaller. The pressure on the point of the drawing pin is therefore 100 times larger than the pressure of your thumb.

Finger
pressure = force ÷ area
pressure = 100 N ÷ 1 cm^2
pressure = 100 N per $metre^2$

Drawing pin
pressure = force ÷ area
pressure = 100 N ÷ 0.01 cm^2
pressure = 10 000 N per $metre^2$

Q3 The pointed end of a nail has an area of 0.5 mm^2. Calculate the pressure on the point of the nail when a force of 300 newtons is used to hammer it into wood.

Reduction of pressure can be calculated in the same way. Fig 4 shows the pressures under the feet of a person standing on snow with and without snowshoes.

▶ ***Fig 4*** *Snowshoes spread the force. Spreading a force reduces the pressure.*

Key Words

pressure – force in newtons exerted on a measured area

SUMMARY

- Pressure is decreased by spreading the force over a large area.
- Pressure is increased by concentrating the force on a small area.
- Pressure is defined as the force per unit area.
- Pressure is calculated by dividing the force by the area.
- Pins, nails and sharp blades concentrate forces.
- Snowshoes, skis, large tyres and caterpillar tracks all spread forces.

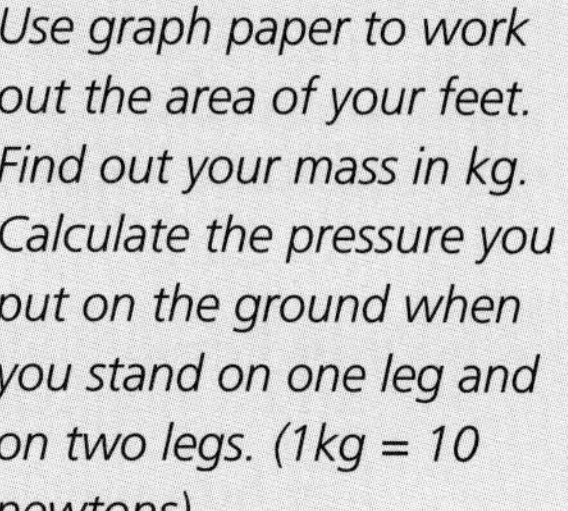

SUMMARY *Activity*

Use graph paper to work out the area of your feet. Find out your mass in kg. Calculate the pressure you put on the ground when you stand on one leg and on two legs. (1kg = 10 newtons)

83 The Sun and other stars

In this section of the book you will learn the following things:

- **what stars and galaxies are;**
- **how the Sun produces light and heat;**
- **that the planets are visible because they reflect sunlight.**

▲ *Fig 1*

◀ *Fig 2 Orion is supposed to look like a hunter and Leo is a lion.*

The stars have fascinated people since very early times. Patterns of stars – or **constellations** – are given names, and legends have been made up about them. Over 1800 years ago 48 constellations were known and more have been added since then. The stars are not arranged in these groups. They are very far apart and only appear to form a shape when seen from Earth.

Q1 What are constellations?

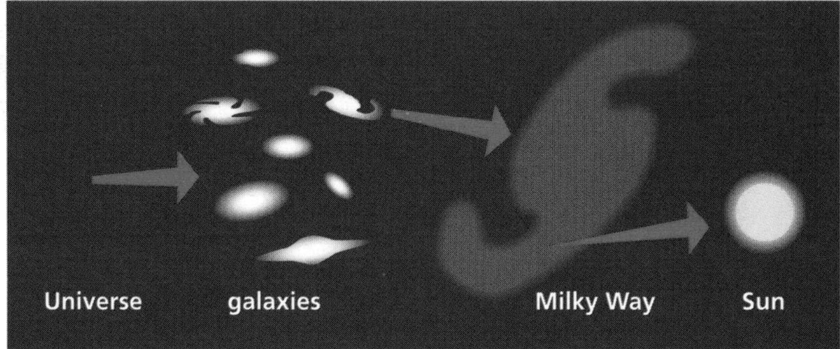

▲ *Fig 3*

Stars and galaxies

Stars shine by their own light. Our own Sun is a star. Nuclear reactions taking place inside the Sun and other stars also produce a great deal of heat and other forms of energy.

Clusters of stars form **galaxies**. There are billions of galaxies in the **Universe**. Our Sun is part of a galaxy called the Milky Way. The Milky Way contains approximately 100 000 million stars and the Sun is just one of these. Our Earth is just one tiny planet circling a single star in the Universe.

The Sun

The Sun supplies the Earth with energy. Without the Sun, there would be no life on Earth. Plants use sunlight to make food (see Unit 23) and during the day we use sunlight to see. The Sun also warms our world.

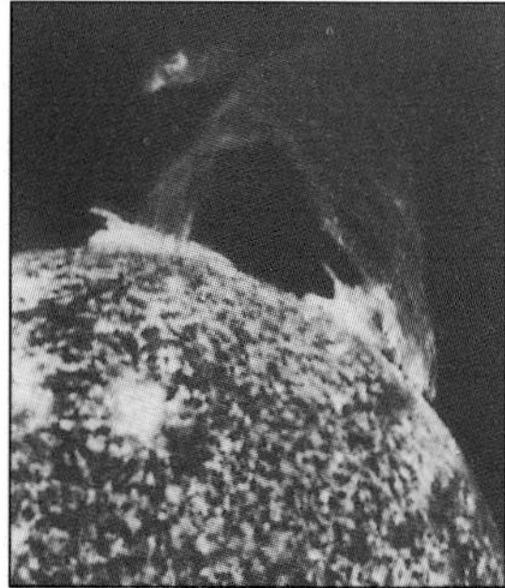

The Sun's hot core reaches temperatures of 15 million degrees Celsius but its surface is much cooler – only about 6 thousand degrees.

◄ ***Fig 4*** *Flaming gases leap from the Sun's surface. At the same time, invisible radiation also escapes.* ⚠ ***Never look at the Sun directly.***

Q2 How does the Sun produce light, heat and other forms of energy?

Seeing objects in space

The light from distant stars and galaxies takes years to reach the Earth. Distances in space are too great to be measured in kilometres. Figures as large as this are even hard to imagine. Scientists measure these distances in **light years**.

One light year is the distance light travels in a year. Light travels at 300 000 kilometres a second and it would only take 1/8th of a second for a flash of light to circle the Earth. There are more than 30 million seconds in a year and the second nearest star to Earth is 4.2 light years – 40 billion kilometres – away. Light from the far side of the Milky Way takes over 100 000 years to reach us.

Other objects in the Solar System are visible because they reflect the Sun's light. When you see the Moon it is reflecting light from the Sun to Earth.

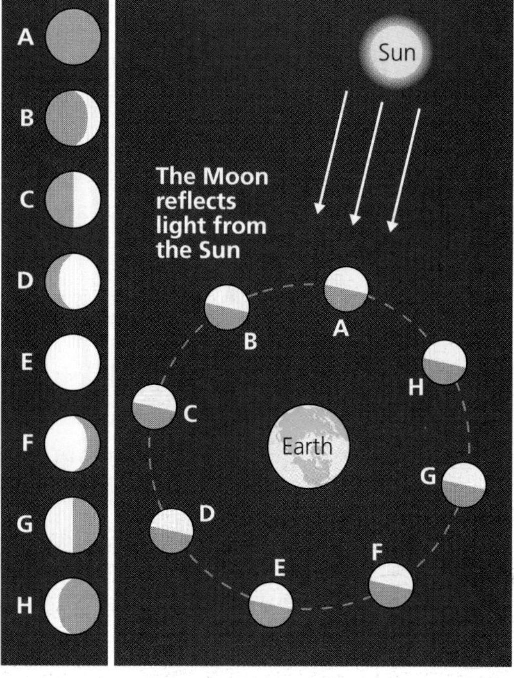

▲ ***Fig 5*** *The Moon appears to change shape as its shadow moves. (Not drawn to scale.)*

Q3 What is the name of the nearest star to Earth?

Q4 Mars does not give out light. How are we able to see it from Earth?

Key Words

constellation – a named 'shape' among the stars
light year – the distance light travels in one year
galaxy – a cluster of millions of stars
Universe – the total amount of material and energy in existence

SUMMARY

- The Universe contains thousands of clusters of stars called galaxies.
- Stars are spheres of gas that give out energy including heat and light.
- Distances in the Universe are so large they are measured in light years.
- The Sun is the nearest star to Earth.
- Stars are visible from Earth because they are light sources.
- Other objects in the Solar System are seen by light reflected from the Sun.

SUMMARY *Activity*

Find out your star sign and look up the pattern of stars that form its constellation. Copy the stars and add your own version of the whole picture, like the ones in Fig 2.

84 The Solar System

In this section of the book you will learn the following things:

- **that the Sun is at the centre of the Solar System;**
- **the names of the planets in the Solar System;**
- **the relative positions of the planets in the Solar System.**

The **Solar System** contains nine **planets**. Each planet moves in an **orbit** around the Sun. The four planets closest to the Sun are called the inner planets. The other five, called the outer planets, are a very long way away.

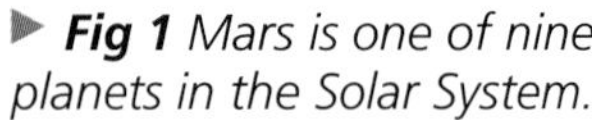

▶ ***Fig 1*** *Mars is one of nine planets in the Solar System.*

Planets are not the only objects in our Solar System. There are thousands of minor planets and debris known as **asteroids**. Most of them orbit the Sun between Mars and Jupiter. The largest asteroid is only 700 kilometres in diameter. Some planets also have their own moons.

Q1 Name the five outer planets.

Q2 Which two planets are nearest to the Earth?

Mercury is not much bigger than our Moon. It is only 50 million kilometres from the Sun and its surface temperature can reach 350°C. Venus is twice as far away but its surface is even hotter. This is because Venus has an atmosphere containing carbon dioxide, which traps heat (see Unit 67).

The Earth is 150 million kilometres from the Sun. The surface temperature on our own planet varies between 40°C and –40°C.

Pluto and Neptune are the planets furthest from the Sun. Neptune orbits the Sun once in 165 years. Pluto's orbit takes 247 years. These outermost planets are very cold and it is probably very dark there. From the surface of Neptune your view of the Sun would be 30 times smaller than it is from Earth – and a thousand times less bright.

Remember that planets do not give out light. We can only see them because they reflect light from the Sun. Planets near to the Sun look brighter than the outermost planets. Venus is the third brightest object in our sky. Pluto is so dim that it was not seen until 1930.

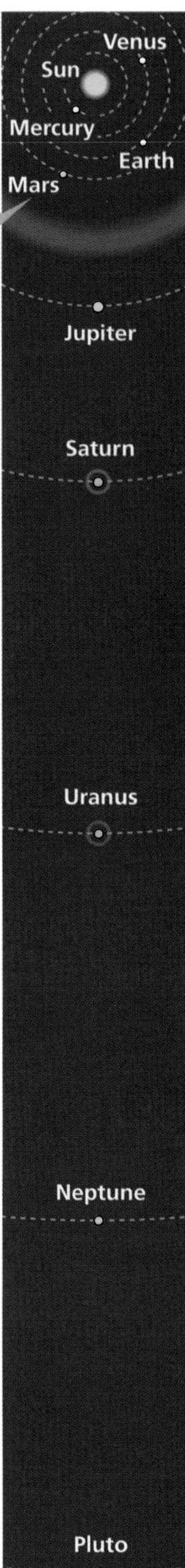

▶ ***Fig 2*** *The nearest star on the same scale as this would be a kilometre away.*

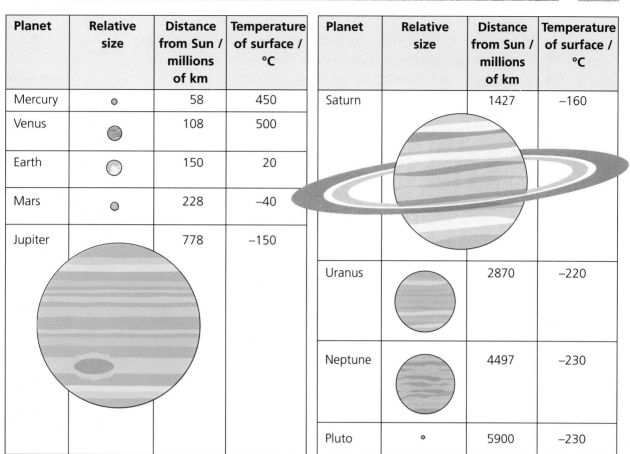

Planet	Relative size	Distance from Sun / millions of km	Temperature of surface / °C
Mercury		58	450
Venus		108	500
Earth		150	20
Mars		228	–40
Jupiter		778	–150
Saturn		1427	–160
Uranus		2870	–220
Neptune		4497	–230
Pluto		5900	–230

Mercury, Venus, Mars, Pluto and Earth are small planets. Jupiter and Saturn are giant planets. Jupiter is more massive than all the other planets added together.

Q3 Why are Uranus, Neptune and Pluto the coldest planets?

Q4 Name the largest planet in the Solar System.

Key Words

asteroid – a small rock or minor planet

orbit – the path of a planet around the Sun

Solar System – the Sun and all the planets and asteroids that move around it

SUMMARY

- The Solar System consists of our Sun and nine planets plus many smaller asteroids.
- There are four inner planets.
- There are five outer planets.
- Planets close to the Sun are much hotter than those further away.
- The planets are different sizes.

SUMMARY *Activity*

Make a model of the Solar System. Take 2 metres of string, nine pieces of card and nine paper clips. Write the name of a planet on each piece of card and clip the planets onto the string the following distances from one end: Mercury 1 cm; Venus 2 cm; Earth 3 cm; Mars 4 cm; Jupiter 20 cm; Saturn 35 cm; Uranus 70 cm; Neptune 110 cm; Pluto 145 cm.

85 Gravitational forces

In this section of the book you will learn the following things:
- **how gravitational forces control the movement of planets;**
- **how comets are affected by gravitational forces.**

▲ ***Fig 1*** *Gravity pulls us down to Earth no matter how hard we try to escape. Gravity also pulls the Earth towards the Sun.*

Planets in the Solar System orbit the Sun (Fig 2). But what prevents them from flying out into Space? They are held in position by gravity.

All objects have gravity. The pull of gravity is greater between massive objects than between small objects. The pull between you and the Earth is about 500 newtons but the pull between you and another person is about 500 million times smaller. Most of the gravity that holds us on the ground is due to the mass of the Earth. The Sun contains almost all of the mass in the Solar System. The Sun's mass is great enough to create a pull that holds the planets in their orbits.

Q1 What is the name of the force that acts between you and the Earth?

Q2 What is the name of the force that acts between the Earth and the Sun?

Orbits

The size of the Sun's gravitational pull on a planet depends on two things:
- the distance between the planet and the Sun;
- the mass of the planet.

This means that:
- an inner planet will be pulled towards the Sun more strongly than an outer planet;
- a massive planet like Jupiter will be pulled towards the Sun more strongly than a small planet.

▼ ***Fig 2***

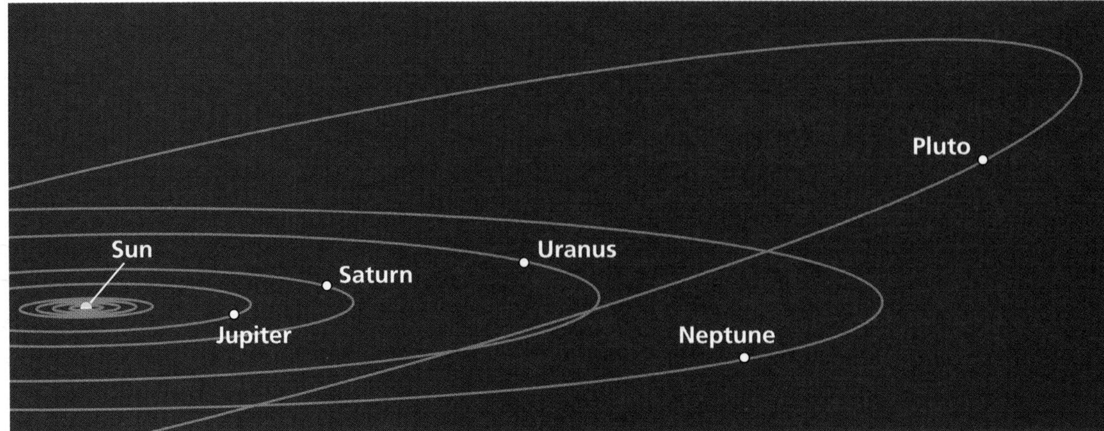

Planets close to the Sun take less time to travel around it than planets further away. The Earth makes one complete orbit of the Sun in one year. Jupiter's 'year' is 12 of our years and Pluto takes 247 Earth years to go once round its orbit. Orbits are not usually perfect circles. Most of the planets have orbits that are **ellipses**.

Q3 Why does Pluto take much longer than the Earth to orbit the Sun?

Comets

Comets move around the Sun in elongated orbits that are long ellipses or parabolas. Unlike the planets the orbits do not have to be in the same plane. It may take many years for a comet to slowly orbit the Sun. Halley's comet comes close to the Sun and Earth every 76 years. As it approaches the Sun it speeds up. As it moves away it slows down.

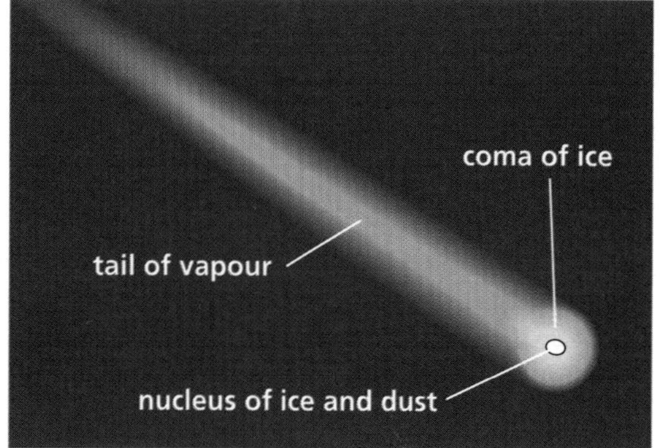

▲ *Fig 3*

A **comet** has a centre of dust and ice called a **nucleus** covered with layers of frozen gases. Out in Space, a comet has no tail. When it comes close to the Sun some of the frozen gases on its surface turn into vapour (Fig 3). This is what we see as a comet's glowing tail. The tail always points away from the Sun, no matter which way the comet is moving.

Q4 What is the centre of a comet called?

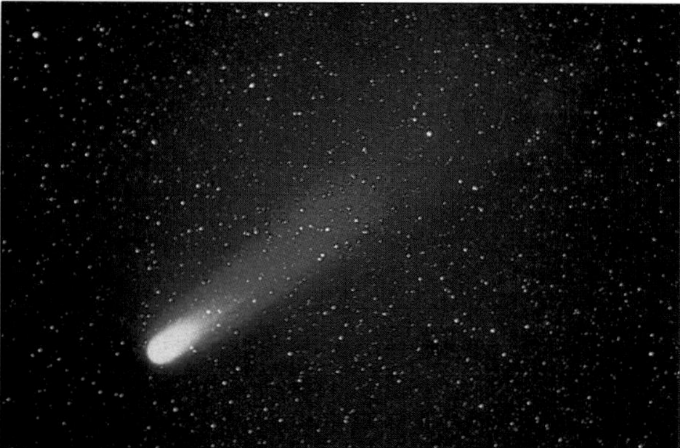

Halley's comet is named after Sir Edmund Halley. Halley saw the comet in 1682, when he was a young man, and used his knowledge of gravitational forces and the movement of the planets to predict when it would be visible again. He was correct, although he did not live long enough to see the comet return.

◄ ***Fig 4*** *Halley's comet.*

Key Words

comet – a body made of dust and frozen gases
ellipse – a slightly flattened circle shape
nucleus – the core of a comet

SUMMARY

- Planets are held in their orbits by gravity.
- Most orbits are ellipses.
- Comets are made of dust and ice.
- A comet's orbit is a long ellipse.
- A comet's tail is made of vaporised gases.

SUMMARY *Activity*

Draw a diagram that shows a comet's orbit around the Sun. Remember to think about which way the tail will point.

86 Days and seasons

In this section of the book you will learn the following things:

- **that nights and days are due to the Earth's rotation;**
- **how seasons are caused by the Earth's movement around the Sun;**
- **why we have leap years.**

Every day, the Sun appears to move across the sky. People once believed that the Sun was orbiting the Earth. Now we know that this is not so. The Earth is simply spinning round on its own **axis**, like a top. It makes a complete turn every 24 hours.

Day and night

One half of the Earth is always in shadow and the other half is lit by the Sun. We have our daytime when the place where we live is turned towards the Sun. Night comes when our region moves out of the light and into the shadow.

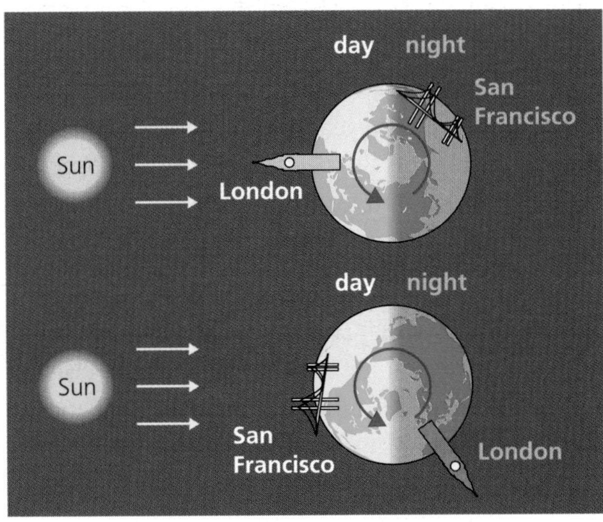

▲ ***Fig 1*** *Daytime for Britain is night-time for the USA.*

During the night, the stars appear to move around the sky. Our Earth is not the centre of the Universe. Remember that it is the Earth's rotation that makes the stars look as if they are moving.

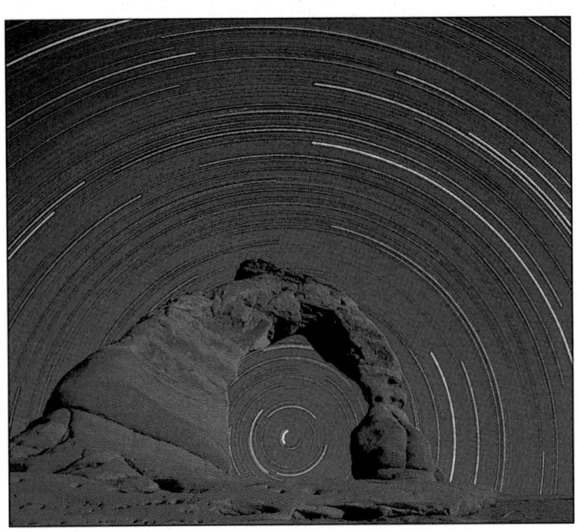

◄ ***Fig 2*** *The North Star is almost directly over the North Pole. It seems to stay still while other stars revolve around it.*

Q1 How long does it take for the Earth to make one complete turn?

Q2 Why do you think the North Star seems to stay still while the Earth spins?

The seasons

As the Earth orbits the Sun (Unit 84) the seasons on the Earth's surface gradually change. This happens because the Earth is not perfectly vertical. Its axis is tilted at an angle of 23.5°.

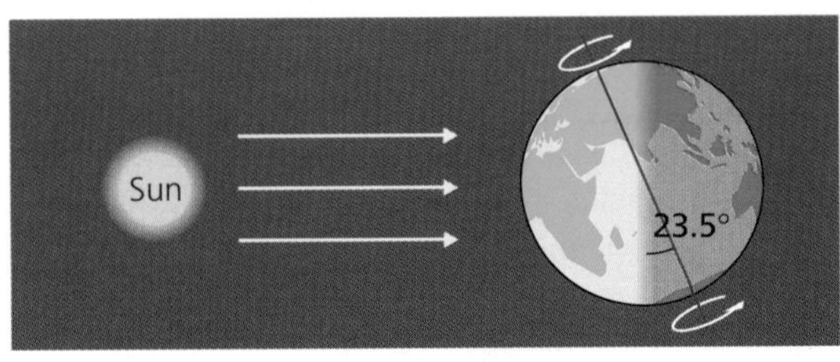

▲ ***Fig 3*** *The Earth is tilted at an angle of 23.5°.*

When the Northern **hemisphere** tilts towards the Sun it gets more light and heat. The days are longer and the Sun is higher overhead. The weather becomes warmer. At the same time, the Southern hemisphere tilts away from the Sun. When it is summer in the Northern hemisphere, it is winter in the Southern hemisphere.

Q3 Why does Europe have summer while Australia has winter?

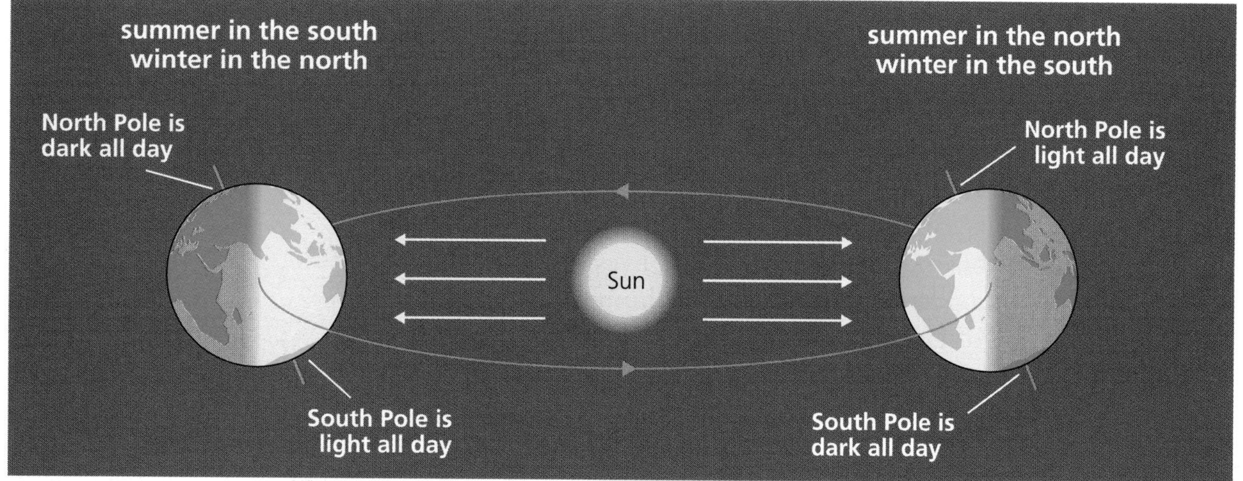

▲ *Fig 4*

At the **equator** there is little difference between summer and winter. As you go towards the **Poles** the seasons become more important. The North Pole gets no sunshine at all in winter but during the summer the Sun never really sets. Study Fig 4 carefully to see how this works.

Leap years

The Earth takes 365.25 days to make a complete orbit of the Sun. We simply save up the extra quarters until we have enough to make one whole day. This is why we have three years of 365 days followed by a **leap year** with 366.

Q4 What would happen to day and night if we added a quarter of a day to each year?

Key Words

axis – the (nearly vertical) centre of the Earth's spin

equator – a (nearly horizontal) imaginary line around the Earth's middle

hemisphere – one-half of the Earth between the equator and a Pole

leap year – a year with 366 days instead of 365

Pole – one end of the Earth's axis

SUMMARY

- The Earth spins all the way round every 24 hours and this gives us night and day.
- The Earth's axis is tilted at an angle of 23.5°.
- The tilt of the Earth as it orbits the Sun creates summer and winter.
- Summer in the Northern hemisphere is winter in the Southern hemisphere.
- The Earth takes exactly 365.25 days to orbit the Sun.
- We make every fourth year a leap year to add on the extra four quarters.

SUMMARY *Activity*

Push a knitting needle through a ball of wool and add a twist of cotton to mark a special spot. Spin it in front of a lamp to show night and day. Try to make a model of the seasons by tilting the ball and orbiting the lamp with it.

87 Satellites

In this section of the book you will learn the following things:

- that the Moon is a satellite of the Earth;
- how artificial satellites are used to observe the Earth;
- how artificial satellites are used to explore the Solar System.

A **satellite** is a **body** in orbit around another body. The Earth is a satellite of the Sun. The Moon is a natural satellite of the Earth.

Natural satellites

The Moon orbits the Earth once every month. We can see the Moon because it reflects light from the Sun. Nothing lives on the Moon but it has been visited by humans. The view of Earth from the Moon in Fig 1 is very clear. The Moon has no clouds or atmosphere to spoil the view.

Q1 What is a satellite?

▲ ***Fig 1*** *Astronauts on the Moon get a wonderful view of Earth.*

▲ ***Fig 2***

Artificial satellites

The Moon is 380 000 kilometres from Earth. It gives a good view of the Earth but it is a long way away. Artificial satellites can give a closer view of Earth. The first one was sent into space in 1957. Since then thousands more have been placed into orbit.

Some satellites can take detailed photographs of people and structures on Earth. They are sometimes called spy satellites. The information they provide is used to find out about what is happening in other countries.

Satellites are used for weather forecasting. **Weather satellites** can detect cloud movements and gathering storms and send pictures down to Earth (Fig 2). These pictures can be used to forecast the weather. Weather forecasts do much more than help us to decide when to go on a picnic or hang the washing out. The lives of those who work at sea may depend on knowing when a storm is coming. Farmers also rely on accurate weather forecasting.

Q2 Why are weather satellites important?

Space exploration

Satellites are not only used to look at Earth. Telescopes placed on satellites can give a much clearer view of stars than a telescope on Earth. The pictures are not spoiled by dust and dirt in the Earth's atmosphere. The Hubble Space Telescope (Fig 3), which was launched in 1990, can see seven times as far as telescopes on Earth.

Satellites have even been sent millions of miles away to orbit other planets in the Solar System. Our knowledge of Mars, Venus and the outer planets has been improved by pictures and other information from exploration satellites.

▲ *Fig 3*

Communications satellites

We also use satellites to pass telephone, radio and television messages around the world. **Communications satellites** in orbit above the Earth (Fig 4) can receive and pass on messages very quickly to and from almost anywhere in the world, without wires or cables. Although a satellite is very expensive to make and launch, the cost can be shared among many different organisations. Once it is in place it can be used for a long time.

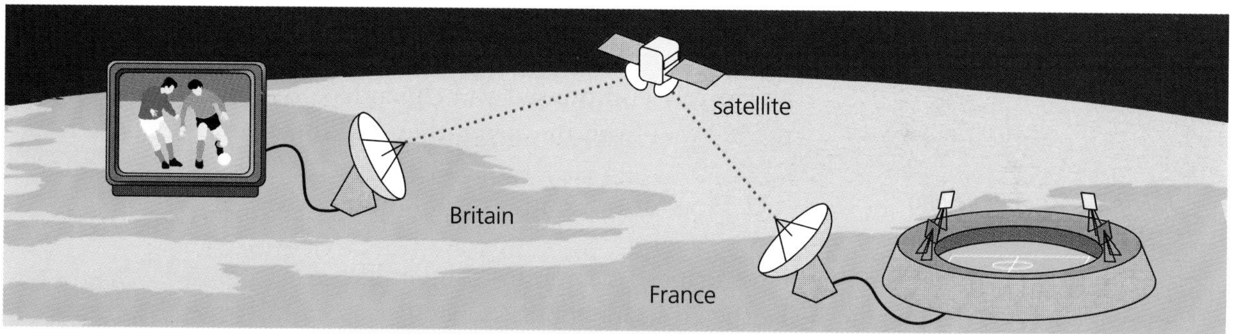

▲ ***Fig 4*** *Live concerts and sporting events can be seen around the world.*

Q3 List some of the uses of artificial satellites.

Key Words

body – an object in Space
communications satellite – a satellite for passing on television, radio and telephone messages
weather satellite – a satellite gathering information to help us to predict the weather
satellite – a body in orbit around another body

SUMMARY

- The Moon is a natural satellite of the Earth.
- Spy satellites can observe people and structures on Earth.
- Weather satellites can help us to predict weather.
- Satellites can give a clear view into Space.
- Explorer satellites gather information about other planets.
- Artificial satellites help to send messages around the world.

SUMMARY *Activity*

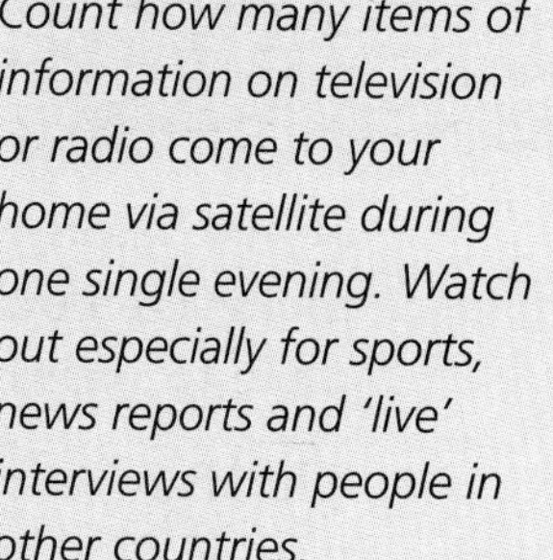

Count how many items of information on television or radio come to your home via satellite during one single evening. Watch out especially for sports, news reports and 'live' interviews with people in other countries.

88 Your hearing

In this section of the book you will learn the following things:

- **what sound is;**
- **how our ears work;**
- **how we describe the loudness of sounds.**

Sound is important to us. We use our voices to speak to one another. Alarms and warning cries protect us from harm. Hearing tells us what is going on around us. Listening to music gives us pleasure. But what is sound?

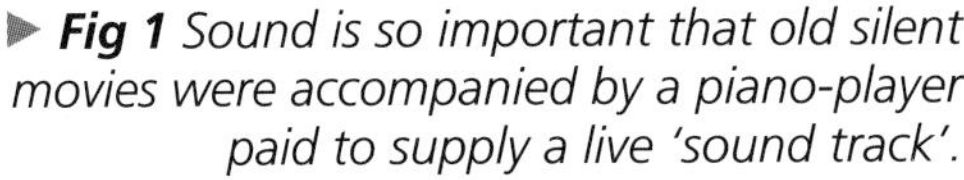

► ***Fig 1*** *Sound is so important that old silent movies were accompanied by a piano-player paid to supply a live 'sound track'.*

Vibrations

Sound is made by something vibrating. When you press a piano key it makes a hammer strike a string inside. This makes the string vibrate. The vibrating string makes the air around it vibrate. Each time the string moves in one direction it pushes air molecules together. When it moves back in the other direction the air molecules spread out again. Sections of air are alternately compressed and expanded. As these sections move away from the string they become sound waves.

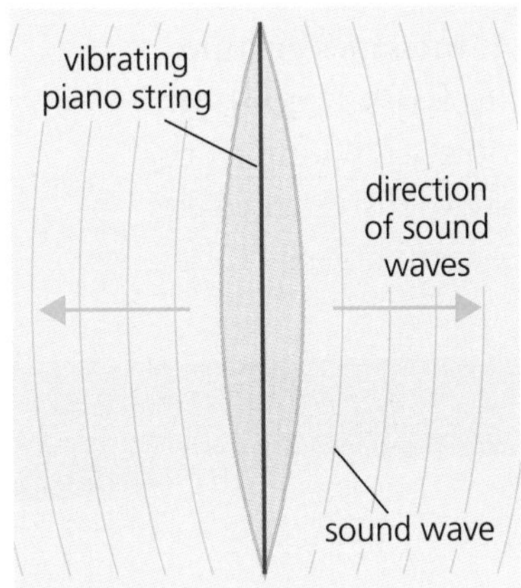

▲ ***Fig 2*** *A vibrating string creates sound waves.*

Q1 How does a guitar make sound waves?

Many instruments do not have strings. A wind instrument like a recorder is designed to make the air inside vibrate when somebody blows into it. Your voice works like a combination of a wind instrument and a stringed instrument. Air from your windpipe passes through your voice-box on the way out. Your voice-box contains vocal cords. These tiny strings vibrate when air passes across them. They make sound waves come out of your mouth.

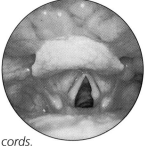

► ***Fig 3*** *Vocal cords.*

Hearing

Sound waves would mean nothing to us if we had no way of detecting them. Luckily, your ears can pick up the vibrations in the air and transmit them to your brain.

The shape of your outer ear helps it to catch sound waves and direct them into a narrow tube behind your jaw. At the end of the tube there is a thin sheet of tissue called your **eardrum**. The sound waves make your eardrum vibrate. The vibration is passed on to three tiny bones deeper inside. They amplify the sound and transmit it even deeper, to a curly region called the **cochlea**. The cochlea contains fluid and nerves. Amplified sound makes the fluid vibrate. Finally, the nerves transmit vibration messages to your brain.

Q2 Why are the three small bones in the middle ear important?

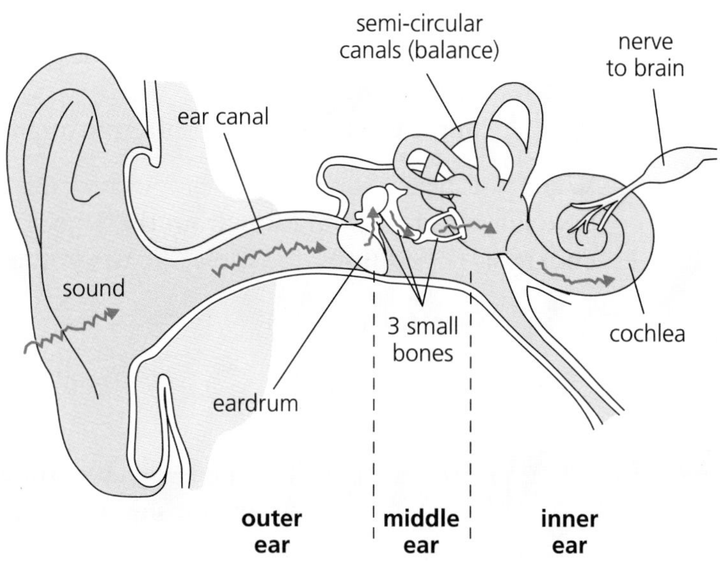

▲ ***Fig 4*** *The human ear.*

▲ ***Fig 5*** *Loud sounds can damage your hearing. People in noisy work places must protect their ears.*

Turn it down

Some sounds are very quiet. Some sounds are so loud they can make our ears hurt. Whether we like a particular sound or not depends on many things. Regular, soft sounds are usually soothing. Irregular, loud sounds can be disturbing. We describe an unpleasant sound as a **noise**. The loudness of a sound can be measured in units called decibels. The sound of a jet plane taking off is about 110 decibels.

Q3 What is the difference between sound and noise?

Key Words

cochlea – part of the inner ear where vibrations become nerve messages

eardrum – a membrane that transmits sound waves from the air

noise – an unpleasant sound

SUMMARY

- Sound is produced by vibration.
- Vibrations create sound waves in the air.
- Our ears collect sound waves and transmit them to our brain.
- Three small bones of the middle ear connect the eardrum of the outer ear to the cochlea of the inner ear.
- Loudness can be measured in decibels.

SUMMARY *Activity*

Make a list of all the devices in your home that are meant to create sound. Make a separate list of devices that produce noise. Do any of the devices on your lists vibrate?

89 How sound waves travel

In this section of the book you will learn the following things:

- **how to find the speed of sound in air;**
- **how echoes can be useful;**
- **how sound travels through different materials.**

When you hear a sound, the air molecules that make your eardrum vibrate have not travelled all the way from the object that made the sound. **Sound energy** is passed from one molecule to another like a baton in a relay race.

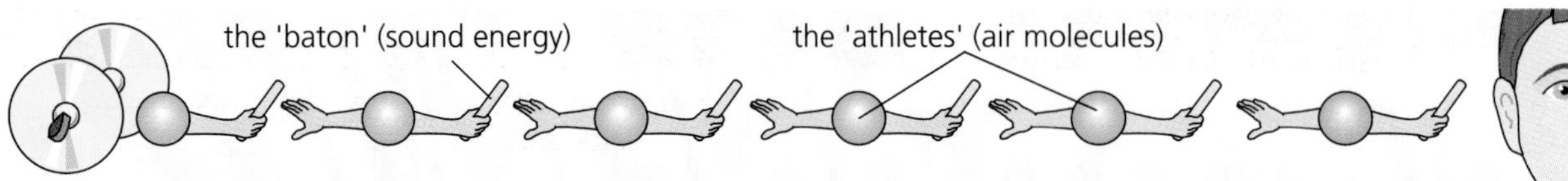

▲ ***Fig 1*** *Sound energy is passed from air molecule to air molecule. The energy eventually makes air molecules near your ear vibrate.*

Sound energy takes time to travel through the air. When you shout near a big building, you may hear an **echo** when the sound waves bounce back to you. You could even use an echo to measure the speed of sound.

Echo timing

Fig 2 shows a way to measure the speed of sound by timing an echo. Stand exactly 200 metres from a high, wide building. Clap your hands once and listen for the echo. The time between the clap and its echo is the time it took for the sound to travel to the wall and back again. Now try to clap in time with the echo, so that your next clap covers the sound of the echo from the previous clap. The time between your claps will allow somebody with a stopwatch to measure how long sound takes to travel to the wall and back.

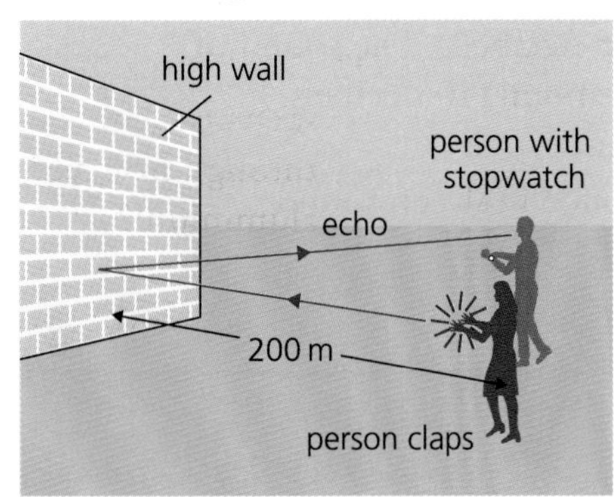

distance one clap travels = 200 metres × 2
= 400 metres

time between claps = 1.2 seconds

therefore sound travels 400 m in 1.2 s

speed of sound in air = distance ÷ time
= 400 m ÷ 1.2 s
= 333 m/s

◀ ***Fig 2*** *This is not an easy experiment because it may be hard to find a suitable place to try it.*

Echo-sounding

Sound waves can be used to locate wrecks and submarines underwater. This is called echo-sounding or **sonar**. Sound waves from the ship travel through the water and bounce back from any sunken ships or submarines (Fig 3). Echo-sounding can also be used to check whether the water is deep enough for a ship to proceed safely.

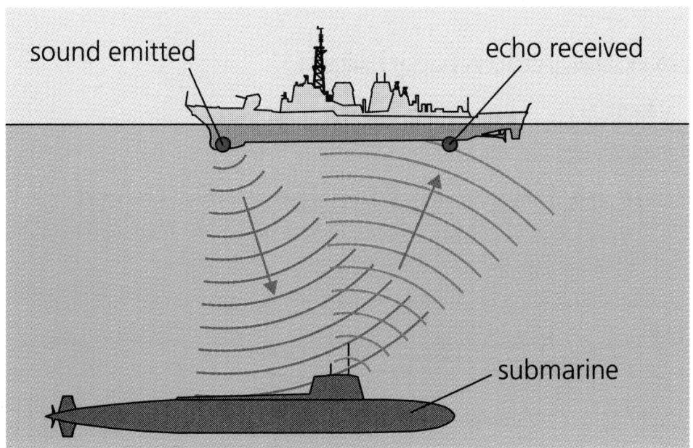

▲ *Fig 3 Echoes can help to locate the sea bed and any objects above it.*

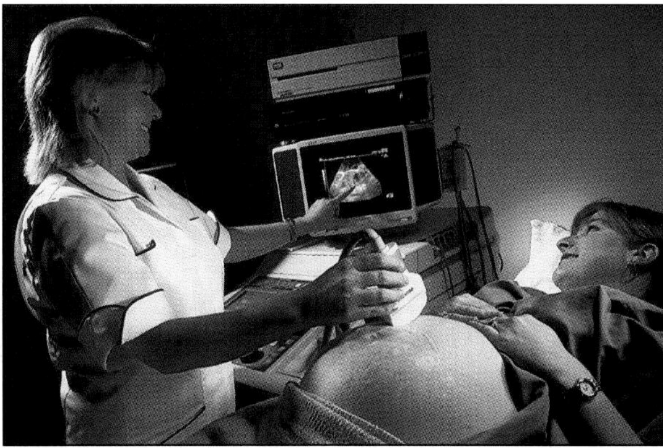

▲ *Fig 4 An ultrasound scan can show how well a baby is growing.*

Ultrasound

Very small sound waves called **ultrasound** are used to examine an unborn baby. The waves pass through the fluid in the womb and bounce back from the baby's body.

Q1 Name two places where echoes can be helpful.

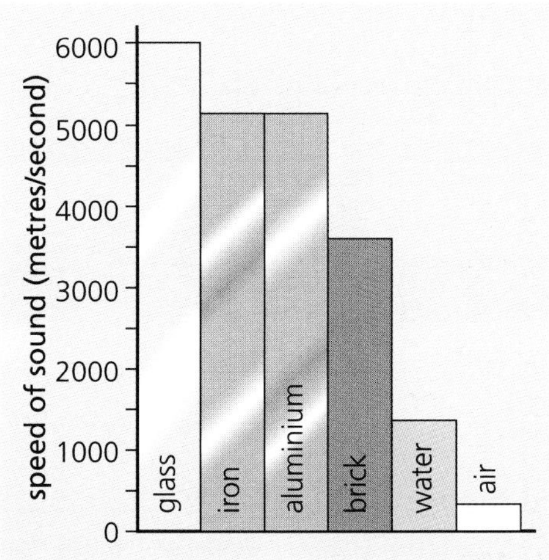

▲ *Fig 5*

Sound and materials

Sound travels through anything that can vibrate. This includes gases, liquids and solids (Fig 5). We can hear sounds through walls and floors, in swimming pools and in the air. Sound waves travel well through water. Whales can call to each other over many kilometres. If you tap very softly on a long bench and ask a friend to place his/her ear to the other end of the bench he/she will hear the tap through the bench but not through the air. Sound travels very well through solids.

Q2 What is the speed of sound through iron and aluminium?

Key Words

echo – a sound bouncing back from a solid surface
sonar – a way of finding objects by listening for echoes
sound energy – energy transmitted in sound waves
ultrasound – sound waves too small to hear

SUMMARY

- Sound bounces back from objects to make echoes.
- The speed of sound in air is around 340 m/s.
- Echoes can be used to locate wrecks and submarines.
- Ultrasound is used to examine babies in the womb.
- Sound travels further through solids and liquids than through gases.

SUMMARY *Activity*

Explain why walls with air spaces in the middle of them are more soundproof than solid walls. What else can help to keep sound out of a building?

90 Loudness and waves

In this section of the book you will learn the following things:

- **that sound cannot travel through a vacuum;**
- **what is meant by the amplitude of a wave;**
- **what is the link between the amplitude of a wave and loudness of a sound.**

Sound and a vacuum

We can hear a bell ringing inside a glass jar perfectly well. Sound travels through air and glass. Removing all the air from the jar makes a **vacuum** inside. If the bell is rung now, you will not be able to hear it. There are no air molecules inside to be vibrated by the bell. You can see the striker hitting the gong but you cannot hear the sound.

Sound cannot travel through a vacuum.

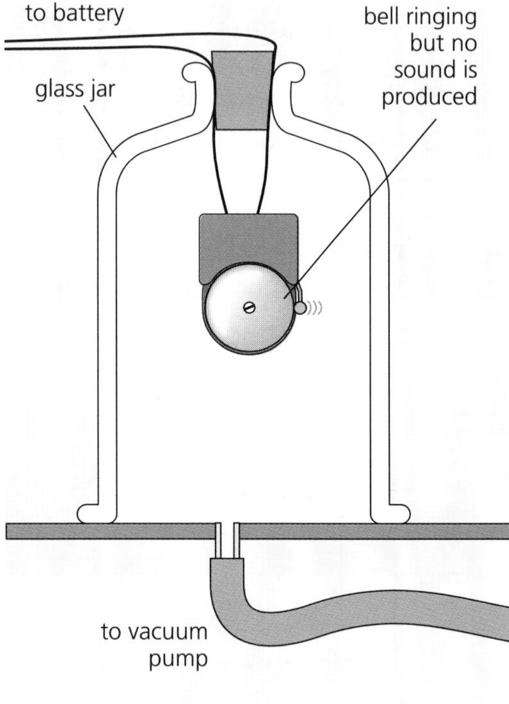

▲ *Fig 1 Bell in a vacuum.*

◄ ***Fig 2***

Q1 As sound cannot travel through a vacuum, how do astronauts (Fig 2) communicate in the vast vacuum of space?

About waves

The energy from a vibrating object travels outward as waves (Unit 88). If you have ever watched a ball floating on waves you will have seen the ball bobbing up and down. The waves do not push the ball along. This is because the waves move but the water just moves up and down. Sound waves in air behave in a similar way but this time they move backwards and forwards. The wave moves but the air does not. Sound waves can be seen by attaching a microphone to a machine called an **oscilloscope**. This shows the wave on a small screen (Fig 3).

Sound waves have crests and troughs just like a wave in a pond. As a wave becomes bigger it rises higher and higher above the normal (silent) level.

The distance above or below normal is called the **amplitude**. The amplitude of a wave is the distance from the crest (or the trough) to the middle. The larger the amplitude, the larger the wave. High waves in the sea have more energy. They can do more damage. This is also true of sound waves. A very large vibration will cause large sound waves. Large waves have a large amplitude. Waves with a large amplitude give a louder noise.

Sound waves with a large amplitude produce loud sounds.

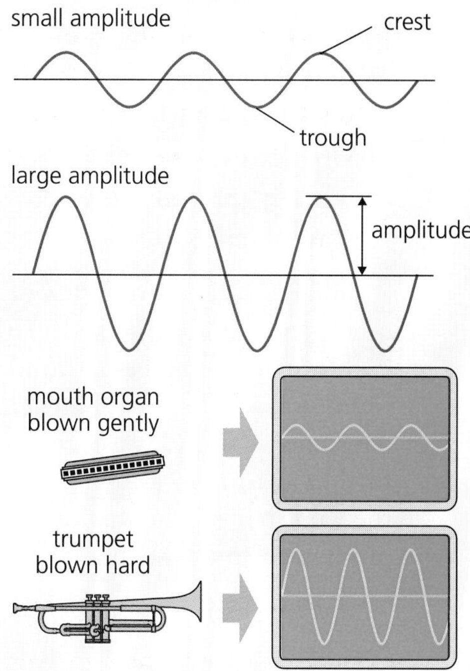

▲ *Fig 3*

Q2 Which instrument do you think produces sound waves with the largest amplitude, a trumpet or a flute?

Tuning forks and explosions

A tuning fork vibrates very fast. It is small and does not move very much air. The waves that the fork makes have a very small amplitude. The sound is not very loud. We can make it sound louder by pressing the base onto a hollow box. The vibration from the fork is **amplified** by the box. The box moves more air than the fork can.

A vast amount of air is moved by an explosion. The sound waves moving out from an explosion are very big. An explosion makes a very loud bang.

Q3 Why does an explosion make a louder noise than a tuning fork?

Key Words

amplify – to make a bigger wave with a louder sound
amplitude – the height of a wave
oscilloscope – a machine to show the shape of waves
vacuum – an area empty of free molecules

SUMMARY

- Sound cannot travel through a vacuum.
- The amplitude of a wave is the distance from the crest (or the trough) to the middle of the wave.
- A wave's amplitude increases as the amount of energy contained in the wave increases.
- The larger the amplitude of a sound wave, the louder the sound.

SUMMARY *Activity*

Use a washing up bowl to create waves of different amplitudes. Which are the waves that require most energy from you?

91 High and low notes

In this section of the book you will learn the following things:

- **what wavelength is;**
- **what is meant by the frequency of a wave;**
- **what is meant by the pitch of a sound;**
- **what is the link between the pitch of a sound and the frequency of the wave causing it.**

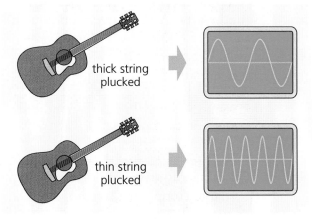

A guitar has strings of different thickness. The thinnest string vibrates very quickly when it is plucked. This creates sound waves that are close together. A thin string produces a sound with a high **pitch**. The thickest string vibrates more slowly when it is plucked. This creates sound waves that are further apart than the ones made by the thin string. The thick string produces a sound with a low pitch.

The wave shapes produced by these two strings are shown in Fig 1.

The pitch of a sound depends on how quickly or slowly the object making the sound is vibrating.

▲ ***Fig 1*** *The thinnest string produces sound waves that are closer together.*

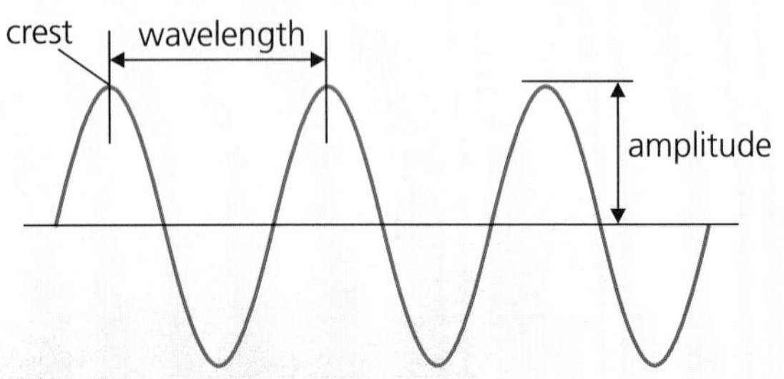

▲ ***Fig 2***

The distance between waves can be measured. It is the distance between two neighbouring crests or troughs. This is called the **wavelength** (Fig 2).

Q1 Which guitar string produces sound waves with the shortest wavelength?

Frequency

The **frequency** of a sound is the number of vibrations per second. Frequency is measured in **Hertz** (Hz). The thin string of a guitar vibrates 660 times per second. The frequency of the sound it makes is 660 Hz. The thickest string of a guitar vibrates 165 times per second. Remember that the pitch of a sound depends on how quickly or slowly the object is vibrating. The thin string has the highest frequency because it vibrates faster than the thick string. It will give a higher pitched sound.

The higher the frequency of a sound, the higher its pitch.

Q2 What is the frequency of sound produced by the thickest guitar string?

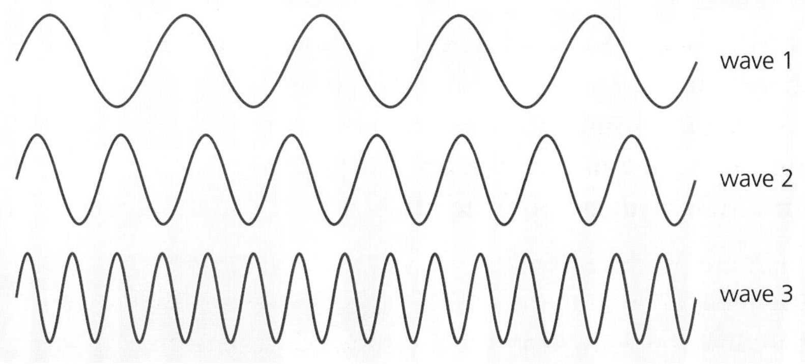

◀ ***Fig 3*** *Waves that are closer together have a higher frequency. They make a higher pitched sound.*

Changing the pitch of a string

The pitch of a guitar string depends on its thickness. It can also be altered by changing the length of the string (Fig 4). A short string vibrates more quickly than a long string. A short string therefore makes a sound with a higher frequency. A high frequency makes a high pitch. All the strings of a guitar are the same length but a guitar player can make notes of many different pitches. The frets across the neck of the guitar allow the player to press down and shorten the vibrating part of any string (Fig 5).

20 cm
string
vibrates slowly
10 cm
vibrates twice as quickly
double the frequency

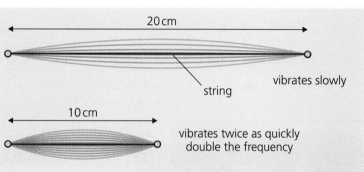

▲ ***Fig 4***

Q3 Describe how a guitarist changes the pitch of a string.

▶ ***Fig 5***

Key Words

Hertz – the unit for measuring frequency
frequency – the number of vibrations per second
pitch – how high or low a note is
wavelength – the distance between neighbouring wave crests

SUMMARY

- Wavelength is the distance between peaks or troughs of a wave.
- Frequency is the number of vibrations per second.
- Waves with a high frequency give high pitched sounds.
- Heavy, thick strings make lower pitched sounds than thin strings.
- Short strings make higher pitched sounds than long strings.

SUMMARY *Activity*

Hold a ruler firmly on top of a desk so that it overhangs the edge. Twang the ruler so that it makes a sound. Experiment to see how the length of the ruler changes the sound. What does this tell you about the frequency and the pitch of the sounds?

92 Taking care of your hearing

In this section of the book you will learn the following things:

- **that high-pitched sounds have more closely packed waves;**
- **that many animals hear sounds that we cannot hear;**
- **that different people have different ranges of hearing;**
- **how loud sounds can damage your hearing.**

High pitched sounds are produced by waves that have a high frequency. High frequency means that there are many waves per second. The unit for the number of waves per second is the Hertz (Hz). The Hertz number increases as the frequency increases. This means that high notes have a higher Hertz number than low notes. One thousand Hertz equals one kiloHertz (kHz).

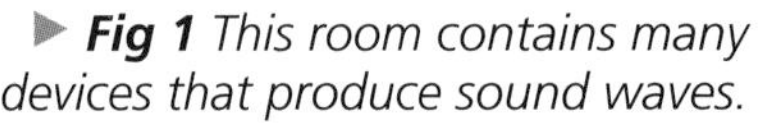

▶ ***Fig 1*** *This room contains many devices that produce sound waves.*

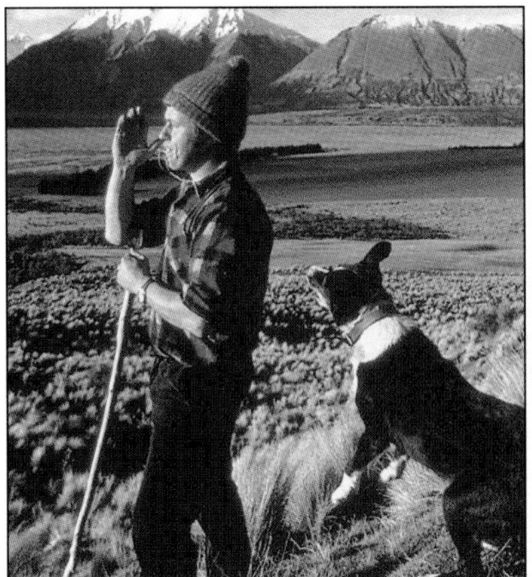

▲ ***Fig 2*** *The note from a dog whistle is too high for us to hear.*

Beyond our hearing

We can hear sounds that have a frequency between 20 Hz and 20 000 Hz (20 kHz). We say that these sounds are **audible**.

A large drum produces a very low note. This could be as low as 20 Hz. A shrill whistle may produce a note as high as 20 kHz. A dog whistle produces a note above 20 kHz. We cannot hear a dog whistle, but dogs and many other animals can (Fig 3).

Higher frequencies than we can hear are called **ultrasound**. Lower frequencies than we can hear are called **infrasound**.

Bats use ultrasound to 'see' in the dark (Fig 4). They make very high-pitched squeaks and use the echoes to avoid obstacles, like a ship using sonar (Unit 89). Bats also hunt with sound. They use echoes to find moths and other insects in the air. Hunting this way is called **echo location**.

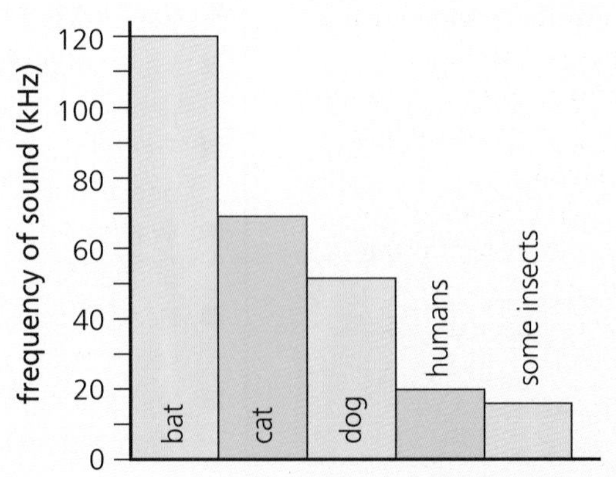

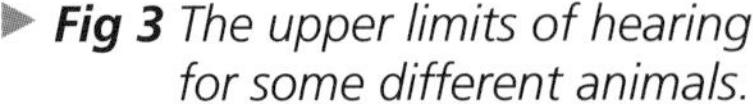

▶ ***Fig 3*** *The upper limits of hearing for some different animals.*

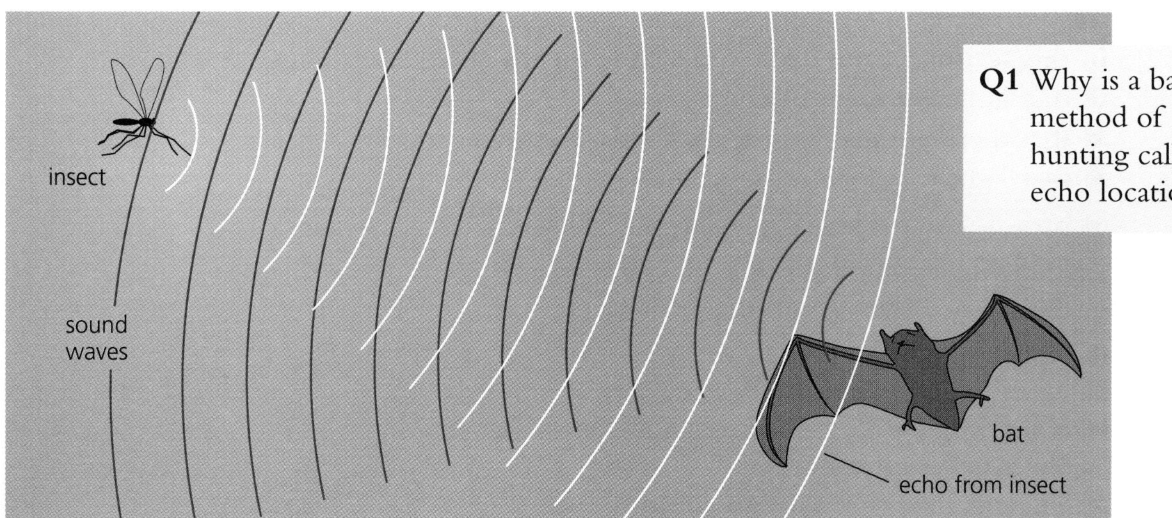

Q1 Why is a bat's method of hunting called echo location?

▲ *Fig 4*

Protecting your hearing

Our range of hearing becomes smaller as we get older. Old people cannot hear some of the sounds that they could hear when they were younger. Nerves in the cochlea (Unit 88) become less sensitive as time passes. Loud noises can also damage these nerves directly. The nerves in our ears cannot switch themselves off for a short while. Once they stop working, they stop for ever. Workers in noisy places must wear ear protectors that shut out some of the sound. Loud music can damage a person's hearing just as easily as a loud and unpleasant noise. A very loud noise such as an explosion can even break a person's eardrum. This is very painful. It also makes a hole where infection can enter. After it heals, the eardrum may be thicker and less sensitive than it was before.

Q2 Why is it important to check the volume of a personal stereo before you put the earphones on?

Key Words

audible – a sound that a person can hear
echo location – finding objects by listening to echoes
infrasound – a sound too low for a person to hear
ultrasound – a sound too high for a person to hear

SUMMARY

- Our range of hearing runs from 20 Hz to 20 kHz.
- Some animals can hear higher or lower sounds than we can.
- Bats use sonar or echo location to hunt and steer in the dark.
- Our range of hearing becomes smaller as we grow older.
- Our hearing can be permanently damaged by loud sounds.
- Very loud noises can damage the eardrum in our ear.

SUMMARY *Activity*

Use your hand to make waves in a shallow tray of water. Adjust your hand movements to demonstrate how increasing the frequency of the waves decreases their wavelength.

93 Light

In this section of the book you will learn the following things:

- **that light is a form of energy;**
- **that there are many sources of light energy;**
- **that light travels in straight lines.**

The caver in Fig 1 would not be able to see anything at all without a lamp. The photograph gives us several clues about the way light behaves.

- A light beam is straight.
- Light bounces off the walls of the cave.
- Light from outside cannot get in by following bends in the tunnel.
- The region outside the light beam is dark.
- There are dark shadows behind lit up rocks.

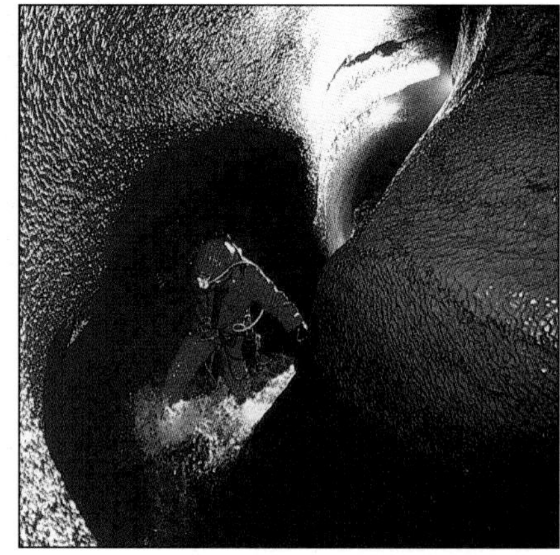

▲ ***Fig 1*** *Natural light never shines into this cave.*

What is light?

Light is a form of energy. The caver's lamp contains a battery which produces electrical energy and a light bulb that changes the electrical energy into light energy. Burning gases also give out light energy. The Sun gives out light energy.

Q1 List three sources of light energy.

Straight lines

We cannot see round corners. Our vision depends on light travelling from an object to our eyes. The reason why we cannot see round a corner is because light cannot bend around a corner.

We can use three cards to show that light travels in straight lines. This experiment is shown in Fig 3.

The light source can only be seen when the holes in the card are in a perfectly straight line. If one of the cards is not in line the light disappears. When you can see the light bulb a piece of cotton threaded through the holes will be perfectly straight. If the cotton is not straight you will not be able to see the light.

Q2 Explain why we cannot see round corners.

▲ ***Fig 2*** *Sometimes it would be useful to be able to see around corners.*

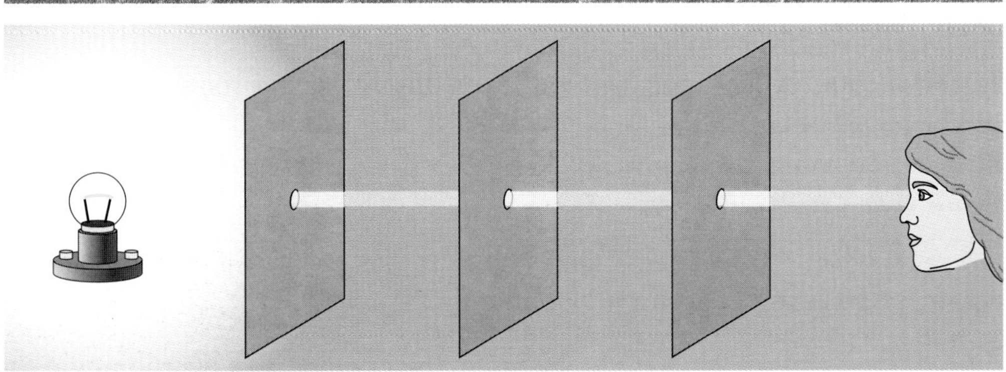

Fig 3

Pinhole camera

The fact that light travels in straight lines makes it possible to project a picture onto a screen at the cinema or a slide-show. We can even use a hole in a card to make a picture on a screen.

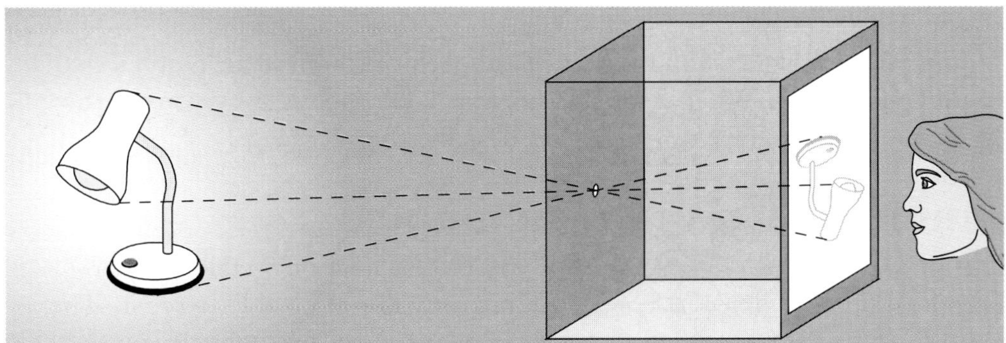

Fig 4

A **pinhole camera** is made from a box with one side cut out and replaced with a sheet of tracing paper. This is the screen. A single pinhole is made in the side opposite the screen. When the pinhole is pointed at a light source such as a lamp, an image of the lamp will appear on the screen (Fig 4).

The image on the pinhole camera screen is upside down. This is because the light from the top of the lamp travels in a straight line through the pinhole. It continues to go in a straight line until it hits the screen. This means it must land at the bottom. Light from the bottom of the lamp lands at the top. A pinhole camera gives us more proof that light travels in straight lines.

Q3 How does a pinhole camera help to prove that light travels in straight lines?

Key Words

pinhole camera – a simple camera with no lens

SUMMARY

- Light is a form of energy.
- Light travels in straight lines.
- The three card experiment and the pinhole camera help to prove that light travels in straight lines.

SUMMARY *Activity*

Make your own pinhole camera from a small box. Point it towards some light sources. Draw the images that appear on the screen.

94 Light to see by

In this section of the book you will learn the following things:

- the speed of light;
- how surfaces reflect light;
- how we can see objects;
- why sight is useful for animals.

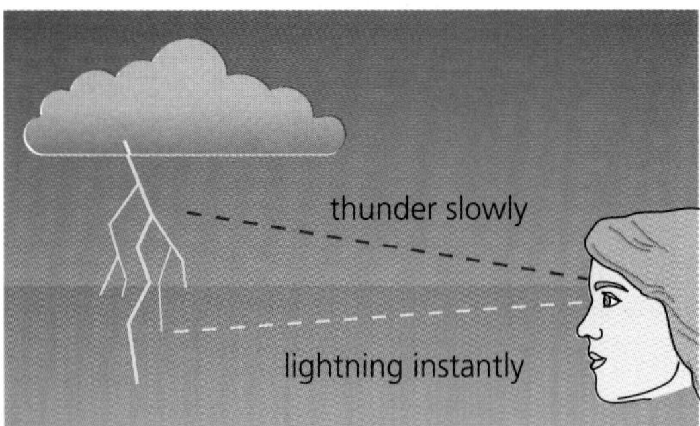

▲ *Fig 1*

The speed of light

Light travels very fast. The light from the Sun only takes 8 minutes to travel 150 million kilometres to the Earth's surface. This means that the speed of light in space is approximately 300 million metres per second. Most of the light we see arrives so quickly that it seems to take no time at all.

Compared with light, sound is slow. The speed of sound in air is about 340 metres per second. When a thunderstorm is 2 kilometres away you see the lightning almost 6 seconds before you hear the thunder (Fig 1).

Luminous and non-luminous

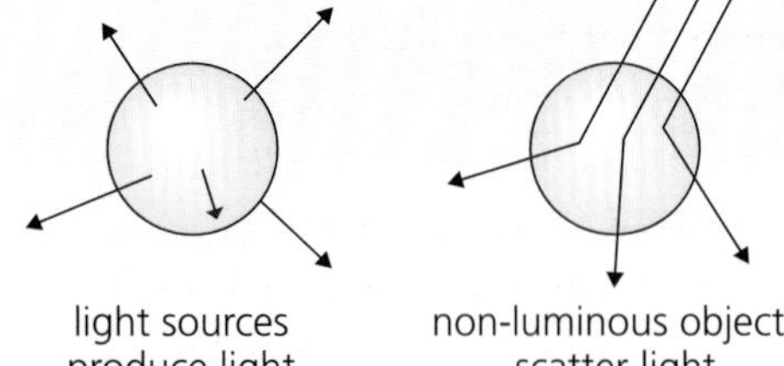

▲ ***Fig 2*** *Luminous objects emit light. Non-luminous objects reflect light.*

If you place a coat on a table in a dark room you will not be able to see it. The coat does not give out light. If you switch on a lamp you will be able to see the lamp and the coat. The lamp gives out light. It is **luminous**. The coat does not give out light. It is not luminous. The coat becomes visible because it **reflects** light given out by the lamp.

Scattered light

If you walk round the table you will still be able to see the coat. Even if you walk to the other side of the room you will be able to see the coat. When the light from the lamp hits the coat it is scattered in all directions.

The surface of the coat is rough. If you look closely (Fig 3) you will see that the surface is broken up into mountains and canyons. The light is scattered from this surface in all directions.

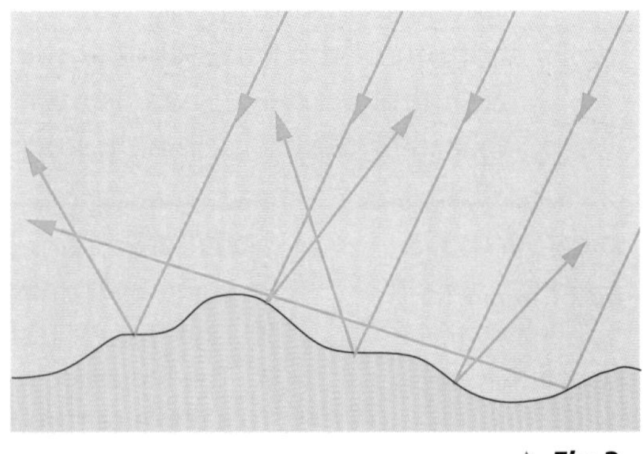
▲ *Fig 3*

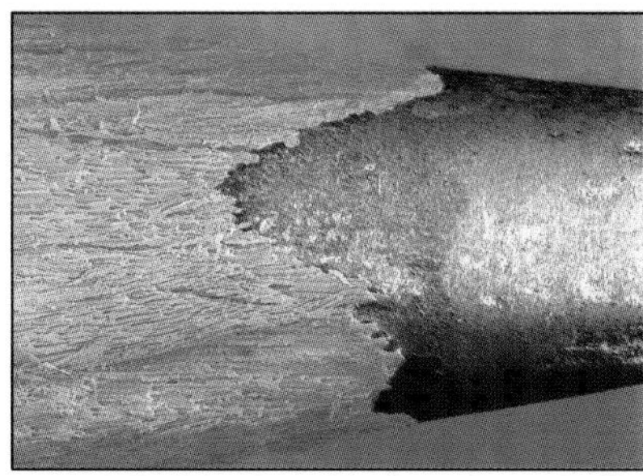

Even objects that may look very smooth have tiny hills and valleys on their surface. You can see a shiny new pencil from every part of the room. Under a microscope (Fig 4) the surface looks like the surface of the Moon.

◀ ***Fig 4*** *Under the microscope, a smooth surface is rough.*

Q1 Explain why every person in your class can see the teacher, even though you all sit in different places in the room.

Q2 Why is the Moon visible from different parts of the Earth?

Animals and sight

We have complicated eyes that can see the world in great detail. Many other animals have eyes that can make use of reflected light. Their eyes enable them to find food, to move around safely, or to escape from enemies. Bees can use the Sun's position to find their way home. Some moths use the Moon's position to fly in a straight line. Some birds can navigate by the stars. Cats' eyes are so sensitive that they can see by starlight.

Some animals do not need to see a picture. Many invertebrates (Unit 30) have very simple eyes that cannot tell them much more than whether it is light or dark. This information may be essential for their survival. Earthworms live in the dark but being aware of light helps them to stay underground. It also helps them to hide from animals that do need light to see by.

◀ ***Fig 5*** *Earthworms cannot see but they can detect light.*

Q3 Why is the ability to detect light important to animals?

Key Words

emit – to give out

luminous – an object that emits light

reflect – to bounce off the surface of an object

SUMMARY

- The speed of light in Space is approximately 300 million metres per second.
- Luminous objects emit light.
- Light is reflected from non-luminous objects.
- We see non-luminous objects by the light they reflect into our eyes.
- Most objects have rough surfaces and scatter light in all directions.
- Scattered light makes objects visible from all directions.

SUMMARY *Activity*

Make a list of objects in your home that emit light. Make a list of 10 objects that you can see because of reflection from these light sources.

95 Reflecting light

In this section of the book you will learn the following things:

- **what a plane surface is;**
- **how light is reflected by a mirror;**
- **the main law of reflection of light.**

Most objects have a rough surface which scatters light. Objects can therefore be seen from many directions (Unit 94). A mirror is an object. It can be seen from many directions, but the image reflected from its surface changes when you move or when the mirror moves. This is because the glass of a mirror is perfectly flat and very smooth. It is called a **plane** surface. A plane surface does not scatter light.

▲ ***Fig 1*** *You cannot see the camera that took this picture. Where was the camera?*

Q1 Why is light not scattered by the surface of a mirror?

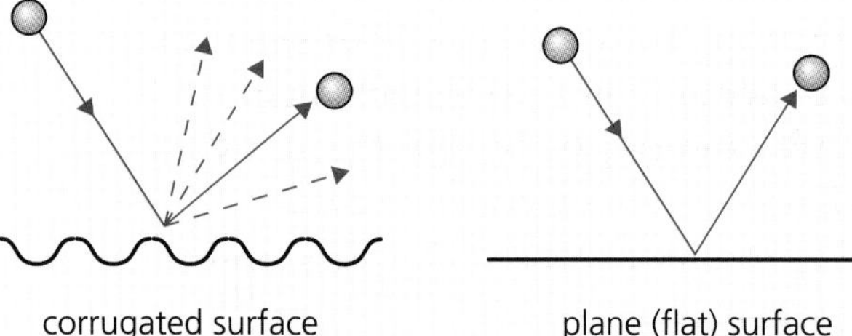

◀ ***Fig 2*** *A ball bounces off a corrugated surface at different angles. It bounces off a flat surface at a regular angle.*

If you stand in front of a mirror you can see an **image** of yourself. If you stand to one side of the mirror you see a different part of the room.

When light hits the plane surface of a mirror it bounces off at a regular angle. This is called regular reflection. We can show this by shining a thin beam of light onto a mirror and marking where its reflection lands (Fig 3).

The light hitting the mirror is called the **incident ray**. The angle at which it hits the mirror is called the **angle of incidence**. The light leaving the mirror is called the **reflected ray**. The angle at which it leaves is called the **angle of reflection**. These two angles are always the same.

angle of incidence = angle of reflection

Q2 What does the term angle of incidence mean?

plane mirror
a
b
incident ray
reflected ray
ray box
normal line (right angles to the mirror)
angle a = angle b
angle of incidence = angle of reflection

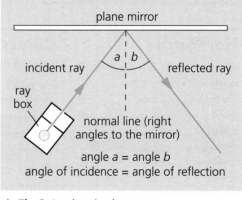

▲ ***Fig 3*** *Angle a is always the same as angle b.*

The image in a mirror looks the same size and shape as the object that is reflected. It is not exactly the same because right becomes left and left becomes right (Fig 4). The image is the same distance behind the mirror as the object is in front of the mirror. We say that the image is **virtual** because we cannot capture it on a screen the way we can capture an image passing through a pinhole (Unit 93).

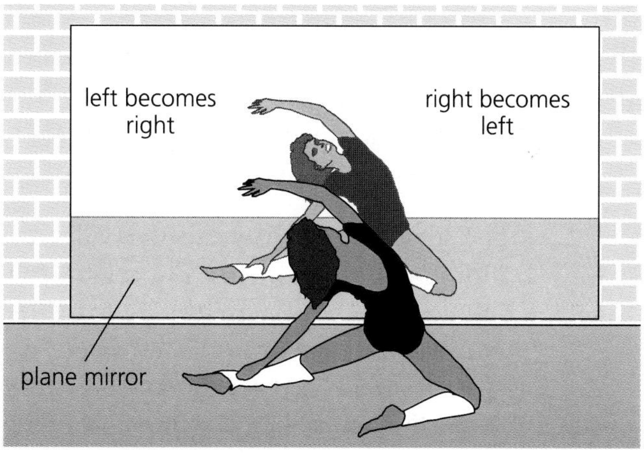

left becomes right

right becomes left

plane mirror

▲ ***Fig 4***

Using reflection

Mirrors are very useful for seeing round corners and inspecting places that are difficult to reach. A dentist uses a mirror to see the back of your teeth. The dentist will have to remember that left becomes right in a mirror image! Mechanics use mirrors to examine pipes and engine parts that they cannot see directly.

◀ ***Fig 5*** *The mirrors in a periscope allow us to see round corners.*

Q3 How would you use a periscope to make your own life easier?

Key Words

image – a copy of an object
incident ray – a ray of light hitting a surface
plane – a very flat, smooth surface
reflected ray – a ray of light reflected from a surface
virtual – something that is not real

SUMMARY

- A very flat, smooth surface is called a plane surface.
- A plane surface reflects light at a regular angle.
- Light rays hitting a plane surface are called incident rays.
- Light rays leaving a plane surface are called reflected rays.
- The angle of incidence at a plane surface is always the same as the angle of reflection.

SUMMARY *Activity*

Use two small mirrors and some tubes of cardboard to design and build your own periscope.

96 Refraction of light

In this section of the book you will learn the following things:

- **what refraction is;**
- **what happens when light crosses between different substances;**
- **some problems and uses of refraction.**

The straw in Fig 1 is perfectly straight. The photograph is not a trick photograph. The straw only looks bent because the light we see it by was bent when it came out of the water. When light passes from air into a different substance, such as water or glass, it changes direction. This is called **refraction**.

▼ ***Fig 1***

The rays of light entering a clear substance are called **incident** rays. The rays of light leaving a clear substance are called **refracted** rays. Rays hitting the surface at right angles are called **normal** rays.

Any light ray passing at an angle from air into water or glass bends towards the normal. This is because water and glass are more dense than air.

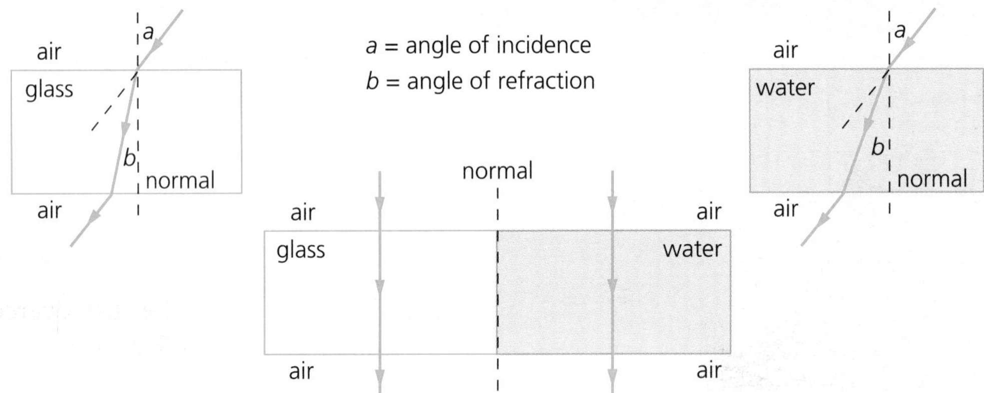

▲ ***Fig 2*** *A single ray going through a block of glass or a fishtank is bent twice, first when it enters and again when it leaves.*

When the light rays leave the glass or water they bend away from the normal. This is because air is less dense.

- Light rays passing into a dense material bend towards the normal.
- Light rays passing into a less dense material bend away from the normal.

Q1 What is the term for a ray of light when it emerges from a clear substance?

Effects of refraction

You can try the coin trick (Fig 3) at home. Simply drop a coin into an empty cup and find a position where you can see about halfway into the cup without seeing the coin. Now sit someone else in the same place and tell them that you can make the coin appear without touching it or the cup. All you need to do is add some water. Not magic, only refraction.

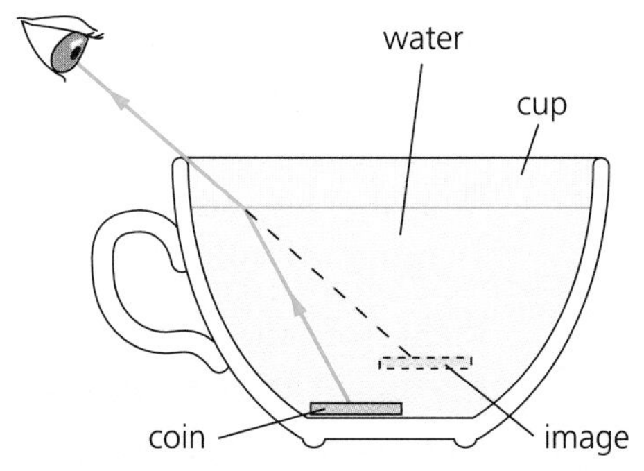

▲ *Fig 3*

Refraction makes a swimming pool look shallower than it really is. If you have ever tried to scoop a fish out of a pond, you will know that refraction can also make all kinds of underwater objects seem closer to the surface than they really are (Fig 4).

▼ *Fig 4*

Q2 Why is it more difficult to snatch a coin from the bottom of a swimming pool than you expect it to be?

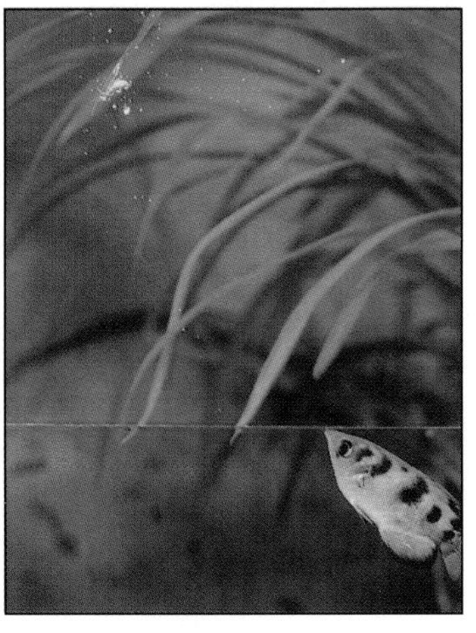

◀ *Fig 5*

Archer fish

The archer fish of Central America catches dinner by firing a jet of water at an insect in the air (Fig 5). This knocks the insect into the water where the fish can eat it. Hitting a target on the other side of a refracting surface is difficult. The archer fish solves this problem by having two parts to its eyes. The upper part is for seeing in water and the lower part is for seeing in air.

Q3 How does the archer fish overcome the problem of refraction?

Key Words

normal – a line at right angles to the surface
refracted ray – a light ray leaving a clear object
refraction – light bending at the surface of a transparent substance

SUMMARY

- A ray of light bends when it enters a different transparent substance.
- The change of direction is called refraction.
- Light bends towards the normal when entering a denser substance.
- Light bends away from the normal when entering a less dense substance.
- Refraction makes objects in water seem closer than they really are.

SUMMARY *Activity*

Use what you have learned about refraction to try to explain how a magnifying glass works.

97 Light and colour

In this section of the book you will learn the following things:

- **what white light is;**
- **that white light can be split to give a range of colours.**

▲ *Fig 1*

Light from the Sun is white. It does not appear to contain any colours. So where do colours come from?

White light is really a mixture of colours. The range of colours that make up white light is called the **spectrum**. When light from the Sun hits a dewdrop it may sparkle with all the colours of the rainbow (Fig 1). The colours of a rainbow are:

red orange yellow green blue indigo violet

You can remember the correct order by learning this phrase:

Richard **O**f **Y**ork **G**ave **B**attle **I**n **V**ain

Little phrases like this are a good way to remember lists. You can invent some of your own to help you with your science.

Q1 Cover up your book and write down the colours of the spectrum from memory.

The light from the Sun is refracted or bent when it passes from the air into water (see Unit 96). Different colours bend at slightly different angles. Violet light bends through a bigger angle than red light. Each of the colours in between has its own angle.

Q2 Which of the colours in white light is refracted least?

Isaac Newton's prism

In the 17th century Sir Isaac Newton created a spectrum in his laboratory. He used a triangular **prism** made of glass (Fig 2). The angle of the glass faces in a prism is perfect for splitting white light into bands of colour.

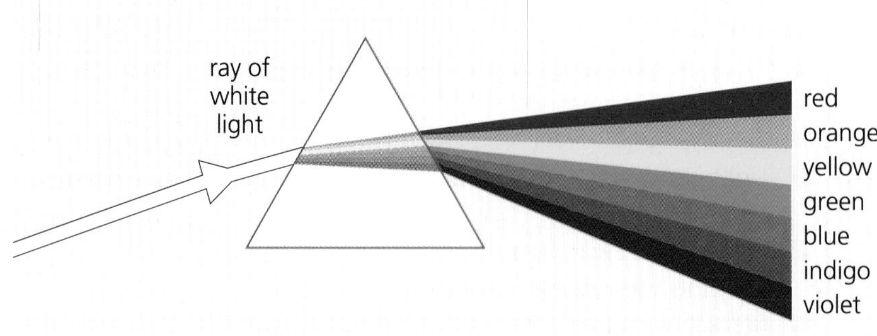

◄ *Fig 2*

Mixing colours

Three of the colours of the spectrum are called **primary colours**. They cannot be made by mixing any other colours together. The primary colours of the spectrum are red, blue and green. All the other colours in the rainbow can be made by mixing these three primary colours.

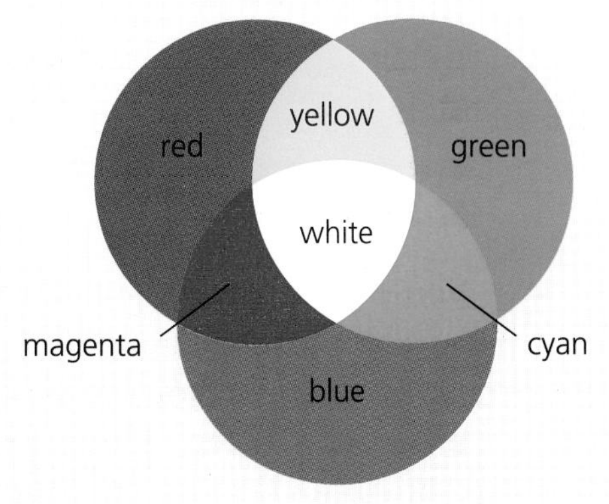

▲ ***Fig 3*** *The primary colours of light and how they mix.*

Light colours work differently from the colours in a paintbox. Paint colours reflect light (see Unit 98). Light colours *are* light.

We can make white light by adding different coloured lights together. We do not need a whole rainbow. Mixing the primary colours – red, green and blue – will give us white light.

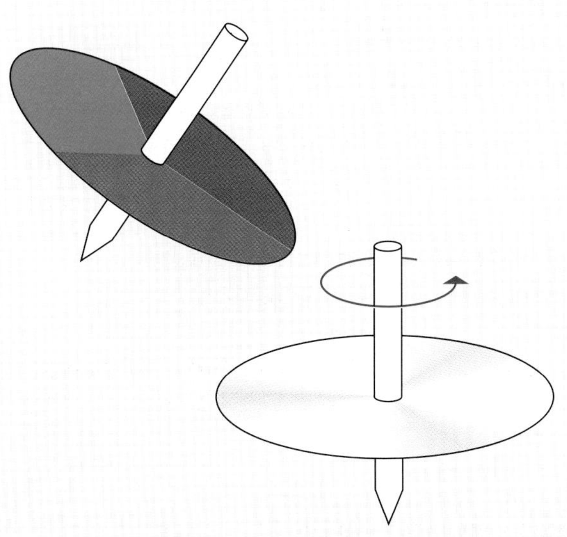

Colours can also be combined by spinning a cardboard disk. The disk is split into three equal sections. Each section is a different primary colour. When the coloured disk is spun very quickly, your eye sees all the colours at once and the disk appears to be white.

◀ ***Fig 4*** *Our eyes do not work fast enough to separate the colours when a disc is spun. Red, green and blue combine to make white.*

Q3 How would you colour a spinning disk so that it would look cyan when it was spun?

Key Words

primary colour – a pure colour containing no other colours

prism – a triangular block of glass for splitting light

spectrum – the range of colours in white light.

SUMMARY

- White light is made up of many different colours.
- The range of colours in white light is called the spectrum.
- Refraction through glass or water can split white light into its spectrum.
- Red, blue and green are primary colours of light.
- Colours can be mixed to make other colours and white light.

SUMMARY *Activity*

Use a circle of card and coloured pencils to make a colour disk. Spin the disk by pushing a pencil through the exact centre of the card.
Try to make disks that appear: a) yellow; b) magenta; b) white when they are spun.

98 Colours we see

In this section of the book you will learn the following things:

- **how coloured filters change white light;**
- **how objects get their colours;**
- **the effect of different coloured light on coloured objects.**

Some substances give out coloured light when they burn. Sodium burns with a yellow flame. Orange-yellow street lights are often called sodium lights. Coloured light can also be obtained from white light by passing it through a transparent **filter**. The colour of the filter is the same as the colour of the light that comes through it. A filter does not add colour to white light. The colour is already contained in the light (Unit 97). The filter works by absorbing some colours from the light and allowing the rest to go through. A red filter looks red because it absorbs all colours except red.

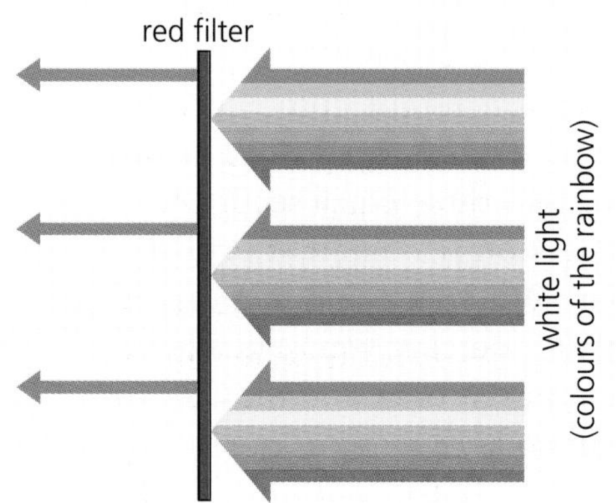

Filters are used to create lighting effects on the stage and in films. They make the green, amber and red traffic lights that motorists have to obey. A rear bicycle lamp contains a red filter.

◀ ***Fig 1*** *A red filter absorbs all the colours of the spectrum except red.*

Q1 List three examples of colour filters you have seen being used.

Coloured objects

Most substances do not let light through them. They are **opaque**. Opaque objects **absorb** some colours of light and **reflect** others. Their colour depends on the colour of the light they reflect. White objects reflect all the light landing on them. Black objects absorb all the light landing on them.

Leaves look green because they absorb red and blue light. Only the green light bounces off leaves. A blue hat absorbs all the colours of white light except blue. It looks blue because the blue light bounces off. A white hat (Fig 2) looks blue if you shine blue light on it. It cannot make white light. It can only reflect all the light that hits it.

▶ ***Fig 2***

Q2 How could you make a white hat look like a red hat?

If you shine blue light onto a green hat none of the light will be reflected. The hat has no green light to reflect so it looks black (Fig 3).

- White objects reflect all the light that falls on them.
- Black objects objects absorb all the light that shines on them.
- Coloured objects reflect some of the light that shines on them.

Q3 What colour would a blue cap be in red light?

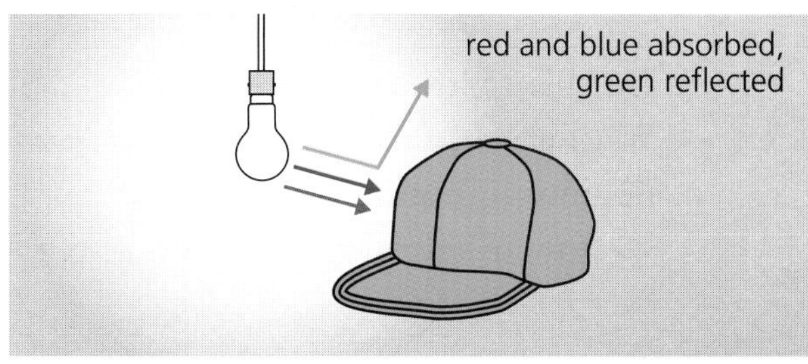

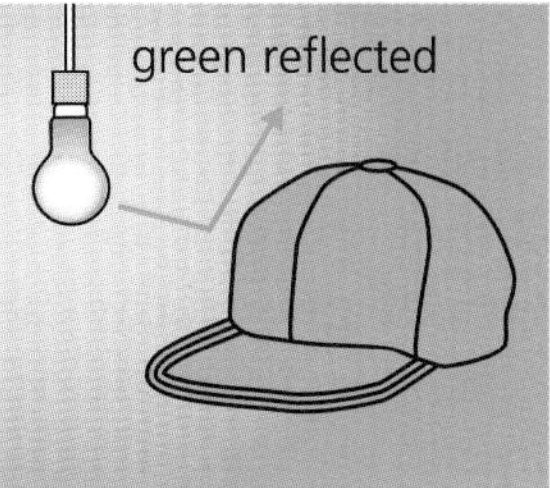

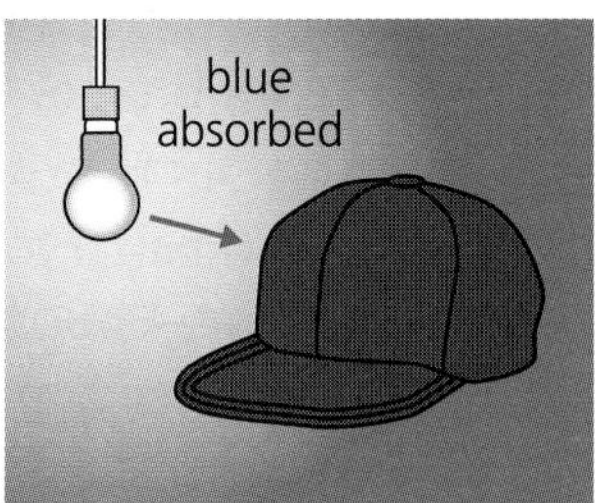

▲ *Fig 3*

▲ *Fig 4*

Q4 Why are divers advised to wear white markings and paint their equipment white rather than red?

Water absorbs some of the light passing through it. Pure water absorbs a lot of red, some yellow and some green light. This is why deep clear water looks blue (Fig 4). Objects underwater also look blue because the water filters out other colours they reflect. Divers need to be able to see one another underwater for safety reasons. They never wear bright red. Bright red is only bright in white light. Red is absorbed by a blue filter. Red can look black under water.

Key Words

absorb – to soak up
filter – a substance that holds back part of what lands on it
opaque – not allowing light to pass through
reflect – bounce back from a surface

SUMMARY

- Colour filters absorb some white light and only allow one colour through.
- Objects that reflect all the colours in white light look white.
- Objects that absorb all the colours of white light look black.
- Opaque objects do not emit colour.
- The colour of an opaque object depends on the colour of the light it reflects.
- Water absorbs more red, yellow and green light than blue light.

SUMMARY *Activity*

Using coloured sweet wrappers as filters, look at different colours through different coloured filters. Make a chart to show your results.

99 Electricity on the move

In this section of the book you will learn the following things:

- **that static electricity can be powerful;**
- **how lightning forms;**
- **how a lightning conductor works;**
- **that electricity can flow.**

You may remember looking at static charges in your previous study, for example the small charges that produce sparks when brushing clean hair. Not all static charges are as small as this. A **Van de Graaff generator** can build up a very large static charge on the outer surface of the dome at the top. The volunteer in the photograph (Fig 1) is insulated from the floor so the charge passing into her body cannot escape to Earth. Her whole body is negatively charged. Each strand of hair is negatively charged. The hairs move away from her body and from each other.

▶ ***Fig 1*** *The Van de Graaff generator can build a charge of millions of volts. Fortunately, this is only a small model.* ⚠ ***Caution:*** *thick soled shoes should be worn during this experiment.*

Electrical storms

Thunder clouds contain tiny ice crystals. They are also full of violent movement. As the clouds churn around, the ice crystals rub past one other. The friction between them creates an electric charge. The charge grows bigger and bigger, like the charge in the Van de Graaff generator. Each flash of lightning we see during a storm is a giant electric spark jumping from one cloud to another or across the gap to the ground.

◀ ***Fig 2*** *These flashes of lightning are electric sparks jumping across the gap between the clouds and the earth.*

Q1 How do thunder clouds become charged?

Moving charge

Metals conduct electricity (Unit 49). Rubbing a metal rod cannot charge it, but a metal rod can conduct electricity from a charged glass or plastic rod to a metal-covered ball (Fig 3).

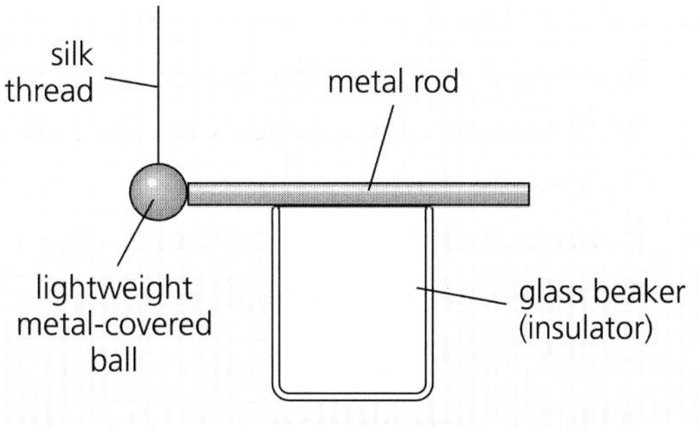

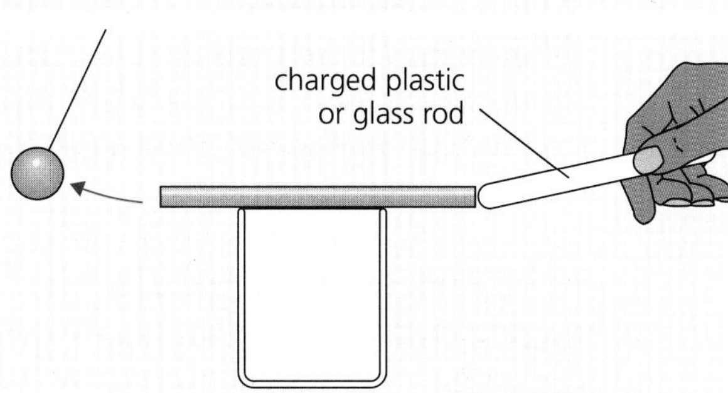

▶ ***Fig 3*** *The static charge from a non-conductor can be conducted through the metal rod to the ball.*

Q2 Why is the metal rod in Fig 3 balanced on a glass beaker?

Q3 Why does the girl in Fig 1 wear thick soled shoes?

Lightning usually strikes tall and pointed objects. High buildings and church spires often have a strip of metal called a **lightning conductor** running from top to bottom. This allows the electricity to flow safely into the earth and protects the building from being damaged by lightning.

Q4 Why is it unwise to shelter under a tall tree during a thunderstorm?

Q5 Why it is unwise to stand in an open space during a thunderstorm?

Most of the electricity we use is generated in power stations. It flows through metal wires into our homes. Many of the devices we use at home rely on this **current**. If the wires are broken anywhere between the power station and our home the electricity stops flowing.

A torch or a personal stereo uses electricity from a small chemical power station called a battery. It is connected to the battery with wires.

Q6 Make a list of 10 devices that use electric current.

Key Words

current – the flow of electricity

lightning conductor – a metal strip to protect a tall building from lightning

Van de Graaff generator – a machine for making a large static electric charge

SUMMARY

- A Van de Graaff generator can make a large electric charge.
- Ice crystals rubbing together in thunderclouds can make a large electric charge.
- Lightning is caused by electricity jumping between two clouds or between clouds and the ground.
- Electricity flowing along wires is called an electric current.

SUMMARY *Activity*

Explain why you sometimes get goose-pimples during a thunderstorm.

100 Conductors and insulators

In this section of the book you will learn the following things:

- that some materials conduct electricity and others do not;
- how materials conduct electricity;
- why conductors and insulators are important.

Metals are conductors. They conduct electricity. Non-metals do not conduct electricity. They are insulators. This is why the wires that carry electric current are made of metal covered with plastic insulation (Fig 1).

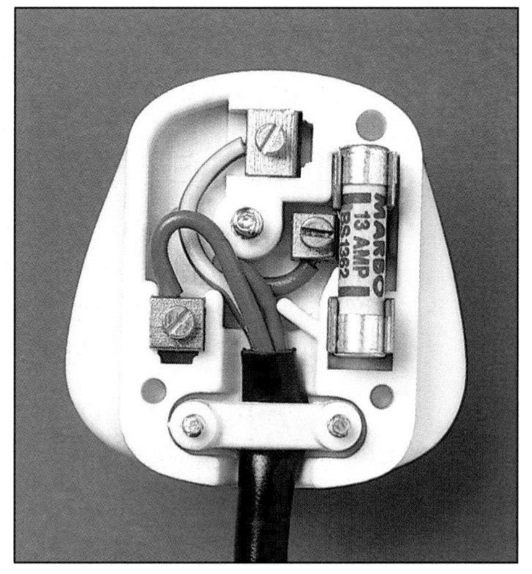

▲ *Fig 1*

Testing materials

We can test a substance to find out whether it conducts electricity. The substance is placed across a gap in a circuit. If the substance is a conductor it will light up a bulb in the circuit. If it is an insulator it will not light up the bulb.

Table 1 shows that:

- metals are conductors
- most non-metals are insulators

Q1 Name one non-metal that can conduct electricity.

substance	conducts electricity
silver	✔
copper	✔
aluminium	✔
graphite	✔
pure water*	✘
glass	✘
rubber	✘
plastics	✘

◀ *Table 1*

*Water at home and in the laboratory is not pure. **Impurities** in water allow it to conduct electricity from a wire to your body.

How metals conduct electricity

Electric current is caused by a flow of electrons. The atoms in a metal are packed closely together. Electrons often change places between atoms in a metal. If they are given energy they can be pushed along. Electrons are pushed away (repelled) from a negative charge and attracted towards a positive charge (Fig 2).

▼ *Fig 2*

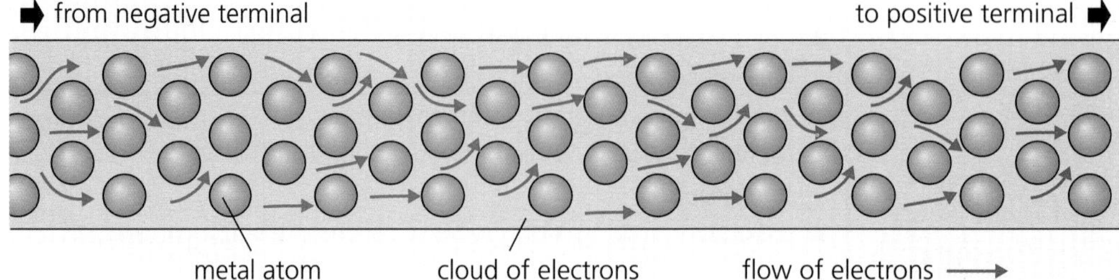

Electrons can move easily through metal wires connected together. They pass between the atoms of the metal and rarely collide with them. When the electrons in a thick wire are pushed through a narrow section of wire they have to move faster. They collide with the atoms more often. This can make the metal become hot. It may become hot enough to give out light. A light bulb contains a very thin **filament** of metal.

Electrons in insulating materials do not move freely. They are firmly held by their atoms. When an insulator is put into a circuit the current cannot pass through it. No current will flow.

▶ ***Fig 3*** *The thin filament heats up when the electrons pass through it. This makes a light bulb glow.*

Electricity and safety

The electricity in your home is dangerous. If you touch a bare wire you will receive a shock. This can kill you. Insulation helps to protect us from being hurt by electricity. Wires, sockets and plugs are covered with plastic insulation. Many tools have plastic or rubber handles so that if they do touch a wire the electricity will not reach the person using the tool.

There are many safety rules for living with electricity. Some of the most important are:

- always ask a trained electrician to repair faults
- never allow water to touch electrical equipment
- always switch off any faulty electrical equipment
- stay away from power cables.

Q2 Why do insulating materials not conduct electricity?

Q3 Name two substances that would make a good handle for an electrician's screwdriver.

Key Words

filament – very thin wire in a light bulb

impurity – any unwanted substance mixed with another substance

SUMMARY

- Metals are conductors of electricity.
- Most non-metals are insulators.
- Electric current is the flow of electrons.
- The electrons in metals are free to move.
- Electrons in insulators are not free to move.
- Electricity can be very dangerous.

SUMMARY *Activity*

Design a safety poster that explains some of the dangers of electricity. Include the words 'conductor' and 'insulator'.

101 Electric circuits

In this section of the book you will learn the following things:

- **how to set up an electric circuit;**
- **how to measure current;**
- **how to measure current in series and parallel circuits.**

Bicycle lamps (Fig 1) allow us to take electricity with us. Each lamp needs a cell, often called a battery, a bulb, wires and a switch. These components make up the electric circuit of the lamp. Electricity only flows if the wires are joined in a complete ring. This ring is called a **circuit**. If any of the components are missing or broken the lamp will not work.

▲ *Fig 1*

Electric circuits

Fig 2 shows an electric circuit for a bicycle lamp. The battery pushes electric current through the circuit. Electrons flow from the negative terminal of the battery. The flow of electrons is the current. Wires link the battery to the bulb. The bulb lights up when the current passes through it. If the circuit is broken the current will stop. The switch stops and starts the current.

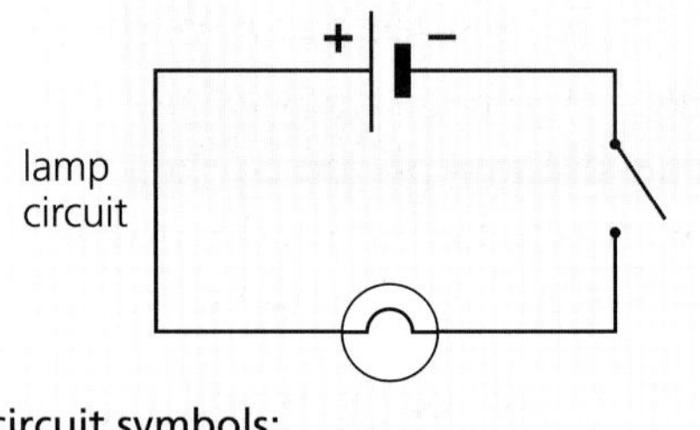

circuit symbols:

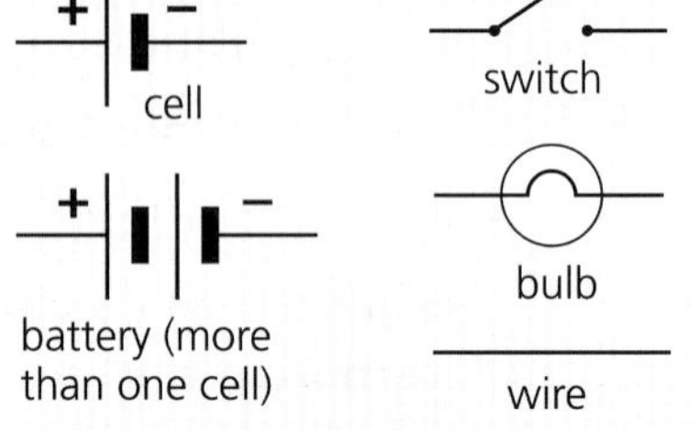

◀ *Fig 2*

Q1 Why is a switch an important part of an electric circuit?

Measuring current

The size of an electric current depends on the number of electrons flowing in the circuit. It is measured in amperes or **amps**. One amp (**A**) is about 1 million billion electrons per second flowing around the circuit. We use a meter called an **ammeter** to measure the size of the current. The circuit in Fig 3 has a current of 2 amps. This is written as 2A.

Q2 What is the flow of electrons in a circuit called?

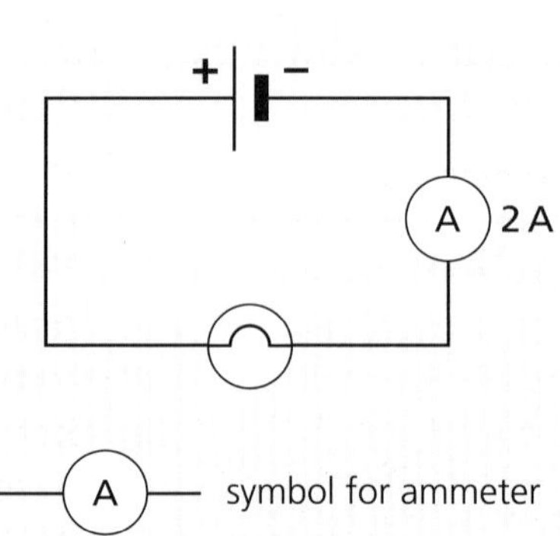

▲ *Fig 3*

Series and parallel circuits

There are different ways of arranging electric circuits. A circuit with two bulbs can be arranged in two different ways (Fig 4).

You could connect the bulbs up in a row, one after another. This is called a **series**. You could connect the bulbs up side by side, with each one having its own part of the circuit. This is called a **parallel** circuit.

The current in a series circuit has to pass through both bulbs. It does not matter where you place an ammeter in a series circuit. The current is the same everywhere on the circuit. If one bulb fails it will break the circuit. The other bulb will go out even if it is not damaged. This is what sometimes happens with the lights on the Christmas tree.

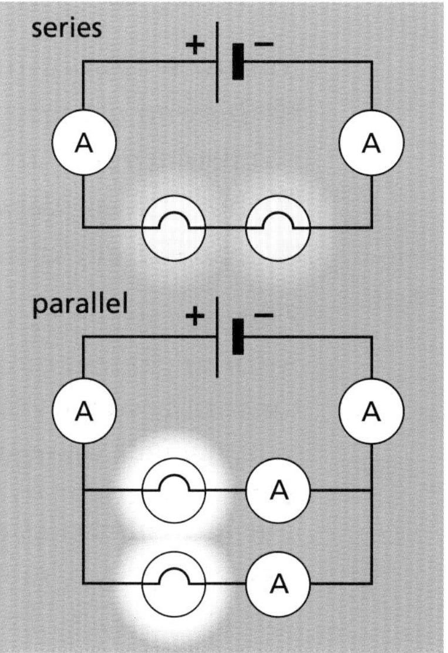

▲ ***Fig 4*** *Parallel circuits have less resistance so more current flows.*

The current in a parallel circuit depends on the number of parallel lines it has. An ammeter shows a different reading depending on where it is placed in the circuit and how many lines are being used at the time. If one bulb fails, the other will continue to work. A parallel circuit allows you to switch separate lights on and off without affecting the others. Parallel circuits are used for house lights and power points.

- In a series circuit the same current flows through the entire circuit.
- In a parallel circuit each branch takes a separate share of the current.

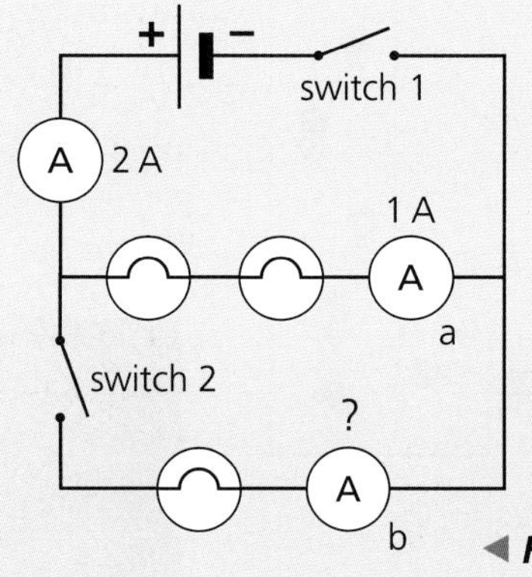

◄ ***Fig 5***

Q3 Study the circuit in Fig 5. What will happen to each bulb when switch 1 is closed and switch 2 is open?

Q4 What would be the reading on ammeter b if both switches were closed?

Key Words

ammeter – a meter for measuring current
ampere – the unit for measuring current, also amp or A
circuit – a complete ring of conducting materials
parallel – side by side
series – one after another

SUMMARY

- The flow of electric charge is called the current.
- Current is measured in amps. The equipment for measuring current is called an ammeter.
- Components of a circuit can be connected in series or in parallel.
- In series circuits the components are connected in a row and the current is the same throughout the circuit.
- In parallel circuits the components are connected side by side. The total current is the sum of what the parallel components take.

SUMMARY *Activity*

Do you think that street lights are wired in series or in parallel? Explain your answer.

102 Changing the current

In this section of the book you will learn the following things:

- **that the current in a circuit changes if batteries are added or taken away;**
- **that current depends on other components of the circuit;**
- **that current is not used up by components in a circuit.**

A battery works by changing chemical energy into electrical energy. An arrangement of chemicals that generates electricity is called a **cell**. One battery may contain one or more cells (see Fig 2, Unit 101).

chemical energy ⟶ electrical energy

The current carries electricity from the battery to wherever it is needed. This energy can be used for lighting a bulb or turning a motor. Power stations generate electricity on a large scale for homes and factories. The chemical energy in a power station comes from burning fuels.

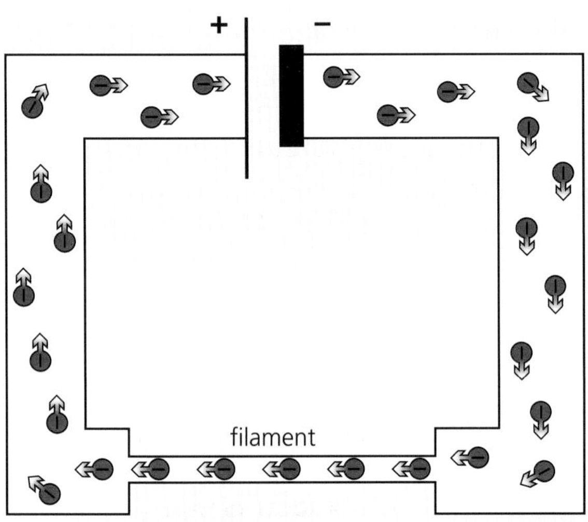

Current and energy

A light bulb in your home is heated up to 2000° C by the energy in the electric current (Fig 1). Adding more energy increases the current. An ammeter reading will rise. A bulb in the circuit will glow more brightly.

◀ ***Fig 1** The electrons pushed through a thin wire, or filament, cause the filament to heat up.*

Take care when building a circuit. Too many cells can make a bulb 'blow'. This happens when the filament becomes hot enough to melt or burn away

Q1 What happens to the current in a circuit if more battery cells are added? *Hint:* look at Fig 2.

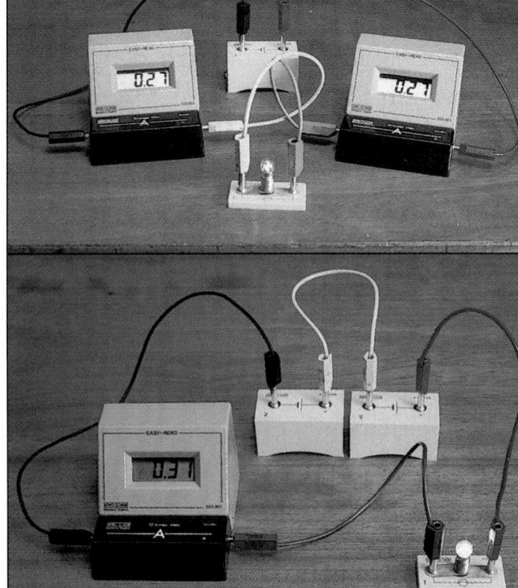

▶ ***Fig 2***

Current and components

Electricity passes through all the components of a series circuit but the components are not all the same. Some of them allow the current to pass through easily. Others slow the current down. This is called **resistance**. The more a component resists the flow of electrons the lower the current in the circuit will be.

Device	Current in amps
lamp	0.2
motor	0.4
heater	0.6

▲ ***Table 1***

Q2 Which of the components in Table 1 is the best conductor?

Components in a circuit do not 'use up' the current. Exactly the same number of electrons enter and leave each component. Some components resist the current by making it more difficult for the electrons to flow.

In a parallel circuit more of the current will flow through the easiest route. More current in Fig 3 flows through bulb c than bulbs a and b. Two bulbs have twice as much resistance as one bulb. Two amperes pass through bulb c and only one ampere passes through bulbs a and b.

If a copper wire is added to a circuit to make another parallel line it will carry a much larger current than the light bulb. Only a small amount of current will pass through the bulb and it will not glow. The copper wire has caused a **short circuit.**

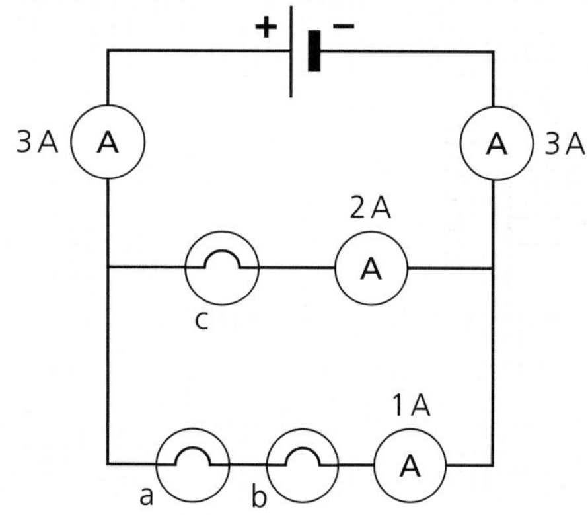

▲ ***Fig 3*** *Three components are resisting the current but it is not used up.*

Q3 How do you think a short circuit can 'blow' a fuse?

Key Words

cell – the part of a battery where chemical energy becomes electrical energy

resistance – a component that reduces the flow of current

short circuit – a wire that gives the current an easier route

SUMMARY

- Battery cells change chemical energy into electrical energy.
- Current in a circuit carries electrical energy to where it is needed.
- Adding cells to a circuit increases the current. This makes bulbs glow more brightly.
- In a parallel circuit more current will flow through the easiest route.
- Current is never used up by the components of a circuit.

SUMMARY *Activity*

Design a circuit that you could use to show that current is not used up by the components of a circuit.

103 Measuring voltage

In this section of the book you will learn the following things:

- **that cells and batteries are a source of electrical energy**
- **that it is the voltage of a battery or cell which pushes the current around a circuit;**
- **how to use a voltmeter to measure the voltage across components in a circuit;**
- that there is a link between voltage and energy in a circuit.

As you will recall (Unit 101), a battery works by changing chemical energy into electrical energy.

chemical energy → electrical energy

It is the electrical energy produced in the battery that is used to push the current around the circuit. When the current flows through a component the electrical energy is converted to another form of energy.

Remember, current is not used up in an appliance. The current carries the energy that is used.

Voltage

The electrical energy produced by a battery or other power source is called **electrical potential energy**. On its journey round the circuit this energy is used to power components such as bulbs or motors. The current returning to the battery or power source has less energy than when it began to travel around the circuit.

The difference in the energy at the start of the journey round the circuit and the energy at the end is called **potential difference**. This is often just called **voltage** and is measured in **volts (V)**. It is the voltage of a supply that pushes the current around a circuit. Voltage can be thought of as an 'electrical push'. The bigger the push, the more current flows around the circuit. Different batteries produce different voltages. As a general rule:

A battery of double the voltage may provide double the energy if all else is the same.

Q1 A torch battery only produces 1.5 V. How could you use torch batteries to produce 6V for an appliance?

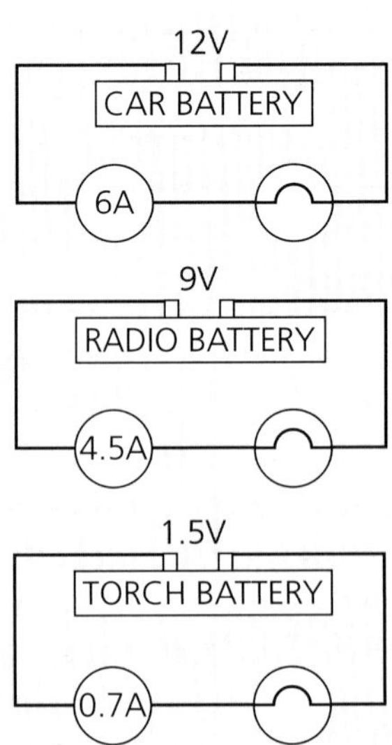

▲ ***Fig 1*** *Different circuits with different batteries.*

Measuring voltage

A voltmeter is similar to an ammeter. However, how they are used is very different. A voltmeter is used to measure the difference between the energy entering a battery or other component and the energy leaving it. The circuit does not need to be broken when using a voltmeter. The meter is connected across the component.

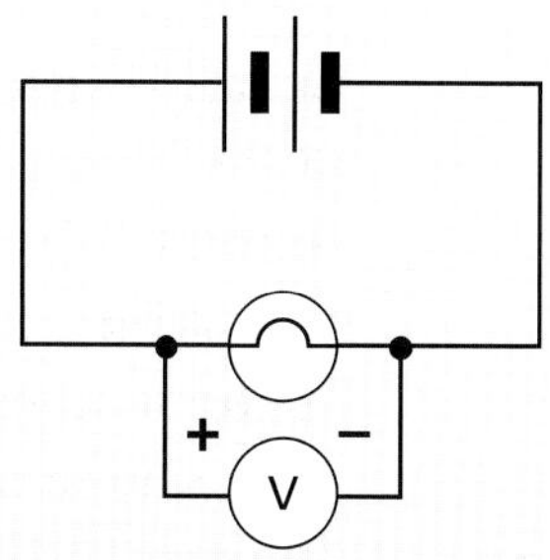

▲ ***Fig 2*** *Voltmeter connected in parallel.*

Q2 Why do we say the voltmeter is connected in parallel?

In a series circuit (Unit 101) the voltage across each individual component adds up to the supply voltage. Each component uses energy so there is a potential difference across each one.

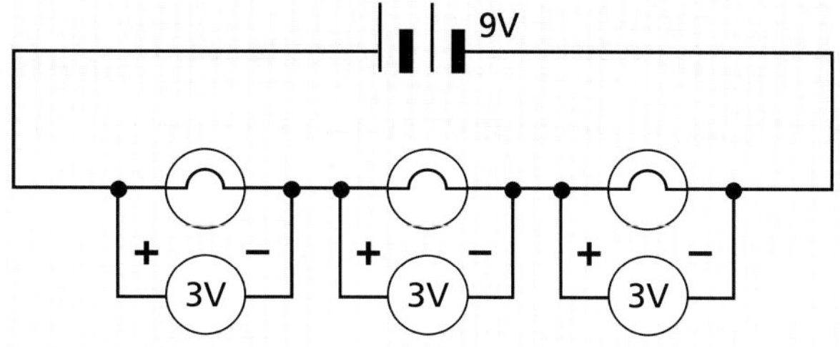

▲ ***Fig 3*** *Measuring voltage in series circuit.*

In a parallel circuit each meter shows the full supply voltage.

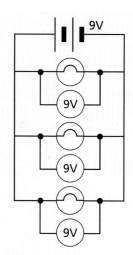

▲ ***Fig 4*** *Measuring voltage in a parallel circuit.*

Current and voltage

It is the voltage or 'electrical push' from a battery that pushes the current around a circuit. As voltage increases the current increases. There is not a simple mathematical link between the two because different components of the circuit can heat up and confuse the result.

Key Words

electrical potential energy – the electrical energy produced by a battery or other power source

potential difference – the difference between the energy at the start of its journey around a circuit and at the end

voltage – a shorthand way of writing potential difference

volts – the units used to measure voltage

SUMMARY

- Cells and batteries are a source of electrical energy
- It is the voltage of a supply which pushes the current round a circuit. Voltage can be thought of as an 'electrical push'.
- A voltmeter measure the voltage across components in a circuit;
- As the voltage of the power source increases the current in the circuit increases.

SUMMARY *Activity*

Using three torch batteries it is possible to connect them up in a circuit in ways that give voltages of either 4.5 V or 1.5 V. Draw circuit diagrams to show how this could be done.

104 Magnets

In this section of the book you will learn the following things:

- **that some materials are magnetic and others are not;**
- **some uses of magnets;**
- **what a magnetic field is;**
- **the field pattern of a bar magnet.**

◀ *Fig 1*

We often use small magnets to attach notes to the refrigerator. They may also help to keep cupboard doors closed. Magnets have many more important uses in industry and other activities.

Navigation and magnets

One of the oldest uses for magnetism is the compass needle (Fig 1). If you dangle a small magnetic bar on the end of a thread it will turn until it lines up in a north–south direction. One end of the magnet points north. It is called the **north-seeking pole** or **north pole**. The other end of the magnet points south. This called the **south-seeking pole** or **south pole**.

The compass needle points north–south because the Earth is also a giant magnet. The compass lines up with the Earth's **magnetic field** (Fig 2). Knowing that the north pole of the compass needle always points to the Earth's North Pole can help us to move in a straight line in any direction we wish.

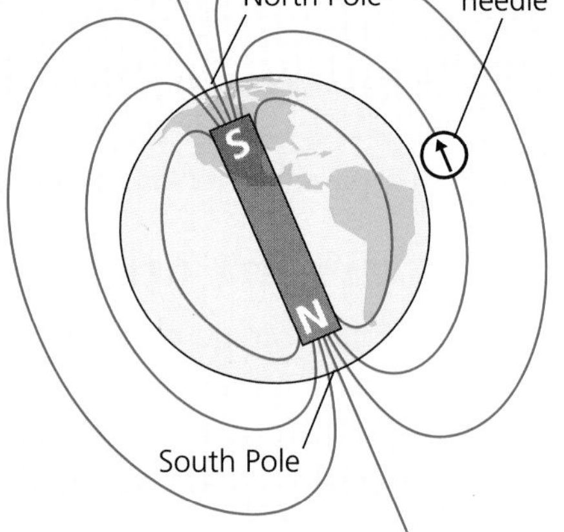

▶ *Fig 2*

Q1 Why does a compass needle line up north to south?

Magnetic substances

Most substances are not magnetic. Non-metals are not magnetic. Iron and steel are the most important magnetic metals. Nickel and cobalt are also magnetic.

We can use a compass to find out whether a substance is magnetic. One end of the compass needle normally points to the North. If a magnetic substance comes close to the needle, it will make the needle turn. If you ever need to use a compass to find your way it is important to make sure that there is no magnetic metal nearby. Some electrical equipment is magnetic (Unit 107) and some rocks also contain magnetic minerals. In parts of Scotland, a compass could lead you round in circles.

Q2 How can magnetic objects make a compass unreliable?

Magnetic fields

When you slowly bring a metal object towards a magnet you will notice the pull of the magnet before the object touches the magnet. Magnetism must be reaching out into the air around the magnet. We can use iron filings to make a pattern around a magnet.

The lines in Fig 3 show how iron filings fall into place around a bar magnet. Each filing behaves like a tiny compass needle. The lines show the **magnetic field** around the magnet. Objects within this magnetic field will be affected by the force of the magnet. Tightly packed lines show where the magnetic field is strongest. Widely spaced lines show where it is weakest.

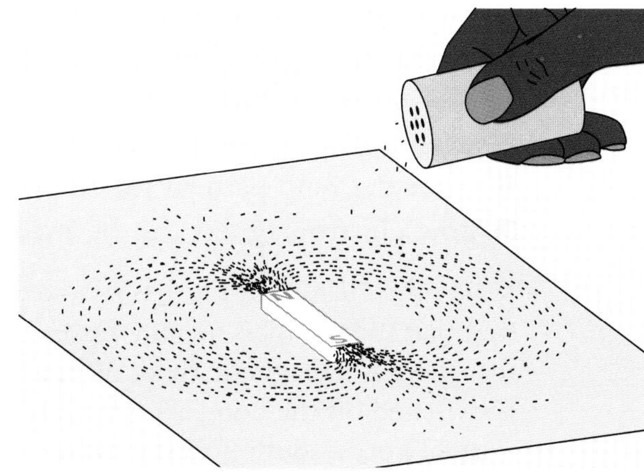

▲ ***Fig 3*** *Compare this pattern with Fig 2. (Wear goggles if you do this experiment yourself.)*

Q3 Where is the magnetic field around a bar magnet strongest? Where is it weakest?

The north pole of one magnet will repel the north pole of another magnet. The magnets will push apart. If the north pole of one magnet is pointed towards the south pole of another magnet they will be pulled together (Fig 4).

- Similar poles repel.
- Opposite poles attract.

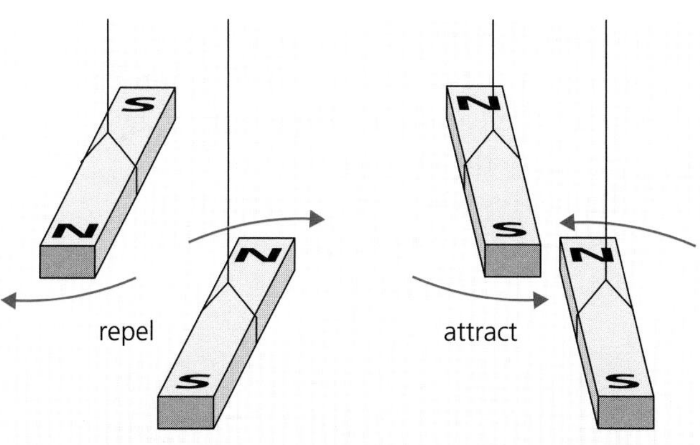

◄ ***Fig 4***

Key Words

magnetic field – the shape and size of the area affected by a magnet

north pole – the end of a magnet that points northwards

south pole – the end of a magnet that points southwards

SUMMARY

- Iron, steel, cobalt and nickel are the magnetic metals. Some of their ores are also magnetic.
- A magnet has a north pole and a south pole.
- Magnets are useful for navigation.
- Similar poles repel and opposite poles attract.
- The force of magnetism reaches out beyond the magnet as a magnetic field.
- This field can be traced using iron filings or plotting compasses.

SUMMARY *Activity*

Use a small compass to find out how many articles in your home are magnetic. Can you see any difference in the strength of magnetic fields?

105 Electricity and magnetism

In this section of the book you will learn the following things:

- **that there is a link between electricity and magnetism;**
- **what an electromagnet is;**
- **what the field pattern for electromagnets is like;**
- **how electromagnets can be made stronger.**

When the current in Fig 1 is switched on we find that the compass needle moves. This shows that there is a magnetic field. When the current is switched off the compass needle returns to its normal north–south position. The magnetic field was only there while the electric current was flowing. This must mean that electricity and magnetism are linked in some way.

When a current flows through a wire, the wire has a magnetic field round it.

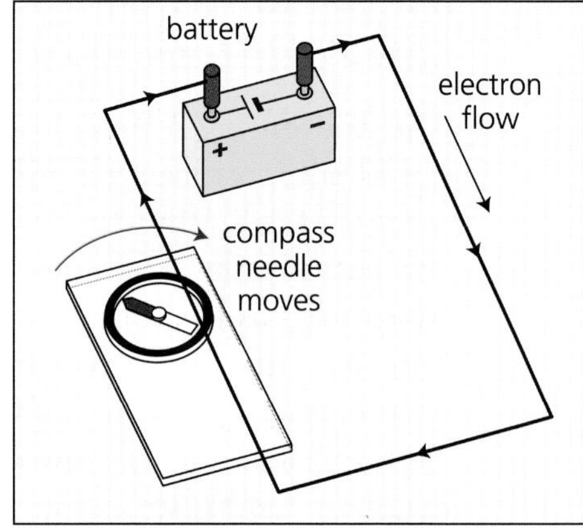

▲ ***Fig 1***

The magnetic field around an ordinary electric wire is not very strong. We can draw the field around a thick wire carrying a large current by setting up the arrangement in Fig 2. The field is too weak to move iron filings so we need to use sensitive plotting compasses instead.

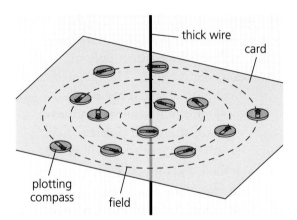

▲ ***Fig 2*** *Finding the magnetic field around a straight wire.*

Q1 List two differences between the magnetic field around an electric wire and the field around a bar magnet.

Electromagnets

A coiled wire (Fig 3) makes a much stronger magnetic field. If the wire is coiled around a rod of iron the field becomes even stronger. The iron inside the coil is called the **core**. The coil and the core together make an **electromagnet**. The field pattern is like the pattern for a bar magnet.

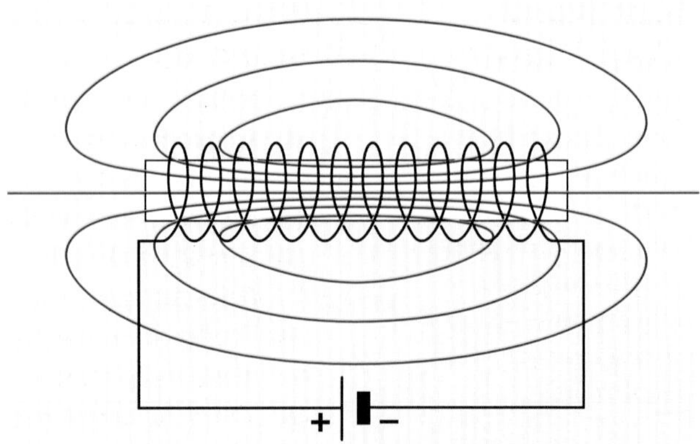

▶ ***Fig 3***

If the core is made of soft iron the magnetic field will disappear when the current is switched off. This means we have a magnet that can be turned on and off.

If the core is made of steel it remains magnetic after the electricity is switched off. This is one way of making magnets.

Q2 Why is it useful to have a magnet that you can turn on and off?

Making the field stronger

A stronger electromagnet can attract more magnetic material. One way to make an electromagnet stronger is to pass a larger current through the coil. Another way to make an electromagnet stronger is to increase the number of coils around the core.

The substance used to make the core can also affect the strength of the field. Fig 4 shows how many paperclips could be attracted by three electromagnets with different cores. The magnets have the same number of coils and are carrying the same current. Only the core materials are different.

All three of these methods are used to make different kinds of electromagnets for use in medicine and industry. Some of these uses are described in Unit 106.

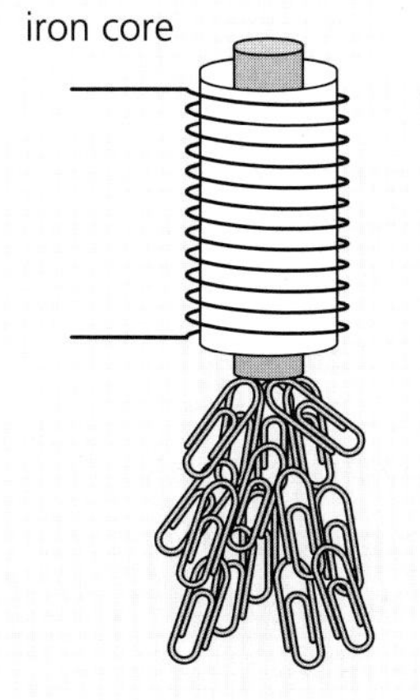

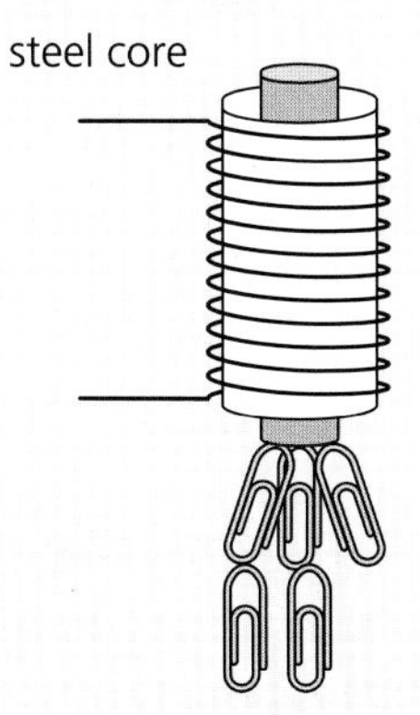

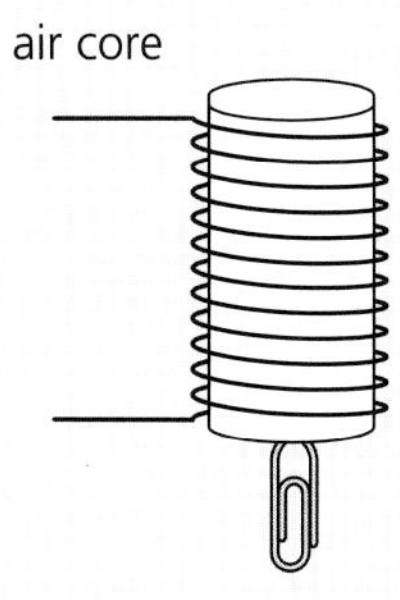

◀ ***Fig 4*** *Different cores can change the strength of an electromagnet.*

Q3 Why would a glass core not improve the strength of an electromagnet?

Key Words

core – the iron or steel rod in the centre of an electromagnet

electromagnet – an electric wire coiled around a metal core

SUMMARY

- An electric current flowing along a wire makes a weak magnetic field.
- A coiled wire makes a stronger field.
- Coiling a wire around an iron or steel core makes an electromagnet.
- A soft iron core loses its magnetism when the current is switched off but a steel core remains magnetic.
- An electromagnet can be made stronger by increasing the current, by increasing the number of coils, or by changing the core metal.

SUMMARY *Activity*

Design an investigation to show that the number of coils increases the strength of the magnetic field around an electromagnet.

106 Using electromagnets

In this section of the book you will learn the following things:

- **how electromagnetism can be useful;**
- **how electromagnets do different jobs.**

Electromagnets have many uses. One reason for this is that they can be made more powerful than ordinary magnets. Another important reason is that an electromagnet can be switched on and off. This means that it can be used to pick up a metal object from one place and drop it somewhere else, just by turning the electricity on and off.

Electromagnets are used in scrapyards to move heavy cars around. They are also used to separate magnetic substances from non-magnetic substances. This is a good way of sorting out metals for recycling.

▶ ***Fig 1*** *Electromagnets can pick up heavy metal objects and drop them again.*

Q1 How can an electromagnet help to separate steel cans from aluminium cans for recycling?

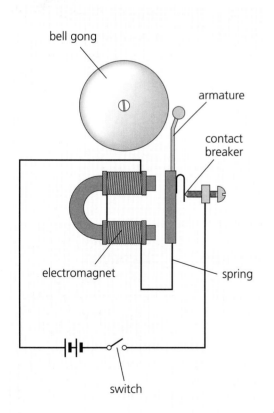

Electric bells

An electric bell contains an electromagnet. Fig 2 shows how the circuit is arranged. The circuit is closed by pressing the bell push. When the current starts to flow, it turns on the electromagnet. The electromagnet immediately attracts a metal arm called an **armature** which hits a gong and makes the bell ring once. As the arm is pulled towards the electromagnet the circuit is broken.

As soon as the circuit is broken the electromagnet stops working. This allows the armature to spring away from the gong. When the armature swings back to its original position it closes the circuit again, the electromagnet is switched back on and the armature is pulled towards it again. This goes on happening for as long as you press the bell-push. The bell is struck many times in a few seconds.

◀ ***Fig 2***

Q2 Why does an electric bell go on ringing as long as you press the button?

Q3 This type of arrangement is often called a 'make and break' circuit. How do you think it gets this name?

Transport and medicine

Some modern trams and trains use electromagnets. The Maglev train at Birmingham airport rides just above the surface of the track. It is held there by electromagnets. The ride is very smooth and quiet because the train stays 15mm away from the track and does not touch it. As well as being quiet, this saves wear and tear on the wheels and the track.

Electromagnets are also used in medicine. Metal splinters can be eased out of a wound with a small electromagnet. This causes much less damage than probing around with a pair of tweezers. If you did not wear goggles when using iron filings you might need to have some sharp pieces of iron removed from your eye in this way.

Q4 Why is an electromagnet better for surgery than a normal magnet?

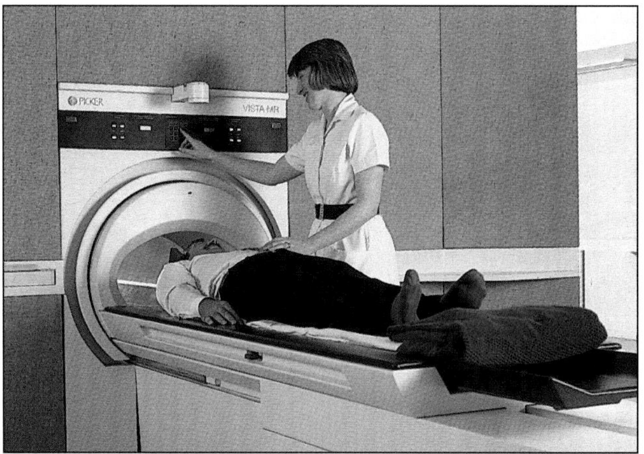

▲ ***Fig 3*** *A lot of modern medical equipment, like this Magnetic Resonance Imaging (MRI) scanner, uses electromagnetism.*

Entertainment

Loudspeakers and television tubes contain electromagnets. The way they work is much more complicated than an electric bell. It is important to know that there are electromagnets in many household articles because strong magnetic fields can spoil computer discs and audio and video tapes.

Key Words

armature – the metal arm carrying the clapper that hits the gong in an electric bell

SUMMARY

- Electromagnets can be switched on and off and this makes them useful for many jobs.
- Electromagnets are used to move heavy metal objects such as cars in scrap yards. They can also separate magnetic metals from non-magnetic materials.
- An electric bell contains an electromagnet that makes a metal ball hit a gong.
- Electromagnets are used in medicine and transport.
- Magnetic fields can damage magnetic tapes and discs.

SUMMARY *Activity*

Draw a circuit that uses an electromagnet to ring an alarm bell whenever somebody opens a door.

107 Energy resources

In this section of the book you will learn the following things:

- **that we use many different energy resources;**
- **that most of the energy on Earth comes from the Sun;**
- **some examples of energy resources.**

Your body uses food as a source of energy. Modern towns and cities also need large amounts of energy. Transport, industry, heating, lighting and entertainment all use up energy.

▲ ***Fig 1*** *Cities use up a lot of energy.*

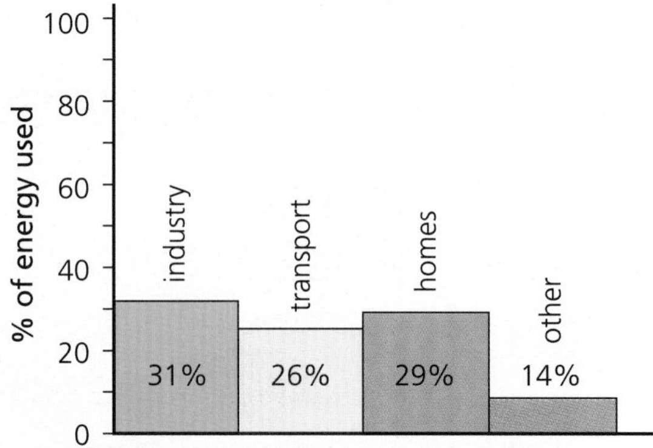

▲ ***Fig 2*** *How energy in the UK is being used.*

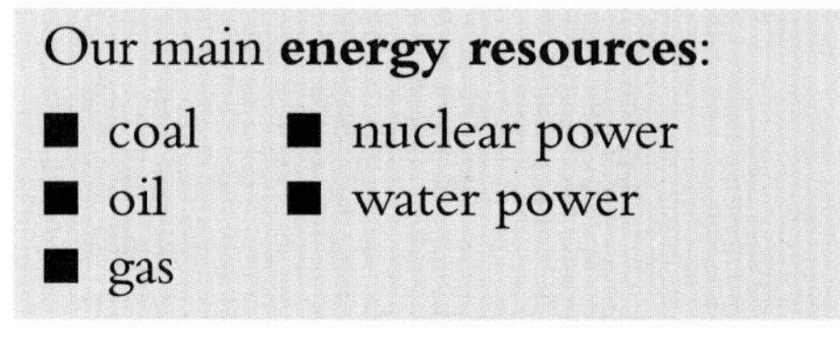

Our main **energy resources**:

- coal
- oil
- gas
- nuclear power
- water power

Coal, gas and oil are called fossil fuels because they come from prehistoric animals and plants (see Unit 67). Water power is mainly used to drive **generators** that make electricity. This is called **hydroelectric power** (see Unit 109).

The way we manage our energy resources is changing all the time. We now use more gas and less coal but fossil fuels are still our main energy resource. Burning them can cause pollution and damage the environment.

Q1 What are some of the disadvantages of using the main energy resources listed above?

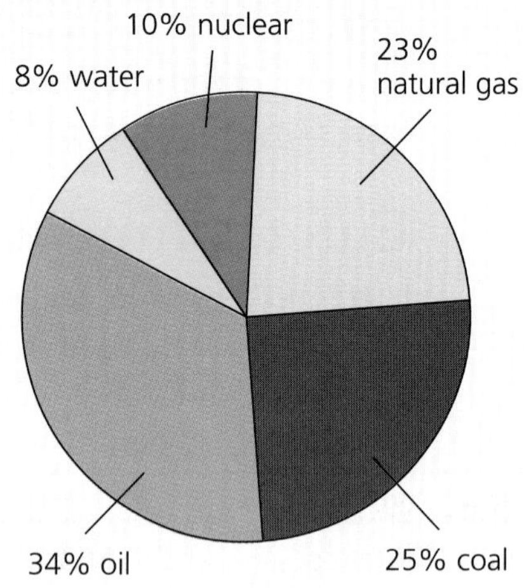

▲ ***Fig 3*** *Sources of energy in the UK.*

The Sun

The Sun supplies nearly all the natural energy on Earth. Plants use the Sun's energy to make food. When a plant is eaten by an animal the energy from the Sun goes into the animal's body. When plants and animals die, the energy is passed on to other living things that eat them. Some dead plants and animals may be trapped under layers of rock. Over millions of years the plants can become coal and the animals can become oil. When we burn fossil fuels we are really getting energy that came from the Sun millions of years ago (see Unit 67).

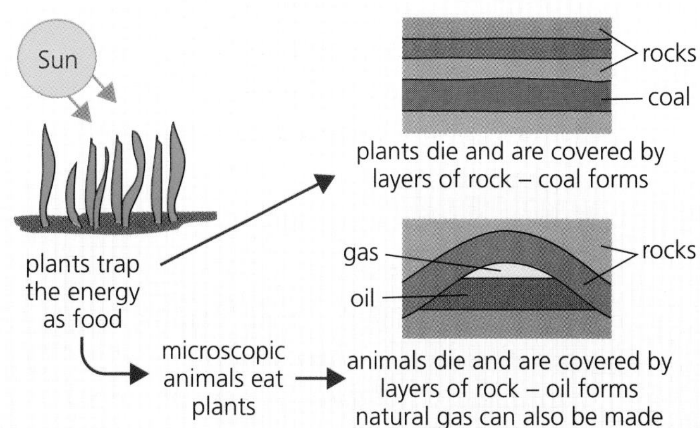
Sun
plants trap the energy as food
microscopic animals eat plants
rocks
coal
plants die and are covered by layers of rock – coal forms
gas
oil
rocks
animals die and are covered by layers of rock – oil forms natural gas can also be made

▶ *Fig 4 How coal and oil form.*

Q2 Why can we say that most of our energy resources come from the Sun?

Other energy resources

▲ *Fig 5*

People have used wind power to move ships and turn windmills for hundreds of years. Running water has also turned water wheels to supply power for mills and other machines. Even the energy of tides has been used to drive mill-wheels. More recently, the Thames Barrier (Fig 5) was built to protect London from dangerously high tides. It also makes use of the energy in normal tides. Wheels in the barrier are turned by the tide rushing past. The turning wheels are used to generate electricity.

Batteries convert chemical energy into electrical energy. We use batteries to supply power for light bulbs and and to start cars. A battery can also drive a car.

Wood and straw can also be burned to release energy. They are called **biomass**. Biomass can be changed into a more concentrated energy source such as alcohol. Alcohol made from plants can be burned to drive an engine. Other fast-growing plants, such as oilseed rape, make oil that can be used for fuel.

Q3 List five different energy resources.

Key Words

biomass – a quantity of plant or animal material
energy resource – a source of energy
generator – a machine that turns movement into electrical energy
hydroelectric power – electricity generated by flowing water

SUMMARY

- The Sun is the ultimate source of most energy resources.
- The energy resource used by plants and animals is called food.
- The energy resources most commonly used by industry are coal, gas, oil, nuclear power and hydroelectric power.
- There are many other energy resources including batteries, wind, waves and tides.
- Biomass is also an energy resource.

SUMMARY *Activity*

Make a list of all the electrical appliances that you switch on in a single day. How could you reduce the amount of energy you use?

108 Generating electricity

In this section of the book you will learn the following things:

- **what turbines and generators do;**
- **how energy resources are used to generate electricity;**
- **how electricity is spread around the country.**

▲ ***Fig 1*** *Power stations generate electricity.*

Most of the 'smoke' you see coming from a power station is water vapour. Smoke and other gases that are produced when a fossil fuel burns come out of thinner, taller chimneys.

Inside a power station

▲ ***Fig 2*** *The fans on the turbine are hit by steam. This makes the turbine spin round.*

Many power stations burn fossil fuels. The pictures here show a power station that uses coal. The coal arrives by train or truck and then it is stored. When it is needed the coal is tipped into a large furnace. Inside the furnace the coal burns to give out heat. The heat is used to boil water. This turns the water to steam.

Jets of very hot steam travel along pipes until they hit the **turbine**. A turbine is like a water wheel for steam. Large fans on the turbine make it spin round when the steam hits them. The turbine is attached to the generator. When the turbine twists the generator, electricity is made (Fig 3).

Q1 What is a turbine?

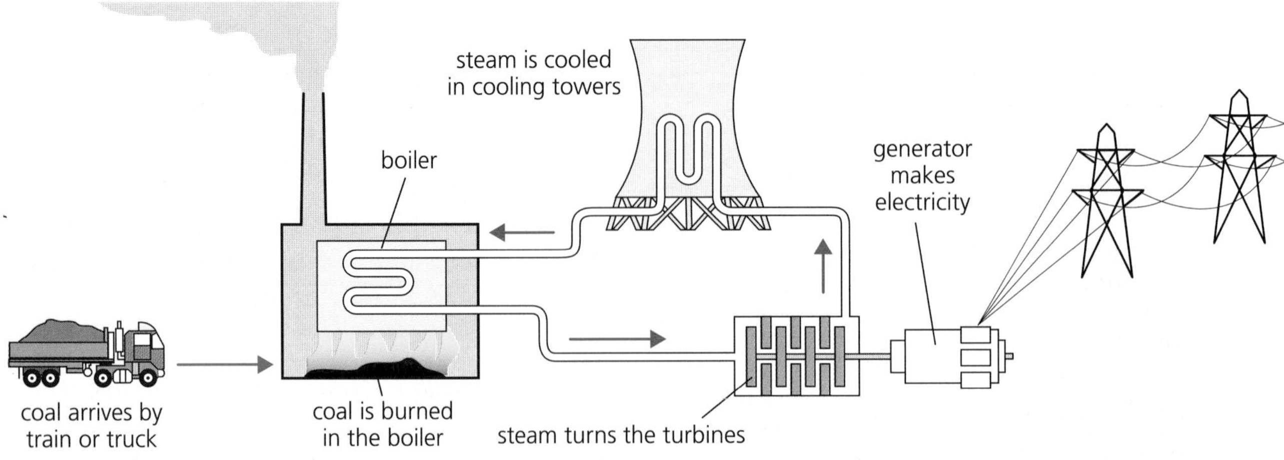
steam is cooled
in cooling towers
boiler
generator
makes
electricity
coal arrives by
train or truck
coal is burned
in the boiler
steam turns the turbines

▲ ***Fig 3***

After hitting the turbine the steam is still very hot. It needs to be cooled before it can go back into the boiler. The steam is cooled in a **cooling tower**. Here, cold water is poured over the pipes that contain the steam. It is the cooling water that we see evaporating from the power station, not the steam that drives the turbines.

Q2 Why do many power stations need cooling towers?

Efficient use of resources

No machine or factory is perfectly efficient. There is always some waste. All power stations lose some of the energy they take from the energy resource they use. Most of the waste is in the form of heat lost through the cooling towers and in waste gases. Some power stations are more efficient than others. The efficiency of four different types of power stations is shown in Fig 4.

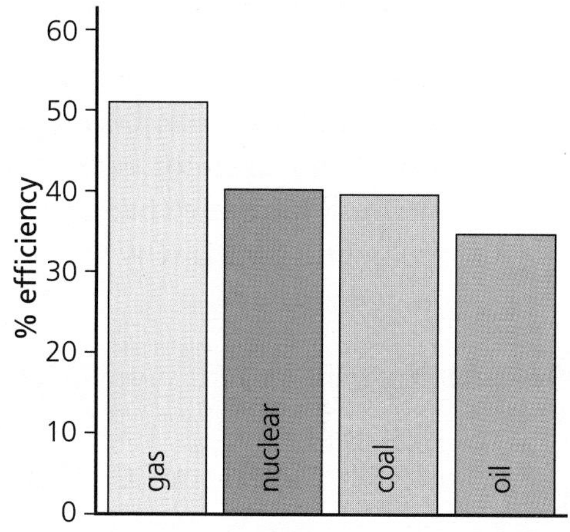

▲ *Fig 4*

Coal power stations have a maximum efficiency of 40%. This means that for each kilogram of coal burned, the energy from at least 600 grams is wasted.

Gas power stations have a maximum efficiency of 50%. This means that for each kilogram of gas burned, the energy from at least 500 grams is wasted.

Q3 Why are gas burning power stations becoming more popular than coal burning power stations?

Electricity where we need it

Electricity has to be sent from the power stations where it is generated to other places where it is needed. We have a network of power cables called the National Grid. You have probably seen parts of it. Many of the cables are carried across the countryside on tall **pylons**. When the cables reach your home they are much smaller. They may also be buried underground.

Key Words

cooling tower – a wide chimney where steam is cooled

pylon – a tall tower carrying electrical cables

turbine – a wheel that is turned by jets of steam

SUMMARY

- Power stations burn energy resources to make electricity.
- The heat from burning fossil fuels is used to make steam.
- The steam turns turbines. Turbines turn generators.
- The steam is cooled in cooling towers.
- Power stations do not make very efficient use of energy resources.
- Electricity reaches your home through a network of cables called the National Grid.

SUMMARY *Activity*

Find out the name of your nearest power station and the energy resource it uses.

109 Renewable energy resources

In this section of the book you will learn the following things:

- **that some energy resources can be used up;**
- **what the term 'renewable energy resource' means.**

Fossil fuels took millions of years to form. When we burn a fossil fuel it is destroyed. It cannot be used again. Fossil fuels are **non-renewable** energy resources.

People are still searching for new supplies of coal, gas and oil. Once they have been used we will need to find more. Our need for energy is also increasing. When all the fossil fuels have been used up there will be serious problems. This is why scientists are developing other energy resources.

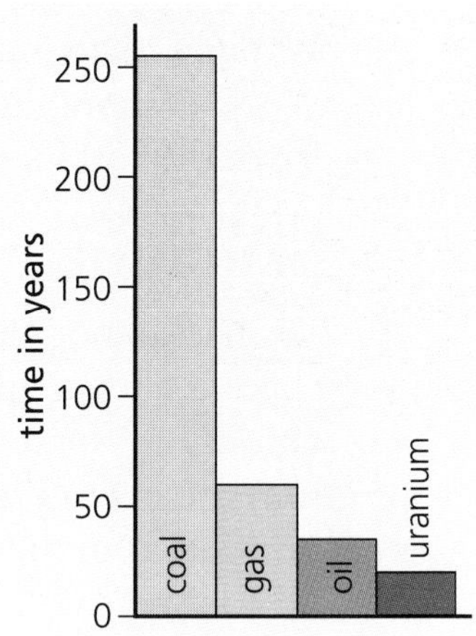

▲ ***Fig 1*** *Estimated stocks of non-renewable fuels.*

Q1 How long are current supplies of oil expected to last?

Renewable energy resources

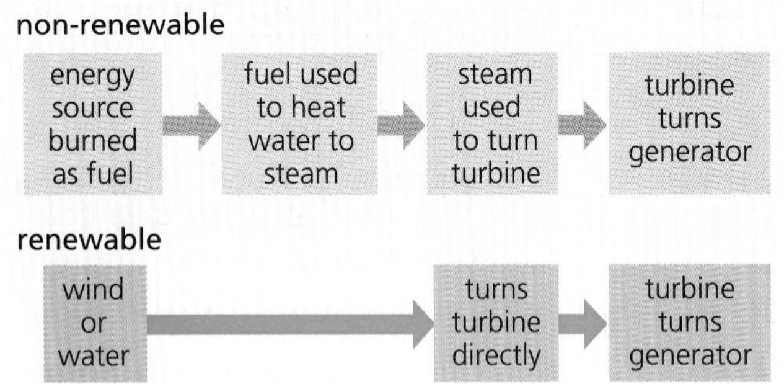

▲ ***Fig 2***

Fossil fuels are burned to make steam. The steam is then used to drive a turbine. Some energy resources can drive turbines directly. No fuel has to be used up.

Energy resources that are not used up are sometimes called **alternative energy**. Alternative energy resources do not run out when they are used. These energy resources are **renewable**.

The tides go on rising and falling and the wind goes on blowing. The Sun goes on shining. Taking energy from wind, water and sunlight does not involve burning anything. It makes no smoke or steam or waste products. Some renewable energy resources are shown in Table 1.

Any turbine can turn a generator. The wind can turn a turbine. Wind generators make electricity in the same way as steam generators in power stations. Wind power is quiet and does not produce much pollution. Many small wind generators (Fig 3) are needed to make the same amount of electricity as a power station.

Renewable energy resource	How is it used
wind	moves boats and turns wind generators
tides and waves	turns a turbine to generate electricity
hydroelectricity	water current turns turbines. When valves open, electricity is generated
geothermal	heat from underground rocks turns water to steam which can turn turbines or heat houses
solar panels	can heat water or generate electricity

▲ ***Table 1***

▲ **Fig 3** *A wind farm.*

Some people think that wind turbines spoil the appearance of the environment.

Solar panels are used to recharge batteries in many small appliances such as calculators and wrist watches. Larger solar panels can be built into the roof of a house. They use the energy in sunlight to heat water or to generate electricity.

▲ **Fig 4** *Solar panels.*

In some parts of the USA there are large fields of solar panels making electricity for whole towns. The panels are turned by small motors so that they always face the Sun. Even in the UK, where the weather is often cloudy, solar panels on a roof can generate more electricity than one house needs.

▼ **Fig 5**

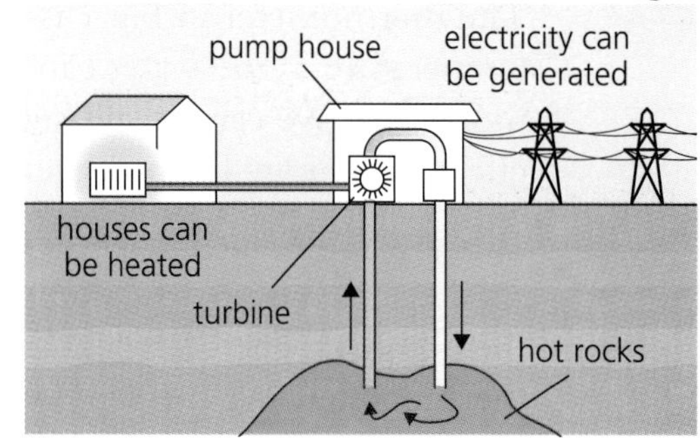

In some parts of the world **geothermal** energy is taken from hot rocks underground. Water is pumped down into the rocks (Fig 5). The heat from the rocks turns the water into steam. The steam is pumped back to the surface. Here it can be used to heat homes or make electricity.

Hydroelectric power

Running water can turn turbines. The water can be stored in a reservoir until it is needed. When valves are opened the water flows downhill past the turbines and makes them turn. The reservoir can be refilled naturally by rainfall or by using spare electricity to pump water back up at night.

Q2 List some differences between renewable and non-renewable energy resources?

Q3 Why do we need to find ways of using alternative energy resources?

Key Words

alternative energy – a renewable energy resource
geothermal – ground (geo) heat (thermal)
non-renewable – something that cannot be replaced
renewable – something that can be replaced

SUMMARY

- Non-renewable energy resources are destroyed when they are used.
- Fossil fuels are non-renewable energy resources.
- Renewable energy resources are not destroyed when they are used.
- Some renewable energy resources are wind, moving water and sunlight.
- Geothermal energy comes from natural heat underground.

SUMMARY *Activity*

Design a poster to show some renewable energy resources and some non-renewable ones.

110 Temperature and energy

In this section of the book you will learn the following things:

- **the difference between the words heat, energy, and temperature;**
- **some different ways of measuring temperature.**

The word **heat** is used to describe a form of energy. The word **temperature** is used to describe how hot or cold an object is. These words are connected but they are not the same.

Temperature

A thermometer can be used to find out how hot a person is or how cold a refrigerator is. You may have used a thermometer at home or in a laboratory.

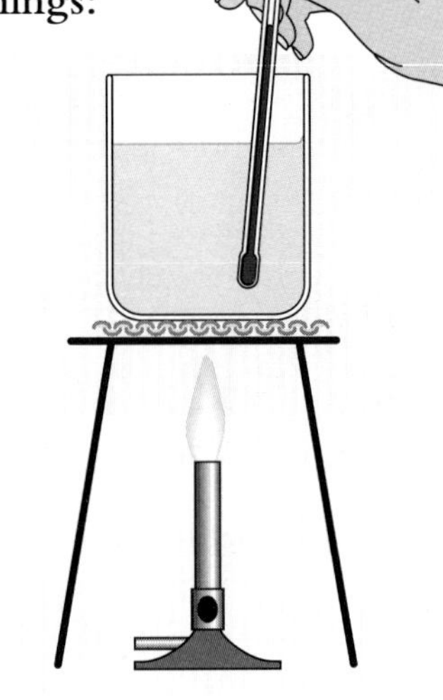

▲ *Fig 1*

The thermometer in Fig 1 is measuring the temperature of the water. The temperature of the water can tell us how much energy is in the water molecules. We cannot measure the energy directly. We have to find out what effect the energy has on other substances.

Heating a substance makes it expand (Unit 40). Liquids expand more then solids. Thermometers contain a small amount of liquid. Heat energy makes the liquid expand. As it expands, the liquid moves up the thin tube of the thermometer. We can see how far it moves by reading the scale.

The scale on a thermometer is set by using two fixed points:

- the boiling point of pure water;
- the freezing point of pure water.

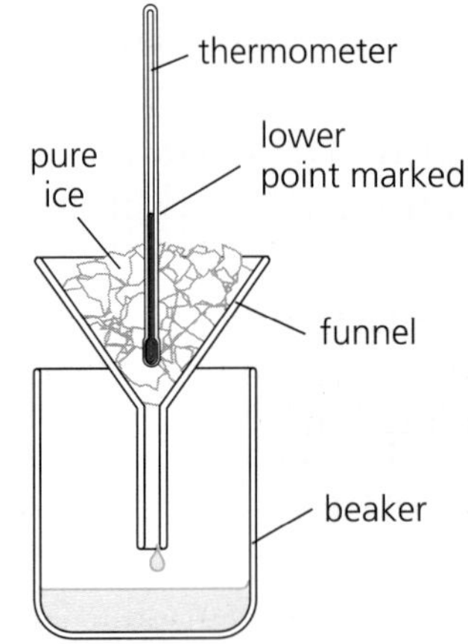

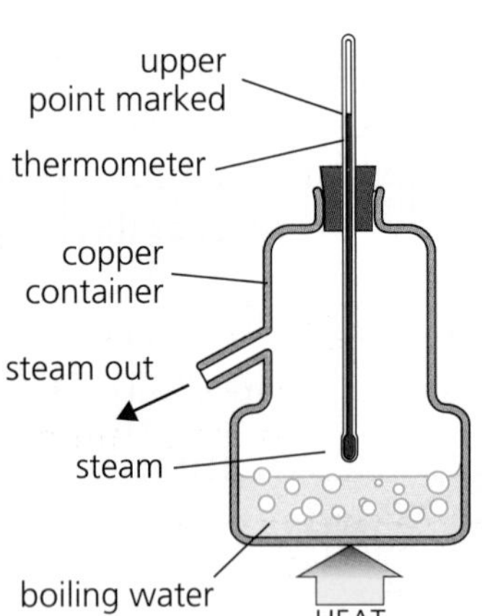

▲ *Fig 2*

The freezing point is fixed by putting the thermometer in ice and marking the top of the liquid. The boiling point is fixed by putting the thermometer in steam and making another mark. The gap between the upper and lower marks is divided into 100 equal parts. Each part represents one degree **Celsius** (°C). The freezing point of water is therefore 0°C and the boiling point of water is 100°C.

Q1 What are the two fixed points on a mercury thermometer?

Q2 How are the fixed points found when a new thermometer is made?

Different thermometers

Scientific thermometers often contain mercury. Some thermometers contain alcohol. Alcohol is cheaper than mercury. A bimetal strip can also be used to measure temperature (Unit 55). It is less accurate than a liquid-filled thermometer.

Thermometers can also be made in other ways. Very accurate thermometers work electronically. Some thin plastic strips or discs contain dyes that change colour at different temperatures.

Q3 Which thermometer in Table 1 would be better for measuring the temperature inside a freezer?

Mercury	Alcohol
expands easily, is accurate	sticks to glass, may not be accurate
high boiling point (360°C) and high freezing point (–37°C)	low boiling point (78°C) and low freezing point (–110°C)
warms up quickly	takes time to warm up
expensive	cheap
easy to see	needs added colour

▲ ***Table 1***

Energy and heat

A substance can contain a lot of energy without being hot. Sugar and coal are fuels. They contain energy all the time but this energy is only released when they burn. Burning fuels release heat energy that can raise the temperature of objects around them. Heat energy is measured in **joules** (J).

- Temperature is a way of describing how hot or cold a substance is compared with freezing and boiling water. We use a thermometer to measure temperature. The unit of temperature is the Celsius degree.
- Energy may be contained in a substance without giving it a high temperature. Energy is measured in units called joules.

Q4 Sugar and fat contain a lot of energy. Ice cream contains a lot of sugar and fat. Why is ice cream not boiling hot?

▲ ***Fig 3*** *Coal needs to be burned to release heat energy to melt snow.*

Key Words

Celsius degree – a unit for measuring temperature

heat – a form of energy

temperature – how hot or cold a substance is

SUMMARY

- The temperature of a substance is measured by seeing what effect it has on a thermometer.
- A thermometer shows the distance between the temperature of freezing and boiling water, divided into 100 sections called degrees.
- Thermometers may contain expanding liquids, bimetal strips or some other substance that changes when its temperature changes.

SUMMARY *Activity*

Make a diagram of a mercury thermometer. Watch the weather forecast and mark all the temperatures that the forecaster mentions on your diagram.

111 Energy transfer

In this section of the book you will learn the following things:

- **how energy moves from place to place;**
- **how energy can help us to do work;**
- **that energy can be stored.**

▲ *Fig 1*

Work is done whenever a force makes something move. A cyclist has to work hard to make a bicycle go fast. The amount of work that the cyclist in Fig 1 is doing depends on:

- the distance she travels;
- the mass of what she is moving, which is the bicycle and herself.

Expensive bicycles are made of light metal alloys. They also have many different gears. This helps the cyclist to use energy more efficiently.

Doing work requires energy. A cyclist gets chemical energy from food. Energy can be in many other different forms (Table 1).

▼ *Table 1*

Energy	Description	Example
Wave	Waves carry energy. This can do work.	Radio, sound and light
Heat (thermal)	Molecules are made to move faster when heated. The molecules can do work.	Steam, hot air and hot coal warming a house
Electrical	Electric current is a flow of electrons. These can do work.	Torch and house circuits
Nuclear	Energy in the nucleus of an atom is released.	Nuclear power station
Chemical	Energy locked in chemicals is released.	Food and fuel
Gravitational potential energy	Objects lifted above the ground gain energy. Work can be done when these objects fall.	Water flowing from a reservoir
Kinetic energy	The energy in moving objects. If they hit other objects work is done.	A moving racing car or cyclist
Strain energy	Energy stored in a material that has been stretched or compressed.	The string of a bow; a coiled spring

When a machine does work it often changes energy from one form to another. The change from one form of energy to another is called **energy transfer**. We can follow a series of energy transfers like a story (Figs 2, 3 and 4).

Wind power

Energy comes from the Sun as **thermal** energy (heat). This becomes **kinetic** energy (movement) in the wind. The wind turns a turbine, which makes electricity.

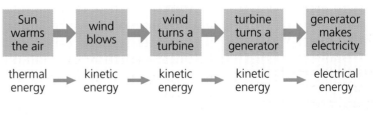

Sun warms the air → wind blows → wind turns a turbine → turbine turns a generator → generator makes electricity

thermal energy → kinetic energy → kinetic energy → kinetic energy → electrical energy

▲ *Fig 2*

Food for energy

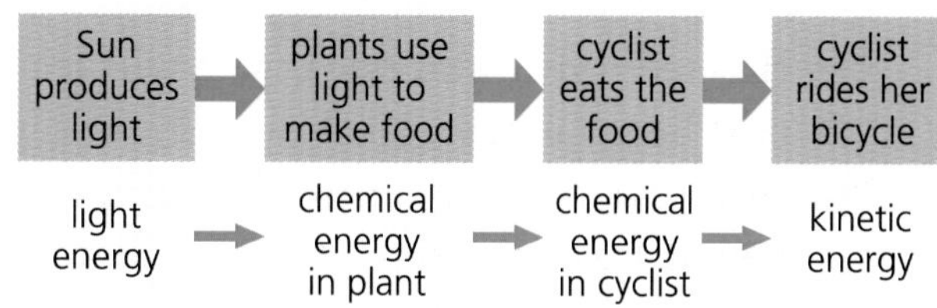

▲ *Fig 3*

The Sun's **light** energy is changed into **chemical** energy by green plants such as wheat. When a cyclist eats some spaghetti the chemical energy it contains goes into his or her own body. It is then changed into many different forms of energy. Kinetic energy moves the cyclist around the track and thermal energy makes her hot.

A coal power station

▼ *Fig 4*

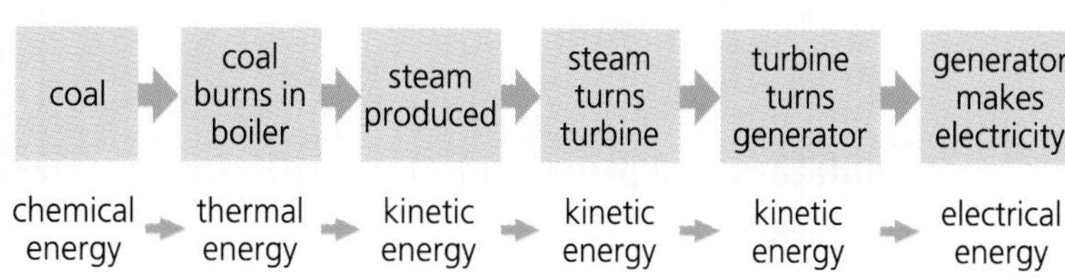

The chemical energy in coal changes into thermal energy when it burns. This changes into kinetic energy when water is heated until it expands into steam. Steam passes the kinetic energy on to the turbines. They pass the kinetic energy on to the generators. The generators change the kinetic energy into electrical energy.

Q1 What happens to electrical energy after it comes out of a power station?

Energy stores

Energy is stored in food and fuels. Energy can also be stored in other ways. Water in a high reservoir acts as a store of energy. It contains **potential energy**. When the water runs downhill, gravity converts the potential energy into kinetic energy. Energy can also be stored in a spring or stretched elastic. An archer uses the energy stored in a stretched string to shoot an arrow. Animals and plants also store energy (Unit 33).

Q2 Where did the energy to stretch an archer's bowspring come from?

Q2 Where does a bungee jumper's energy come from?

Key Words

energy transfer – one form of energy changing into another form
kinetic energy – energy of movement
potential energy – stored energy
work – the movement of an object by a force

SUMMARY

- Work is done when a force makes something move.
- Energy gives living things and machines the ability to do work.
- Energy exists in several different forms.
- Energy can be changed from one form to another.
- Energy can be stored as potential energy.

SUMMARY *Activity*

Draw an energy story to show all the energy transfers involved in making hydroelectricity.

112 Conduction, convection, radiation

In this section of the book you will learn the following things:

- **that heat energy can flow from one place to another;**
- **that heat transfer occurs through conduction, convection or radiation;**
- **that a knowledge of heat transfer can help us to conserve energy.**

The scientist in the photograph (Fig 1) understands that heat energy moves from one place to another. Without his protective clothes he would die very quickly. The molten rock from the volcano is over 1000°C! The heat energy is being transferred to him in different ways. His clothes are **insulators** and protect him from the heat.

▲ *Fig 1*

Sometimes we want to prevent heat from leaving our body. In cold water we would quickly die, so divers and cavers must wear special clothes. These insulate them from the cold water.

These two examples show an important fact about heat transfer. Heat energy will move from a hotter to a cooler place.

Conduction

If you have ever stirred hot tea with a metal spoon you will know that heat can travel through metals. the handle of the spoon can be too hot to touch after a few minutes. This movement of heat through metals is called **conduction**. Metals conduct heat this way because of the way their atoms (Unit 42) are packed together. One atom will start to vibrate because of the heat energy, and this causes the atoms near to it to vibrate also. In this way the heat energy passes along the metal.

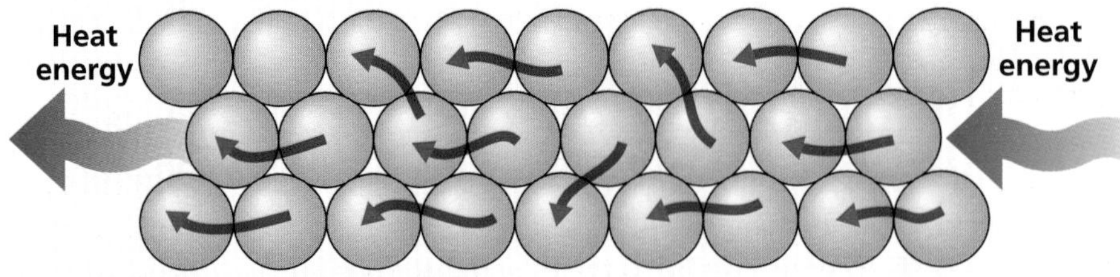

▲ ***Fig 2*** *Metallic structure.*

Materials that do not have this structure will not conduct heat. Plastics, rubber and wood will not conduct heat. They are insulators.

Q1 Why do divers and cavers wear rubber or nylon suits to help them to stay warm?

Convection

Heat energy does not only travel through metals. It can also travel through liquids and gases. If this was not possible you could not heat water or warm up a room. The molecules of the liquid or gas move, and take heat energy with them. This is called **convection**. As the substance is heated it expands (Unit 55) and becomes less dense. This makes it rise. As it does so it starts to cool. This makes it fall. The rising and falling sets up **convection currents**.

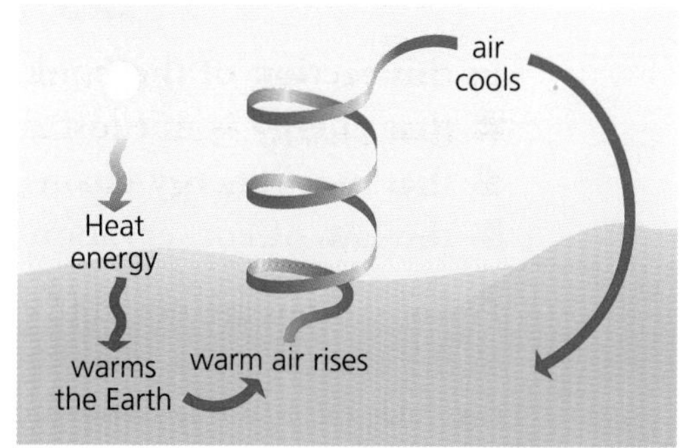

▲ ***Fig 3*** *These currents are important in the generation of weather and are used by birds and glider pilots.*

Q2 Explain why birds find convection currents so useful.

Radiation

When you place toast on a grill it is underneath the heating element. The bread is not being heated by conduction. The bread cannot be heated by convection because the hot air will rise upwards and away from the bread. Some heat is being transferred directly down from the element. This is called **radiation**. The heat is transferred by waves of heat energy.

The Sun (Fig 4) heats the Earth from 150 million kilometres away. This shows that heat can be radiated without needing any particles or materials. Unlike conduction and convection, radiation needs no help in moving heat energy from place to place.

Q3 List three examples of heat transfer by radiation.

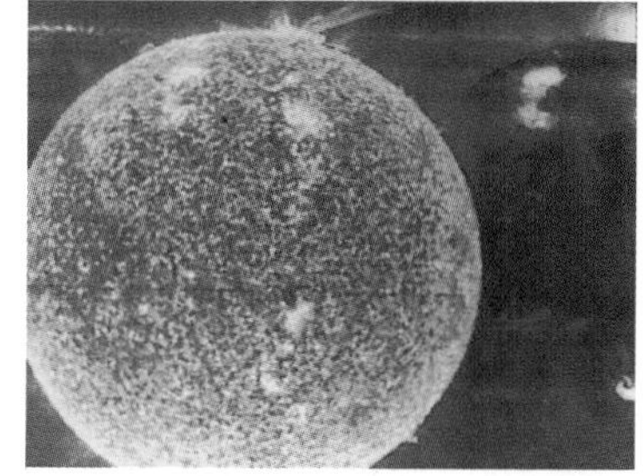

▲ ***Fig 4***

Key Words

insulators – materials that do not easily allow heat energy to be transferred
conduction – the movement of heat energy along a material
convection – a way in which heat energy is transferred in liquids and gases
convection currents – the rising and falling of liquids and gases as convection occurs
radiation – the way in which heat energy is transferred from a hotter to a cooler place without needing any other material

SUMMARY

- Heat energy flows from one place to another.
- Conduction of heat energy is the result of metallic atoms vibrating and passing the energy along the metal.
- In convection heat energy is transferred by moving molecules.
- Heat transfer by radiation involves waves of heat energy that can travel through a vacuum.
- Insulators can reduce heat transfer and help us to conserve energy.

SUMMARY *Activity*

Examine a vacuum flask closely. Make a list of the ways that heat transfer from the hot liquid is reduced. Which design features are there to reduce: a) conduction; b) convection; c) radiation?

113 Energy and efficiency

In this section of the book you will learn the following things:

- **that energy is not lost during an energy transfer;**
- **that most energy chains end up as heat;**
- **the law of conservation of energy.**

Power stations are not 100% efficient (Unit 108). This means that around half of the energy in the fuel does not give us electricity that we can use. A lot of the heat energy released when coal is burned in a power station is wasted in the smoke and steam. Energy can be wasted but it does not disappear.

When a washing machine spins the water away, electrical energy is changed into kinetic energy. Kinetic energy turns the drum. This is the energy transfer we want.

electrical energy → kinetic energy

A washing machine makes a noise when it spins. Some of the electrical energy is becoming sound energy. The motor also gets warm. Some of the electrical energy is becoming heat energy.

electrical energy → kinetic energy + heat energy + sound energy

▲ ***Fig 1*** *The electrical energy flowing into the washing machine is changing into kinetic, heat and sound energy.*

Q1 What forms of energy does a washing machine not produce?

Q2 What forms of energy does a television not produce?

Q3 What forms of energy do both machines produce?

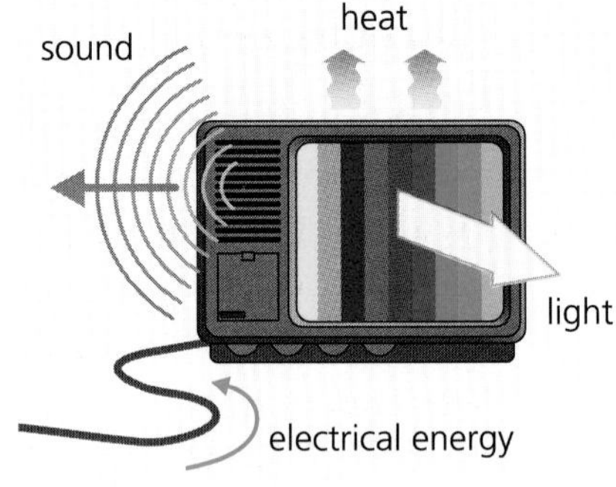

▲ ***Fig 2*** *Electrical energy is changing into heat, light and sound energy.*

Efficiency

What happens to the energy from a small petrol engine when we use it to light up a lamp bulb? This is shown in Fig 3. Burning the petrol makes the motor turn. The motor turns a generator. The generator makes enough electricity to make the bulb light up. Only 1% of the energy in the petrol becomes light energy. The other 99% is transferred to other forms of energy. Using a petrol engine is not a good way to make light.

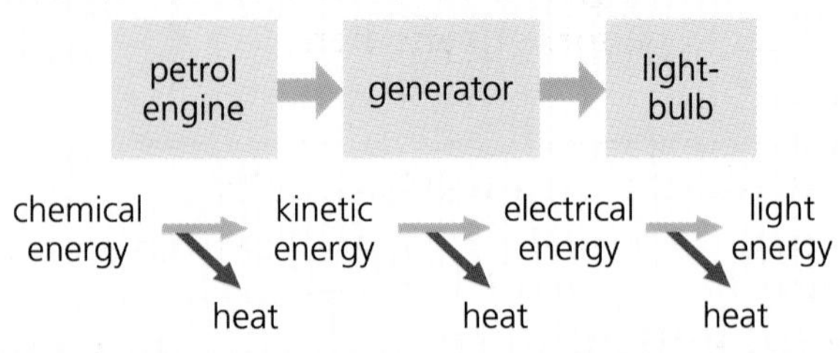

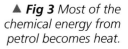

▲ ***Fig 3*** *Most of the chemical energy from petrol becomes heat.*

We try to design machines so that they are as **efficient** as possible. This means they should transfer as much energy as possible to the job. The efficiency of an electric drill is shown in Fig 4.

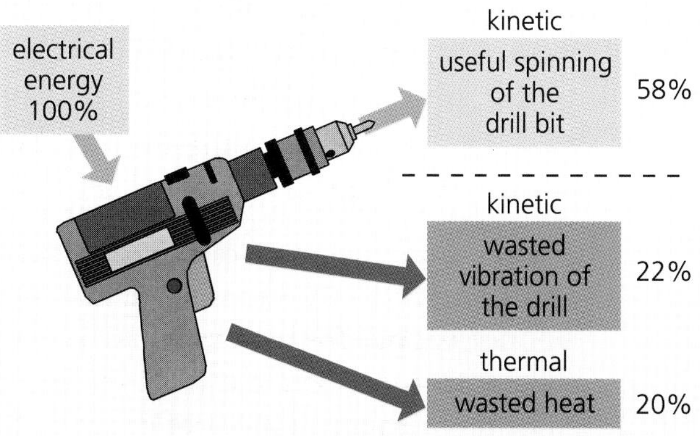

▶ *Fig 4*

Q4 Add up all the energy values in Fig 4. What is the total?

Heat as waste

Notice that 20% of the electrical energy in an electric drill (Fig 4) immediately becomes heat energy. Most energy chains end up as heat. An electric cooker ring converts electricity to heat and light. The light from the cooker ring hits objects around it. This warms the objects up slightly so even the light from the cooker eventually becomes heat.

▲ *Fig 5*

A light-bulb probably started the fire at Windsor Castle. Even though the light-bulb was designed to transfer electrical energy into light energy it also produced heat. Eventually the bulb in the light became hot enough to set fire to a long curtain that was next to it. The burning curtain released enough heat energy to set light to wood. Soon a large part of the Castle was in flames (Fig 5).

Q5 Why must you never put paper or cloth over a light-bulb?

The law of conservation of energy

Energy cannot be created or destroyed. It can only be changed from one form to another.

Key Words

efficient – wasting little energy

law – a basic fact of science

SUMMARY

- Energy can be transferred in more than one form at the same time.
- Efficient machines waste as little energy as possible.
- Energy cannot be created or destroyed. This fact is called the law of conservation of energy.
- Most energy chains end as heat.
- The heat from a light-bulb can be dangerous.

SUMMARY *Activity*

Describe some of the energy transfers that take place in your body when you use the chemical energy in your food.

114 Using energy sensibly

In this section of the book you will learn the following things:

- **how energy can be wasted in our homes;**
- **how we can make the best use of energy.**

An electric drill is inefficient (Unit 113). It wastes more than 40% of the electricity it uses. This means that it wastes more than 40% of the money we pay for the electricity it uses. All the equipment in our home wastes some energy. The more energy a piece of equipment wastes, the more money we waste buying energy for it.

Inefficient equipment costs us more than money. Electricity is made by burning fuels. Inefficient equipment wastes fuel at the power station. This also increases pollution.

Q1 How can using a more efficient electric iron help to make the air cleaner?

▲ ***Fig 1*** *You can tell how much electricity is being used right now by seeing how fast the pointers move.*

A car can be made more **fuel efficient** by having a lighter body and a more efficient engine. The old car in Fig 2 needs a litre of fuel to travel five miles. A litre of fuel takes the modern car three times as far.

▲ ***Fig 2*** ▶

Q2 How far does the modern car travel on one litre of petrol?

Q3 Apart from money and petrol, what else does an efficient car save?

Saving energy in industry

More than 30% of UK energy resources are used in industry. A lot of this energy is wasted as heat. Some industries can capture heat energy and use it again. Spare heat energy from the cooling tower of a power station can be sent to nearby factories and homes (Fig 3).

▼ ***Fig 3***

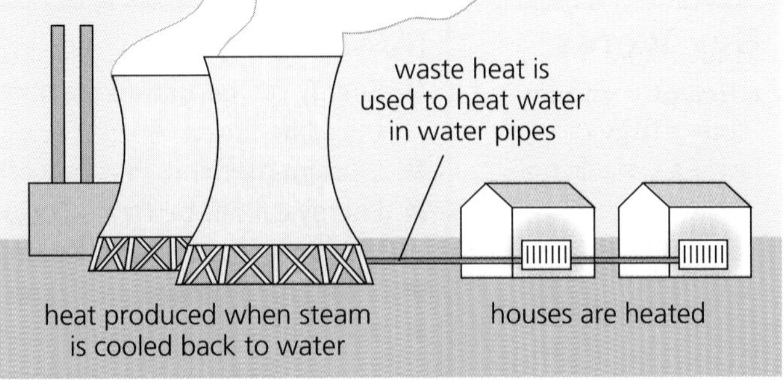

Saving energy in transport

More than 25% of UK energy resources are used for **transport**. Fuel can be saved by making engines more efficient. Energy can also be saved by using transport more sensibly. A car can only hold a small number of people. Trains and buses can move more people with one litre of fuel than a car can. They are more **economical**. Another way to save energy in transport is by using energy directly from the Sun. Scientists are working towards building cars with solar panels.

Q3 How does a car sharing scheme help to save energy?

Saving energy at home

More than 29% of UK energy resources are used in our homes. We can all use less energy, especially by saving heat. **Insulation** helps to keep heat inside our homes instead of leaking out through the roof, walls, doors and windows. Thermostats can prevent radiators from becoming hotter than they need to be. Turning the heating down just a degree or two saves energy without making much difference to how we feel.

Q4 How can insulating a house save money and reduce pollution?

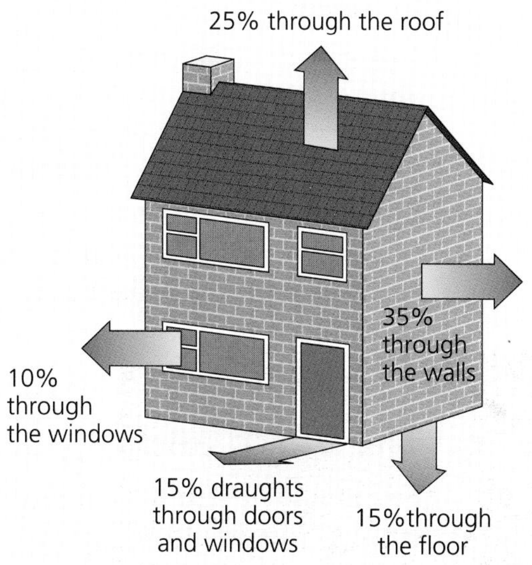

▲ ***Fig 4*** *Where a house loses heat.*

Why bother?

We need to make our energy resources last as long as possible. We also need to reduce pollution. We can do both of these things by saving energy. Saving energy is sometimes called energy conservation. This does not mean the same as the law of conservation of energy (Unit 113). Energy cannot be destroyed but it can be wasted. Conserving energy means trying not to waste it.

Key Words

economical – using a resource efficiently
fuel efficient – getting more useful energy from a fuel
insulation – a substance that does not conduct heat
transport – vehicles that move people or goods around

SUMMARY

- Wasting energy costs us money, wastes resources and increases pollution.
- Energy is often wasted as heat.
- Energy can be saved by having more efficient industries.
- Energy can be saved by inventing more efficient transport.
- Insulating our homes can save a lot of heat energy.

SUMMARY *Activity*

Make a list of as many ways as possible to use energy resources more efficiently in: a) industry; b) transport; c) your home.

Summary – Physical processes

This part of the book should have helped you to understand some of the important forces and processes of the physical world.

Forces and motion

You should understand how forces can move objects. You will know how to measure speed and be able to link speed, distance and time. You should also understand that forces can be balanced and unbalanced.

- If an object takes 30 seconds to travel 90 metres, what is its average speed?
- How long would it take for a car moving at 100 km/hr to travel 350 km?
- Gravity is one type of force. Name two others.

You should understand how friction affects movement and be able to give some everyday examples. You should know the law of moments which describes how forces can be used to make things turn. You should also understand the connection between pressure, force and area.

- Explain how a parachute works.
- Describe two ways of reducing friction between two objects.
- Write down the law of moments.
- Why do we unscrew a nut with a spanner rather than with our fingers?
- How do snow shoes help you to walk on snow?

The Earth and beyond

You should be able to explain the physical reasons for night and day and the seasons. You should be able to describe the positions of the planets in the Solar System and their sizes and temperature. You should be able to describe what artificial satellites are, how they move, and how we make use of them.

- Sketch a diagram that shows why we have night and day.
- Name the inner planets of the Solar System.
- Name the largest planet in the Solar System.
- Describe two uses of artificial satellites.

Sound and light

You should know about the properties of light and how shadows form. You should also know the laws of reflection and refraction. You will understand how white light can be split into the colours of the spectrum and how coloured filters work. You should also be able to explain how coloured objects reflect light.

- How would you show that light travels in straight lines?
- Why does a swimming pool look shallower than it really is?
- Explain why a green cap looks black in blue light.

You should understand that sound is caused by vibrations and be able to draw sound waves to show the difference between loudness and pitch. You should know and understand terms such as 'amplitude', 'wavelength' and 'frequency'.

- Sketch some sound waves to explain amplitude, wavelength and frequency.
- How can whales many kilometres apart hear one another?
- How can sound waves be used to find sunken ships?

Electricity and magnetism

You should know how static electricity is formed and be able to give some examples. You should also understand how electricity is conducted, and why insulators are important. You should be able to draw simple electrical circuits. You will understand that components in a circuit do not use up electricity.

- Explain how an insulating material is charged by friction.
- Draw the circuit symbols for a bulb and an ammeter.
- Design a circuit that has three bulbs in parallel.

You should understand the link between electric current and magnetic field and be able to draw the field pattern around a bar magnet and a coil. You should know how the strength of an electromagnet can be increased and be able to give some examples of ways in which we use electromagnets.

- Draw the field pattern around a bar magnet.
- Write down three practical uses for electromagnets.
- Describe two ways to increase the strength of an electromagnet.

Energy resources and energy transfer

You should understand where our energy comes from and how electricity is generated. You should know the difference between a non-renewable energy resource and a renewable one. You should also be able to name some renewable sources of energy.

- Where does most of the Earth's energy originally come from?
- What are fossil fuels? Write down three examples.
- List four types of energy that are renewable.
- Sketch a diagram that shows how electricity is generated from coal.

You will know the difference between the temperature of a substance and the energy that a substance contains. You will also know how energy can be transferred and stored. Finally, you should understand that although energy can be transferred it is never created or destroyed.

- List five different forms of energy.
- Draw a diagram to show the energy transfers that make a television work.
- Write down the Law of Conservation of Energy.
- Draw a diagram of a house that shows where heat energy can be lost.
- Explain why it is important to conserve energy.

Useful formulae and tables

Photosynthesis

carbon dioxide + water $\xrightarrow[\text{chlorophyll}]{\text{energy from sunlight}}$ glucose + oxygen

Respiration

glucose + oxygen → carbon dioxide + water + energy

Reactivity Series

most reactive

- potassium
- sodium
- calcium
- magnesium
- aluminium
- zinc
- iron
- lead
- copper
- silver
- gold

least reactive

Reactions of acids

acids + metals → salt + hydrogen

acids + metal oxides (bases) → salt + water

acids + alkalis (soluble bases) → salt + water

acids + carbonates → salt + water + carbon dioxide

Velocity, distance and time

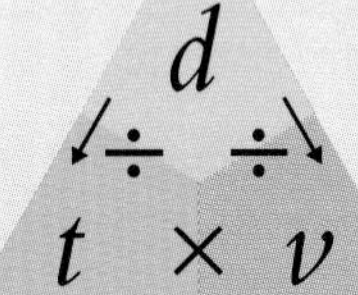

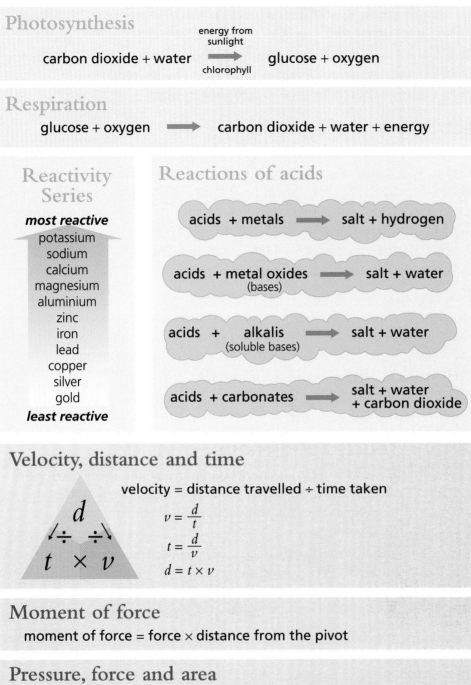

velocity = distance travelled ÷ time taken

$$v = \frac{d}{t}$$

$$t = \frac{d}{v}$$

$$d = t \times v$$

Moment of force

moment of force = force × distance from the pivot

Pressure, force and area

F
÷ ÷
P × A

pressure = force ÷ area

$$P = \frac{F}{A}$$

$$F = P \times A$$

$$A = \frac{F}{P}$$

The Periodic Table

Period	Group I	Group II											Group III	Group IV	Group V	Group VI	Group VII	Group 0
1						1 **H** Hydrogen 1												4 **He** Helium 2
2	7 **Li** Lithium 3	9 **Be** Beryllium 4											11 **B** Boron 5	12 **C** Carbon 6	14 **N** Nitrogen 7	16 **O** Oxygen 8	19 **F** Fluorine 9	20 **Ne** Neon 10
3	23 **Na** Sodium 11	24 **Mg** Magnesium 12											27 **Al** Aluminium 13	28 **Si** Silicon 14	31 **P** Phosphorus 15	32 **S** Sulphur 16	35.5 **Cl** Chlorine 17	40 **Ar** Argon 18
4	39 **K** Potassium 19	40 **Ca** Calcium 20	45 **Sc** Scandium 21	48 **Ti** Titanium 22	51 **V** Vanadium 23	52 **Cr** Chromium 24	55 **Mn** Manganese 25	56 **Fe** Iron 26	59 **Co** Cobalt 27	59 **Ni** Nickel 28	64 **Cu** Copper 29	65 **Zn** Zinc 30	70 **Ga** Gallium 31	73 **Ge** Germanium 32	75 **As** Arsenic 33	79 **Se** Selenium 34	80 **Br** Bromine 35	84 **Kr** Krypton 36
5	85.5 **Rb** Rubidium 37	88 **Sr** Strontium 38	89 **Y** Yttrium 39	91 **Zr** Zirconium 40	93 **Nb** Niobium 41	96 **Mo** Molybdenum 42	99 **Tc** Technetium 43	101 **Ru** Ruthenium 44	103 **Rh** Rhodium 45	106 **Pd** Palladium 46	108 **Ag** Silver 47	112 **Cd** Cadmium 48	115 **In** Indium 49	119 **Sn** Tin 50	122 **Sb** Antimony 51	128 **Te** Tellurium 52	127 **I** Iodine 53	131 **Xe** Xenon 54
6	133 **Cs** Caesium 55	137 **Ba** Barium 56	139 **La** Lanthanum 57	178.5 **Hf** Hafnium 72	181 **Ta** Tantalum 73	184 **W** Tungsten 74	186 **Re** Rhenium 75	190 **Os** Osmium 76	192 **Ir** Iridium 77	195 **Pt** Platinum 78	197 **Au** Gold 79	201 **Hg** Mercury 80	204 **Tl** Thallium 81	207 **Pb** Lead 82	209 **Bi** Bismuth 83	210 **Po** Polonium 84	210 **At** Astatine 85	222 **Rn** Radon 86
7	223 **Fr** Francium 87	226 **Ra** Radium 88	227 **Ac** Actinium 89	– **Db** Dubnium 104	– **Jl** Joliotium 105	– **Rf** Rutherfordium 106	– **Bh** Bohrium 107	– **Hn** Hahnium 108	– **Mt** Meitnerium 109									

d-block transition elements

f-block

139 **La** Lanthanum 57	140 **Ce** Cerium 58	141 **Pr** Praseodymium 59	144 **Nd** Neodymium 60	147 **Pm** Promethium 61	150 **Sm** Samarium 62	152 **Eu** Europium 63	157 **Gd** Gadolinium 64	159 **Tb** Terbium 65	162.5 **Dy** Dysprosium 66	165 **Ho** Holmium 67	167 **Er** Erbium 68	169 **Tm** Thulium 69	173 **Yb** Ytterbium 70	175 **Lu** Lutetium 71
227 **Ac** Actinium 89	232 **Th** Thorium 90	231 **Pa** Protactinium 91	238 **U** Uranium 92	237 **Np** Neptunium 93	242 **Pu** Plutonium 94	243 **Am** Americium 95	247 **Cm** Curium 96	247 **Bk** Berkelium 97	251 **Cf** Californium 98	254 **Es** Einsteinium 99	253 **Fm** Fermium 100	256 **Md** Mendelevium 101	254 **No** Nobelium 102	257 **Lr** Lawrencium 103

key

atomic mass
symbol
name
atomic number

Glossary

A

absorption – the passage of nutrients from the gut to the blood
acid rain – rainwater that is more acid than normal
aerobic respiration – using oxygen to get energy from glucose
air resistance – friction caused by air molecules
alkali – a solution made by dissolving a metal oxide in water
alloy – a mixture of metals
alternative energy – a renewable energy resource
alveolus – a tiny air sac in a lung
ammeter – a meter for measuring current
ampere – the unit for measuring current, also amp or A
amplitude – the height of a wave
antibiotic – a chemical that kills bacteria
artery – a blood vessel that carries blood from the heart
atom – the smallest particle of an element
atomic number – the number of protons in an atom

B

base – a metal oxide
bimetal strip – a strip made from two metals joined together
biomass – a quantity of plant or animal material
boiling point – the temperature at which gas bubbles form in a liquid
bronchiole – a small air tube in a lung
bronchus (plural: bronchi) – one of two main tubes branching off the windpipe

C

camouflaged – blending into the background or looking like something else
capillary – a tiny thin-walled blood vessel
catalyst – a substance that helps a chemical reaction without becoming a product
cell – the basic building block of living things **or** the part of a battery where chemical energy becomes electrical energy
cell membrane – flexible covering of the cell
change of state – a change between a solid, liquid or gas state
chemical change – a change into a new substance not easily reversed
chlorophyll – the green pigment in plants that traps the energy in sunlight
chloroplast – a structure in a plant cell that contains chlorophyll
cilia – tiny moving hairs attached to cells
circuit – a complete ring of conducting materials
comet – a body made of dust and frozen gases
community – the collection of animals and plants that share a habitat
competition – one or more living things requiring the same food, mate or shelter
compound – a chemical substance made of different elements
condense – change from a gas to a liquid
conductor – a substance that transmits heat and electricity
conservation of mass – no alteration in mass during a change
constellation – a named 'shape' among the stars
consumer – an animal that feeds on plants or other animals
contact force – the force between colliding objects
contraction – shrinkage caused by cooling
corrosive – able to attack other materials
current – the flow of electricity
cytoplasm – the liquid part of a cell

D

decompose – to break down into smaller parts
diffusion – the movement of one substance through another substance
digestion – chemically breaking down food into smaller molecules
distillation – a method of separation using evaporation
division of labour – sharing out the functions needed to maintain life

E

eardrum – a membrane that transmits sound waves from the air
echo – a sound bouncing back from a solid surface
eclipse – a shadow on the Earth cast by the moon, seen from Earth as a hole in the Sun

ecosystem – a self-contained community interacting with the environment
effervesce – fizz with gas bubbles
electric force – the force between electric charges
electrical conductivity – the ability to conduct electrical energy
electrolysis – splitting chemicals with electricity
electromagnet – an electric wire coiled around a metal core
electron – a small negatively charged sub-atomic particle
element – a substance made of one type of atom
embryo – the first 2 months of development of a new baby
endothermic – taking in heat
environment – geographical, geological and biological surroundings
erosion – the movement of weathered rock
evaporate – change from a liquid to a gas
exothermic – giving out heat
expansion – growth caused by heating

F

fertilisation – the point when a sperm cell enters an egg and genetic material is combined
filament – very thin wire in a light-bulb
filtration – separating a mixture by passing it through a filter
foetus – a human embryo after 2 months
food web – a network of food chains
fossil – evidence of living things preserved in rocks
fractional distillation – a method of separating liquid mixtures by evaporation
freezing point – the temperature at which a liquid becomes a solid
frequency – the number of vibrations per second
frictional force – force between objects sliding past each other
fuel – a substance that combines with oxygen to give out heat in a way we can use

G

galaxy – a cluster of millions of stars
gamete – male or female sex cell (animal or plant)
gas exchange – the process of oxygen entering the blood and carbon dioxide leaving the blood
gene – a very large molecule carrying a code for one characteristic
genus – a group of organisms just above species level
global warming – an increase in the Earth's average temperature
gravitational force – the force of the Earth's pull
greenhouse effect – how carbon dioxide keeps the Earth warm

H

habitat – the home for a living thing that provides everything it needs to live
haemoglobin – the red pigment inside red blood cells
heat – a form of energy
herbivore – an animal that only eats plants
Hertz – the unit for measuring frequency
hydroelectric power – electricity generated by flowing water

I

igneous – rock formed when magma cools
incident ray – a ray of light hitting a surface
indicator – a chemical that indicates pH
infection – the result of disease-causing bacteria entering the body
insoluble – unable to dissolve in a liquid
insulator – a material that does not transmit heat and electricity
invertebrate – an animal without a backbone

K

key – a table or chart that helps you to identify living things
kilojoule – the unit for energy
kinetic energy – energy of movement
kingdom – one of the five major divisions of living things

L

lever – a rod used with a pivot to increase force
luminous – an object that emits light

M

magma – hot liquid rock
magnetic field – the shape and size of the area affected by a magnet
melting point – the temperature at which a solid becomes a liquid

menstrual cycle – the monthly cycle of the female sex organs
metamorphic rock – rock changed by heat or pressure
mineral – an element needed to make some body chemicals
mixture – substances mixed but not chemically joined
molecule – a group of atoms chemically joined
moment – the turning effect produced by a force
multicellular – made of more than one cell
mutation – a sudden change in the structure of a gene

N

natural selection – survival of well-adapted organisms and death of badly adapted ones
negatively charged – having extra electrons
neutral – having no charge
neutral – pH 7, neither acidic nor alkaline
neutron – a sub-atomic particle with no electrical charge
nocturnal – belonging to the night
normal – a line at right angles to the surface
nucleus – the central core of an atom **or** the control centre of the cell
nutrient – any food substance needed by the body

O

opaque – not allowing light to pass through
orbit – the path of a planet around the Sun
ore – a natural metal compound
organ – a group of tissues working together
ovary – part of the female reproductive system producing eggs
oxide – an element chemically combined with oxygen

P

particle – a very small part of a substance
penumbra – the pale border of a shadow
Periodic Table – a useful chart of elements
pH number – a measurement of acidity or alkalinity
photosynthesis – the process of making glucose by using energy from the sun
physical change – a change affecting the appearance of a substance but not its chemistry
pitch – how high or low a note is
pivot – the point around which an object turns
placenta – the structure made by an embryo to obtain food and oxygen from its mother
plane – a very flat, smooth surface
plankton – tiny plants and animals found in surface waters of oceans
pollen – the male sex cell of a flowering plant
population – the number of individuals of one species in one area at one time
positively charged – short of electrons
potential energy – stored energy
predator – an animal that eats other animals
pressure – force in newtons exerted on a measured area
prey – a specific animal eaten by a predator
producer – a green plant making food by photosynthesis
product – a substance produced by a chemical reaction
proton – a positively charged sub-atomic particle
puberty – the time when sex organs begin to work
pyramid of biomass – a diagram showing the mass of organisms at each stage of a food chain
pyramid of numbers – a diagram showing the number of organisms at each stage of a food chain

R

radioactive – the ability to give out radiation
reactant – a substance changed by a chemical reaction
Reactivity Series – the league table of metals that shows how reactive each one is
reduced – having oxygen taken away
reflect – bounce back from a surface
refraction – light bending at the surface of a transparent substance
residue – the part of a mixture that is trapped by a filter
resistance – a component that reduces the flow of current
respiration – the process of breaking down foods for energy
rock cycle – the repeated breaking and building of rocks
root hair cells – root cells adapted to take in water

S

salt – a compound formed from a metal and an acid
satellite – a body in orbit around another body
sedimentary – rock formed from sediment
selectively or partially permeable – allowing only some chemicals through
sex hormones – chemicals that cause the changes of puberty
shadow – an area where light is blocked
Solar System – the Sun and all the planets and asteroids that move around it
soluble – able to dissolve in a liquid
solute – the substance that dissolves in a liquid
solution – a mixture of a solute in a solvent
solvent – a chemical that dissolves other chemicals
sound energy – energy transmitted in sound waves
species – an organism that is genetically distinct
spectrum – the range of colours in white light.
speed – distance divided by time
stoma (plural: stomata) – a pore in the lower surface of a leaf
sublimation – a direct change of state from solid to gas without passing through the liquid state

T

tap root – a plant's main deep root
temperature – how hot or cold a substance is
thermal conductivity – the ability to conduct thermal energy
thermal decomposition – chemical breakdown caused by heating
tissue – a group of similar cells grouped together
tumour – a lump made by cells dividing too quickly
turbine – a wheel that is turned by jets of steam

U

ultrasound – a sound too high for a person to hear
umbilical cord – the connection between embryo and placenta
umbra – the dark inner region of a shadow
Universe – the total amount of material and energy in existence
uterus – womb

V

vaccination – an injection of a weak or dead micro-organism to create immunity
vacuum – an area empty of free molecules
vapour – a gas at the same temperature as its liquid state
variation – a small difference between members of the same species. A larger difference between members of different species
vascular system – the plant's transport system
vein – a blood vessel that carries blood back to the heart
velocity – speed (v)
vertebral column – the spine or backbone
vertebrate – an animal with a backbone
villi – small folds in the lining of the small intestine wall
vitamin – a ready-made chemical essential for health

W

wavelength – the distance between neighbouring wave crests
weathering – physical and chemical breakdown of rocks
work – the movement of an object by a force

Y

yield – the edible amount of a plant produced from an area of land

Index